The

Unknown Travels

and

Dubious Pursuits

of

William Clark

The

Unknown Travels

and

Dubious Pursuits

of

William Clark

Jo Ann Trogdon

UNIVERSITY OF MISSOURI PRESS
Columbia

Copyright © 2015 by Jo Ann Trogdon
University of Missouri Press, Columbia, Missouri 65211
Printed and bound in the United States of America
All rights reserved. First paperback printing, 2023.

Library of Congress Control Number: 2015940589
ISBN: 978-0-8262-2049-3 (hardcover : alk. paper)
ISBN: 978-0-8262-2302-9 (paperback: alk. paper)

∞™ This paper meets the requirements of the
American National Standard for Permanence of Paper
for Printed Library Materials, Z39.48, 1984.

Frontispiece: Charles Willson Peale's 1807 portrait of William Clark
Typeface: Caslon

To William Least Heat-Moon:

For his steadfast belief in this book

Contents

Illustrations

Foreword

James J. Holmberg

The Lewis and Clark Expedition of 1803 to 1806 is recognized as the greatest exploring venture in United States history. The Corps of Discovery's journey across the American West to the Pacific Ocean and back covered some eight thousand miles. For Meriwether Lewis, William Clark, York, and others who began the trip east of the Mississippi and continued to destinations east of that river after arriving in St. Louis, the journey covered as many as ten thousand miles. These early nineteenth-century explorers were among the greatest travelers in history.

People in the late eighteenth and early nineteenth centuries were often on the move. By necessity or for pleasure, in a day when it was time-consuming and often difficult, travel was accepted as a matter of course. Travelers were experienced in the ways of the road, river, and trail. When Meriwether Lewis set out from Washington, D.C., in July 1803 to rendezvous with his partner-in-discovery, William Clark, in Louisville and the nucleus of the Corps, he was already a seasoned traveler. And when Clark boarded their keelboat in October 1803 and set off down the Ohio River with his fellow explorers, he was even more experienced. For Clark it was just the latest journey in what had been a life of frequent travel since moving to Kentucky from Virginia in 1785. Working on survey crews, campaigning with the Kentucky militia against Indian nations north of the Ohio, four years of travel and missions in the Army, trips back and forth to Virginia, and at least one trip to New Orleans had made Clark an experienced and knowledgeable traveler. He was so accustomed to life on the road and river that he referenced the expedition to the Pacific as his "western trip."

None of William Clark's pre- and post-expedition travels (he regularly traveled in the years after his epic journey) is as well-known as the "western trip." Among these travels, one in particular stands out, his 1798 trip to New Orleans. Leaving Louisville in March, Clark returned on Christmas Eve, having covered some four thousand miles by way of river, sea, and road. He was no stranger to travel on the Ohio and parts of the Mississippi, but from New Orleans he took ship and sailed around Florida and up the East Coast to New Castle, Delaware. From there he went by land to Virginia and home to Kentucky by way of Ohio.

The practice of keeping a record of events and expenses had been instilled in Clark as a youth. His father, John, and brothers, Jonathan, George Rogers, and Edmund, all kept journals and records. William learned by example. Keeping at least a basic account of his travels—recording events, mileage, expenses, observations, and sometimes drawing maps—was useful and prudent. As he had done in the past and would do in the future, most famously on the Expedition, Clark kept a written account of his 1798 trip. In his frequently taciturn style he recorded events, observations, miles traveled, and expenses and also drew maps of sections of the Mississippi. But if the reader scratches below the surface of this seemingly routine and rather mundane account and places Clark in the context of the events of the day swirling around him, it is anything but routine or mundane. And it is this that Jo Ann Trogdon does for us.

In 1798 the young United States, only fifteen years removed from the end of the American Revolution, was still feeling its way as a nation. It was by no means certain that it would one day stretch across the continent and be a great union of states. Westward movement beyond the Appalachians was in its infancy. The "western" states of Kentucky and Tennessee had only joined the Union in 1792 and 1796, respectively. Its western border was the Mississippi. It was surrounded by European powers—the British in Canada and the Spanish in Florida and Louisiana—that were generally ambivalent, if not hostile, to the young nation. In the

1780s and 1790s, it was by no means certain that Kentucky and Tennessee would even join—or, once joined, remain in—the United States. European agents, self-serving adventurers, and frustrated westerners, tired of the federal government's perceived inattention and inability to address their most important needs, fomented dissatisfaction, dissension, and schemes for possible independence.

The most infamous of these schemes came to be known as the Spanish Conspiracy, a persistent effort by Spain in the 1780s and 1790s to separate Kentucky and other western American territory from the United States and ally them to it. Such schemes were never realized, but they were a serious concern in the nation's early years. Who said what, who intended what, and who did what resulted in accusations, charges of conspiracy and treason, and legal action. In Kentucky the Spanish Conspiracy played out in newspapers for years, long after the possibility of it joining Spain in a western alliance had passed. The affair helped make careers for those who championed the American cause and helped ruin careers and reputations of those tainted with the suspicion of treason. Some—like James Wilkinson, an American Army general who was a paid agent of Spain for many years—proved slippery enough to continue in important positions. Others unwittingly might have played a role in this drama. Was one of them William Clark?

Did fortune smile on William Clark that he was never identified as part of the cabal scheming to separate Kentucky from the Union? Was he ever a party to such scheming and possible treason? As unlikely as this might be, it is a question worth asking about him and others. The early years of the Republic were an uncertain time. It was a time of growing pains for the nation and its citizens. There could be a blurred line between loyalty and disloyalty. Making one's name and making one's fortune did not necessarily conflict with one's governmental duties. They could be intertwined to some degree. What is now considered unethical, if not illegal, was not necessarily the case then. If William Clark could himself avoid Spanish taxes and fees or help a friend or associate avoid them, he almost certainly would have been happy to oblige, especially as a private citizen, which he was in 1798. If he trusted and respected that person, such as his former commander James Wilkinson and family friend Benjamin Sebastian, he would not have hesitated to be of service to them. If he believed what they were doing to be treasonous, would his sense of loyalty to them cause him to act differently? Or was he an unwitting pawn in this game of international intrigue? What did Clark know? As unlikely as it is that William Clark knowingly assisted these Spanish conspirators, it is a question that bears asking, and Trogdon delves into the subject in search of answers.

Through William Clark's 1798 account of his trip to New Orleans, Jo Ann Trogdon places him in the much larger important events of the day, times of uncertainty that helped decide the fate of a nation. We learn much from Clark's journal and its maps. We learn much more thanks to Trogdon's narrative and thorough research. Clark could be frustratingly brief in his entries, ignoring or neglecting to mention people and events that he encountered and witnessed. Were they not worth mentioning? To others then—and to us today—the information would be significant. Did Clark intend anything conspiratorial or devious by such omissions? Clark could be a hard man to impress, and information deemed significant to others was not always so to him. All one need do is read his journals from his journey to the Pacific to rue the lack of detail about many of the people and events of that adventure. But even in his briefest journal entries on his 1798 trip, the information accumulates, and with the patient, ever-probing research of Jo Ann Trogdon, Clark and his journal become a focal point of a crucial period in American history.

William Clark became famous for the journey he co-led to the Pacific. But his New Orleans journey of 1798 is important in its own right. Not only did it hone his travel and cartography skills for the epic Lewis and Clark Expedition and play an important part in its success but it placed the explorer on the historical stage, as a player in a turbulent time in American history, with schemes and shifting alliances that potentially threatened the stability, growth, and very future of the young United States.

Preface
The Unknown William Clark

By all accounts it was a splendid funeral, the grandest ever since the founding of St. Louis. So many citizens turned out to honor General William Clark on that hot September morning in 1838, the cortege extended more than a mile along the road. Opening the way was a military band, followed by a company of volunteer soldiers and Clark's fellow Masons, then by four black-caparisoned white horses pulling the hearse. Behind it, a slave led William's own mount; on the saddle it bore his sword and holstered pistol, and in the stirrups, his spurs and boots. A group of riders succeeded by mourners in dozens of carriages brought up the rear.[1]

The procession wound north out of the city toward the estate of Clark's nephew John O'Fallon; there William had selected for his interment a tract overlooking the bottomlands flanking the confluence of the Missouri and Mississippi rivers, the two longest waterways in North America. That the panorama included the Mississippi was more fitting than he might have intended. Although his co-leadership of the famous 1804–1806 exploration up the Missouri River and beyond it to the Pacific Ocean had won him lasting renown and led to appointments as superintendent of Indian Affairs and governor of the Missouri Territory, a nearly forgotten journey he began on the Mississippi River in 1798 had, in all likelihood, helped to make those and other assignments possible. The throngs lining the funeral route, however, had no idea of that long-ago trip; few people beyond Clark's children knew anything of it, and even they had little inkling of its effect on his development as an agent of national expansion or on the shape of his subsequent life.

But, according to an obscure journal in Clark's own hand, a voyage he made down the Mississippi to Spanish Louisiana—rather than up the Missouri—had significantly sharpened his abilities in mapping, navigation, command of an often unruly crew, and adaptation to a foreign sovereignty, culture, and language. Those capacities would make him an ideal complement to Meriwether Lewis, the partner whose name would be forever linked with his because of their western reconnaissance, and with whom Clark would thereafter administer federal policy in that region.

Given such momentous consequences from Clark's Mississippi River journey, why were so few of his contemporaries—and hardly anyone in succeeding years—aware of it? So I wondered when, in 1992, I first read "William Clark's Notebook, 1798–1801," the eighty-eight-page journal composed in large part of diary and ledger entries from the 1798 trip. Also containing Clark's 1798 map of the Mississippi, quartermaster tables from his earlier days as a soldier, and five pages of notes from a journey he made in 1801 from his Kentucky home to the cities of Philadelphia and Washington, the book has been in the keeping of the State Historical Society of Missouri since 1928.

The story he recorded in that tastefully marbled volume—which I will call the Mississippi Journal—fueled my curiosity. Not only do Clark's entries help to answer the long-debated question of why Meriwether Lewis wanted William Clark, more than anyone else, to assist him in leading the great Expedition, they prove he possessed broader practical experience than he was thought to have. But the logbook also presents the first of several mysteries we will encounter. That is, on some matters in it Clark writes with more verve and less caution than was his customary practice, yet on other topics, including those that usually animate his pen, he is oddly silent. Clearly, the William Clark taking literary shape in the Mississippi Journal was a fully human individual, one having little in common with his eventual image as a stolid and uncomplicated explorer-turned-government-official.

Because there was yet no complete, published biography of him nor a monograph concerning his activities in 1798 and 1801, the focus years of the Mississippi Journal, I determined to check collateral sources that might clarify the activities mentioned in that logbook. Clark having penned most of those entries while in or near Spanish Louisiana, I started with the Archivo General de Indias (the General Archives of the Indies), an immense collection of documents concerning the governance of Spanish holdings in the New World. Relevant sections of the Archivo are available in facsimile at numerous American historical societies and universities.

Having already written (as Jo Ann Brown) the only book yet to explore and illuminate the Spanish roots of St. Charles, Missouri—the same town from which Clark, Lewis, and the Corps of Discovery set off up the Missouri River in 1804—I had an idea where in the Archivo to look. Soon I found more pertinent information than I'd ever guessed existed. Further searching in American sources heretofore unconsulted about William Clark during this early period of his life yielded additional and unexpected knowledge. Whether in Spanish, English, or the cryptic symbols used in communications between high government officers who wanted the utmost secrecy, the records that turned up not only dovetailed almost exactly with Clark's writing, they shattered any notion of him as a person of little depth or complexity. What emerged instead was a richly nuanced portrait of a young man determined to get on in the world, at times through highly questionable means.

To my profound surprise, such measures included dealing with principals in what is often called the Spanish Conspiracy, a multi-phased intrigue contrived mainly by corrupt Kentuckians seeking Spanish money. To obtain the money they engaged in a succession of plots, even one to sever Kentucky from the Union and to ally it in some fashion with Spanish Louisiana. The Union being much younger then, talk of withdrawing from it, especially for economic reasons, was more common than it is now. Still, Clark's own writings link him with men scheming to diminish the United States—hardly the background one might expect of a future agent of American growth.

At this point I began to wonder whether his Mississippi Journal had become obscure because of any deliberate effort on his part, particularly after he returned from the great Expedition and found himself celebrated as a hero and destined for illustrious appointment in government. Having long hoped for such advancement, he was surely not about to let past writings sink his prospects or sully his reputation; exposure of the 1798–1801 logbook may well have done both. But because he was evidently averse to destroying his effects (a granddaughter of his was to inherit so many of them that she would keep them in an apartment separate from her own), he may simply have stored the volume away. Whatever he did with it, he concentrated instead on serving the public, yet presenting a proper image, no matter how two-dimensional it made him seem. Although that persona helped him carry out official duties, which included penning at least twenty-two books of transactions concerning Indian affairs and hundreds of letters, records, and legal papers, it likely increased his innate reluctance to reveal much of himself, especially in writing.

Those closest to him were unable to help him do so. In 1808 he married Judith (Julia) Hancock, a sixteen-year-old Virginian he had scarcely known before the Expedition made him a luminary. Having no experience of their father as a young man, the children (and those born to Harriet Kennerly Radford, the woman Clark married after Julia died) paid scant attention to his earliest letters and logbooks. And by the time Clark's adult grandchildren laid claim to his voluminous correspondence and many dozens of his maps and journals, they also had no reason to question what had by then become the predominant but quite circumscribed view of him—or to scrutinize his logbook of 1798–1801.

In the early 1920s, historical societies around the country vied for the favor of Julia Clark Voorhis, William's elderly, childless granddaughter, because she possessed the largest array of his valuable documents and artifacts. Resisting all entreaties, she instead left those things to her executor, Arthur J. Martin, having advised him on how she wanted them distributed. Following her death in December 1922, he honored her wishes by sending numerous crates of her grandfather's relics to the St. Louis institution then known as the Missouri Historical Society.[2]

The Mississippi Journal was not among them. Instead, in May 1923, an elderly Missourian named William Clark Breckenridge (no kin to Clark) purchased it for fifty cents but failed to note its past ownership. After he died in 1927, the State Historical Society of Missouri in Columbia acquired the book as a tiny fraction of a lot holding 1,030 other historical items, many of them esteemed more highly than the Mississippi log. If

William Clark had wanted it to continue being overlooked long after he died, he could hardly have devised a series of events more likely to guarantee that outcome.[3]

* * *

But in early March 1798, Clark had big plans for the journal. Because it was sturdy, nearly unused, and contained plenty of blotting pages for protection from dampness, he would take it with him on his longest journey yet. As a twenty-seven-year-old veteran whose static rank and failure to achieve the distinction he craved had, along with family obligations, prompted him to resign his Army commission, he was assembling cargoes of tobacco, peltries, and cured pork to take on a flatboat voyage to New Orleans.

He wanted more than to try his luck at commerce, although that was certainly one motive. Having been a junior officer devoted to General James Wilkinson (the secret architect of the Spanish Conspiracy, and the most insidious traitor the United States has yet produced, far surpassing Aaron Burr, the infamous accomplice he betrayed), Clark anticipated earning a large number of Spanish pieces of eight. He also hoped to smuggle them out of Louisiana and to gather exactly the sort of intelligence General Wilkinson wanted for his own seditious ends.

Perhaps to ensure success in those endeavors, Clark was to note only their essentials, keeping details so minimal they could not cause alarm if his journal fell into unfriendly hands. Nonetheless, he and a handful of associates were to leave enough of a record for the story of what he was doing to be reconstructed.

To do this I employ a wide array of evidence, some of it never before viewed with regard to William Clark because it comes from sources not previously recognized as relevant to him. Much of what I demonstrate will challenge established notions by linking him to the ringleaders of the Spanish Conspiracy, a profound, early threat to national unity. Unfortunately, the depth of those connections is not clear and probably never will be unless a good deal of further information comes forth. Even so, my goal in this book is not so much to judge him as it is to present the most fully human and three-dimensional portrait of him yet.

Nevertheless, in researching Clark's life before the great western exploration, I have turned up enough evidence of his relationship to those conspirators for him to be examined in light of the conspiracy itself. Key among the materials I present—and here appearing in print for the first time—are his own journal entries and two of his letters from 1798; although for ninety years these writings have been available for scrutiny, to my knowledge they have not until now been evaluated with regard to any intrigue. A considerable amount of the evidence I disclose in this book, however, comes from the papers of Clark's contemporaries—both those who were hoping to get rich through scheming against the United States and others who suspected them of doing so.

Just as in the courtroom, judges and juries weigh the merit of testimony, documents, and other exhibits in order to discern in such evidence a preponderance on which to base a proper decision, in the following pages I offer for examination all pieces of evidence I have found that are germane to the story, allowing them to accumulate so the reader can draw a sound conclusion. This process of point-by-point inquiry and evaluation applies not just to uncertainties about what Clark was doing but also to questions about what his intentions may have been. Where gaps in the evidence militate against drawing indisputable conclusions I refrain from doing so, instead indicating—through qualifying language or simple questions—that a matter is open to interpretation. I hope in this work to encourage the discovery of further detail about William Clark's activities and motivations during the years covered here. For too long he has been portrayed as a simpler individual than the documents will reveal.

PART I

A Small Adventure of Tobacco
March 8 to April 23, 1798

1

My Wish Is on the Mississippi

ON March 8, 1798, two well-worn vessels roped to the muddy riverbank just below Louisville, Kentucky, were nearly ready to commence their last voyage. That both of them were still afloat must have seemed surprising; each sported new boards patched over gouges and tears, and each sagged under the weight of filled crates and barrels. The flatboats were cumbersome and almost unsteerable wooden boxes slapped together for the sole purpose of conveying cargoes and people downstream. Although these particular vessels appeared unlikely to carry a passenger much farther than beyond the next bend, their owner, William Clark, planned to take them more than a thousand miles to New Orleans, the grand emporium of Spanish Louisiana. He had only lately acquired the boats, planking them over and caulking the hulls for what he intended to be a quick descent of the Ohio and Mississippi rivers. Proprietors usually named their vessels, but there is no record whether Clark did. To distinguish them for what he hoped to accomplish on the voyage, though, he might well have called them *Fortune* and *Connections*.

That fleet of two fulfilled an ambition he had long cherished. Four years earlier, while still in the Army, he had disclosed (in uncharacteristically good orthography and legible penmanship):

> I have some intentions of resigning [his military commission] and get into some business in Kentucky or on the Mississippi. my wish is on the Mississippi, as I think there is great oppening for an extensive & sucksessful Trade in that River could a man form Valuable Connections in New Orleans, which I make no doubt could be accomplished, particularly at this early period.[1]

3

Notions of a downriver venture had so sustained Lieutenant Clark that during idle moments, while other officers amused themselves playing cards or plotting their next foray from camp, he laid plans to become an international trader. That ambition might seem incongruous with his military background, but business concerns—much more than soldierly feats or geographical discoveries—occupied his mind and animated his pen. If on a certain day he pondered the optimal dimensions of a flatboat, on another he doodled possible revenues on varying amounts of tobacco and other goods acquired near his Kentucky home and sold at a profit, perhaps in Spanish New Orleans.[2]

As he was keenly aware, no other market promised as high a return on either tobacco or the peltries and cured meats he also wished to sell and all to be paid for in Spanish silver dollars. Counted out in increments officially designated *reales de á ocho* but known in English-speaking regions as pieces of eight, those coins stamped with the image of King Carlos IV would remain the preferred currency in the United States for some years. As Clark must have known, though, Spain punished anyone attempting without permission to take its money beyond Spanish territory.

The voyage about to begin was not his first effort at foreign commerce. Upon resigning from the Army in July 1796, Clark had tried to put together a cargo fleet to New Orleans but a debilitating illness forced him to call off the journey and to find a local buyer for his tobacco. Since then, he'd been tending to family duties, which often kept him close to Mulberry Hill, the rambling, six-room log house on the South Fork of Beargrass Creek in Jefferson County, Kentucky, where he and his forty-five-year-old brother, George Rogers Clark, lived with their aging parents, John and Ann Clark. Most of William's obligations sprang from a financial crisis originating during the Revolutionary War, with debts George had taken upon himself in order to feed and equip his troops. George's command of Virginia forces in the Ohio River valley earned him lasting fame as the "Hannibal of the West" for he secured for the United States many thousands of square miles east of the Mississippi River and north of the Ohio. Much of that area in 1798 comprised the old Northwest Territory.[3]

Neither Virginia nor the national government assumed responsibility for these crucial expenses—necessary to the favorable outcome of the

War in the West—and the debt undermined George's sterling reputation, leaving him vulnerable to the covert manipulations of his envious rival James Wilkinson. What's more, George's chronic financial woes helped motivate him to seek escape in drink. Happily for William, his exertions to allay George's creditors succeeded for a while and freed William to set off downstream.

Before he did, he looked over his flatboats one last time. They were certainly not the proud vessels he had once dreamed of but they would have to do. He had purchased them for only fifteen dollars each (much less than they must have cost when first assembled), and he spent another forty dollars to repair them. One may have been longer than the other, but both were likely near the typical size—from twelve to fifteen feet wide and forty to sixty feet long—and capacious enough to carry nearly thirty tons of payload. Wooden gunwales several feet high surrounded the decks. A roof probably covered a large portion of each craft, forming a shelter for

Contemporary print of an early nineteenth-century Mississippi River flatboat. The tent-like structure provided shelter for the crewmen.

himself and crewmen, most of the cargo, and a rude kitchen consisting of a fireplace built over a sand-filled box. Equipped with yards of rope cable and perhaps a mast and sail apiece, the flatboats—also called arks or broadhorns—likely had capstans to reel lines in or out; buckets served to bale water should a boat run against submerged trees. In the event those safeguards failed, Clark carried extra planks.

Seven deckhands awaited his order to push the vessels away from shore. Directed by William G. Basey (one of only four of them able to scrawl his own name), those boatmen probably resided in the Ohio River valley when not transporting cargoes to and from Spanish Louisiana. Clark promised prevailing wages (fifty dollars to Basey and forty-five to the others who would stay on to New Orleans), in addition to meals and a daily ration of liquor. In return, he expected vigilance, prudence in reading the often deceptive Mississippi, and herculean labor when necessary to get the boats safely past the countless hazards.[4]

Because Clark had in his soldier days commanded several voyages on the Ohio and at least two on the Mississippi, he may have planned to share navigational duties with Basey. Clark probably brought along his slave York (who would several years later accompany him to the Pacific). The journey would provide them an ideal training in skills key to the success of the subsequent Expedition, particularly in boatmanship, teamwork, and survival in foreign territory. That Clark was to make not a single logbook reference to York in either 1798 or 1801 does not indicate York's absence; during their shared travels over the next decade, Clark would seldom chronicle anything about him. What's more, Clark's silence on this subject typifies his accustomed practice of not mentioning properties—human or otherwise—except when buying or selling them.

He called the impending voyage "a small adventure of tobacco," but there was nothing minor about it, to him or to the men who muscled fifty-seven hogsheads of Kentucky tobacco up gangplanks, rolled them across creaking decks, turned them upright, and shoved them into place. Empty, the barrels weighed more than a hundred pounds, but packed with compressed tobacco they averaged well over a half ton apiece. Each container bore a number and the initials of the neighbor who had culti-vated the leaves.[5]

Among those growers was Richard Taylor, father of thirteen-year-old Zachary, the future president. According to Clark's sometimes problemat-ic handwriting, another barrel belonged to a "Mrs. Meriwether," probably related by marriage to his Army friend Meriwether Lewis. But the largest supply came from Alexander Scott Bullitt, a native Virginian then pros-pering as the grandee of a large plantation a short distance from Clark's comparatively small Mulberry Hill.

Those and other neighbors had consigned the tobacco to William's brothers-in-law Richard Clough Anderson and William Croghan, and they in turn asked Clark to take it to New Orleans. Having a decade earlier secured one of the first Spanish passports ever issued to Americans, those Louisville-based partners had since developed their trade with Spanish Louisiana. They especially liked to route Kentucky goods through two in-fluential New Orleans agents, both named Daniel Clark. They were uncle and nephew to each other, and not kin to William, although he hoped to establish a working relationship with them.[6]

Croghan and Anderson surely knew of the former lieutenant's business ambitions. By putting him in charge of transporting the tobacco and sell-ing it for reales, they evinced an implicit trust in his practical abilities, a desire to help him see the world, and an interest in exposing him to inter-national commerce. In exchange, they wished to profit not just from the tobacco sales but from his expertise in other matters too. Because Wil-liam was a sharp judge of horses, Anderson authorized him to select and purchase a string of Virginia colts. And further, because William was also a licensed, deputy Kentucky surveyor (an almost forgotten aspect of his career), Croghan, a surveyor who ran a land office, commissioned him to determine the boundaries of claims located on three islands in the lower Ohio River.[7]

Carrying out such a task stood to benefit Clark as well; it lent plausi-ble reason to bring along surveying instruments also useful in gathering sensitive intelligence about Spanish defensive works, should he so dare. Accordingly, he found room onboard not only for the documents concerning the real estate but also for his surveyor chains, pins for holding them together, sextant or octant, ink powder, quill pens, a watch, a compass, and probably a staff to mount it on. In addition, he stowed a drafting set (including rules, scales, and pencils) and probably brought a drawing board, a field desk, and a leather shoulder pouch for carrying instruments needed to perform the surveys. The tools he loaded must have included axes of various sizes, a machete-like instrument, and a scribe for notching trees growing near corners of areas to be measured.

He brought seventy dollars, believing that sum sufficient to get him to New Orleans. For a reason he did not explain he forbore writing much about the tobacco or anything of the other cargoes (fifty pounds of beaver furs, ten pounds of otter pelts, dozens of bear skins, nearly fifteen hundred deer hides, and a quarter-ton of salted pork), but he noted paying four dollars to load all those items. To supplement provisions of flour, cornmeal, biscuits, and potatoes he also brought along kegs of sugar and coffee, tropical products sold at New Orleans and sometimes shipped upriver to hide the ill-gotten Spanish revenues of American officials secretly working against the interests of the United States. Brigadier General James Wilkinson, the ranking officer in the U.S. Army, and his close friend Judge Benjamin Sebastian of the Kentucky Court of Appeals—both of whom had intricate ties with Clark and his family—were rumored to have sold Spain their allegiance. Whatever Clark may have thought about those stories, however, he kept to himself.[8]

Last of all, he stowed three dozen candles to use during the voyage, for it was often only after sundown that he would have time to write in his logbook, the most crucial possession on the flatboat. With sheets of thick absorbent material sewn between each writing page, the journal seemed ideal for a river trip. We don't know where he got the volume, but it was handsomely bound in marbled cloth and trimmed with leather. Opening at the top like a stenographer's pad (an advantage allowing Clark to write from top to bottom, perhaps even while balancing the journal on his knee as he would do on occasion during the voyage to the Pacific), the book was also supremely practical.

It bore a few marks dating back to 1794. The first page contained instructions from the enterprising Captain Maxwell Bines about money he'd advanced certain soldiers, and Clark, Bines's regimental paymaster, now planned to call on him in Delaware. Neither the miles between them nor the fact that Bines had left the Army twenty months before Clark did had broken a mutual affinity formed during the long period of preparation leading up to the August 20, 1794, Battle of Fallen Timbers, where Major General Anthony Wayne defeated Indians trying to defend lands north of the Ohio River. But Clark, Bines, and a number of their fellow officers had much more in common than mere participation in that fateful campaign; weeks or even months earlier they formed a close mutual rapport seasoned with the belief that General Wayne was a harsh and capricious dolt—an unfair opinion nurtured in them by his Machiavellian second-in-command, James Wilkinson.[9]

Though no admirer of Wayne, Clark had been careful to keep written denigrations of him and praises of Wilkinson mostly confined to a journal unlikely to draw notice. By contrast, the attractive logbook he was to take down the river in 1798 yet contained nothing more remarkable than several tables concerning rations issued to Bines and his fellow captains of their regiment. The few other entries appeared equally innocuous, most of them reflecting data useful to surveying and celestial navigation: the circumference of the Earth, its degree of tilt from the sun, distances between Earth and the planets from Mercury to Saturn. Astronomers then referred to Uranus as "Herschel," for the astronomer who discovered it in 1781; and Clark also used that name, adding simply that Herschel revolved around the sun "at a greater distance" than that between the other known planets and the solar hub.[10]

In the manner of Thomas Jefferson, the vice president of the United States and the embodiment of the political philosophy to become known as Democratic-Republicanism, Clark, his adherent, appreciated the practical applications of that sort of information. It could serve not only for precise surveying but also, were he so inclined, for plotting the coordinates of strategic locations. Well aware the Spanish expelled anyone caught gathering such intelligence, Clark would have to be careful that his journey appear nothing more than a commercial venture.

To convey such an impression he had to maintain a tight schedule. Although departing at the earliest opportunity was essential to beat other traders to New Orleans, leaving too soon could end with his boats locked in a frozen grip or battered to flinders by ice floes. For days he watched the Ohio as ice broke loose to force its way downstream, and by March 8 what little ice remained was washing quietly toward the Gulf of Mexico. For the next several weeks the river would run high. The Ohio beckoned.

Of March 9, Clark wrote in his logbook, "Set out from the Rapids of Ohio at 6 oClock, well all night." The hour apparently refers to an evening rather than a morning departure. Because he wrote nothing about them we can assume the weather was seasonable and the river calm, although on other occasions he articulated natural observations with perceptiveness and often with grace. For now, what mattered most to him was simply getting under way; to write about anything beyond immediate concerns—distances, directions, strength of the wind, speed of the current—would occur later.

* * *

To accomplish all the goals he set for this journey, Clark needed his run of bad luck to improve. His luck had been unfavorable for so long now, he may not even have remembered when his fortunes began to turn against him, but they did perhaps in 1784 when his parents took him and his three unmarried sisters from their home in Virginia to start a new life near the Falls of the Ohio. William was then fourteen, youthful enough to be excited about a future along the frontier but sufficiently mature to expect little opportunity in Kentucky to improve his education—a virtual necessity were he to measure up to the impressive example already set by his brothers.

Once there had been five. Jonathan, the firstborn, was a prosperous Virginia farmer and county magistrate who, during the Revolution, won a reputation for bravery and leadership at Monmouth, Germantown, and Brandywine and who rose to the rank of lieutenant colonel. He lived in Spotsylvania County, close to the house his parents left behind when they moved to Kentucky. Two years younger than Jonathan, George had attained the commission of a brigadier general in the Virginia militia by the time the war drew to a close. The next Clark boys were John and Richard; though they died not long after the Revolution, each had served his coun-

Opening entries, March 9–15, 1798, of William Clark's voyage to New Orleans, on page 9 of his 1798–1801 Notebook.

try honorably as an officer. Edmund, the youngest but for William, rose rapidly to become a lieutenant before the fighting ended, then he farmed and operated a mill in Spotsylvania County.

William resembled his brothers, especially Jonathan and George. No portrait of Jonathan exists, but two are known to have been painted of George during his life; he sat for these likenesses within a few years of his death in 1818, at age sixty-five. Contemporary descriptions tell us that all three of those Clarks stood around six feet tall, had high foreheads and deep-set eyes, and hair and brows a tint between sand and rust. From portraits of William, though, we can see he also possessed a long, bumpy nose and full lips almost feminine were it not for a certain tightness of expression, as though he were perpetually holding himself in check.

During their youth in Virginia, Jonathan and George had attended classes taught by their uncle Donald Robertson, who also instructed James Madison and other future leaders. Afterward, those brothers passed along what they had learned to the younger members of their family, but by the time William—the penultimate of ten children—was old enough for instruction, Jonathan had gone to fight the British, and George had migrated west where he led campaigns against the British and their Indian allies. William's parents and elder siblings still at home must have taught him what they knew; in a well-worn copybook he left calculations showing his progress in arithmetic. Later, in Kentucky, he augmented his rudimentary academic knowledge with surveying, cartography, techniques for survival in the woods, and other practical skills imparted by George and perhaps also by Croghan and Anderson.[11]

William's journals from the great 1803–1806 Expedition show he struggled mightily with the elements of English composition—syntax, punctuation, and spelling in particular. But, rather than avoid those perplexities by putting away his pen, he determined to improve his writing by seizing every opportunity for practice. He often sent long letters to Jonathan and Edmund, and when they responded, tried to reply promptly. On William's nineteenth birthday (August 1, 1789), he inaugurated the earliest logbook we know about today. In it he describes travels and activities during a militia operation in what is now Indiana. He took obvious care in making the journal, applying iron gall ink to loose papers he had previously folded into folios and afterward stitched together. In the volume he outlined his doings and noted his impressions of the lands around him but seldom chronicled the lurid realities of combat. His later diaries would reflect the same restraint.[12]

Because he looked to his brothers for advice in all sorts of matters, especially those concerning judgment or propriety, he may have learned his journalistic discretion from them. George's problems with debt and alcohol were to complicate their relationship, but William often relied on Jonathan and Edmund for the sort of advice other men derived from their fathers. There is no evidence, however, that William did not esteem John Clark.

Of greater importance to this story, when Jonathan and Edmund were not available, William looked to others for guidance. During his early years in the military he received a large measure of that from General James Wilkinson—an officer midway between Jonathan and Edmund in age—who perhaps also exposed William to what was to become known as the "Spanish Conspiracy," a series of seditious intrigues linking officials of Spanish Louisiana with Wilkinson and other venal Kentuckians, including Benjamin Sebastian and Samuel Montgomery Brown. Before taking William into his confidence, though, the canny Wilkinson must have made certain William was unaware that Wilkinson himself had probably ruined George's financial and political prospects. In addition, Wilkinson fostered young William's receptivity by favoring him with agreeable duties. Still, William surely realized that his brothers disliked this commander, suspecting him of causing George's fall from national prominence. As we will see, William may have made a practice of concealing from them his admiration for, and reliance on, General Wilkinson.

Even so, William found life in the Army a source of frustration, and he resigned in 1796 when four years of striving to rise above his own lieutenancy failed. In further contrast with his brothers' service, William's conferred neither glory nor eminence but instead revealed his prowess at a variety of nonviolent skills. That is, he excelled not at rallying troops, planning master strokes, or killing enemies but, rather, at overseeing construction projects and transporting men, provisions, and materiel from fort to fort along the Ohio. Without ever losing his cargo or bearings, he made a name for himself conveying money and messages among Army installations. A superb marksman, he trained other men to shoot, including Ensign Meriwether Lewis. Even William's pastimes had peaceable applications: sketching maps and diagrams of architectural works. And, as coming chapters will show, he was unparalleled at conducting sensitive or covert missions down the Mississippi and into Spanish territory.

Such talents were not likely to lead to a lucrative post-military career, and indeed they did not. Well before William left the Army in 1796, he believed civilian success could begin in New Orleans with a commercial coup, especially one blessed by a close relationship to men familiar with the Spanish Conspiracy. The journey beginning March 9, 1798, just might bring about a long-awaited lucky break. Certainly his hopes had never been higher.[13]

2

Wind Rose, Blew, and Snowed

THE flatboats made steady progress as the river carried them almost due south for the first twenty miles of the voyage. An inexperienced boatman on that stretch of the Ohio might think he was shooting straight toward the Gulf of Mexico when he was in fact bearing into a sharp turn to carry him nearly an equal distance to the northwest before angling back again. Clark realized there were no shortcuts to Spanish Louisiana. He had floated the Ohio many times while serving in the Army and had at least twice descended the river all the way to the Mississippi, the most evident boundary between the territory of Spain and the United States.

The deckhands settled into a cooperative routine. To guide the vessels they maneuvered "sweeps," which were poles with boards attached to their lower ends. The longest and most important of those oversized oars was connected with the stern and determined the general course of the boat, but smaller sweeps helped the deckhands on each side to steer through eddies and crosscurrents. In addition, a crewman stationed near the bow of each vessel probably kept ready a stubby pole called a gouger to shove off from hazards. If Clark followed the custom of the era, his men worked six-hour shifts followed by a rest of equal duration.[1]

Although there was often little for anyone to do beyond staying alert to changing conditions, vigilance could spell the difference between a completed voyage and an early wreck. From the breakup of ice until late spring, the Ohio usually ran swiftly, reaching a speed of up to six miles per hour, and after a hard rain the river could rise high enough to wash

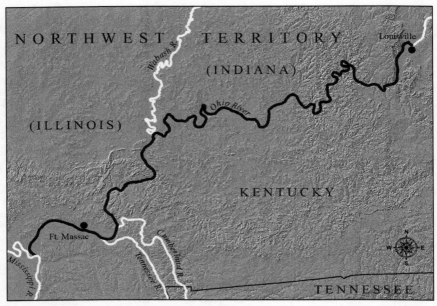

William Clark's 1798 route on the Ohio River from below Louisville to the Mississippi confluence, 428 river miles. Parentheses indicate future states.

vessels up into the lower reaches of tributary streams. Clark surely trusted his hired help to maintain a safe distance from those dangers, but because he knew the Mississippi was much more hazardous to navigate than the Ohio, he kept an eye out for additional lumber to make repairs, knowing he could sell unused planks in New Orleans.

During the first twenty-four hours of the journey the weather was tranquil, but in the late afternoon of March 10 the boats headed into chilling, contrary winds. Near Doe Run Creek (thirty-six river-miles below the Falls), Clark first wrote about blustery conditions, and on the following day he continued in the same concise style: "Wind rose, blew & snowed all the evenning." The next morning was quiet, ushering in a period of clement weather enabling him to stay on the water for three days and two nights, the longest uninterrupted stretch of floating between his departure and his arrival in New Orleans.

By the time Clark passed the mouth of Green River and the nearby village of Red Banks (the future Henderson, Kentucky), hills flanking the Ohio were giving way to a broad forested floodplain interspersed only here and there with settlements. He kept his journal entries brief. Although he frequently noted confluences and villages, he made special mention of rises of the land, as if he thought them of strategic importance. On March 14, after viewing the mouths of the Wabash, Saline, and Tradewater rivers, he wrote: "Passed Waubash, (a high land on the S. Side opposit the first Island below) passed Saline & trade water (high Land on both Sides of it) wind rose & obliged us to Land."

The next day Clark searched the horizon until he found three-mile-long Cumberland Island, the site of real estate claimed by William Croghan, according to a Kentucky treasury warrant purchased in 1786. Croghan had no intention of building on the low-lying tract, but he hoped it would eventually appreciate and become useful, perhaps for a ferry crossing such as the one he owned near Louisville. Unable to secure full title until he had the acreage surveyed, he entrusted that responsibility to Clark, one of the few men in the state who were able to help him. As an official deputy surveyor, Clark was sanctioned to measure tracts and set boundaries anywhere within Kentucky, a fact previous biographers have not mentioned despite his recorded surveys signed "William Clark, D. S."[2]

To assist him, he selected William Patton, John Rogers, and Joseph Cleghorn, probably local men of some education, and he perhaps brought some of the deckhands along to help. Having observed relatively high ground at the upriver end of the island, Clark decided to begin the survey at a trio of sycamores there. Next to them he planted a wooden support and mounted his compass on it, forming a Jacob's staff, the tool George Washington used decades earlier to apportion and plat the Virginia wilderness. On aligning the needle of the compass with the first segment of the tract he wished to survey, Clark sent his helpers in that direction to cut away vegetation. After they finished, he extended his surveyor's chain along the cleared line and continued measuring until he wished to go in a new direction, whereupon he moved the staff to the intended corner, notched an adjacent tree, adjusted the compass, dispatched the axmen, and figured the length of that segment. So the work progressed

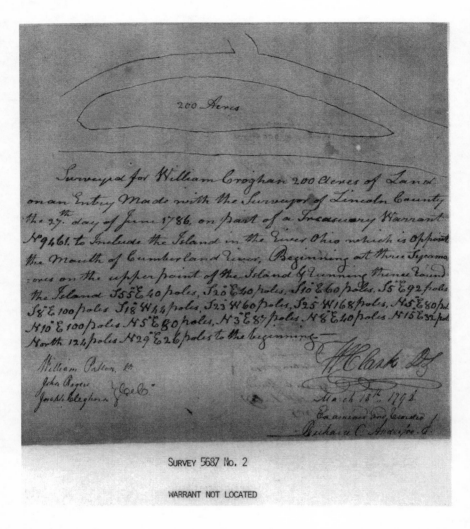

SURVEY 5687 No. 2

WARRANT NOT LOCATED

One of the surveys done by William Clark, deputy surveyor for Kentucky, while descending the lower Ohio River in 1798.

until Clark had laid out a sixteen-sided expanse of two hundred acres, compiling courses and distances on a sheet of paper he would then give to another man to take back to Croghan.[3]

Afterward, Clark and crewmen descended the river a couple of miles to a smaller island Croghan also claimed. Judging that it held perhaps only twenty acres worth his effort, Clark positioned the Jacob's staff at three hickories near the upstream end and had boatmen George Beaty, James Scott, and perhaps others assist by cutting brush, blazing corners, and carrying the chain. Together they worked their way down the northwest beach and came back up the opposite side, clearing and plotting a hexagon of twenty-two acres. Clark entered field notes into his journal, dated them March 15, 1798, and asked Beaty and Scott to sign the page.[4]

The sun was sinking and the wind blowing hard when they finished, so they remained on the island until the air calmed. No doubt tired from descending the river and from surveying a total of 222 acres that day, Clark nonetheless resumed the voyage at three o'clock in the morning.

A few hours later his boats pulled to the northern shore beneath a low bluff some fifteen river-miles above the last great bend of the Ohio. Clark had reached Fort Massac, today near Metropolis, Illinois. Having visited the outpost as a soldier, he was probably familiar with its history. In 1757 the French had built the first defensive works there, calling them Fort de l'Ascension for the holy day of their dedication, but in 1759 changed the name to honor the Marquis de Massiac, minister of marine for Louis XV. After France lost the French and Indian War and withdrew, Chickasaw Indians destroyed Fort Massiac.[5]

Although William's brother George had rendezvoused his troops on the site during the Revolutionary War, it remained uninhabited until a detachment sent by Major General Anthony Wayne arrived in 1794 and rebuilt the fortification, reducing the name to "Massac." In subsequent years the Army reinforced its structures with palisades and a deep, outer trench. By the time Clark arrived, however, Fort Massac had yet to see combat.[6]

Just outside the complex was a village of Indians and French Canadians and perhaps some Americans; it was frequented by George Drouillard, a young Shawnee métis already well-known as a hunter and an interpreter fluent in English, French, and at least two Indian languages. If Clark met Drouillard then, he was duly impressed because, five years later, he and Meriwether Lewis would seize the opportunity to hire him as translator for the Corps of Discovery. Of his 1798 visit, however, Clark recorded only: "March 16th, Friday. Arrived at Fort Massac at 10 oclock, all day & night." During that time he must have become reacquainted with the commander, Captain Zebulon Pike of the Third Infantry Regiment. Pike was a fellow veteran of the Fallen Timbers campaign and a friend of James Wilkinson.[7]

Surely Clark also encountered Pike's eponymous son, the nineteen-year-old post quartermaster known by his middle name, Montgomery. For months, young Pike had been stockpiling materiel, provisions, and every vessel he could find; his fleet probably included a battered but serviceable canoe Clark purchased for fifty cents. If so, that transaction was more momentous than either party could have realized. When Clark began exploration of the rivers of the northern Louisiana Purchase, Montgomery Pike was carrying out private orders of General Wilkinson to locate the source of the Mississippi, then to reconnoiter the Arkansas and Red rivers. In turn, Wilkinson would curry favor with President Jefferson by submitting the results to him—after extracting details of possible use to himself. Even in 1798, Montgomery may well have shared Clark's admiration for Wilkinson despite the latter's questionable goals.[8]

At Fort Massac, Clark prepared the notes of the second survey for William Croghan and gave them to a merchant navigator, Ransom Eastin, to deliver when he returned east. That same day, Clark spoke with the captains of four flatboats bound for the Mississippi River and decided to accompany their convoy. Shortly after midnight when the wind died down, he took to the dark water with his new companions.[9] He listed them as "Mr. Jones, Brown, Lind, & OHarro." Although the omission of given names makes precise identification impossible, the third man was probably a supplier referred to in Army records as "Mr. Lynn," and "OHarro" was probably Edward O'Hara, brother of chief Army contractor James O'Hara, a Revolutionary War veteran and former quartermaster general. "OHarro" and the others were transporting military uniforms and hats, casks of wine and brandy, and barrels of foodstuffs, all destined for American posts on the east side of the Mississippi. It seems a number of soldiers traveled with them.[10]

No one at Fort Massac having heard whether Spanish forces still occupied a couple of those sites, Clark did not know in advance whether he would be able to stop at either of them. There was a possibility the little fleet would have to halt many miles upriver at the Chickasaw Bluffs, the only Mississippi River installation Americans knew for sure to be occupied by the Army. The cause of the uncertainty—and of increasing animosity in the United States for Spain—was the long Spanish delay in carrying out most terms of the Treaty of San Lorenzo, a 1795 agreement nonetheless intended to reverse twelve years of deteriorating relations between the two countries.

* * *

That troubled history, on the other hand, produced the very economic conditions prompting Clark to take his tobacco, furs, and pork to New Orleans. Not long after the Revolutionary War, King Carlos III barred Americans from traveling on portions of the Mississippi running through Louisiana, at that time a vast, underpopulated, and poorly defined region that Spain had received from France in 1762. Although aware that Louisiana lacked precious minerals, Carlos III considered it useful as a barrier between the English-speaking settlements along the Atlantic seaboard and the silver mines of New Spain. On that understanding, he—then his son and successor, Carlos IV—had governed the province for three and a half decades, keeping it from going bankrupt but never spending enough money to make it able to defend itself or even to grow enough food for its inhabitants.

By contrast, residents of the Ohio River valley, having crops and products in abundance but no affordable way to transport them across the Appalachians to eastern markets, desired Louisiana goods such as coffee and sugar and preferred Spanish silver dollars to the handwritten orders and IOUs that substituted for cash in the United States. But Americans taking their goods down the Mississippi after 1784 often lost them to confiscation by the Spanish government—which on June 26 of that year declared it had the right not only to use the lower part of the river but also to keep everyone else off it. As a result, resentment against Spain ran high west of the Appalachians, particularly in Kentucky.

Such animosity spawned a succession of plans for paramilitary projects against Spanish Louisiana. For various reasons none of them ever came to fruition, but they were familiar to William Clark. In 1793 his brother George had organized the best-known of those schemes, having two years earlier collaborated on a similar one with a brother-in-law, James O'Fallon. Such plots were so dangerous to Spanish-American relations that, in 1794, President Washington's secretary of war, Henry Knox, had the Massiac site refortified to keep Americans such as George from making "hostile inroads into the dominions of Spain."[11]

In 1795 Spanish secretary of state Manuel de Godoy, to whom Carlos IV had entrusted foreign relations, decided that Louisiana was too expensive as a buffer zone and was useless for any other purpose except as a pawn. Until the right circumstances for getting rid of the territory arose, however, he sought to quiet anti-Spanish sentiment in the United States by giving Americans all they had been demanding since the end of the Revolutionary War. And so, on October 27, 1795, when he convened in Spain with U.S. envoy extraordinary Thomas Pinckney of South Carolina, Godoy assented to everything Pinckney asked for, rendering their pact (called "Pinckney's Treaty" in America) a string of outright grants to the United States. Spain agreed to allow Americans to trade along the Mississippi and also promised to retreat from east of the river above the thirty-first degree of latitude (only seventy-five miles north of New Orleans), thus turning that parallel into an international boundary and adding many thousands of acres, gratis, to the United States. In addition, Spain assented to withdraw from her former Indian alliances, to open Louisiana markets and warehouses to tobacco, pork, furs, and many other American goods; and to allow an American consulate in New Orleans.[12]

Shortly after the accord was ratified in early 1796, however, Godoy learned that President Washington had also approved another treaty, one that U.S. Envoy John Jay had reached with Great Britain, enemy of Spain and France. In retaliation for what seemed to him a betrayal of Spanish good faith, Godoy secretly nurtured a closer association with France and resolved to delay compliance with the terms of Pinckney's Treaty. In turn, France reacted to Jay's Treaty by allowing her citizens to seize any privately owned U.S. ship holding even a single item of English manufacture. Because Britain then led the world in industrial production and exported much of it to the United States, all American ships were at risk. By 1798 French depredations against them were so frequent and expensive, vessels of other countries were hoisting the French flag to join in the plundering. Having all the characteristics of war except a formal declaration, those maritime hostilities would become known as the Quasi-War.[13]

Late in 1797 President John Adams sent to Paris envoys John Marshall, Elbridge Gerry, and Charles Cotesworth Pinckney (brother of Thomas) to seek a peaceable solution, while he tried to quell the increasing clamor at home for war with France. Little did Adams yet understand, such a conflict was just what former treasury secretary Alexander Hamilton was hoping for. As the guiding force behind the Federalist party, Hamilton would argue for turning American anger against France into grounds for overrunning the Louisiana territory of her ally, Spain, in order to seize the busy, strategic port of New Orleans.[14]

General Wilkinson, however, had been contemplating that series of events for a much longer time. A man who changed his own politics to suit those in power, Wilkinson professed Federalist views when they stood to benefit him. Provided that Spain and the United States stayed at peace, he had no legitimate excuse to send the Army across the southern border, but a declaration of war could give cause for an incursion—perhaps even a march to the silver mines of New Spain. To inform his actions, Wilkinson required solid information on Louisiana geography, troops, and military works—just the sort of intelligence a skilled surveyor going down the Mississippi on a trading venture could gather surreptitiously, whatever that surveyor intended to do with it.

* * *

An hour after midnight, Clark's boats and those of O'Hara's agents swung away from Fort Massac and drifted through the dark while the crews steered around sandbars and skirted a low place called the Big Chain of Rocks. On the northern shore close to that location, General Wilkinson less than three years later would erect Cantonment Wilkinsonville, a military facility Hamilton intended as a base of operations against Louisiana and perhaps even Latin America, but those plans were in the future. Clark proceeded on and by daybreak had reached the broadest, deepest, most remote stretch of the Ohio.[15]

He tied his vessels to the last island of any size; it contained fifty acres of a third Croghan claim. Clark took with him crewman George Beaty and also William McFarland, probably a hand from one of the contractor's boats. The three of them (and perhaps others whose names Clark did not record) commenced a survey at a large maple near the upstream end. After measuring the eastern portion of the island, adding field notes to his journal, and trekking up the other side, Clark deemed his work sufficient and returned to the boats. He set off one last time down the Ohio. He had finished surveying for Croghan, but he kept his instruments close by to plot the coordinates of key positions in Spanish territory.[16]

Clark was approaching the end of the Ohio River and the beginning of his journey down the Mississippi. Beyond flowed water so wide he could scarcely see across it. Having covered 428 miles since setting off ten days earlier, he probably hoped to make even better time on the more swiftly flowing Mississippi; it often ran at six miles per hour, double or more the rate of the Ohio.

Clark might have imagined that on such an accelerated current he'd have less time to devote to his travel account; until now he had penned an average of sixteen words for every day on the water. But he would have been wrong. Once on the Mississippi, the western border of the United States and the entrance to the Spanish empire, his overall progress would slacken considerably, giving him a chance to add three times as much text as before to his logbook. More importantly, the slower pace would allow him to chart the river and to ascertain the coordinates of thirteen places essential to any penetration of the lower Mississippi valley.

He reached the confluence of the Ohio and Mississippi at noon on Saturday, March 17, 1798. Some two hundred river-miles to the north, the Missouri—the longest drainage in the western part of the continent—emptied into the Mississippi, injecting it with enough silt and perversity to make the lower river turbid, contrary, and relatively fast. Above that union, the Mississippi resembled the Ohio in clarity and deportment, but below it raced muddy and rough, devoured its banks, and lurched for the Gulf of Mexico in tight, exaggerated curlicues likely to spin a boat in all directions.

The occluded color of the waters he saw revealed their distant origin. Beneath him swirled sands from islands and banks two thousand miles to the west, mingling with sediment from the Nishnabotna, the Knife, and the Mussellshell rivers, grindings from the Rocky Mountains and Great Plains. So thick was the silt in each jugful dipped from the Mississippi, he had to let the contents settle, then sip only the top layer to avoid tasting too much mud. Indeed, Clark drank the West before he traveled it.

Except for the increased velocity under his fleet, the first few miles of the Mississippi might have seemed more like the last stretch of the Ohio. Every now and then, placid currents still broke the surface to remain momentarily suspended, powerful boils of muddy, unruffled liquid sediment. At other times, deep whorls of ooze made upper waters appear to seethe, and if such vortices formed under a vessel they could rotate it in circles or push it shoreward, toward obstructions.[17]

As Clark well knew, though, drifting or snagged trees were much more numerous and unpredictable than eddies and boils; for every cottonwood or sycamore borne straight downstream on the Mississippi, another one drifted crosswise, forming a huge low wall. Even worse were snags, that is, trees embedded on one end in the riverbed. If the opposite extremity bobbed in a sawing motion, such "sawyers" could tear into a hull. He had to be careful near land, too; stories abounded of vessels wrecked and lives lost when the Mississippi cut beneath a bank and caused it suddenly to collapse into the water.

Once on the big river, Clark became cautious about proceeding in inclement weather or with poor visibility. Although spring runoff accelerated the flow and increased his progress, he must have hoped that coming rains would not be excessive. He had only to look at the forest on each side to see drifted debris still clinging to upper branches long after a flood.

Before floating beyond view of the Ohio he surely scanned the western horizon to verify the absence of the Spanish freshwater navy; until sometime in 1797, the royal galiots *La Flecha* and *La Activa* had patrolled the middle Mississippi to stop American intruders. Clark knew this from experience. In 1795 he had reconnoitered that section of the river, surreptitiously producing a map showing a Spanish naval station on the west bank, just opposite the mouth of the Ohio. In addition, he'd indicated barracks for royal boatmen by drawing three small squares and captioning them "Spanish Guard of 6 Men." But now, seeing no sign of any Spanish vessel, he prepared to make the first in a long series of topographical observations.[18]

He was surely aware, though, that performing such an inspection could get him in trouble. Two years earlier, American newspapers had reported that Spanish authorities in Louisiana arrested, imprisoned, then expelled French general Georges-Victor Collot for recording details about Louisiana fortifications. (Three decades later, Collot's observations and maps were published as *A Journey in North America*.) When confident that no one but Americans might see what he was doing, Clark opened his journal in the middle, flipped to four successive blank leaves, and pressed an inked nib to the top of the first one, tracing to the left a dual set of lines he labeled "Ohio." Into those he merged a wriggling pair of contours captioned "Mississippi" and thereby commenced a chart of that river, committing the first of numerous violations of Spanish law.

To allow room on paper for the initial 550 river-miles he was to travel, he would squeeze two stretches of the Mississippi averaging 70 miles each onto a page. He would keep to the same scale by fitting the second half of the river onto another four pages. Because his journal opened like a stenographer's pad, he would begin each section at the top of a double page and draw downward and over the gutter until reaching the bottom of the adjoining page. The result was to resemble a modern mariner's chart, with islands of various shapes and sizes, tributary rivers and creeks, sandbars, oxbows, and bluffs sketched as if seen from above.

For added precision he would tally distances between major bends, later totaling those figures at the foot of each double section. Sure of his ability to reduce the contorted stream to accurate calibrations, he allowed himself no extra paper. Only where the Mississippi trends more to the east than to the south, as it does from above New Orleans to the Gulf, would he

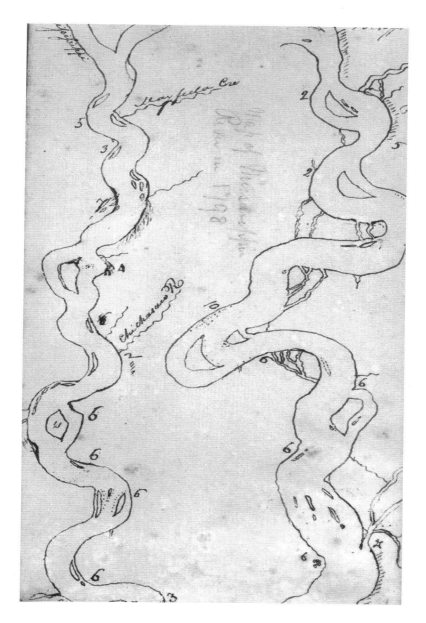

Clark's map of two reaches of the Mississippi River not far below the Ohio confluence, on page A01 of his 1798–1801 Notebook.

adjust his predominantly vertical map by breaking the river up into separate lateral pieces, stair-step fashion. Even with that accommodation, the chart was to remain remarkably accurate. It provides evidence to dispel the once common assumption that Clark was not a cartographer until the 1803–1806 Expedition. On the contrary, the 1798 map proves he was already adept at figuring positions based on compass readings, dead reckoning, and perhaps even observations made with an instrument such as a sextant or an octant; all were effective means he would employ during the journey to the Pacific.[19]

On this voyage, however, he would draw the Mississippi without the shading, arrows, and trigonometry he used to embellish his maps of the great West, making the chart in his journal appear more a preliminary effort than a finished product. Why was he bothering to map the river at all? Regardless of his long-standing wish to trade on it, he had never before charted it beyond New Madrid, a Spanish gateway some seventy miles below the mouth of the Ohio.

Might he have intended the map for someone else? It is a fair question. Having served under General Wilkinson for four years in the Army and during previous militia campaigns, Clark surely knew of Wilkinson's unflagging desire for information, especially details about Spanish lands bordering the United States. If the Mississippi map was in fact for him—a point that may never be proved—Clark was still trying to serve the officer whom General Anthony Wayne once termed "the worst of all bad men."[20]

3

Big Little Man

JAMES Wilkinson moved to Kentucky, then the western district of Virginia, in 1783, more than a year before young William Clark arrived with his parents and sisters. Born and raised in Maryland on a plantation near Plum Point on Chesapeake Bay, Wilkinson found his new surroundings agreeable and soon became known and liked throughout the territory. Even Humphrey Marshall, a lawyer later to become his bitter enemy, used favorable language to describe him, saying he possessed "a countenance open, mild, capacious, and beaming with intelligence; a gait firm, manly, and facile; manners bland, accommodating, and popular; an address easy, polite and gracious. . . . By these fair forms he conciliated; by these he captivated." Whether practicing medicine, his study before the Revolution, or selling groceries, dry goods, and hardware for a Pennsylvania firm doing business in Lexington, Kentucky, Wilkinson spoke with fluency and aplomb, employing clever turns of phrase and classical allusions revealing a solid education. Linked in marriage with the illustrious Biddle family of Philadelphia (one of whom would prepare some of the Corps of Discovery journals for publication in 1814), he purchased land near the Falls of the Ohio. From time to time he visited his close friend and attorney Benjamin Sebastian in Louisville.[1]

Wilkinson was ready for a fresh start in Kentucky. Having abandoned his medical education in order to take part in the Revolution, he joined Washington's forces at Cambridge, Massachusetts, and within months became a captain. After serving in the siege of Boston, he participated in the Canada campaign of Benedict Arnold, becoming friends with him

Charles Willson Peale's 1797 portrait of General James Wilkinson.

and with Aaron Burr, one of a number of individuals Wilkinson would later double-cross. His brilliant rise continued. Named aide-de-camp to General Horatio Gates, he attained a colonel's commission, then that of deputy adjutant-general. A few months afterward, at the age of twenty, he became a brigadier general.

A lifelong predilection for intrigue, however, began to assert itself. Named secretary to General Gates, president of the Board of War, Wilkinson took part in the machinations of that officer and his followers known as the "Conway Cabal" (for Thomas Conway, a minor figure in the group) to replace George Washington as commander in chief. On realizing that Washington's leadership and popularity would probably cause the plot to fail, Wilkinson gave it away, setting a perfidious pattern he would repeat throughout his life and earning Washington's suspicion.

Resigning from the Board of War, Wilkinson accepted the post of clothier general to the Continental Army. Within two years, though, problems with his accounts prompted Washington to question Wilkinson's honesty. Congress reacted by eliminating half his salary, at which point Wilkinson left the military altogether.[2]

He migrated to Kentucky, at that time the center of westward expansion. Finding George Rogers Clark—then widely acclaimed as a hero—his rival for influence, Wilkinson, it seems, set out to destroy George's reputation and supplant him as a leader. The means to do both arose in a controversy caused by George during 1786 in Vincennes, a French-speaking town founded more than a half-century earlier on the Wabash River in what is now Indiana. While preparing for a campaign against nearby Indians, George fed and supplied his troops with goods confiscated from three merchants visiting Vincennes from Spanish territory. Although he complied with martial law, George's use of the items provoked an uproar in Louisiana; officials there considered it retaliation for the Spanish practice of seizing American wares on the Mississippi.

Cook's portrait of George Rogers Clark, ca. 1810.

As a professed military officer of Virginia, George asked Governor Edmund Randolph of that state to let a court of inquiry review the matter, having no idea Wilkinson would get himself appointed to chair that very proceeding. Wilkinson also, it seems, anonymously accused George of "playing hell" and of being "constantly drunk and yet full of design," opinions that eventually influenced the other investigators to condemn George's action. As a result the governor did so too, spoiling George's superb prospects in politics and for military command. This ruling also made him liable to the Spanish merchants for thousands of dollars and left him little hope of recouping any portion of the twenty thousand dollars Virginia owed for his Revolutionary War expenses. Because those events occurred when William was a teenager, they must have perplexed his feelings for his brother.[3]

But Wilkinson was only just beginning. To the Spanish commandant of St. Louis he dispatched a letter deploring George's action at Vincennes, warning of an alleged—and probably bogus—attack contemplated against Spanish Natchez by George and an associate named Thomas Green, and offering to help thwart their supposed plan. Afterward, Wilkinson set off from Kentucky for Louisiana on a flatboat carrying tobacco and a pair of thoroughbred horses. Lacking a passport, he boldly presented the animals to Natchez commandant Carlos de Grand Pré who, having heard of Wilkinson's reputed role in protecting Natchez, awarded him a written recommendation to Governor Esteban Miró at New Orleans.

Wilkinson pulled ashore there on July 2, 1787, received a warm welcome from Miró and Intendant Martín Navarro, and sold his tobacco. He then asked permission to return the next year with tons of Kentucky wares; he wanted an exclusive exception to the law restricting foreign trade to Spanish subjects only. To induce approval from the Spanish Court (the ultimate arbiter of his request), Wilkinson shockingly penned a long memorial in which he proposed to advance the fortunes of Spain by helping populate Louisiana with emigrants from the western United States. If Spain wished him to accomplish this end through violent means, he would urge fellow citizens to break away from the Union and ally themselves with Spain. If that nation instead preferred a more peaceable method, he would persuade western Americans to defect across the river. In this manner Wilkinson stealthily launched the initial phase of the Spanish Conspiracy.

To increase the odds of success for either alternative, he advised Spain to keep the Mississippi closed to all Americans but himself. He went on to stress the need for Spanish fortifications along the U.S. frontier, especially on the west bank of the Mississippi and not far below the mouth of the Ohio. Then, capping those acts of treachery, he made a solemn secret declaration shifting his allegiance from the United States to Carlos III, upon whose death in December 1788 the monarchy would devolve to son Carlos IV. This was a move so potentially damning to Wilkinson's reputation in the United States, he would thereafter correspond with Louisiana by means of codes and cyphers. Because Miró and Navarro's next report to Spain included a number of documents, the thirteenth of which concerned Wilkinson and his proposals, the Crown assigned him a secret identity as Agent 13.

Miró and Navarro promised to seek royal approval of the monopoly sought by Wilkinson and awarded him the right to come back the next year with thirty-five thousand dollars' worth of goods to sell. So favorably disposed were they to his proposals, Wilkinson did not expect the Spanish court would eventually rule against many of them. Until that discouraging news reached him, he continued trying to limit the ability of other Americans to profit from dealing with Spanish Louisiana.[4]

He applied quite another standard to potential accomplices. In the hope of wringing more benefit for himself, Wilkinson sent Governor Miró a list of twenty-two such "notables," describing each by his views, means, and the amount of money Wilkinson thought necessary to purchase his compliance in the intrigue. Those assessments were to prove remarkably prescient of the following men—all of them known in person or by reputation to William Clark, and all of them key to the events about to unfold.[5]

Benjamin Sebastian was born in 1741 in Virginia and served as an Anglican minister before the Revolutionary War. Afterward, he moved to Louisville and became a lawyer. For his military service he received a warrant entitling him to more than two hundred acres in Kentucky; he eventually settled at Belmont, an estate not far from the Clarks' Mulberry Hill. He won the esteem of John Clark whose youngest son's technical prowess caught Sebastian's attention. That is, in the spring of 1795, when "Billy" was home on leave from the Army, Sebastian asked for him to come over with "the plat & certificate of his survey on Cumberland." Tall and gaunt, Sebastian conveyed an impression of Revolutionary-era gentility, tying his hair behind his back, wearing breeches fitted at the knees with silver buckles, and carrying himself with dignity despite chronic financial need deepened by his spendthrift wife and children.

Wilkinson listed Sebastian—a fellow advocate of separating Kentucky not just from Virginia but also from the other states—as the first of his "confidential friends," requesting that Spain favor him with a thousand dollars. Soon Wilkinson began instructing Sebastian on the use of secret cryptographs and pseudonyms in correspondence with that nation.[6]

Harry Innes was born in 1752 in Virginia and grew up close to the Caroline County home of John and Ann Clark and their large family. In his early twenties Innes became a lawyer and soon developed a busy practice. Not long after becoming attorney general for the Kentucky District in 1784 he moved there, helping to organize the Indian-fighting militia that William Clark joined. In 1789 Innes was appointed U.S. district judge for Kentucky, a position that made him cautious about—but not opposed to—receiving an illicit salary from Spain. For him, Wilkinson also requested a thousand Spanish dollars.[7]

John Brown was a Virginian born in 1757 who attended the College of New Jersey (now Princeton University) but graduated from the College of William and Mary. In 1782 or the following year he settled in Kentucky, established a law practice, and became involved in the political maneuvering that would eventually produce statehood. Before it did, however, he secretly corresponded with Spanish minister Diego de Gardoqui about advantages to be gained by having the Kentucky District break away from the Union. Toward that end he conspired with Wilkinson who, correctly perceiving Brown's timidity, judged a thousand dollars necessary to lure him into more active participation.[8]

George Muter was a Scottish immigrant. As Harry Innes's fellow on the U.S. District Court, he drew an annual salary of a thousand dollars; Wilkinson therefore recommended that sum, plus two hundred additional dollars, necessary to win him over to seditious causes. Having neither family nor the ability to husband his judicial income, he came to depend heavily on lawyer Thomas Todd who, as Harry Innes's cousin, was willing not just to join them in the intrigue with Spain but also, as we will see, to use it in order to seize control of Kentucky commerce.[9]

George Nicholas was born in Virginia in or around 1754 and moved in 1790 to Kentucky where he practiced law and became active in politics. Possessing properties scattered among six Kentucky counties, Nicholas was so wealthy that Wilkinson judged at least two thousand dollars necessary to turn him into a tool of the Spanish monarchy. Nicholas was a William and Mary graduate who fought in the Revolution, married well, and spent most of the 1780s as a Virginia politician. He eventually followed his friend Harry Innes to Danville, Kentucky, where they worked as attorneys, but Nicholas also taught law and composed much of the first Kentucky constitution. As will be revealed, by failing to destroy his clandestine correspondence with Spain he posthumously would touch off a media frenzy that William Clark may have viewed as a threat to his own reputation.[10]

Conspicuously absent from the roster was George Rogers Clark. Though never to learn the extent of Wilkinson's treachery against him, George distrusted him and his friends, referring to them as "big little men." No doubt George did so around William as well.[11]

* * *

Wilkinson was so encouraged by the support his treasonable proposal received at New Orleans that in 1788 he routed there twenty-five flatboats bearing tobacco, salted pork, butter, and flour. He spent the proceeds on imported luxuries—sugar, brandy, fine fabrics, brass housewares—to sell in Kentucky. Around the same time he also entered Kentucky politics, spearheading the movement to separate that district from Virginia (but secretly, leading his Spanish contacts to believe he was working instead to sever Kentucky from the United States). Late in 1789 he moved to Louisville where he and Benjamin Sebastian became municipal trustees, a position to enhance James Wilkinson's aura of success. If nineteen-year-old William Clark had not yet heard much about Wilkinson, he certainly did now. In a town then consisting of only a handful of streets and fewer than a thousand residents, William must have encountered the charismatic Wilkinson from time to time.[12]

Little did anyone but he realize, however, his sources of revenue were already ebbing. Expenses of all sorts, including the partial loss of his fleet to river hazards, reduced his profits from the Louisiana trade nearly to nothing, and imprudent land speculations in and around Kentucky put him deep in debt. The most crushing news came in 1789: Rather than grant Wilkinson a monopoly, the Spanish Court would instead open trade on the Mississippi to select Americans, including William Croghan and Richard C. Anderson. And, in lieu of having Wilkinson foment secession, Spain would prompt Americans to settle west of the river by giving them land and more religious toleration than it allowed in other parts of the realm. Clearly, Spain did not want Wilkinson as a secret agent.[13]

His finances tilting toward bankruptcy, he sold thousands of prime Kentucky acres but was unable to live for long on the proceeds. Desperate for money, he agreed in 1791 to serve as the second-ranking officer of the Kentucky militia. His commission soon put him in charge of William Clark who since 1789 had been fighting in skirmishes against Indians of the Ohio River valley.[14]

At Wilkinson's order on June 2, 1791, Clark's unit of 360 men launched a surprise attack on the large Indian settlement of Kethtepeconunk, near the site of Logansport, Indiana. They burned it to the ground, achieving one of the few victories of that era against tribes of the old Northwest. Similar results following at the nearby native village of L'Anguille, Wilkinson expected to receive a high Army appointment.[15]

In weighing whether to recommend him for one, President Washington considered his own reservations about Wilkinson as well as more recent rumors of his conniving with Spain. Lacking proof of any disloyalty, though, Washington decided to gamble on Wilkinson. After all, he was a popular Kentuckian whose leadership in the Army could help reconcile western Americans to remaining in the Union—a point of monumental importance to the survival of the early republic. Indeed, Wilkinson's minor victories were among the only successes in those years against the Indians; the Army had been reeling since the 1790 defeat of General Josiah Harmar's force of fifteen hundred men.[16]

The president named Wilkinson lieutenant colonel in October 1791, and the following year he promoted him to brigadier general. By entrusting him with those commissions, Washington inaugurated a practice his successors until James Madison were to follow. They would keep Wilkinson in conspicuous positions of power while wagering that the harm he might do would not exceed the benefits to the federal government—especially those of gaining increased control over the Army and of improving relations with the western states.[17]

William Clark joined the Army in March 1792, and in May reported for duty to Fort Washington at Cincinnati. From the very beginning he worked for Wilkinson, Clark's first assignment being to carry Wilkinson's correspondence from that post to Kentucky. Other plums followed, such as recruiting duty that allowed Clark to wear a fine, new uniform, to improve his prowess at billiards (taverns were prime locations for enlisting soldiers), and to remain close to Louisville. As Wilkinson shrewdly calculated, kinship to the famous George Rogers Clark helped William attract men to the Army, and granting him pleasant tasks surely cemented his loyalty to Wilkinson.[18]

In the spring of 1792, President Washington charged Anthony Wayne, the Revolutionary War hero of Stony Point, New York, with putting an end to Indian attacks north of the Ohio River and appointed him major general. Unfortunately, by ignoring George Rogers Clark, perhaps the ablest commander of all, Washington further alienated him from the country they had both freed from England; thereafter, George would ally himself with the French Republic. And, by passing over Wilkinson, the president inadvertently aroused in him an abiding enmity for his new superior.

Before Wayne assumed command at Fort Washington in May 1793, Wilkinson was already sowing insubordination and disrespect for him. Soon a schism split the Army into mutually opposed factions, as men in each of them quarreled, dueled, and even killed those in the other. Such discord was exactly what Wilkinson wished; to a secret contact in Louisiana he professed aiming "to keep down the military establishment, to disgrace my commander, and to secure myself command of the Army."[19]

Once Wayne and his troops reached the Ohio River valley, Wilkinson began engaging in all manner of sabotage. On occasion he sent influential civilians letters revealing strategic secrets; at times he dispatched to the press anonymous messages full of vituperation for Wayne and contempt for his system of transforming the Army into a force capable of winning a major battle with the Indians. Circumstances permitting Wilkinson cover, he may have managed for a while to hinder provisions and supplies from reaching Wayne's troops, an unconscionable and potentially deadly endeavor.[20]

Wilkinson often accomplished his devious purposes through the efforts of loyal junior officers. To win them over, he liked to ascertain and then take advantage of their individual weaknesses and desires. According to him: "Some men are sordid, some vain, some ambitious. To detect the predominant passion, to lay hold and to make the most of it is the most profound secret of political science." Evidence suggests that as the Army prepared for a decisive campaign against the Indians, Wilkinson made ready to score a pivotal blow against Wayne, in part by having a handful of trusted supporters keep diaries critical of his tactics and decisions. If this is so, Wilkinson must have planned to circulate that biased and often erroneous information among members of Congress.[21]

William Clark was to keep such a journal. Already a partisan of Wilkinson (known during that time as the most popular officer in the Army), Clark had reason to think he would benefit from a close relationship with him. And the longer Clark remained in the service, the more evidence he could have seen linking Wilkinson with the Spanish Conspiracy.

4

No Sort of Trick Is Involved

NOW, as civilian Clark and his flatboats of mercantile goods entered the Mississippi, he observed on the eastern shore the first of several locales that were key to the development of that series of plots. This particular place was a boggy and nondescript but strategic tract that Thomas Jefferson had once asked George Rogers Clark to fortify in order to keep Spanish troops off the Ohio River and to arrest the influence of the British in the Mississippi valley. In 1780, finding the area too flood-prone for construction, George built on higher ground, five miles downstream, an outpost called Fort Jefferson and an adjacent village known as Clarksville. More than five hundred soldiers and civilians soon took up residence there, but disease, hunger, and Indian hostilities caused them all to leave in 1781. Still, the experience of founding a colony on the Mississippi awakened George and his countrymen to the advantages of living along the western boundary and relatively close to the markets of New Orleans.[1]

Even after 1784, when Spain closed the river to American trade, George's settlement ideas gained in popularity. Having no doubt heard of Wilkinson's seeming commercial coup at New Orleans in 1787, George proposed the following year to Spanish minister Diego de Gardoqui a plan to establish across the Mississippi from the deserted Fort Jefferson a "numerous and flourishing colony of faithful [Spanish] subjects" composed mostly of American émigrés who, because of their time in the states, were accustomed to representative government and to worshiping openly as Protestants. Although Gardoqui knew of Wilkinson's accusa-

William Clark's 1798 route on the Mississippi River from the mouth of the Ohio to Walnut Hills, 591 river miles. Parentheses indicate future cities and states.

tions concerning George's controversial actions at Vincennes, he refused the request because Spain was yet unwilling to grant such measures of religious or political freedom. Consequently, George gave up the idea of colonizing Spanish territory; thereafter he would aim to conquer it.[2]

In 1790, talk spread on both sides of the Mississippi concerning the South Carolina Yazoo Company, a business association put together by land speculators wishing to settle the east side of the Mississippi, from the mouth of the Yazoo River (near the present city of Vicksburg) to Natchez. Company directors took care to secure the permission of Georgia, whose western boundary then stretched to the Mississippi, but Spain and various Indian tribes also asserted rights to the same ground. The best-known of several speculative bubbles of that era, the South Carolina Yazoo project attracted dozens of businessmen, politicians, and schemers, including James Wilkinson and the Irish-born James O'Fallon, a medical doctor more interested in intrigue than in treating patients (he was soon to marry Frances Clark, William's younger sister). The South Carolina Yazoo scheme also won support from George who, hoping to profit as a soldier of fortune, offered to take fifteen hundred men down the Mississippi to crush Spanish resistance. But because the Yazoo plan was sure to antagonize Spain and alarm Indians between Georgia and the Mississippi, President Washington issued a proclamation against it, causing it to collapse before any settlement could occur. Later, as Spain continued to claim the right to control the east side of the Mississippi as far north as the Ohio River, George looked anew for paramilitary projects to lead against Louisiana. Wilkinson stayed alert for ways to profit from betraying them.[3]

Because accurate intelligence would determine his course, Wilkinson kept an eye out for maps and data concerning the western frontier, often relying on talented, youthful associates to compile such information. Equipped with sextant, compass, and training provided by Wilkinson, adventurer Philip Nolan—a man of approximately William Clark's years—was already spying out terrain beyond the Sabine River. Soon Zebulon Montgomery Pike of the Army would reconnoiter for Wilkinson a vast Spanish expanse northwest of Nolan's travels.[4]

But now, Clark adjusted his scientific instruments once more and determined the coordinates of what he described simply as the "sandy Island before you come to the mouth of the Ohio." He meant the first major island below the confluence; that landform had the distinct advantage of close proximity to the abandoned Fort Jefferson and to at least one large cannon still there. But the order in which Clark was to list this geographical position and the other ones he would record downstream indicates he had in mind a party heading *up* the Mississippi. Because few commercial vessels of that day were able to ascend the river, we must ask what other sort of mission he may have been thinking of.[5]

When finished taking observations, he stowed his instruments and continued the voyage. Before nightfall he tied up at what he called "Chalk Bank," although bluffs of that designation probably lay some eleven miles downstream. Instead, he must have been referring to the Iron Banks, lofty cliffs of tremendous strategic potential in that low-lying region. Clark did not record what he did there. At noon the next day he set off despite a contrary wind. Landing in the evening opposite a large island, he got back on the water shortly after sunup. Two and a half hours later, his boats drifted within view of New Madrid.

In front of the town stood what was left of the original Fort Céleste, a Spanish stronghold erected nearly a decade previously and named to honor the wife of then-governor Esteban Miró. Once a third of a mile from the river, the post had by that time been eroding into the current for several years, obliging its occupants to move key military structures away from the Mississippi before they fell into it. Fort Céleste being the essential checkpoint for detecting and opposing invaders from upstream, the most important duty of its commandant was to pull ashore every passing vessel and to inspect those he thought might imperil the interests of Spain.[6]

Clark wrote of that day: "at 9 oClock landed at <u>New Madrid</u> wind rose obliged us to Stay all day. obtain permission to pass. &c." He also noted that during those hours he had six of his more valuable pelts cleaned. Locating someone to perform that work must have been easy; for years the fur trade had been the predominant business along the horseshoe-shaped river loop occupied by New Madrid. Decades earlier, so many deer, bears, and other creatures of marketable peltry and flesh abounded there, hunters and trappers called it L'Anse à la Graisse (Greasy Bend) for the animal oils they rendered. Having paused at New Madrid in 1793 and 1795 as he carried out confidential Army missions, Clark was knowledgeable about the area.[7]

New Madrid had changed little since his last visit; the population was still incongruously low for a well-laid-out town of such obvious possibilities. To Clark's eye, its overall design—broad, tree-lined streets bordering lots nearly square, the traditional land-use pattern of cities in the East—was harmonious and familiar. But the inhabitants did not seem to reflect their setting; they consisted of fewer than two hundred families, most of whom spoke French or an Indian tongue. The American influence was obvious, but where were the Americans? As Clark must have known, nearly all of them—including George Morgan, the Revolutionary War colonel who in 1789 founded New Madrid—had long since returned to the United States.

Clark probably knew something of Morgan's story. Encouraged by Minister Gardoqui, who approved of offering American emigrants acreage at no charge, commercial freedom, and religious tolerance, Morgan asked permission to lay out and establish an elegant community not far from the mouth of the Ohio. Gardoqui endorsed that project and asked Spain to do so as well, but he failed to notify Governor Miró of Morgan's plans although they concerned part of Miró's jurisdiction. In the meantime, Morgan and seventy men hoping to settle at what would become New Madrid went to work there, clearing timber and building a town in keeping with Morgan's vision.

While they did so, Wilkinson, an investor in the rival South Carolina Yazoo Company, slyly lied to Miró, calling Morgan's plan a ruse to seize navigation of the Mississippi or perhaps to collude with Spain's enemy, Great Britain. To protect Louisiana, Wilkinson urged, Spain must erect a fort at New Madrid and restrict immigration there to those willing to submit to the authority of the Crown and of the Catholic Church. Confident such measures would stunt the colony, Wilkinson also ruined Morgan's reputation with Spain by revealing he had a history of insolvency.

Thus informed, Miró approved land for Morgan's settlement but no civil liberties beyond those Spain usually allowed her subjects. Soon Morgan left for the United States, never to return nor to have anything of substance to do thereafter with New Madrid. Within a short time, most of his followers also abandoned the settlement. Spain sent Lieutenant Pierre Foucher of the Louisiana Regiment to take military and civil command of New Madrid, and Foucher completed Morgan's designs for streets and public works. In conformity with Wilkinson's recommendation, Foucher also constructed Fort Céleste, an impressive installation befitting a gateway to the Spanish realm. Surrounded by a moat and a palisade, the fort had bastions, barracks for a hundred men (although usually twenty or fewer were stationed there), a galleried residence for the commandant, a powder magazine, an infirmary, a jail, a guardhouse, and storerooms. Captain Tomás Portell, a native Catalonian, relieved Foucher in 1791.[8]

To keep Americans and other invaders out of Louisiana and to pacify Indian allies, Spain went on to invest even more money in New Madrid. By 1796, Portell commanded twenty regular soldiers and a body of militiamen and possessed an artillery of eight cannons firing eight-pound shot. Occasionally the heavily armed Spanish galiots *La Flecha* and *La Activa* paused at Fort Céleste while patrolling the Mississippi, but when foreign vessels hove within sight, Portell and his successor, Carlos Dehault Delassus, dispatched soldiers in a large canoe to direct them to shore.[9]

Clark does not mention whether that happened on March 20, 1798, when the boats in his convoy rounded the last bend above New Madrid. If Delassus's troops subjected those vessels, especially the Army boats, to rigorous scrutiny, they would have done so not only because turncoat Wilkinson advised Spain to take such precautions but also because of a confidential mission his adherent, Lieutenant William Clark, had previously made to New Madrid. Let us examine what happened during that critical earlier expedition.

* * *

In May 1793, while General Anthony Wayne was preparing for battle with Indians north of the Ohio, he received War Secretary Henry Knox's orders to convey five hundred muskets, a score of rifles, a ton of gunpowder, thousands of flints, two tons of lead, fifteen hundred bushels of corn, a hundred bushels of salt, and great quantities of whiskey to a group of Chickasaws 225 miles down the Mississippi from the Ohio. Those Indians had requested the supplies and provisions, and prompt delivery was crucial. Because the Chickasaws occupied lands that would become Tennessee and northern Mississippi but were virtually the only Indians who might assist the Army in the coming engagement, Knox and President Washington wanted to establish ties of amity with them as soon as possible.[10]

At twenty-four hundred total members, the Muskogean-speaking Chickasaws comprised the smallest tribe of the four major ones occupying what was then the southern territory of the United States; the others were the Creeks, Choctaws, and Cherokees. (Often associated with those groups are the Seminoles, then residing in the Spanish Floridas.) Far outnumbered by the Choctaws, the Chickasaws were generally of larger stature and of a fiercer and more independent disposition. Unlike nearby tribes, they remained neutral during the American Revolution but afterward had been wooed by both Spain and the United States with gifts of clothing, food, tools, armaments, and other items. The Chickasaws were therefore split into factions over which nation to support.

Chief Ugulayacabe led the one favoring Spain. Preferring an American alliance, Chief Payemingo spoke for the Chickasaws requesting the items enumerated in Knox's letter; they needed them in order to fight the Creeks and Choctaws. But because those neighboring tribes were also friendly to the Spanish, Payemingo and his followers were really asking the United States, a nation at peace with Spain, to help arm its enemies. Washington was willing to do so, but only on the condition that the true nature of the operation remain unknown, especially at New Madrid.[11]

When Wayne received Knox's order he had not yet made William Clark's acquaintance, but he understood that the young lieutenant had successfully directed several Army convoys on the Ohio. What's more, Wayne knew that, because William was the brother of the disaffected George (a man notorious in Spanish regions for his interest in conquering them), William was likely to command respect there. Having little idea yet of Wilkinson's deceits or of his reliance on others to carry out his trickery, Wayne ordered Clark to hasten downstream with the goods for the Chickasaws.[12]

At first, Clark did as he was told. Having proceeded past the Falls of the Ohio, he and two dozen soldiers on three loaded flatboats reached the

Mississippi the following week. Because Spain had not yet stationed a patrol at the mouth of the Ohio, Clark and his men entered the Mississippi unimpeded.[13]

Just above New Madrid, however, Clark began to deviate from instructions. Ordered by Wayne to pass Fort Céleste *only under cover of darkness* in order "to prevent any difficulty or disagreeable consequence" that might develop should the Spanish discover his party in the act of running guns to foes of Spain, Clark instead did the opposite, approaching the post at midday on July 5, 1793, when Commandant Portell's forces would be sure to stop him. Clark's diary account and subsequent report to General Wayne having served until now as the principal sources of knowledge about this series of events, historians have either taken for granted that Clark passed New Madrid by night—an impression his laconic entries of that mission do not dispel—or, taking a deeper look, have accepted at face value his explanation for why he did what he did. That is, to General Wayne, Clark excused his blatant advance on New Madrid by claiming he had heard that Portell knew about his mission and was expecting him. But was Clark telling the truth?[14]

Portell's hurried, unpolished account—nearly forgotten in the Spanish Archives until now—raises the possibility that, in fact, Clark was not. Portell wrote: "About eleven-thirty in the morning, the Corporal of the Guard notified me that three flatboats were in sight, and some minutes later a corporal for the rifleman division of the American infantry came ashore and delivered to me the attached [a notice announcing Clark's arrival]." Portell thought quickly, devising a plan to find out what Clark was trying to accomplish:

> I ordered the Sub-Commandant of the Militia Company of this Port to go in the King's Canoe with the large flag, so that the first flatboat could see its nationality, and to do as much as possible to get Clark to dine with me, while I observed at that same time what I could of the three said boats. Having succeeded only at getting Clark's consent to dine with me, I did as much as possible to detain him somehow. Thus I proposed a horseback ride, excusing myself from going along because of feeling unwell.
>
> Having thus delayed him, I take advantage of this occasion to tell you that the three said boats carry about fifteen hundred bushels of corn, seven

standard crates of rifles, about seven hundred pounds of gunpowder, and some barrels of whiskey and salt, all of which I was able to observe, but beneath the corn much [more] could have been hidden.

Clark himself has told me that no sort of trick is involved . . . and that his mission is to leave what he brings on behalf of his nation with that of the Chickasaws, *without having to deal with any chief in particular* [emphasis added].[15]

Given the gunpowder and rifle boxes that Portell and his deputies *did* see, why did he not search the boats? Surely he refrained from doing so because finding munitions onboard would have touched off a confrontation that might have led to war. What's more, although the Spanish had cannons in Fort Céleste, the Americans obviously possessed plenty of guns and ammunition within reach. Portell must also have feared that a clash of this sort would bring Payemingo's warriors down on his isolated post. Portell therefore allowed Clark and his vessels to pass, but first he quietly dispatched a report of the episode to Governor Carondelet in New Orleans.

Unaware that such intelligence was proceeding downriver ahead of him, Clark continued his journey, landing near the mouth of the Wolf River where 150 of Payemingo's men awaited. Clark accompanied them inland to their settlement some eighty miles away, then rode on again with a Chickasaw escort to a camp near Fort Washington. Soon he reported to General Wayne. The immediate outcome for the United States seemed positive; Payemingo continued east and met with President Washington, and his warriors commenced scouting for the Army.[16]

Wayne believed Clark deserved the "highest approbation," but it seems Wayne had little idea that Clark, by departing so drastically from his orders (for whatever reason), was helping precipitate a military buildup on the Spanish side of the river. In turn, those preparations for war would inspire Wayne to send Clark back to New Madrid on an even more sensitive and important mission.[17]

5

A Grand Tribute to General Wilkinson

WHEN Commandant Portell reported the events of July 5, 1793, he referred to the leader of the American party simply as "Clark," as if confident that this surname alone would disconcert Governor Miró's successor, the credulous Hector, el Baron de Carondelet. It did. Duly alarmed to learn that a kinsman of the dreaded George Rogers Clark had just achieved a military penetration of the Mississippi corridor, Carondelet took swift action.[1]

He ordered Captain Pierre Rousseau, a Frenchman commanding the Spanish freshwater squadron, to prevent U.S. troops from returning to occupy the Chickasaw Bluffs. Carondelet also dispatched word to Portell to search for weapons—other than those for sale by legitimate traders—on any American boats carrying corn to the Chickasaws. Should such acts provoke an assault on New Madrid, Spanish forces from St. Louis and Cape Girardeau, a hamlet some forty-five miles above the mouth of the Ohio, were to rush to that settlement and defend it.[2]

Carondelet likewise intended to carry out Wilkinson's sub-rosa recommendations for securing the mid-Mississippi valley for Spain. Before the governor could erect a stronghold at the Chickasaw Bluffs, though, rumors arrived of a formidable operation being developed against the southern parts of Louisiana by George Rogers Clark and the French Republic. Those stories soon proved true. Having grown bitter against his own country and sympathetic with the republican coalition replacing the French monarchy, George had renounced his allegiance to the United States and declared himself a citizen of France.[3]

In the spring of 1793, not long after the execution of Carlos IV's cousin, Louis XVI of France, the infant French Republic declared war on England and Spain and sent Minister Edmond Charles Genet—sometimes called "Citizen" Genet—to the United States. Genet's declared purpose was to win support for his government, but he had secret orders to stir up Americans against Spanish Louisiana and to use their ports to launch French attacks on the British fleet. He received a warm welcome at Charleston, South Carolina, before traveling north to carry out his clandestine instructions. Apprised that George wished to liberate not only Louisiana but also West Florida and Santa Fe from the Spanish, Genet enthusiastically embraced his project, calling Clark "Major General in the Armies of France and the French Revolutionary Legions on the Mississippi River." George swore to uphold the French Republic and commenced recruiting men and preparing to conquer Louisiana, the stepping-stone to other Spanish regions.[4]

Whispers of the Clark-Genet collaboration reaching Philadelphia before Genet did, President Washington made a formal statement of neutrality in April 1793, warning Americans not to participate in foreign aggressions. Genet arrived the following month and openly started outfitting French privateers to plunder British shipping. Fearing that those actions would draw the United States into war with England, Washington warned him to desist and, when he did not, pressed for his recall.[5]

At around the same time, Spanish diplomats at Philadelphia cautioned Carondelet to prepare for a French naval assault by way of the Mississippi delta. Further intelligence told of American freebooters soon to head downstream for New Orleans. Both warnings, especially the second one, frightened Carondelet. He knew George Rogers Clark persisted in his warlike preparations but was unaware that the presidential proclamation and trouble within the Clark-Genet scheme were causing it to wither.[6]

Enter James Wilkinson, again. Seeing in George's illegal activities the means to revive what Wilkinson called his own "villainous, confidential connexion" with Spain, he sent Carondelet an encrypted letter in which he claimed to have foiled George's design against Louisiana. As a reward, Wilkinson asked that the two-thousand-dollar annual salary the Spanish Court had approved for him as Agent 13 in 1791 be doubled, and he requested timely reimbursement of the thousands of dollars he said he'd spent in frustrating George's "piratical plan." As if to reprise his duplicity in the Vincennes affair, Wilkinson also sent to Philadelphia tidings of the "audacious proposition" of General Clark and Citizen Genet, calling on the federal government to put out their "seditious flame."[7]

But Wilkinson had much more in mind than merely collecting for past services; he envisioned the most ambitious and potentially lucrative conspiracy yet—one so thoroughly traitorous he might be hanged if it ever became known to the federal government. On April 30, 1794, he unveiled that plot to Carondelet, having first put him in a receptive mood by playing on his fear of war with the United States. Spain, Wilkinson explained, could forestall that turn of events by paying a secret operative such as himself two hundred thousand dollars to bring about a violent removal of Kentucky from the Union—a devilish recommendation without precedent in U.S. history. In case that amount seem exorbitant, the general added, the royal treasury ought to compare it with the cost of fighting the United States or of putting down an assault on Louisiana. He pointed out that until the secession of Kentucky should take place, Spain must invest in turning Indians against the Americans, bolstering frontier defenses, and building new fortifications, especially near the mouth of the Ohio River and at the Chickasaw Bluffs.[8]

Carondelet embraced all these proposals, sending them on to Spain with his own pleas for appropriate funding. Receiving this correspondence around the same time as he learned of the threat to Louisiana posed by George Rogers Clark and Genet, Secretary of State Manuel de Godoy considered Wilkinson's less expensive proposals, referring the two-hundred-thousand-dollar secession project to the Council of State. Meanwhile, Carondelet set aside enough money to pay Chief Ugulayacabe's band for acreage atop the Chickasaw Bluffs, and in the spring of 1795 sent Natchez governor Manuel Gayoso de Lemos there to consummate the purchase and to oversee construction of a military post intended to keep Americans from occupying the middle Mississippi. Completed that summer, the installation was named San Fernando de Las Barrancas (Saint Ferdinand of the Bluffs), a tribute to Ferdinand, prince of Asturias and son of Carlos IV.[9]

Fort San Fernando indeed reinforced Spain's claim to the Mississippi, but its presence was to provoke General Anthony Wayne to send Lieutenant William Clark back down the river in 1795 on another confidential assignment. First, though, Wayne gave full attention to his mission of suppressing Indian resistance to large-scale white settlement north of the Ohio River. Upon arriving in that region in 1793, he commenced recruiting and drilling a force capable of achieving such a victory. An unsurpassed tactician, he was at times prudent and thoughtful; at others, unforgiving and prone to pique. Having been friends during the Revolution with Wilkinson, Wayne refused for a long time to think that subaltern might be trying to discredit him in order to gain for himself Wayne's superior rank.

But this is exactly what Wilkinson was doing. Behind Wayne's back he ridiculed him to their soldiers; in unsigned letters he caviled against the major general's no-nonsense preparations for battle. As the time for armed conflict drew closer, Wilkinson may have had William Clark and other friends in the officer corps keep journals portraying Wayne in the worst possible light, as if Wilkinson planned to use those words as evidence against Wayne. Although on August 20, 1794, Wayne's forces routed the Indians at what came to be called the Battle of Fallen Timbers, just outside what is now Toledo, Ohio, Clark continued disparaging him in his logbook. So biased and negative are those entries, historian R. C. McGrane, editor of Clark's Fallen Timbers diary, propounded that he wrote it for Wilkinson's self-serving purposes.[10]

Meanwhile, Wilkinson was secretly redoubling his efforts to grow rich from his treasonable relations with Spain. Having requested twelve thousand pieces of eight, more than two-thirds of them for allegedly saving Louisiana from attack by the forces of Genet and George Rogers Clark, Wilkinson sent minions Henry Owen and Joseph Collins down the Mississippi to retrieve the coins. Owen took delivery of half of them at New Madrid. He was proceeding by canoe up the lower reaches of the Ohio River when his crewmen, all of them Spanish subjects, killed him and absconded with the valuable cargo.[11]

By contrast, Collins collected the other six thousand pieces of eight at New Orleans and sailed with them across the Gulf of Mexico and up the Atlantic coast, until problems with the ship caused him to disembark and proceed by land. Months later, after dissipating most of the money on his own outlays, he turned the balance over to Wilkinson who in turn promptly billed Carondelet for twenty thousand dollars as reimbursement of the total lost by Owen and Collins and as payment of his secret salary approved by the Spanish Court. This time, though, Wilkinson had a fool-proof plan for receiving the cash: He would depend on the quick wits and plausible manner of Thomas Power, a Spanish secret agent to become the most successful money-runner in the long history of the Spanish Conspiracy. By August 1795, when the tribes vanquished at Fallen Timbers met with General Wayne at his Fort Greenville headquarters and ceded large chunks of their territory to the United States, Wilkinson was growing impatient for Power to bring the money.[12]

* * *

In September, Wayne was angry to learn about the construction of Fort San Fernando. As did many Americans, he believed the Spanish had no claim to the east side of the Mississippi at that latitude, although the French, their predecessors in interest, had once asserted rights to the entire river valley. On September 10, Wayne directed William Clark to take a detachment downriver and look for the officer commanding the Spanish troops at Fort San Fernando. On finding him, Clark was to deliver Wayne's protest of the occupation and ask on what authority Spain had built the post. Wayne shrewdly expected that the notoriety in Spanish territory of George Rogers Clark would induce proper regard there for his brother's mission.[13]

Wayne also instructed William to notify the Spanish commander about the Greenville peace agreement and the recently concluded Jay's Treaty, by which Britain was to relinquish her Northwest Territory posts and to grant the United States use of the upper Mississippi. In addition, Wayne ordered Clark to bring back details on navigable streams and strategic positions below the mouth of the Ohio, and to gather figures on Spanish troops, galleys, and munitions, especially those at the Chickasaw Bluffs.[14]

Perhaps most important, Wayne warned Clark not to bring along any person, package, or written message, for any reason. Having recently learned that Wilkinson was scheming against him, Wayne must have suspected he was also intriguing with Spanish officials and might somehow use William Clark as a go-between. But because Wayne lacked hard evidence of the conspiracy, he had little knowledge of the cabal to separate Kentucky from her sister states and to ally her with the Spanish empire.[15]

Wayne was therefore unaware that Wilkinson had alerted Carondelet to the George Rogers Clark–Citizen Genet project against Louisiana. Wayne may have heard rumors of Owen's ill-fated mission and of Collins's courier service for Wilkinson, but he had no proof they were true. Nor did he realize that Wilkinson, as Agent 13, was continuing to pass the Spaniards U.S. military secrets such as the decision to refortify Massac, or that he was urging those same contacts to furnish Kentucky ten thousand stands of arms and twenty cannons to use in the contemplated war of secession.

Cognizant of all these facts, however, Governor Carondelet was sending Agent 13 sub-rosa notice of upcoming talks on that secret matter. If things went according to plan, Carondelet promised Wilkinson, he would become chief executive of the nation formed by Kentucky and adjacent territories also leaving the Union. In the meantime, Carondelet was forwarding him 9,640 pieces of eight, to reimburse the losses incurred through Owen and Collins, and had approved secret salaries for Wilkinson's conspiratorial associates. In exchange, Carondelet asked that Wilkinson or a delegate of his come to New Madrid and meet with Natchez governor Gayoso de Lemos in order to advance the plot against Kentucky. In late August, Gayoso reached New Madrid aboard *La Vigilante*, his armed galiot.[16]

Late in the afternoon of October 2, 1795, his barge displaying banners to indicate a peace mission, William Clark arrived and handed Gayoso the communications of General Wayne. Promising a response on the following day, Gayoso invited Clark to remain overnight. He accepted. The next morning he received Gayoso's letter, then proceeded upriver. For his own protection he went in the company of a "man of information" whom he did not otherwise identify except to say he was a Vincennes-bound trader who had just visited the Chickasaw Bluffs. From him Clark may

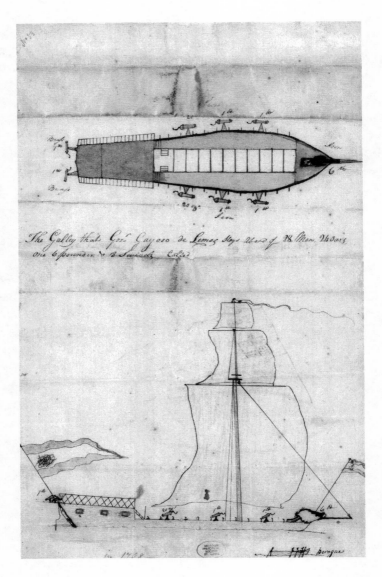

William Clark's pen-and-ink sketch of Governor Gayoso's Mississippi River galley *La Vigilante*, drawn in 1795. Meriwether Lewis's later design for the keelboat he, Clark, and the Corps of Discovery would take up the Missouri River shows a remarkable resemblance to this earlier craft.

well have gathered specific details on Fort San Fernando, for he drew a skillful pen-and-ink diagram of that installation, captioning it in English as well as in Spanish and French, languages Clark never learned. The records of Gayoso identify the "man of information" as Manuel Lisa, an opportunistic businessman fluent in English, Spanish, and French (whom the governors of Spanish Louisiana trusted to carry their top-secret correspondence to Wilkinson).[17]

On November 4, 1795, Clark reported back to Wayne, turning over to him a written account of the mission, entries from Clark's diary, and several pages of data concerning Spanish defenses atop the Chickasaw Bluffs and at other strategic points on the river. Pleased with that information, Wayne granted Clark a long furlough.[18]

But had Clark witheld information? It seems that his submission to Wayne may have lacked the layout of Fort San Fernando and the drawing Clark produced of *La Vigilante*. It also appears he might have said nothing about the Spanish gunboats patrolling the mouth of the Ohio River, although, according to Gayoso, Lisa provided Clark with safe passage beyond those very hazards. Clark's report also failed to mention a docking station being built on the western bank of the Mississippi for those vessels—despite the fact that a map he drew around this time depicts what he terms a "Spanish guard" of perhaps six men at the same place. In a little-known account of their meeting, Gayoso recorded that Clark gave his crewmen liberty, went ashore, and took dinner with Commandant Portell, all the while entrusting his boat to a hired pilot—one *not* bound by General Wayne's instructions against accepting unsolicited letters or packages. Whether the Spanish took advantage of that lapse is unknown.[19]

We will probably never learn how much Clark and the canny Lisa knew about the conspiracy to sunder Kentucky from the United States and to place it within the Spanish orbit, or whether they shared such information with each other. Whatever they discussed, however, they discovered in each other the qualities necessary in an associate. Lisa would go on to help supply the Corps of Discovery and, later, to become Clark's partner in the Missouri Fur Company and his subagent in Indian business. It seems they both owed Gayoso thanks for arranging their first collaboration.

Most significant of all are the nearly fifteen hundred words Gayoso composed about Clark's mission. One sentence is especially revealing. It relates a conversation in which Clark—forbidden to pass along any writing other than General Wayne's—repeats Wilkinson's ideas, all the while conveying his characteristic bombast. "We spoke of unimportant matters," writes Gayoso, "until [Clark] mentioned General Wilkinson by name, *giving me many of his expressions and delivering a grand tribute to his concept of the Army and to his being in command at Fort Washington* [emphasis added]." Such obvious dedication to Wilkinson—possibly in addition to a willingness to furnish Wayne incomplete information and to disregard the spirit if not the letter of his instructions—raises questions about Clark's deepest loyalty.[20]

6

These Infernal Bluffs

HOWEVER much Clark thought of that mission or of his 1793 gun-smuggling operation, he would see fit during his 1798 journey not to record anything more about them. Late in the afternoon on March 21, 1798, he got ready to leave New Madrid and to head back into the wind. For reasons unknown, an American soldier deserted from one of the contractor's boats, and of that day, Clark added only that the voyage progressed a mere three miles below the point of departure. Blustery conditions on March 22 forced him and the others to land "with great Dificullty," as he puts it. A man on O'Hara's vessel then stole undisclosed items from it and fled into the forest, but Clark relates no more of that fugitive than he does of the first one.

As the weather continued to deteriorate, Clark employed an atypical number of words to describe it. Of Friday, March 23, he reports in nearly unpunctuated style: "the wind rose verry high obliged us to land with much Dificullty & Danger the boates much Scattered, wind continue all night Some rane." Of the following day he says: "wind blew violently in the morning Some rane continued windy all day and night. No account of the boats to day." Other entries are similar. The next day, Clark took to the water at noon. Tying up that evening to an island he did not name, he and his crew enjoyed an unusually dry and placid night.

During the next week he refrained from describing topography but added to his map some major features of the river. For instance, although he made no textual mention of a fur-trading settlement called Little Prairie (near the present Caruthersville, Missouri), he inscribed "Prairie" at the corresponding location on his chart. He also sketched clusters of sandbars and towheads in river bends where numerous hazards lurked. As he must have known, of the approximately 1,450 river-miles he was to navigate, the next two hundred posed the greatest threat to his vessels and cargoes.

Clark was now far enough from home to see animals unknown in Kentucky, but because he records almost nothing about the zoology of that section of the Mississippi valley we must look to the journals of other travelers to know what he might have beheld. During the previous year, Englishman Francis Baily observed in that vicinity strings of pelicans gliding overhead and alligators sunning on the banks. A decade later, French visitor Fortescue Cuming saw abundant swans, cranes, and bitterns in those parts. As we will see later, during Clark's voyage through the Gulf of Mexico, he was curious about unfamiliar animals, especially several species of fish caught from his ship. Although the more formally trained Meriwether Lewis was to overshadow him as a naturalist on the Western Expedition, Clark would still produce from his own observations both accurate drawings and descriptions of indigenous flora and fauna. On this journey, however, he was to write almost nothing on these topics.[1]

He probably disregarded other considerations as well in order to concentrate on navigating the "Devil's Race Ground," a snag-filled chute some forty miles above the present Memphis, Tennessee. Farther along, he would have to contend with the "Devil's Elbow," a narrower, crooked passage eventually to accrete to the Arkansas side, opposite the present-day Meeman-Shelby Forest State Park of Tennessee. At low water both stretches were thick with dead trees that sometimes forced boatmen to steer close enough to the bank to risk burial under chunks of collapsing loess.

Because Clark wrote nothing of such difficulties, we can assume he passed unscathed through those stretches of diabolic designation. On the evening of March 26, he found the Army contractor's boats tied up below the third of the four Chickasaw Bluffs (near the northwestern edge of what is now Shelby County, Tennessee), and pulled ashore nearby. Soon his hands were celebrating as if they'd completed the entire voyage rather than merely paused to rest at a place less than halfway through the most tortuous part of their route. The wind was rising again, and Clark called his own vessels to shore near the others. He notes "Mad Meriment &tc," then "Mr. Jones Sick" but writes nothing further about that day or tells whether he joined in the festivities. Convivial when occasions warranted, Clark nonetheless got back on the water early the next morning; other loaded boats were passing his own. By sundown he had floated 156 miles from New Madrid and was ready to see the first of the U.S. Army installations along his Mississippi River route.

Directing his crewmen to stop at the foot of the Fourth Chickasaw Bluff, he disembarked and proceeded up a low declivity until he stood at what was to become the northwest corner of Auction Avenue and North Front Street in the future city of Memphis, Tennessee. He had reached what was officially designated Fort Adams, a name used by few (apparently Clark did not use it either). That location, however, was heavy with significance to the Spanish Conspiracy and to his own, closely held plans for this journey.[2]

* * *

Scattered throughout the area were some of the Chickasaws. The division among their members remained as before: Ugulayacabe led the partisans of Spain, Payemingo represented those of the United States, and others still based their loyalty on the quality and number of gifts received from each nation. But now, because Pinckney's Treaty had given Americans exclusive control of the overall area, Payemingo's faction predominated. Fearing retaliation if they were to cut off all largess, the Spanish continued bestowing gifts on the Chickasaws but did so on a lesser scale than they had done previously.

Spanish forces had abandoned the Chickasaw Bluffs more than a year earlier, yet paradoxically, they retained control of their forts at Walnut Hills and Natchez even though Pinckney's Treaty made those places U.S. territory. Despite what many Americans suspected (that Spain was implementing a nefarious plot to hold on to the region it had bargained away), Governor Carondelet had instead been responding to contradictory orders. The initial set of orders came shortly after news arrived of the treaty; they implemented its terms by requiring the prompt withdrawal of Spanish troops from those three posts. The second set of orders came shortly after the first but were radically different. Carondelet was to delay abandoning those strongholds, as Spain had just learned of agreements linking England and France, enemies of Spain, with the United States. Carondelet had time to countermand the orders he had already sent for evacuating the forts at Walnut Hills and Natchez but not for doing the same at the Chickasaw Bluffs. Accordingly, Spanish forces there emptied Fort San Fernando and put it to the torch in the spring of 1797.[3]

Pinckney's Treaty said nothing about destroying existing defenses, but Carondelet deemed it prudent to do so because Ugulayacabe, having for years opposed American rule, wanted nothing left behind for U.S. troops to use against him and his people if they should choose to do so. To keep the Chickasaws from feeling abandoned, the Spanish transported across the Mississippi a couple of blockhouses from Fort San Fernando, thereby establishing on the swampy western bank a small garrison optimistically named Campo de la Esperanza, a name later anglicized to "Hopefield" and applied to a nearby settlement.[4]

In July 1797 Captain Isaac Guion of the Third Infantry reached the site of Fort San Fernando in order to carry out the official instructions of General Wilkinson. A veteran of the Revolutionary War and of the Fallen Timbers campaign, Guion was one of Wilkinson's staunchest supporters. But because Wilkinson feared the Spanish would reveal his treasonous relationship if the Army pressed to enforce the terms of the treaty, he forbade Guion from doing anything to provoke a confrontation. As a result, Guion found his assignment extremely trying.[5]

His poor health made it even more of a challenge. Just before pulling ashore at the Bluffs he developed what he described as a "violent intermittent" fever, probably a symptom of malaria. Once there, he learned that because the Spanish were still wooing the local Chickasaws with costly presents and had not yet abandoned the royal garrisons at Walnut Hills and Natchez, he would have to remain at the Bluffs for many weeks. During that time he opened a cordial but firm correspondence with Natchez governor Gayoso de Lemos and his superior at New Orleans, Governor Carondelet.[6]

Guion also cultivated Payemingo and other Chickasaw leaders. Believing he might eventually win their allegiance and their permission for him to build a fort on the Fourth Bluff, he shrewdly withheld U.S. beneficence until the Indians had received their Spanish gifts, then showered them with American items of higher quality and treated hundreds of Chickasaws to a banquet exhausting vast measures of beef, flour, and distilled spirits. Afterward, noted Guion, the Indians were "all desirous of our stay and willing that we should put up what works we pleased."[7]

Within a short time his soldiers raised on the site of Fort San Fernando what he called "a snug little cover for one hundred men to maintain a foothold." But, as the summer came on and a majority of his troops (at one time three-fourths of them) fell ill with malarial symptoms, he took to calling the locale "these infernal bluffs." He regretted not building a couple of miles to the south, on a site farther above the miasmatic floodplain. (Although science had yet to prove mosquitoes as vectors of malaria, the link between the lowlands they infested and certain fevers and agues was well understood.) In October 1797, when the fort was nearly completed, he dedicated it to President John Adams, put it in the care of a corps, and in early November resumed his journey toward Walnut Hills and Natchez.[8]

To his chagrin he found those sites still under Spanish occupation. Having already suspected that Spain had entered into Pinckney's Treaty in bad faith, he began thinking that nation was plotting to retake the Chickasaw Bluffs. Both presumptions were wrong; Spain was soon to order full compliance with the agreement. But until it did so, soldiers of the Spanish Louisiana Regiment would tarry north of the thirty-first parallel and east of the Mississippi, and Captain Guion—unaware that Wilkinson's double-dealing helped create such instability—would not be certain which power was really in control.

* * *

Although the Spanish had designed and equipped Fort San Fernando to repulse marauders such as the forces of George Rogers Clark, Captain Guion intended Fort Adams less as a stronghold and more as a way station for soldiers descending the river. For proof of that purpose William Clark had only to compare the number and size of the artillery pieces in place on March 28, 1798, with those he'd earlier sketched of Fort San Fernando (quite possibly from specifications provided by Spanish agent Manuel Lisa). According to that drawing, the Spanish had kept at least two large cannons trained on the Mississippi and also possessed perhaps a dozen guns firing six- or nine-pound shot, whereas Fort Adams had only three six-pounders and a pair of small howitzers.[9]

The post, however, contained a magazine and a barracks sometimes overrun with troops. Captain John Pierce and his unit had of late arrived. They replaced four hundred soldiers led by Major William Kersey who, on learning the Spanish were at last departing Walnut Hills, had set off for that locale a short time before Clark reached Fort Adams. Even Natchez might become fully American before long; by late March 1798, rumor had it the Spanish were also getting ready to give up their fort there.[10]

Clark made good use of his time at what he called "the Bluffs." He sold the Army a half-ton of tobacco for seven dollars per hundredweight, a relatively high price for prime burley leaves. He also hired a deckhand named John Martin and renewed an acquaintance with Captain Thomas Lewis, an officer with whom he'd served at Fort Greenville. A native Virginian and perhaps a distant cousin to Meriwether Lewis, Thomas was a firm Federalist who'd earlier courted a friend of William's sister Frances. Because Thomas had served as General Wayne's aide-de-camp and held Federalist views at wide variance with William's Democratic-Republican politics, their friendship must have been limited, but Clark was no doubt happy to see him and to learn that he was bound for the East by way of Kentucky. Clark neatly copied his survey notes from the island just above the mouth of the Ohio, gave Thomas the transcription, and instructed him to deliver it to William Croghan.[11]

Thomas's ultimate destination was the national capital of Philadelphia. At the request of the U.S. government he had been investigating alleged intrigues, paying special attention to the activities and connections of William Blount, a former U.S. senator from Tennessee. As Thomas and others were in the process of uncovering, in 1797 Blount had schemed with the British and their Indian allies to foment a war in Spanish territory in order to inflate the value of Blount's nearby lands. Having thwarted justice by fleeing to Tennessee where his anti-Spanish notions made him popular and protected him from prosecution, Blount was the latest American to hatch such a project.[12]

James Wilkinson took due notice of this. So did Vice President Thomas Jefferson—whose favor Wilkinson was trying to purchase with maps and data from the Spanish southwest and with specimens of the natural resources and antiquities of that alluring region. As Wilkinson realized, Jefferson possessed an avid interest in such things.[13]

7

A Spy for the British, a Spy for the Spanish, and a Spy for Somebody Else

T HE wind continued rising after Clark reached Fort Adams in 1798, compelling him to remain two days at the Chickasaw Bluffs. Let us take advantage of his enforced idleness to become acquainted in the next two chapters with Thomas Power, a Spanish secret operative whose advances in smuggling money were soon to transform Clark's life. Perhaps even more significant, Power and Clark were to encounter each other on at least three critical occasions.

Born around 1761 to Irish parents in the Canary Islands, Power was a naturalized subject of Spain and an immigrant to Louisiana. He spoke fluent English, Spanish, and French and conveyed an impression of worldliness and culture, attributes one might expect in a man of his Jesuit education, medical training, and scientific accomplishment, particularly in land-surveying. But Power was more interested in indulging his "ruling passion" of travel than in practicing a profession. When Carondelet appealed for a canny individual to visit Kentucky and report back on the paramilitary activities of George Rogers Clark, Power offered to go. Spying drew on all his faculties—especially a prodigious memory, steely nerves, and a certain oily persuasiveness—and earned more money than anything else he was qualified to do.[1]

Early in 1794 he visited many corners of the Ohio River valley while gathering intelligence to confirm Wilkinson's dire reports about George Rogers Clark. Even so, Wilkinson did not begin employing Power in treasonable pursuits until some weeks after the robbery and slaying of Henry Owen, one of the two bearers of thousands of Spanish dollars disbursed for Wilkinson in the summer of that year.[2]

After murdering Owen on the lower Ohio River, the killer and his accomplices—all of them Spanish subjects who had rowed Owen's vessel—split up the money and fled into Kentucky. Their cumbersome loads of coins and their inability to speak English raised suspicions against them, and soon they were under arrest and in the courtroom of Judge Harry Innes, Wilkinson's friend and attorney. Afraid of what they might reveal about his own seditious connections, Innes packed them off to Fort Washington. There Wilkinson, mortified by the risk they posed to his double life, put them under military escort on a boat bound for New Madrid. At his instruction, their keepers tried to slip them past Fort Massac after nightfall, but the boat was nonetheless detected. The suspects were brought before Commander Thomas Doyle, an officer determined not to send perpetrators of a crime in the United States beyond the national boundaries. To gauge the quantum of evidence against them, however, he needed someone able to understand their language; having no Spanish-speaking person in his own camp, he sent to New Madrid for an interpreter. In response came Thomas Power.[3]

To him the men confessed killing Owen and stealing the six thousand dollars in his keeping, but Power omitted from their testimony those details and any others that threatened to bring about additional investigation. Doyle's doubts persisted nonetheless, and he disobeyed Wilkinson's instructions to return the accused to Louisiana. Instead, Doyle sent them back up the Ohio River for judicial inquiry in Kentucky. Power went too. Because he translated and coached the culprits through their trial, it reached an inconclusive result, forcing the court to remand them to Judge Innes. This time he held them for several weeks. When no new witnesses came forward, Innes set the malefactors free on the condition they depart the state. They hurried back to Louisiana where Spanish authorities arrested and tried them, then hanged their leader for Owen's murder.[4]

Wilkinson was so relieved by this outcome, he sang Power's praises to their mutual employer, Governor Carondelet: "his talents, his address, his knowledge of languages and manners, his acquaintance with Kentucky, his zeal, enterprize and discretion all mark him for politic agencys." But Wilkinson also noticed that, by quietly circumventing the American legal system and dodging hidden snares without exposing his covert purposes, Power demonstrated qualities that were indispensable in a secret agent. After Joseph Collins, Owen's more fortunate fellow courier, ran through better than thirty-five hundred of the six thousand Spanish dollars entrusted to him, Wilkinson began regarding Power as a potential smuggler too, especially of money to replace the waylaid amounts.[5]

Power was back in the Mississippi valley in the summer of 1795. Because of his and Wilkinson's intelligence concerning George Rogers Clark, Spain at that time was fortifying the Chickasaw Bluffs and augmenting the river patrol, and Governor Carondelet was seeking to lure Wilkinson into a new chapter of the intrigue to detach Kentucky from the states. Carondelet committed his thoughts on the subject to paper, disguised them with enigmatic symbols to which Wilkinson held the key, and forwarded the correspondence to New Madrid for Gayoso to pass along to courier Manuel Lisa. When Lisa failed to show up promptly, Gayoso gave those letters and some of his own to Power, who on September 6, 1795, set off for Fort Washington, General Wilkinson's Cincinnati headquarters. After two weeks sidelined from his route by illness, Power reached Fort Washington on October 3, the day Lieutenant William Clark, in the company of Manuel Lisa, departed New Madrid for the same fort. As soon as Power could do so discreetly, he reported to General Wilkinson and handed him the letters.[6]

The general found some portions of them encouraging. Not only did Governor Carondelet applaud Wilkinson's proposal of a "reciprocal intercourse" of Kentucky products for "the precious metal of Spain," he endorsed his request of Spanish incomes for Wilkinson, Sebastian, and other key associates.[7] But the missives also gave the general much to think about. Clearly, the Spanish governor believed that tearing Kentucky from the Union not only was necessary to the survival of Spanish Louisiana but was feasible in its own right. (It was, but only so long as the Mississippi remained closed to American navigation.) To that end, Carondelet wanted Wilkinson to send delegates to a secession conference at New Madrid. To compel his cooperation, Carondelet assured him of riches and honors to be his when Kentucky at last would withdraw from the United States and become allied with Spain: "G[eneral] W[ilkinson] can aspire to the same dignity in the western states that P[resident] W[ashington] has in the eastern." Believing the Spanish would continue paying princely sums for his alleged service no matter what else happened, Wilkinson responded accordingly by asking for an increase in his secret salary and compensation for those attending the meeting. In addition, he recommended that the Spanish not just augment their defenses on the Mississippi but also make available to him and like-minded Kentuckians ten thousand stands of arms, field artillery, and ammunition.[8]

And he wanted Power to bring him the Spanish dollars (more than twenty thousand of them) that Carondelet had promised. To deflect attention while he and Power plotted that smuggling operation, Wilkinson had him pretend to be a business traveler merely stopping by Fort Washington on his way upstream, and affected an interest in topics unrelated to the intrigue. Long after everyone else had retired for the night, however, Power met Wilkinson in his quarters, and they drew up plans. Word of those meetings nevertheless got back to General Wayne. At a public dinner he announced his suspicions, calling Power "a spy for the British, a spy for the Spanish, and a spy for somebody else," no doubt meaning Wilkinson.[9]

Wary of the vigilance of his commanding officer and other Americans, Wilkinson had, with the help of Spain, developed a sophisticated system of codes and ciphers for communicating in confidence. His lengthy and detailed correspondence with Carondelet and Gayoso, and previously with Miró and Navarro, demonstrates that money and his own security were uppermost in his mind. The Kentucky scheme needed an immediate twenty thousand dollars, he wrote Gayoso, otherwise "millions may not repair the consequences." The general added that he was authorizing "the Honourable Sebastian" to treat on the subject of Kentucky separatism, arguing that the judge's Spanish surname and "intimate knowledge founded on 10 years acquaintance, his judgment & . . . his discretion" made him the ideal representative. Having just conferred with Sebastian on those same points, Wilkinson recommended him for a salary of two thousand Spanish dollars per year, full repayment of expenses, and a generous sum for future services.[10]

Wilkinson proceeded to outline the next steps. He related that, in mid-December, Sebastian would descend the Ohio to the village of Red Banks (the future Henderson, Kentucky), to wait for the Spanish to send a boat bound for New Madrid. Once there, he and Gayoso de Lemos would work out the remaining details of the Kentucky-secession project.[11]

Then Wilkinson set down in writing a revised set of "Reflections." Like those he penned in 1787 to launch the first phase of the Spanish Conspiracy, this later version demonstrated an astonishingly transparent disloyalty to the United States. He reiterated that to inflame Kentuckians against the eastern states Spain must curtail use of the Mississippi. Then, to increase the odds of sundering Kentucky from the Union, the Spanish must further fortify that river and establish a post at the mouth of the Ohio. Under no circumstances should they give up Fort San Fernando. He added, "Iron ordnance may be procured in Kentucky and also laborers. . . . Spain should make no public advance to the people of Kentucky tho' she should insinuate by secret agents her disposition and readiness to serve them whenever they may think it proper to apply for her aid and indulgence."[12] For such "Reflections" Wilkinson asked an advance on his own clandestine salary, repayment of the sums lost by Owen and Collins, and additional funds to hold in readiness for contingencies. By repeating his request of twenty thousand dollars (whether to "bribe a Governor or to destroy a convoy of provisions" for American soldiers), he committed to paper proof sufficient to ruin his career and perhaps send him to the gallows should those words be revealed in the United States.[13]

Next, he nominated Thomas Power to convey those secret payments from New Madrid. Power must come up the Ohio "in the character of a Merchant with grossery from New Orleans," that is, on a flatboat loaded with kegs and barrels seemingly full of Louisiana goods but also containing hidden stashes of coins. Wilkinson elaborated, saying, "The money that it may be judged proper to introduce into the country will be kept out of sight, even of the crew, and the real object of the expedition kept secret. . . . The cargo ought to consist of gun-powder, sugar, coffee, brandy, wine, segars, &c."[14]

For years, Wilkinson had been experimenting with various means of transporting reales to Kentucky; he wished to avoid the hazards, delay, and expense of having them sent by oceangoing vessel to an eastern port and then freighted west. Moving the money along inland routes, however, presented a different set of problems. Roads of that era were often lonely, narrow paths through the forest, and concealing hard cash in anything larger than saddlebags would make transit by pack animal difficult or perhaps impossible. Although in 1789 a commercial transaction at New Orleans had yielded Wilkinson two mule-loads of Spanish dollars carried to Kentucky, that smuggling mission succeeded only because a second courier was able to take over when the first one became ill. Wilkinson also realized he would have to be careful in selecting such an agent. It seems that in 1792 the general had forfeited fourteen hundred pieces of eight, probably when Michel La Cassagne, a Louisville businessman to whom he owed that amount, deducted it for himself from the four thousand such coins he brought to Kentucky for Wilkinson that August.[15]

Cognizant that only sixteen of those minted pieces weighed a pound and took up a good deal of space (when stacked, they nearly filled a wine glass), Wilkinson concluded he had little choice but to try hiding them in commodities typically shipped upriver from Louisiana. A less determined man than he might have refused to consider such a risky venture after what had happened to Henry Owen, but Wilkinson learned that Owen had inadvertently brought about his own end by letting his boatmen know his casks held valuable contents. As Wilkinson realized, a more accomplished operative would avoid making such a basic mistake. Power, by contrast, seemed an excellent candidate; he'd succeeded at all his confidential assignments, earning the trust of Louisiana officials. Wilkinson gave him the job.

Before Power left Fort Washington for Louisiana, he and Wilkinson worked out the details of a smuggling plan and then reduced it to a series of steps beginning the moment Wilkinson received word his reales were finally coming up the Mississippi to New Madrid, the last Spanish stop on their journey. They agreed that, before Power took possession of the money, he would purchase barrels and kegs of sugar, coffee, and other Louisiana products in great demand in Kentucky. Power described what he would do next:

> I would wish to put a bag of one thousand dollars in a barrel of coffee or sugar, so that although the difference of the respective gravity, between silver, sugar, and coffee, be very great, the quantity being so small, it would not be easily known. It will likewise be prudent to carry some barrels without money, in order to sell them before arriving at Cincinnati, if it should so happen that any one should offer to buy those goods; because not to sell them, when it might be done to advantage, would excite suspicion.[16]

He and Wilkinson went over those points until they knew them by heart.

* * *

Power was temporarily absent from Fort Washington on November 2, 1795, when William Clark returned from New Madrid, but General Wilkinson was present and must have been eager to find out what the lieutenant had seen and heard. Although there is no known record of a meeting between them on this occasion, Army protocol—and Wilkinson's personality—practically guaranteed some sort of encounter. If one took place, the general must have been secretly gratified to learn that the Spanish were implementing his seditious advice to fortify the Mississippi at the mouth of the Ohio River. In addition, he no doubt understood that such a construction project lent Gayoso a plausible excuse to linger nearby until Wilkinson's delegate Sebastian and any fellow intriguers arrived.[17]

Maybe Clark showed Wilkinson the drawings of *La Vigilante* and of Fort San Fernando de las Barrancas (in another journal, it seems Clark had already sketched Wilkinson's barge). Perhaps Clark added that he had repeated to Gayoso the general's views of the American military. Whatever Clark may have said, though, he departed for Fort Greenville where, on November 4, 1795, he conveyed to General Wayne what appeared to be comprehensive findings on the distribution of Spanish forces and vessels in the mid-Mississippi valley. As we have seen, however, Clark's report failed to mention the Spanish gunboat patrol and its headquarters, omissions so out of character for the usually systematic lieutenant, we must consider whether he held them back for a reason known only to him.[18]

Clark had scarcely resumed his accustomed duties when Ensign Meriwether Lewis joined his rifle squad, thereby inaugurating their official association. Because Clark was acclaimed throughout camp for his Mississippi River missions, Lewis first knew him as a man adept at spiriting guns and ammunition past the Spanish, and at reconnoitering their territory.[19]

Clark stayed at Fort Greenville the rest of November, asking on November 27 for an extended furlough to visit Virginia "under <u>views</u> that are Lucrative," and to take care of "private business." Lacking further idea of Clark's plans, Wayne approved the request, and Clark left camp in early December. Later that winter, Wayne commenced a long-delayed trip to Philadelphia, having compelled Wilkinson to move to Fort Greenville and direct the Army in his absence. By now Wayne expected nothing honorable or even impartial from that subaltern, but he would have been shocked to know he was to advance the Spanish Conspiracy while using Wayne's own headquarters.[20]

Meanwhile, Power was striving to carry out Agent 13's secret instructions. Having left Fort Washington on November 14, 1795, Power reached New Madrid in early December, purchased a pirogue, and took it back up the Ohio to Red Banks in order to fetch the men who would represent Wilkinson at the secession conference. Finding no one but Benjamin Sebastian awaiting him there, Power asked about the other conspirators, particularly Judge Innes, Attorney George Nicholas, and a merchant named William Murray. Either "family concerns" or "indisposition," said Sebastian, prevented Innes from coming; Nicholas's fear of discovery kept him away; and Murray's "habitual state of inebriation" convinced his associates not to let him go. But because Sebastian possessed their complete trust, they authorized him not only to speak for them but also to find out on what conditions Spain might grant them the all-important right to navigate the Mississippi.[21]

Sebastian and Power set off downstream. At the mouth of the Ohio they found Gayoso's troops building the docking station. Power described it as "a small triangular stockade fort," a shape William Clark indicated with three diminutive squares captioned "Spanish Guard of 6 Men" on the map he produced around this time. Power also wrote that the construction project gave Gayoso a plausible excuse to linger in the area while awaiting the conspiratorial Kentuckians. Once Sebastian showed up, he and Gayoso proceeded together onboard *La Vigilante*, and Power followed in another royal vessel. The three of them reached New Madrid on Christmas Day.[22]

Soon after their conference got under way, it stalled because Gayoso lacked the authority to decide several important points. Wanting Governor Carondelet to do that, Gayoso and Sebastian continued down the Mississippi to New Orleans. As they traveled, word spread through Louisiana that "a greate Governor [Judge Sebastian] has come from Kentuckey to treat with the [Spanish] Governor . . . respecting a revolt from the United States."[23]

Sebastian basked in the attention he received as an important guest of Spain. Happy to have him close, Carondelet devoted full energy to developing the conspiracy to detach Kentucky from the Union. He and Sebastian were making progress toward this end when news arrived of Pinckney's Treaty, and especially of the Spanish decision to open the Mississippi to American use.[24]

Realizing that provision destroyed the motivation for his fellow Kentuckians to leave the Union, Sebastian gave up on the secession intrigue and made plans to sail to Philadelphia with four thousand dollars, two years' worth of his Spanish salary. But Carondelet stubbornly continued to believe in the plot, no doubt because it offered the only chance of prolonging Spanish rule in Louisiana. With that goal in mind, he ordered Power to accompany Sebastian all the way to Cincinnati and then to offer Wilkinson handsome payments on his account and promises of more, should he subscribe to a new chapter of the conspiracy.[25]

In the early spring of 1796, Sebastian and Power left New Orleans, reaching Philadelphia a few weeks later. From that city they traveled overland to Redstone, Pennsylvania, where they caught a boat down the Monongahela and Ohio rivers. They parted at Cincinnati. Sebastian continued to Louisville while Power, hearing that General Wayne was still in the East, hastened to Fort Greenville. He arrived on June 2, 1796.[26]

As soon as Power could do so without drawing attention, he handed Wilkinson the latest secret correspondence from New Orleans. Pinckney's Treaty having dashed the general's hopes for milking the Spanish Conspiracy much further, he was thrilled to learn that approximately ten thousand pieces of eight were being held for him at New Madrid. He and Power discussed how to sneak those coins—the exact number of which neither of them knew—up the Ohio.[27]

Power spent at least one week in camp. Having returned from his furlough in May or June, William Clark might well have come upon him. If indeed that happened, they would have been surprised to find out how soon they were again to encounter each other.

8

A Spanish Lady Going to General Wilkinson

CARONDELET was sending Wilkinson precisely 9,640 Spanish dollars—full repayment of the amounts forfeited by smugglers Owen and Collins. In January 1796 or shortly thereafter, the royal galley *La Victoria* headed upriver to deliver those reales to the Spanish post at New Madrid. With them came explicit instructions telling the commandant to hold the entire amount in readiness to hand over "the moment an order [for it] may be presented to you by the American General . . . James Wilkinson."[1]

But Tomás Portell—the same Spanish commander Lieutenant William Clark had encountered at New Madrid in 1793 and 1795—did not know when such a communication might arrive or who was to bring it. Unwilling to expose the precious cargo to any risk, he decided the safest place for it was his own residence inside the fort, in the bedroom he shared with his wife. There the Portells stashed the coins in a large chest rather than splitting them up among several hiding places. To prevent those six hundred pounds of silver from causing the floor to buckle, they propped it from beneath with a sturdy beam.

The full amount of money was still there when Elisha Winters, a former Kentuckian living in New Orleans and conducting a brisk mercantile trade between Louisiana and the western states, called at New Madrid in the early summer of 1796. Upon hearing the Spanish-speaking Portell make a comment Winters did not understand, he asked the translator for an explanation. According to Winters, "He answered that the commandant had in his chamber a Spanish lady going to General Wilkinson. This raised my curiosity. I made further inquiry, and found it to be a chest of dollars (as much as four or five men could handle) from the Spanish Government to General Wilkinson." Winters checked the cellar beneath the Portells' bedroom and noticed the beam holding up the floor.[2]

He speedily departed New Madrid and was heading upstream when he came upon Thomas Power on his way down the Ohio. Power acknowledged having left Fort Washington only a few days earlier, saying he was bound for New Madrid to pick up a "cargo of groceries." As Winters explained, "This convinced me that what I had learned at New Madrid was true, and that he was on his way to gallant the Spanish lady to [Wilkinson's] headquarters." As soon as Power resumed his voyage, Winters continued his. At Louisville he forwarded to General Wayne's headquarters notice about "the approach of so valuable a creature" as a chest containing Spanish dollars and, as both Winters and Wayne suspected, some secret communications to Wilkinson from the Spanish government. Wayne, however, would not return from the East until July.[3]

While Winters's report was in transit, Power reached New Madrid, presented himself as General Wilkinson's agent, and asked for the money. Commandant Portell then refused to turn it over, instead requesting the general's written order for it. Wilkinson had deliberately refrained from providing one. Not only was he unaware of the exact amount to be sent, he also feared discovery should such an incriminating document wind up in unfriendly hands.[4]

Power's only hope to retrieve the reales was to win the commandant's confidence. To do this, Power alluded to his own success at carrying the Spanish government's most highly classified messages to Wilkinson, a.k.a. Agent 13. Then he related that he and Wilkinson preferred to cloak their smuggling missions as commercial ventures by concealing quantities of reales among shipments of tropical comestibles. Reminding Portell that Wilkinson had already waited two years for payment and was by now very impatient to receive it, Power closed with more information about the respective weights of sugar, coffee, and silver.[5]

The combination of telling details and subtle pressure proved persuasive, and Portell released the cumbersome chest. From it Power removed thousands of coins, distributing them among nearly a dozen cloth bags, which he stashed inside barrels of sugar and coffee. Once those containers were closed and loaded onto a "barge" (a long, masted vessel with lines and poles for moving it against the formidable current), he and a crew were ready to go upriver.[6]

To appear a licit trader, Power also laid in additional kegs and barrels holding nothing but coffee and sugar to sell should he have an opportunity. To "complete the disguise," as he put it, he brought along other imported goods, particularly rum and gunpowder. Last of all, he hid secret communications for General Wilkinson by stowing them deep within a bucket of spoiled tobacco leaves and placing it atop the cabin of his boat. Then Power set off upstream.[7]

Meanwhile, Wilkinson was hurrying at Fort Greenville to wind up his duplicitous activities before the return of General Wayne. Having done all he could to discredit that officer and win the loyalty of his soldiers, Wilkinson redoubled his efforts to disgrace Wayne with President Washington and the secretary of war. On the last day of June, Wilkinson drew up a written complaint accusing Wayne of incompetence and favoritism, the first overt step in his efforts to supplant him as commander in chief.[8]

To start the defamatory document on its journey, Wilkinson needed someone to take it to Cincinnati. Perhaps he asked William Clark to do so; he was going in that direction the next day, as soon as he resigned from the Army. Disgusted with his own failure to advance in rank and wishing to sort out his brother George's tangled affairs and to visit Spanish Louisiana on a mercantile venture, and perhaps to reconnoiter a strategic position he referred to obliquely in a book kept from his soldier days, Clark planned to leave for home. Because he often visited Cincinnati, located approximately midway between Fort Greenville and Louisville, it is reasonable to assume he stopped there. As a friend and former messenger of Wilkinson, Clark would surely have been amenable to carrying his mail. It therefore seems possible that Clark ended the first phase of his Army career in the same manner he began it—by serving as Wilkinson's courier.[9]

Clark was probably just beyond Cincinnati when General Wayne arrived there on July 5. Several days later that officer reached Fort Greenville, heard about Thomas Power's visit, and read Elisha Winters's letter. Wayne

found the news in it alarming but gratifying too, for it confirmed his opinion that the character of his second-in-command was indeed "vice on vice."
In addition, Winters's account lent weight to what Wayne had learned
only weeks earlier in Philadelphia—that President Washington suspected
Wilkinson of working with Power and others for the interests of Spain.[10]

More determined than ever to secure proof of Wilkinson's treachery,
Wayne sent an officer down the Ohio to intercept the wily Power, and
notified Captain Zebulon Pike at Fort Massac to be on the lookout for
him. Pike received the order too late to intercept Power on his way to
New Madrid, but he directed Lieutenant John Steele to patrol the lower
Ohio in order to catch him on his return. Despite Steele's vigilance, Power
somehow got past Fort Massac.[11]

But on August 8, 1796, Steele caught up with him between Fort Massac and Louisville and had him pull ashore for questioning. Power objected strenuously, producing papers to show he was a Spanish subject on a
commercial voyage. He also said he was planning to purchase horses for
breeders at Natchez. So persuasive was he that Lieutenant Steele refrained
from opening any of his cargoes and from searching the bucket of spoiled
tobacco on the roof, and let him continue upstream. Fearing Steele might
change his mind and pursue him, Power issued his crew extra rations of
liquor to encourage vigorous rowing. When their boat reached Louisville,
Power secured the cargoes and hurried by land to Fort Washington where
he informed Wilkinson about the money.[12]

Delighted, the general directed him to hand over the silver-laden coffee and sugar barrels to Philip Nolan. Power did as he was told. In turn,
Nolan conveyed those goods to the Frankfort store of Samuel Montgomery Brown, an American about whom little is known except that he often
navigated between Kentucky and New Orleans, coveted a career in the
Spanish-American trade, and possessed few scruples.[13]

Power went along to Frankfort to recoup his expenses from the smuggling mission. For that purpose—and with Wilkinson's blessing—he took
640 dollars from the barrels. He also sold the sugar and coffee and, to
lend credence to the story he'd given Lieutenant Steele, bought a blooded
stallion and mare. Before heading back downstream with them, he went

to Cincinnati to commence legal action against Steele for delaying his voyage and checked in one last time at Fort Washington. On hearing he had "delivered the money agreeably" to directions, Wilkinson remarked that "it was well."[14]

And it was. Except for 640 dollars, he had finally received the entire twelve-thousand-dollar reward promised two years earlier for his alleged efforts to thwart the invasion planned by George Rogers Clark and his French associates. That amount, the largest payment Wilkinson had yet received, spoke volumes to him of the profits still to be reaped by exploiting the dire situation of Spanish Louisiana. In addition, the unqualified success of Power's operation made clear the manner in which future shipments of pieces of eight ought to be smuggled to Kentucky.

9

The Gibraltar of Louisiana

OUR story returns to 1798. Early on Friday, March 30, Clark gave up on waiting at the Chickasaw Bluffs for favorable weather, and despite hard rain he headed downstream with O'Hara's fleet. "Wind rose," reports Clark, then, "we continue landed on a Sharp point, a Dangerous part of the river, one Boat far behind and caint get in at the p[o]int, one boat behind came late & landed below, the bank falling in all night." Not long past sunrise he set off into a heavy fog, but as the day advanced, the murk condensed to a drizzle that became an afternoon shower before changing into a thunderstorm. In the night, Clark watched from one of his boats as ever-shortening intervals of thunder accompanied by strong gusts punctuated the dark. He writes: "It litiened [lightninged] for at least 2 hours incesently as one continued blaze."

The next morning, April 1, the atmosphere quieted but rain persisted, washing soil into the Mississippi from both sides; the channel swelled with mud-streaked flows that drove the vessels toward rafts of dead timber scattered between the banks. Just when obstructions seemed to plug the entire waterway, the strong current drew the flatboats into a narrow bend, sometimes whirling them around before releasing them. On days of poor visibility such as this, a steersman had little idea of the depth of the river; in certain reaches, more than a mile of water separated American from Spanish shores, but in others, the distance was only a few hundred yards.

Due no doubt to the need for careful navigation, Clark added little to his map while in this area. Evidently he did not see the mouth of the

St. Francis River, an important tributary rising near the lead mines west of Ste. Genevieve (a town of French origin approximately ninety miles below the juncture of the Missouri with the Mississippi), for he neither drew it nor mentioned it in his journal. Among the only landforms he acknowledged was the Grand Prairie, some of the highest acreage he would observe along the west bank of the Mississippi.

Adversity struck just before noon on that April Fool's Day. As the larger of Clark's broadhorns rounded a wide bend not far upriver from a powerful eddy, the current pushed them toward a nearly submerged tangle of dead trees close to the shore. This was a stretch of river that travelers would be warned about. For example, Zadok Cramer, a Pittsburgh bookseller who soon would begin publishing a series of navigation guides to the Ohio and Mississippi rivers based on the journals and observations of others, in 1814 wrote: "One mile below . . . around a right hand point, is a large bar, having an ugly appearance, being covered with drift wood, snags, willows, and small cotton trees."[1]

Clark and his crew may not have seen the hazard at all. As they bore down on it, an enormous boil lifted the top of a previously unnoticed waterlogged tree and drove its branches into their bow. The hands struggled to maneuver the boat sideways but the rapid current turned the vessel around instead, exposing the hull to another snag. It punctured and sank Clark's canoe and rammed through the stern of one of his flatboats, leaving it stuck fast.

Just then, the ark of Army supplier Lynn entered the same reach and briefly floated above the hidden sawyer before it again broke the surface and stabbed his hull a lethal blow. Clark does not say how Lynn or the others onboard escaped the foundering vessel, nor does he explain by what means their convoy companions managed to navigate the deadly passage. He stayed on his own impaired boat while Lynn's went down, but Jones, Brown, and O'Hara managed to pull theirs ashore. Most of Lynn's cargoes—trunks of blue uniform coats with white lining for the infantry and red for the artillery, bundles of Army-issue linen overalls and white vests, packages of yellow-plumed hats worn by the Third Regiment, and according to an official Army report "two casks of Wine and Brandy"—

disappeared into the water.[2] Despite persistent wind and rain, Clark devotes a great deal of ink to the misfortune:

> My boat run up a Snag which run thro' her bow then un other which nearly sunk her & lodged on a third which hel[d] her fast only injuring the Stern, here I am at 12 o'clock. . . . Mr. Linds boat loaded with Merchandize Sunk on the 2d. Sawyer that I struk. he lost all but a few bales & kegs. all the boats forced to Shore. . . . a Verry Dangerous Situation, the Current runs against the Shore.

The storms continued as he and the deckhands tried to free their flatboat, and in the evening he noticed the men were uneasy, perhaps because they did not want to spend the night aboard such a precarious craft. But the hours of darkness passed without calamity, and by dint of combined effort the following day the crew pried the vessel loose, patched it as best they could, and raised the shattered canoe. Finding unharmed his cargoes and gear—including the surveying and mapping equipment—Clark resumed the voyage. Four miles downstream he dispatched some of his crew members "to collect what property of Mr. Linds which may flote ashore," a neighborly gesture that delayed his own progress. The next morning Clark got under way at seven o'clock, navigated with care around what he termed a "bad Island in the center of the River," and heard Mr. Lynn was recovering more goods.

The following day dawned free of storms, and in a few hours Clark beheld the broad mouth of the Arkansas River. Some fifty miles above this point stood the Arkansas Post, a French-speaking settlement consisting of a few dwellings and a rude Spanish fort with a small garrison guarding that locale, reputedly the gateway to the fabled wealth of Santa Fe. General Wilkinson had for some time been seeking intelligence and samples of minerals and Indian artifacts from that largely unexplored region—eventually his collection must have surpassed that of any other American, except perhaps Thomas Jefferson. Wilkinson was to consider the Arkansas River the best route for invading the Provincias Internas, an expanse covering much of present-day Texas, New Mexico, Arizona, and sections of northern Mexico.[3]

Estimating the mouth of the Arkansas to be three hundred yards wide, Clark drew it broader than any other river junction on his map. In that vicinity he scrutinized the angle of the sun and the headings on his compass to determine the latitude and longitude of a place he calls the "Northern point of 2 Islands," as if unwilling to name so strategic a confluence. If he was indeed exercising such caution, he must have feared the Spanish might catch him in the act of surveillance.[4]

By Thursday, April 5, 1798, the Mississippi had swollen almost to flood stage. Clark's flotilla shoved off early into the swift current and landed that evening on an island he neglects to identify, but the following day he made little distance because of rain and wind. Although he surely was discouraged to find smaller, more streamlined craft—including Indian canoes loaded with skins and furs—overtaking his own in the effort to get to New Orleans before the goods of others drove down prices, he had little choice except to wait. Such times had to frustrate him, but once again he does not voice discouragement. April 7 proving more favorable for travel, he progressed downstream for almost ten uninterrupted hours.

He departed the next morning, a placid Easter Sunday. Soon his boats approached the outflow of the Yazoo River, the center of the failed South Carolina Yazoo swindle and later schemes modeled after it. Just above the confluence he pulled over to await the O'Hara convoy, and there he stayed for the night.

Around sunrise he was under way but paused at the Yazoo long enough to take observations in order to figure the position of such a significant juncture, the opening to much of what is now northern Mississippi. Three hours later he rounded a bend in the river and tied up beneath bluffs topped with naturally occurring groves of *Juglans Nigra*, a tree producing delicious black walnuts encased in adamantine shells swathed with green, aromatic husks. Travelers agreed this place, Walnut Hills, was one of the loveliest on the river. That point being the most defensible one between New Orleans and St. Louis, Clark took readings from which to derive its precise coordinates.

* * *

A decade earlier James Wilkinson had seen firsthand the military potential of Walnut Hills. Upriver, the Mississippi flows almost due east for six miles to the junction with the Yazoo, then abruptly pinches into a ninety-degree bend and veers south, the current deflecting off the eastern shore. Observing those same forces pushing his boat toward that side of the Mississippi, Wilkinson recognized the advantage of having a hilltop fort there, with cannons large enough to hit vessels in the narrowed stream. He urged Manuel Gayoso de Lemos, at that time the governor of what the Spanish called the Natchez District: "pray you to loose no time in making [a military] establishment" at Walnut Hills. Wilkinson also wanted a royal grant of three thousand acres in the area, especially if the South Carolina Yazoo Company or another developer began settling colonists nearby.[5]

Accordingly, Governor Miró sent Gayoso to study the flow of the Mississippi and the lay of Walnut Hills. Concurring with Wilkinson's assessment, Gayoso selected a bluff nine miles below the mouth of the Yazoo as the site for a stronghold. But because the numerous and powerful Choctaws claimed the vicinity, Gayoso took pains to treat with them until reaching an agreement conducive to the harmony of the greater province.[6]

By May 1791, his men had erected El Fuerte de Nogales, roughly translated as "The Walnut Hills Fort." It guarded the Mississippi with four twelve-pound cannons and eight eight-pounders and also housed a powder magazine, barracks for two hundred soldiers, and quarters for their commander. But because an attack might also come by land, Spanish soldiers cleared the surrounding area. On discovering it included some slopes even higher than the one holding the military post, they equipped those hills with guns to protect the lower works, and soon there were five fortified elevations within less than a square mile.

French spy Victor Collot scrutinized El Fuerte de Nogales in 1796, mockingly calling it the "Gibraltar of Louisiana" and deriding the notion that so many separated defenses made it invincible. "Eighty soldiers and a captain are intrusted with the defence of these different forts, which would require at least a thousand men." He went on, "In whatever manner this position be occupied, with the view of protecting Louisiana against the Americans, it will always be ineffectual, unless possession be gained of the whole chain of heights."[7]

In November 1797, when Walnut Hills was still under Spanish jurisdiction, Captain Isaac Guion paused there to purchase beef for his troops as they descended the river. On studying what he called the "much boasted of impregnable post," he decided it could easily be reduced to U.S. possession. Because no such attempt was to occur we will never know whether he was right; but he and Collot ignored the fact that the Walnut Hills stronghold did indeed check American expansion into that quarter and monitored the movements of the Choctaws. So important was El Fuerte de Nogales to Governor Carondelet, he wished to retain it as long as possible.[8]

By early 1798, however, Pinckney's Treaty had vastly decreased the likelihood of an American invasion, and Captain Guion, who since December 1797 had been camping outside the Spanish fort at Natchez, was impatient to assume authority over the full extent of territory ceded by Spain. When he heard that Spain was soon to relinquish the Nogales post intact, and that Gayoso de Lemos (who in the summer of 1797 replaced Carondelet as governor of Spanish Louisiana) wished compensation for it, Guion sent orders to Major William Kersey to estimate the value of the structures there.[9] As Guion knew, Kersey and a detachment of soldiers were already in transit from the fort at the Chickasaw Bluffs to Walnut Hills. On March 23, 1798, the Louisiana Regiment of the Spanish Army at last abandoned Nogales. Nine days later, Kersey and his detachment arrived. They found the buildings in satisfactory condition except that vandals had already stripped them of hinges, locks, and even some timbers.[10]

Such was the state of the outpost—to be designated Fort McHenry after Secretary of War James McHenry—when William Clark pulled his boats there on April 9. He purchased a canoe to replace his damaged one. Then he writes of his two-hour-long stay: "Maj. Kersey & two companies & a Detachment of artillerist & Inft. garrisoned at this place, Which they found at their arrival avaquated [evacuated] by the Spaniards & left in good order a Number of new buildings left, This is a most charming Situation."

Kersey surely was disappointed to hear about the loss of uniforms due to the accident upriver; his men had almost nothing to wear. He also learned the unhappy news that the convoy brought no physician or medicine, or funds to recompense his soldiers for duty dating back at least to 1797. But because the Army was especially delinquent getting the payroll to troops on the distant Mississippi, their commanders often had to rely on pieces of eight to meet such obligations, even though in most cases the Spanish forbade the exportation of their money. Noticing the shortage of hard cash at the forts along his route, the enterprising Clark would in a few weeks come up with a daring means of supplying that need.[11]

But for now, Major Kersey must have been aware that suspicion pervaded the Mississippi River valley; General Wilkinson had disingenuously warned his subordinates against trusting the Spaniards. Captain Guion was of the same mind. At the general's request he was forwarding intelligence from Natchez, the present focus of tensions between Spain and the United States, and he innocently took for granted that Wilkinson was using that information for the good of their country. Both Guion and Kersey were prudent officers, but neither of them realized that, by creating a presumption of Spanish duplicity, Wilkinson was deflecting attention away from his own.[12]

* * *

Shortly after Clark left Walnut Hills and returned to the water, a storm forced his flotilla to shore for a while. In the evening, a southwest wind "nearly blew us out of the river," he comments. Such struggles were to persist almost to New Orleans, making his entries repetitive and occasionally tedious although they helped prepare him for the twenty-eight months of the expedition to and from the Pacific. This particular spell of rough weather kept his vessels idle the next day too, comprising a very long and unwelcome pause, but he writes about its effect on his journey in characteristic uncomplaining fashion: "The Wind Continue this morning, and violintly all day we oblige to

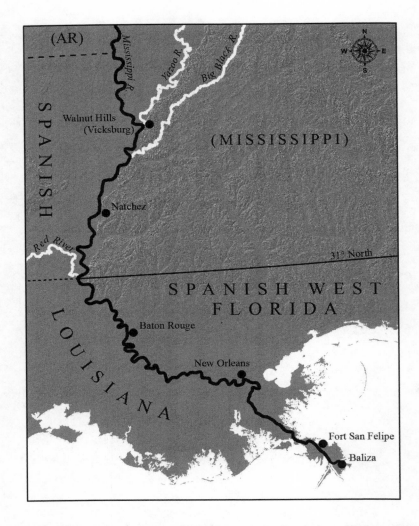

William Clark's 1798 route down the Mississippi River from Walnut Hills to the Gulf of Mexico, 530 river miles. Parentheses indicate future cities and states.

continue here," adding, perhaps with sympathy, "all the hands Drunk in the Contractors boat."

At sunrise on April 11, 1798, the voyage resumed, and Clark's flatboats descended a few miles before the wind once again compelled them to put to land for the rest of the day. Leaving early the following morning, he paused at the mouth of the Big Black, a broad stream pouring into the Mississippi from the east. Thought to rise near waters flowing into the Tombigbee River, the Big Black was a potential avenue to the fortified city of Mobile, capital of Spanish West Florida. No doubt mindful that control of the Big Black might be a key to the region between Louisiana and the Spanish-ruled Floridas, Clark stopped long enough to take another positional fix.[13]

Afterward, he cautiously threaded the Grand Gulf, a pair of large eddies formed below a sharp bend constricting the Mississippi. "This place is Dangerous," he records, "on the left the current runs against the p[o]int of a rock (under a Hill) & [on the] right a large whorl, also below & above the rock on the left side." Not far past the Grand Gulf, which he sketched to resemble a sack cinched in the middle, he again encountered fierce winds. He called a halt at the mouth of Bayou Pierre, a short sluggish creek flowing out of a swamp to the east, and remained there for the night.

Early the next morning, Friday, April 13, the wind still blew: "Set out at 7 oClock the wind continue tho not hard we was obliged to land at 10 oClock after makeing 9 miles. Set out at 1 o'Clock, wind all day." Natchez, the largest town on his route except for New Orleans, lay only a few miles downstream, but he moved cautiously, taking advantage of the slower pace in order to study the terrain.

Five miles below Bayou Pierre he drew the hills of the Petit Gulf, a smaller version of the eddy-filled straits near the end of the Big Black River. After passing this lesser hazard he sketched the Mississippi wide and dotted with few islands. To the east he noted a large bend, then another one turning in the opposite direction, then Cole's Creek pouring in from the east. To indicate bluffs commencing above that stream and proceeding almost due south rather than following the sinuous contours of the Mississippi, he inked a series of short parallel strokes.

The hilltops above him teemed with pines and, below them, the small-leafed magnolia. Because snow and ice were almost unknown at this latitude, he also observed drooping veils of Spanish moss and other flora unlike that of Kentucky. Fields of cotton and tobacco were not far away, but farmers of his era seldom planted to the edge of the river, and Clark probably saw along the banks only willows and canebrakes as high as small trees.

He must have begun to relax. Natchez was but a short distance downstream, and only three hundred river-miles beyond it lay New Orleans. Soon the heights to the east fell away as the river flowed so broad and deep a boatman might descend it simply by keeping to the center of the stream. Having crucial tasks still to carry out, Clark kept his scientific instruments, journal, and writing tools close at hand.

10

That Miserable Natchez Fort

ON Saturday, April 14, 1798, Clark shoved off early, somewhere below the mouth of the Bayou Pierre, and remained on the river until it carried him to Natchez a few hours later. He recognized that location by bluffs looming nearly two hundred feet over a string of houses and shops along a steep road leading to the Mississippi. He directed his boats eastward to a landing lapped by a wide, gentle eddy, secured them, and proceeded up the hill. Because he was to record at Natchez only his monetary dealings, we must look to the writings of his contemporaries, particularly Captain Guion and British traveler Francis Baily, for an idea of what Clark encountered there.

Atop the bluff was a weather-beaten assemblage of structures that until just two weeks earlier had housed the troops and artillery of Carlos IV. Now they held U.S. forces. Despite its dilapidated condition, the fort was a symbol of American sovereignty in the Natchez District, which, on April 7, 1798, entered the Union as the Mississippi Territory. Nevertheless, from almost his arrival at Natchez, Guion believed it less strategically important than a point a few miles downriver on an eminence called Loftus Heights.

France had been the first European nation to assert control over the greater area, much of which the powerful Natchez tribe then claimed. In 1716 the French constructed a fort called Rosalie (for the duchess of Pontchartrain, wife of the French minister of marine) but placed it next to a large settlement of Natchez Indians. Tensions between newcomers and natives gradually increased. In 1729 some Natchez burned Fort Rosalie to the ground, but within a year the French had driven them away and rebuilt the stronghold.[1]

On losing the Seven Years' War, France ceded its lands east of the Mississippi and north of New Orleans to the British, who in turn refortified the Natchez area, settling it with English-speaking families from the colonies along the Atlantic seaboard. After the American Revolution, Britain relinquished the lower Mississippi valley to the confederated United States, a nation as yet too weak to assert control over such distant lands. A conflict with Spain eventually developed. Having received New Orleans and southern portions of the Mississippi valley from France at the end of the Seven Years' War, Spain had until recently governed the Natchez District—and its many Anglophone residents—although it lay east of the Mississippi.

Natchez was strategically important not only for its proximity to New Orleans but also for its topography, which, unlike that of Walnut Hills or Chickasaw Bluffs, did not lend itself to assault by land. To make attack from the Mississippi similarly unlikely, the Spanish crowned the highest riverside eminence with a framework twelve feet tall, packed it with earthen fill, and erected on top of it a hexagonal stronghold with barracks for two hundred soldiers, a powder magazine, and sixteen cannons (eight of them eighteen-pounders, the others twelve-pounders) aimed at the river. On a rise to the east they added a battery of smaller guns; it commanded a defile running between the two sets of works.[2]

Clark could see that these defenses, which had yet to face an armed force, were steadily giving way to natural ones. When the French general Victor Collot was spying on Spanish military works in 1796, he wrote that the Natchez fort was in "a most wretched state; the buildings are falling into ruins, the platforms rotten, as well as the gun carriages." Conditions two years later were even more deplorable. Calling the outpost "that miserable Fort, mouldering and tumbling on every side," Captain Guion stationed in it only several dozen artillerists, sending a much larger number of infantrymen to a nearby tent encampment.[3]

Due to a shortage of military apparel, the soldiers at Natchez did not look much like their brethren stationed along the Ohio River valley. According to Guion, his men were greatly "in want of Clothing, particularly my Company which having been many years detached have been less regularly supplied, and of that more destroyed by an over share of labour on public works than the others." Few Natchez civilians being available for hire, he had to rely on his own troops to rebuild and maintain the fort, and performing those tasks wore out their uniforms.[4]

Replacing such clothing was expensive and often risky; contractors required sturdy flatboats, skilled navigators, and a large measure of luck to transport apparel downriver without sustaining damage to it. For those reasons Captain Guion had few alternatives but to relax the dress code, sometimes allowing soldiers at the posts under his command to wear the coats and hats of other units. Guion was disappointed to learn about the loss of supplier Lynn's cargoes and to receive from him and his companions just a tiny fraction of what the Army needed in the Mississippi valley. Guion suspected that Edward O'Hara, chief of the flotilla, had been negligent and perhaps wasteful in discharging his duties, but from Clark's account we cannot tell whether anyone was to blame.[5]

Guion was especially concerned about how he was to shelter his soldiers and the hundreds of others descending the Mississippi to Natchez. O'Hara's convoy having brought almost nothing in the way of tents or camping gear, Guion had to report to his superior, Colonel John F. Hamtramck: "And I assure you Sir of almost every article are we destitute: Camp equipage we have none, a few old weather beaten and rotten tents excepted; The troops who occupy them having done so since August last."[6]

Little wonder then that Clark probably put up in a "tavern," a term often used to denote an inn for travelers. He gives no specifics, so we cannot be sure where he spent his two nights in Natchez, but he records paying "Expenses" of two dollars. Perhaps this figure reflects the cost of staying in the same house that served Francis Baily in 1797. Baily did not identify his lodging but said it was one of only two or three accommodations in town. It charged a dollar per night and had a billiard table (Clark played billiards at every opportunity).[7]

According to Baily, the town of Natchez contained eighty or ninety separate dwellings, some of them "scarcely furnished beyond the first stage of civilization, when a few boards nailed together have served for a bedstead, and a mattress covered with a few blankets for a bed." Others were "fitted up in the neatest manner possible; but then in the greatest plainness." The orderly layout was similar to what he had seen in Philadelphia, and in the future national capital being raised along the Potomac River, and perhaps reminded him of his native England.[8]

Yet Baily noticed something rather foreign about Natchez too. Many houses there occupied enough ground to appear to be the centers of little plantations. Such a pattern of land use came from the Spanish custom of granting acreage to settlers who, rather than paying for it with cash, dwelled on it and improved it with farms or businesses. Although Spain used this system in other places, it enjoyed the greatest success in the Natchez area, particularly after the 1793 invention of the cotton gin. Baily noted that several of those machines were functioning in 1797, making cotton the predominant crop of the region.[9]

If only Clark had recorded such things! Instead, he writes just of immediate concerns—having his clothes washed, selling some of his bacon, laying in candles, fish, wine, and spirits for the rest of the voyage. His ledger notations also reveal that he compensated deckhand William Orr for his services, hired a replacement named Robert Kates, and advanced hands Cline and Beaty several dollars.

The diary section of his journal is particularly unrevealing; in it he writes only "at the Natchez," for Saturday, April 14, and even less for the following day: "at the N." Such economy of language makes his river entries, even the most repetitive ones, seem rich. Thus far, he had compressed his narrative of the eleven-hundred-mile voyage from Louisville into not quite eight pages by substituting staccato phrases such as "wind rose," "Set out early," or "wind continued" for the ampler, more descriptive prose of which he was capable. On the grand Western Expedition his style would now and then blossom with carefully articulated observations, even if they were also condensed: "Ocian in view! O! the joy." These, of course, he could often compose with a bit more leisure and the help of other observers as he fulfilled President Jefferson's assignment to annotate the territory.[10]

In Natchez in 1798, however, Clark surely kept in mind that in a few days he would cross the thirty-first parallel and enter the Spanish empire where authorities locked up foreigners suspected of spying. General Collot's copious notes about Mississippi River defenses, for example, landed him in a New Orleans jail, and Clark would have to be extremely selective about what he set down to paper until after leaving the province. If, until now, he had recorded relatively little about his activities because doing so was not his wont, soon he would have a more pressing reason to keep such entries to a minimum.[11]

Captain Guion was ready to begin preparing Natchez residents for representative government when the Spanish finally evacuated the fort. But by the time Clark arrived, Guion was learning how difficult that job would be. He reported being "constantly perplexed with all kinds of business, complaints for abuse, slander, arrest for debts, thefts, and the whole Catalogue of vexations," problems exacerbating the blinding headaches he'd begun suffering upriver.[12]

Guion longed for the arrival of the territorial governor though no one along the frontier knew who that might be; many expected General Wilkinson to get the appointment. Wilkinson desired it for the prestige and salary it was sure to bring, but even more for the cover it promised should he resume scheming with Spain. While he'd allowed the Spanish to violate Pinckney's Treaty by remaining at their forts, especially those at Walnut Hills and Natchez, Wilkinson had reason to believe they would do him the courtesy of not revealing his treasonable role as Agent 13. But now they were gone, and he no longer had such assurance.

Until his situation changed, Wilkinson would temporize with Spain by claiming to be holding out for the proper opportunity—and price—to continue passing along U.S. secrets. At the same time, and with diminishing patience, he awaited reimbursement from Spain of the 640 dollars that Thomas Power had kept for the effort and expense of smuggling nine thousand Spanish dollars to Wilkinson in 1796. Two years having passed since then, Wilkinson surely also wanted interest in addition to the principal.[13]

11

The Most Fortunate and Glorious Commotion

JUDGING from his ledger notations, Clark must have found Natchez an agreeable place. But he wrote nothing more about what he did during his two days there. So let us again take his silence as an opportunity to observe in this chapter and the next, how conspiratorial developments soon to affect him were shaping up. Late in the summer of 1796, after General Wilkinson took his nine thousand dollars and Thomas Power accepted 640 dollars for his expenses, Wilkinson instructed Power to bill Spain for that amount and come back with it. No doubt the general expected to receive this money before long; compared with previous payments, it would be insignificantly light, weighing a mere forty pounds.[1]

But the odds against timely delivery were high. Unusually cold weather kept Power at New Madrid during the winter; he was unable to report to New Orleans until May 1797. He then suggested that, because General Wayne's dragnet was looking for him to return to the lower Ohio River, someone other than he should take the 640 dollars to Wilkinson. Carondelet agreed. Learning later that Philip Nolan was unavailable to do so, the governor temporarily set aside the concern.[2]

Uppermost on Carondelet's mind was a violent strategy to make Kentuckians rebel against the Union and align themselves in some fashion with Spain, thereby preventing the enforcement of Pinckney's Treaty and prolonging the Spanish regime in Louisiana and the Floridas. Considering Wilkinson essential to such an undertaking, and Power critical to securing his cooperation, Carondelet promised that if the proposed project succeeded it would cause the "most fortunate and the most glorious commotion." In that event, Power would "cover [him]self with glory" and receive "the most brilliant fortune."[3]

Carondelet outlined the plot: Spain would give Wilkinson, Sebastian, and their comrades an initial hundred thousand dollars—an amount far beyond the aggregate of all sums paid in previous schemes—for launching an insurrection to tear Kentucky from the Union. To guarantee that outcome, Spain would then furnish another hundred thousand dollars and twenty artillery pieces. Once the secession was complete, the conspirators would configure out of their former state a new republic. Guarded by Spanish garrisons at Walnut Hills and Natchez, it would stretch from the Mississippi River to the Appalachians. Carondelet reasoned:

> The [American] public is discontented with the new taxes; Spain and France are enraged at the connexions of the United States with England, the Army is weak and devoted to Wilkinson; the threats of Congress [against France, at that time an ally of Spain] authorise me to succour on the spot, and openly, the Western States; money will not then be wanting to me, for I shall send without delay a ship to Vera Cruz in search of it, as well as of ammunition. . . . If they [the people of the western states] suffer this instant to escape them, and that we should be forced to deliver up the posts, Kentucky and Tennesse . . . will ever remain under the oppression of the Atlantic states.[4]

The opportunistic Power hailed the desperate plan and pledged to promote it with all his "fidelity and zeal," even guaranteeing support for it from Wilkinson, Sebastian, Innes, Murray, and other supposed friends of Spain. Power added, "if I give credit to my presentiment, our success is infallible," thereby encouraging Carondelet to believe that promises of riches and the acclaim of becoming "the Washington of the Western states" would lure Wilkinson into the scheme. No doubt Power thought that for the right price Wilkinson (who, as ranking commander of the Army, was preparing to send troops to take possession of the Spanish forts to be vacated according to Pinckney's Treaty) would resume treasonous pursuits, but he must have known that the general was growing extremely cautious about doing so.[5]

Power immediately set off on horseback; he was equipped with precise instructions and everything else he needed but not with the 640 dollars. He called first at Natchez and then at Nashville where a magistrate had him searched and detained for trying to stir up resentment against the United States. After being released, Power continued to Louisville only to find that his notoriety preceded him: "The inhabitants," he wrote, "were much alarmed at my arrival . . . and were openly threatening me." Despite such opposition he persisted, disclosing Carondelet's seditious proposal to Sebastian, Wilkinson's closest ally in such matters.[6]

Apparently more concerned with what he might lose in the bargain than with the proffered benefits, Sebastian asked a number of questions: Would he and his associates be compensated if complicity in the scheme cost them their legitimate employment? What would Spain do if they asked more protection than a pair of military posts could offer, or different boundaries for the breakaway nation? Would Spain consent *not* to interfere in its government? Exacting affirmative answers on all those points before agreeing to take further action, Sebastian promised to lay the plot before Harry Innes, George Nicholas, Thomas Todd, and other trusted friends, and to report their response to it when Power returned in a few weeks.[7]

Power departed Louisville, crossed the Ohio, and rode north to the Detroit fort to meet with Wilkinson. Finding him temporarily away on an inspection tour of other Army installations, Power settled in, having no idea that the general's attitude toward Spain might have changed since they last saw each other. But it had, drastically. Shortly after they had split up in 1796, Wilkinson had ascended the Ohio to take his vendetta against General Wayne to the seat of government at Philadelphia. Suspecting what his second-in-command was doing, Wayne had set out overland on a journey he intended to culminate in the same city, with his triumph over Wilkinson's calumnies. Instead, Wayne died en route in December 1796, after suffering acutely from gout, stomach pains, and fever.[8]

His demise occurring shortly after the election of John Adams as chief executive, it compelled lame-duck President Washington to consider who ought to command the Army. For years he had heard rumors about Wilkinson's treasonable Spanish connection, but he still had no proof of it. Lacking any other officer of commensurate experience or capability to lead the Army, especially in the West, Washington simply let the position of commander in chief devolve to Wilkinson. A few weeks later, Adams became president and left the situation as it was. At around the same time, Congress reduced the size of the Army and eliminated Wayne's rank of major general. Wilkinson would remain a brigadier. Even so, his top position in the Army made him more watchful than ever about plotting with Spain.[9]

* * *

As we have seen, Wilkinson was away from Detroit when Power arrived in mid-August 1797. If Power expected the hospitality he'd enjoyed the previous year at Fort Greenville, he was soon free of that misconception. Even before Wilkinson returned, he had Power arrested and confined to camp on suspicion of espionage. Wilkinson returned in early September and allowed Power only enough time to present Carondelet's proposition. According to Power:

> General Wilkinson received me very coolly. . . . he exclaimed very bitterly we are both lost, without being able to derive any advantage from your journey, and then asked me if I had brought him the 640 dollars. . . . Having informed him of the proposals of the Baron [Carondelet], he proceeded to tell me that it was a chimerical project which was impossible to execute; that the inhabitants of the Western States, having obtained by treaty all they desired, would not wish to form any other political or commercial alliances, and that they had no motive for separating themselves from the interests of the other States of the Union, even if France and Spain should make them the most advantageous offers.[10]

For once, Wilkinson spoke the truth. Hoping to persuade him to subscribe to the new scheme, Power emphasized that if he did so, his two-thousand-dollar Spanish salary would be doubled, and he'd receive a hundred-thousand-acre grant in Upper Louisiana. Power also appealed to Wilkinson's considerable vanity, asserting that his countrymen would surely name him president of the nation formed from what had been Kentucky. But Wilkinson remained unmoved. Blaming Pinckney's Treaty for his unwillingness to get involved, he said it had "overturned all his plans . . . and rendered useless the labours of more than ten years," adding that he'd "destroyed his cyphers, and torn all his correspondence with our government [Spain], and that his duty and his honor did not permit him to continue it."[11]

Power might take heart, however, as Wilkinson pointed out that he was not necessarily finished with conspiring. On the contrary, if appointed the first governor of the Mississippi Territory, an assignment many people expected him to receive, "he would not want opportunities" to intrigue anew with Spain. Obviously reluctant to cut all ties with his secret handlers, Wilkinson calculated that, so long as they thought him useful, they would refrain from exposing him as a traitor. Therefore, when Power let him know that Carondelet wanted him to delay taking over the Mississippi River forts (in direct violation of his War Department orders), he renewed his resolution not to anger the Spanish lest they expose his treachery. And so Wilkinson assured Carondelet that, although Captain Isaac Guion was already on his way down the river, Wilkinson had ordered him to avoid offending the Spanish as much as possible.[12]

Eager to get free of Power before he drew suspicion down on him, Wilkinson ordered Captain Bartholomew Shaumburgh, one of his most partisan subordinates, to hustle the agent back to New Madrid. Power took exception to their route—by following the chain of frontier posts it would avoid Louisville, preventing him from reuniting with Sebastian and perhaps advancing Carondelet's plan—but Wilkinson refused to alter it.[13]

Power, Shaumburgh, and a military escort left Detroit on September 6, 1797, reaching Fort Knox at Vincennes more than four weeks later. William Clark, who'd gone there to represent his brother George in a lawsuit, came upon Power just when Power needed someone to carry to Louisville a letter telling Sebastian that Power would not be coming to town and asking Sebastian to meet him at New Madrid instead. As we will soon see in further detail, the next day Power sent that communication on to Louisville by means of a special messenger he did not identify, and Clark—whether with or without Power's missive is unknown—departed for the same place. Power continued his westward journey. At New Madrid he waited two weeks for Sebastian to arrive and then proceeded without him to New Orleans.[14]

On December 5, 1797, Power briefed Gayoso de Lemos (who in August had succeeded Carondelet as governor of Louisiana and West Florida) on the mission just completed. Although Power was angry with Wilkinson for rebuffing the plot and for treating him as a potential enemy, he believed the seditious seeds he had planted in the minds of the other Kentuckians might still bear fruit. Sebastian was his main hope. Despite Sebastian's caution, he'd pledged to Spain the continued friendship of Kentucky and promised to discuss the new proposal with his pro-Spanish friends. Power and Gayoso understood Sebastian well enough to expect a response from him as soon as possible, and perhaps in person.[15]

Before taking leave of Gayoso, Power handed him a remarkably accurate description—compiled during his detentions at Nashville and Detroit—of the three-thousand-man U.S. Army. Accompanying that report were a dozen documents, most of them regarding his instructions, expenses, and correspondence from the trip. He made special mention of a crucial paper submitted earlier; it concerned "the 640 dollars, which General Wilkinson [still] so anxiously solicits." As Power and Gayoso realized, there was probably no chance the general would even consider resuming active duty as Agent 13 unless he collected in full on that small yet absolutely essential account.[16]

No question remained of how to smuggle him those coins; Power's 1796 mission, coming so soon after the failed ones of Henry Owen and Joseph Collins, proved the reliability of distributing reales among barrels of Louisiana exports. But who would take charge of the money for the general? Not Power; he was no longer willing to work for Wilkinson nor to risk another arrest, especially on the Ohio River. Philip Nolan was yet unavailable. Gayoso might have decided that until an American of demonstrated nerve, ability, and loyalty to Wilkinson assumed responsibility for his precious cargo, it would have to stay in New Orleans. Such an American was Samuel Montgomery Brown; he was already heading downstream but well behind William Clark.

12

I Could Not Carry Our Plan in Execution

THERE would be little more to tell about how recent developments in the Spanish Conspiracy were to affect Clark's present venture to New Orleans had he not, in 1793, walked away from Fort Hamilton (in what is now southwest Ohio) with a record book he never gave back. Called "An Orderly Book from Fort Washington and Fort Hamilton, 1792–1793," it was strictly a compendium of military orders until he began drafting letters, lists, diagrams, sketches, and even a legal document in it. His motive for some of those additions may never be discovered, but several of them suggest the possibility of heretofore undeduced links between him and General Wilkinson. In light of the Orderly Book and a handful of better-known writings, including a cryptic journal Clark kept in 1797 during a journey to and from the Mississippi River valley, let us review how the months after his return to civilian life may have shaped his 1798 travels.[1]

Clark resigned from the Army on July 1, 1796. Intending to put together a cargo fleet to take down the Mississippi later that year, he instead found family obligations demanding his immediate attention. He had scarcely arrived back at Mulberry Hill when he rode to southwest Kentucky to inspect two thousand acres claimed by his brother Jonathan.[2]

At around the same time, French general Victor Collot, on his way to spy out military defenses in Spanish Louisiana, paused at Louisville. Coming upon "a number of persons who were crowding around something that lay extended on the ground, on which a blanket had been thrown, and which a man was about to take up and carry off," Collot, it seems, learned that the outstretched form belonged to an intoxicated George Rogers Clark. If so, his rescuer was a shopkeeper mindful of George's sacrifices for American independence and determined to protect him from shame.[3]

That binge was probably George's last one as master of his own affairs. On August 15, 1796, he evidently signed a power of attorney (a draft of it in William's hand appears in the Orderly Book) authorizing William to transact for him and to represent him in court. William immediately took the executed document—which, because of its precise phrasing, spelling, and syntax, must have come about with the help of a lawyer, perhaps Benjamin Sebastian—to Lexington, Kentucky, where he attempted to settle a debt George owed to Humphrey Marshall, one of his most demanding creditors.[4]

William wrote Jonathan about those dealings, saying he planned to leave Lexington on August 25 for Cincinnati but not mentioning why he was going there. Explaining he'd recently mustered out of the Army, William comments that the feud between James Wilkinson and Anthony Wayne "rages more violent than ever," adding that both of them were heading to Philadelphia, and Wilkinson was already ascending the Ohio.[5]

But he was not. Wilkinson remained at Cincinnati until heading east on October 3, 1796, shortly after Thomas Power and Philip Nolan spirited to Samuel M. Brown's store Wilkinson's 9,640 Spanish dollars (640 of them, as we have seen, he turned over to Power for his expenses). Although we cannot discern the state of Clark's knowledge, if he was indeed aware the general lingered at Fort Washington (in what is now downtown Cincinnati), why did he indicate otherwise?[6]

Clark proceeded to Cincinnati where on September 8, 1796, he tended to land business on behalf of Bennett Tompkins, a Virginia friend of the Clark family. William also spent an unknown amount of time at Fort Washington. Subsequent to departing for home, he came down with a severe illness, which he mentions in the opening of a letter drafted in the Orderly Book to a recipient he does not identify:

Sir:

Louisville, Jany. 1797

From my promis to you at fort Washington you must certainly expected to have heard from me before this time, on a certain piece of business. the Cause of my not wrighting by Mr. Brown was owing to my indisposition which has continued from the third day after I left you at Cincinnati untill this time. This day is the first that I have ventured out of the house for three weeks, and but seldom for 12 weeks past.[7]

Who was Clark's addressee? Likely a military man, although a relatively small number of civilians made business calls at Army posts. "Mr. Brown," however, might well refer to Kentuckian Samuel M. Brown who, by hiding the pieces of eight in his store in Frankfort, late in the summer of 1796, completed the smuggling mission carried out by Power and Nolan.

Clark goes on to mention an arcane place and a heretofore unknown business venture, both of which he had obviously discussed with the man he was writing: "I have it still in view to visit Point Sarlle mearly to See and find out the Advantage." He adds, "I had procured Tobacco but the State of my indisposition was such that I could not carry our plan in Execution & have parted with the Tobaco. I have recovered I believe."

Tables of figures in Clark's penmanship on other pages in the Orderly Book demonstrate that he was thinking about taking pirogues loaded with tobacco, salt, flour, pork, and whiskey to a downstream destination—and perhaps not just for profit, depending on the location of "Point Sarlle." No such toponym exists in English, but the underscoring suggests that Clark and the recipient of the letter knew where that place was and why it was worth examining (as we will see in chapter 24).

On February 12, 1797, Clark drafted another message in the Orderly Book; it was for someone he addresses only as "Sir." Saying he had not received from that person any answer to his latest communications, Clark asks to be remembered to Army officers he does not name. He also requests reimbursement of amounts, which "your bro. Thomas expended at this place [Jefferson County, Kentucky]," and seems to poke fun at the recent death of General Wayne, the man Wilkinson hated most, saying Wayne was "taken off to the holy land."[8]

Although we cannot say beyond a doubt that letter was for James Wilkinson, if it was, who might "bro. Thomas" have been? (Wilkinson had only one brother, and his name was Joseph.) Could he have been Thomas Power? Let us consider what little known evidence there is on this question. In August 1796 and a few weeks later, Power came to Louisville, first hiding there the 9,640 Spanish dollars long enough to hurry to Cincinnati and tell Wilkinson about them, then returning and sending them on to Brown's emporium in Frankfort, their last hiding place before Wilkinson took them. If Power was "bro. Thomas" (a point that may never be proved), it follows that Clark played a yet undiscovered role in that infamous project.

If Wilkinson was the addressee of any letter drafted in the Orderly Book in early 1797, he probably did not receive it until returning to Fort Washington in the last days of April 1797. Between then and the previous autumn he had spent a great deal of time in Philadelphia. Having traveled there in order to criticize General Wayne, Wilkinson remained longer than planned because news of Wayne's unexpected death raised urgent questions about his own rank, salary, and duties. Once those matters were settled, he stayed as long as possible, so ingratiating himself with the otherwise sagacious John Adams that soon Adams thought the many rumors about Wilkinson were the fabrications of his enemies.[9]

Having such support from the president emboldened Wilkinson—not only to disregard orders about evicting Spanish troops north of the thirty-first parallel but, soon, to disguise such insubordination as patriotism.

* * *

Just as Clark recorded in the Orderly Book, he spent January and February 1797 convalescing at Mulberry Hill. On days of relative health, he went to Louisville where he inquired whether Spanish forces had yet abandoned their posts at the Chickasaw Bluffs, Walnut Hills, and Natchez; the answer to that question was crucial to his planned river trip to New Orleans. On August 18, 1797, he wrote a letter voicing his anxieties on that topic to his brother Edmund: "A detachment of 200 men has Descended the Mississippi a few days a go for to receive the posts to be delivered by Spain on that River. I fear they will not be delivered yet."[10]

Two days later, Clark set off for Vincennes in order to represent George in the lawsuit over his 1786 confiscation of goods for the support and provisioning of his troops. Vincennes stood on the eastern side of the "Illinois Country," a vaguely defined region encompassing much of what is now Illinois and Indiana and eastern sections of Missouri. Despite being the home of Fort Knox (which Clark occasionally visited while in the Army), Vincennes had a mostly French-speaking populace with close ties to communities in the Mississippi valley. With him Clark brought a makeshift journal. It was a large sheet of paper, roughly fifteen by twelve inches, folded into eight pages. He began using it right away; our knowledge of this venture comes almost exclusively from his daily entries into that log.[11]

He reached Vincennes on August 22, 1797, only to learn he needed documents kept by John Rice Jones, George's former commissary who lived 150 miles to the southwest in Kaskaskia, a French-speaking village founded in 1703 near the junction of the Kaskaskia River and the Mississippi. Clark headed in that direction, possibly aware he was entering territory whose inhabitants were feeling the effects of living along the frontier, far from the sure reach of American law.[12]

According to Judge John Edgar of Kaskaskia, numerous residents of New Design, a village thirty-four miles to the northwest, had organized themselves into an association of "French Republicans." As such they planned to "withdraw all allegiance" from the United States, and "plunder all those who would not join them." Edgar reported those stories to the territorial government.[13]

Many rumors of that sort, however, were emanating from Army headquarters at Detroit where Wilkinson was exaggerating reports about a French menace to the Illinois Country. He was trying to create an excuse not just to let the Spanish remain indefinitely at the posts their nation had ceded to the United States but also to send in the Army, thereby making the Mississippi valley more prone to war and to his own exploitation. To Secretary Winthrop Sargent of the Northwest Territory, Wilkinson sent notice of that supposed threat and of his alleged plan to post at Kaskaskia a detachment of artillery and another of infantry, "to keep our neighbors in check, to countenance our friends and confound the Banditti." Wilkinson added dramatically that, "should the clouds thicken, I shall stand ready to repair thither in person, with an additional force, & with all possible Celerity."[14] He gave this letter to Captain Bartholomew Shaumburgh to deliver while Shaumburgh was escorting Thomas Power back to Spanish territory. Afterward, he was to command the troops detached to Kaskaskia. Shaumburgh completed both assignments.[15]

In the meantime, William and two companions departed Vincennes. Four days later they reached Kaskaskia where, on July 4, 1778, George and only 175 volunteers had, without any act of violence, taken the town for the United States. On September 5, 1797, William strolled the streets of town, no doubt inspecting the site of Fort Gage, the British military installation George had captured and renamed Fort Clark, and perhaps visiting the locations of older defensive structures erected by the French. Learning that Jones was temporarily gone, William decided to pass the time until he returned by calling at nearby fortified places, some of them in Spanish Louisiana.[16]

The next day he and three companions crossed the Mississippi and entered that province. They rode a short distance to Ste. Genevieve and on to adjacent New Bourbon, settlements more prosperous than Kaskaskia because they were located on slightly higher ground. (Built along the riverbank, the original village of Ste. Genevieve had nearly been destroyed by the flood of 1785, giving rise to the town William saw; it still stands today.)[17]

Soon he became acquainted with Ste. Genevieve commandant François Vallé and accepted an invitation to spend the night at his house. Vallé's unwillingness to be invaded by forces of Citizen Genet, George Rogers Clark, or other supporters of the French Revolution had impelled him in 1794 to build on a hill overlooking the community what William called "a stockade fort" large enough for a hundred soldiers. A closer inspection of the installation would have revealed that it was built with oak timbers, surrounded by a palisade, and measured nearly two hundred feet square. From every corner protruded a bastion, each likely holding a two-pounder cannon—perhaps those transferred from Fort Massiac when the French abandoned it in 1763. The Ste. Genevieve fort must have lacked barracks, because the handful of Spanish soldiers stationed there slept in quarters rented from Jean Baptiste Vallé , the commandant's brother.[18]

Returning to Kaskaskia on September 7, 1797, and hearing that Jones was still gone, Clark, with a companion, set off the next day for Spanish St. Louis, taking a low-lying road on the American side of the Mississippi. They stopped for lunch at the old French-speaking settlement of Prairie du Rocher and then turned onto a lonely path leading west. Three miles farther they reached Fort de Chartres, a stronghold completed by the French in 1756 and abandoned nine years later. The third and last installation of that name to be constructed in the area, the post must have seemed to William potentially useful for military purposes. As he surely realized, in 1780 George had transported to Fort Jefferson at least one of several cannons originally guarding Fort de Chartres.[19]

While William inspected the spacious complex strategically placed along the Mississippi River, he estimated the dimensions of structures yet standing, as if considering their potential usefulness: "There remains three slides [sides] of a fort of a Stone wall, about 15 foot high 2 1/2 & 3 thick, the curten 75 yds. long hous walls entire and good, this fort is calculated for 600 men." Having toured the place the previous year, General Collot also noted:

> four large and magnificent buildings, one of which was destined for officers, one for the garrison, and the two others for military stores. The whole of these buildings are made of freestone, and raised on arches. This establishment was constructed with so much solidity and care, that in spite of time and the neglect in which it is left, the wall and buildings are still in good preservation: the timber has been taken away.[20]

The afternoon was far advanced when Clark finally left Fort de Chartres. Ten miles up the road he spent the night at the public house of Nathaniel

Hull, a local judge and militia commander who was keeping a close watch on the French sympathizers at nearby New Design. Rather than detour to that community, though, Clark rode the next day to Cahokia, the setting of another bloodless Revolutionary triumph by George. William found the town—which he spelled "Cohos," "Kahokia," "Kohokia," and "Cohoka"—unappealing but in relatively good order, calling it "low & mean . . . houses and much stragled, tho [it] does not appear on the Decline as the other villagies do," and estimating it held two hundred people. He made no mention of a fort, probably because a wooden one built decades earlier by the French had long since crumbled away, leaving little—other than a stone building erected as a mission—for British or American soldiers to occupy.[21]

Soon Clark crossed the river to Spanish St. Louis and, again not recording why, met the commandant. He was Zenon Trudeau, also the governor of Upper Louisiana, and he had recently rebuilt and expanded local defenses. In addition, Clark connected with Charles Gratiot—a Swiss-born businessman who had assisted George in his Illinois campaign—and with Auguste Chouteau, Gratiot's wealthy brother-in-law who in 1764 laid out the central area of St. Louis. Clark dined that evening with Trudeau. Neither of them noted what they talked about.[22]

Evidently Clark made a pleasing impression; on the next day, he underlined in his journal that he "was introduced to most of the gentlemen of Character & pour [power]." He toured the town, which (as yet unknown to him) would become his home for the last three decades of his life. He found St. Louis "to be in a Thriveing state, a number of . . . houses built . . . in the French Stile" (that is, of vertical timbers supported by a stone sill, or planted in the earth). He mentioned "a small fort, one Bastion & 5 Towrs round guards the Town," but surely recognized that such works left lower portions of St. Louis unprotected. No doubt careful not to reveal observations of this type now that he was in Spanish territory, he received what he termed "pressing invertations" to remain. But he departed on September 12, 1797, crossed the Mississippi, rode hard, and reached Kaskaskia at twilight the next day. Soon he was able to collect the papers he'd come for.[23]

Around the same time, General Wilkinson projected that he and a body of soldiers would reach Kaskaskia on October 15. To Governor Sargent, Wilkinson declared of the insurrection allegedly contemplated by the local francophiles: "We must nip the evil in the bud, or the consequences may become extensive & dangerous to the repose of the Western Country." Through such histrionic words, Wilkinson was apparently trying to lay a plausible foundation for an armed conflict contrived to deflect attention from his own questionable actions. So thought Timothy Pickering who, as secretary of war in 1795, had been privy to General Wayne's suspicions of Wilkinson's conspiring with Spain. Pickering therefore let Sargent know—in the vague language often employed in that era for the sake of security—that the general bore watching closely.[24]

Despite having collected the papers for George's case, William lingered several days at Kaskaskia but did not record why. Still there on September 17, 1797, he reported he was developing "large inflematory sores on my legs & thighs" and, on the following day, had "a violent hed ake." From September 19 to 21, he wrote of being "Housed with a boil."[25]

Whatever ailments he may have had, Clark still managed to pay a call on Winthrop Sargent just after Sargent arrived to strengthen the local militia. Neither of them left any lasting mention of their meeting. In addition, the following afternoon Clark had dinner with Judge Edgar and "som of the french sett[l]ers," yet he wrote nothing of substance about that encounter either. Once Sargent and local leaders departed for Cahokia, Clark says of himself only that for the next five days he was "At Kasskassies, sick."[26]

He set out eastward on the last of September. The next day he dispatched an "express," a communication often carried by a special courier, to a party Clark does not name, and for a purpose he does not reveal. He reached Vincennes on October 4 and stayed two days. During that span, Thomas Power and the soldiers guarding him arrived on their journey to Spanish Louisiana. By the time they left, Power had, in his words: "dispatched an express to Louisville, with a letter for Benjamin Sebastian . . . advising him of what had occurred, and informing him minutely of the motives which prevented me from complying with my promise given him [to confer at Louisville]." Did Power realize Clark was heading there, and that he knew Sebastian well? If so, did Clark carry the message? Although Power's mention of using an "express" makes that outcome seem unlikely, the question nonetheless bears asking.[27]

Not long after Clark returned home, Wilkinson abandoned his plan to go to Kaskaskia. Sargent had decided that the threat of criminal prosecution and the presence of a small garrison in that village would suffice to discourage rebellion. Wilkinson instead proceeded to winter quarters at Pittsburgh.[28]

After returning to Louisville, Clark continued to monitor troop movements down the Ohio and to listen for news from Spanish Louisiana. In December 1797 he wrote to Edmund that one of the battalions sent to Kaskaskia was soon to be deployed elsewhere. Upon confiding that "Our [federal] executive oficers . . . have but few friends in this quarter," William adds: "Please to destroy this hasty scrawl, what I rite you [I] do not wish any one else to see."[29]

Clark's fear of being thought an opponent to the Adams administration, however, paled beside Wilkinson's dread of being being proved a traitor. On learning over the winter that the Spanish were at last to abandon their posts at Natchez and Walnut Hills (an event that threatened to destroy his usefulness to Spain), Wilkinson encrypted a terse message to Gayoso, begging that his own name never be revealed in connection with treasonable dealings. Wilkinson passed this communication along to Sebastian who took it with him when he embarked on his own journey to New Orleans—just after Clark, with flatboats, cargoes, and deckhands, set off for the same place.[30]

13

The Door to the Whole Western Country

SECURE in the knowledge that because Natchez had become American territory he was free to record intelligence about it, Clark added the town to his chart. He also determined geographic coordinates, inscribing them on his growing list of important locations along the lower Mississippi. At noon on April 16, 1798, he had his crewmen shove the boats into the current, and they proceeded downstream. For the first time since leaving Fort Massac a month earlier, they were traveling alone, the Army vessels having reached their ultimate destination at Captain Guion's fort.

Clark's flotilla made more than twenty miles before darkness set it. Passing the chalk-colored headlands then called the White Cliffs (now the Ellis Cliffs), he sketched them with a series of short strokes radiating outward from the curve of the Mississippi. He departed early the next morning and made good progress until the wind picked up, then he took advantage of the slower pace to study the terrain. On his map he drew the mouth of the Homochitto River and that of Buffalo Creek, both streams low-lying meanderings rising only a few miles away. He had ample time also to examine the last noteworthy bluff in the series of terrestrial rises and dips—all of them east of the river—that he had been following for hundreds of miles. Perhaps misunderstanding "Loftus Heights" as the official designation of that promontory he instead calls it "Loveless Cliffs." Named for the British major Arthur Loftus, whose upstream-bound party of 350 soldiers was ambushed there in 1764 by Indians (probably of the Tunica tribe), the bluff had never been fortified. Even from the water, Clark must have recognized the strategic usefulness of the site.[1]

Captain Guion knew it well. He wanted to build a military installation there to replace the one falling to ruin at Natchez. General Wilkinson was soon to agree; within a few months he would secure Loftus Heights with an earthwork, a garrison, and powder magazines and then dedicate the outpost to President John Adams. Located only six river-miles above the southern U.S. boundary, Fort Adams was to provide Wilkinson not just with a secure location for defending Natchez and points upriver but also with a convenient perch for monitoring Spanish military movements and for assessing the risks and benefits of resuming his perfidious double life.[2]

When the rain died down later that day, Clark noted "Mr. Ellicotts Camp at the mouth of a Creek," referring to the tenting place of the Americans who, according to Pinckney's Treaty, were to "run and mark" the thirty-first parallel of northern latitude, the new line of demarcation between the United States and Spanish territory. Andrew Ellicott was the astronomer and mathematician who completed the Mason-Dixon line indicating the northern border of Maryland, surveyed much of the Potomac River basin for the national capital, and laid out the town to become Erie, Pennsylvania. He also led the commission to delineate the new boundary. He and his surveyors, trained assistants, and laborers had departed Natchez only eight days earlier to begin the work. He was expecting the Spanish Boundary Commission—required by Pinckney's Treaty—to arrive before long.[3]

Clark passed Ellicott's encampment in the middle of the day, an ideal time for taking positional readings because the sun is at its apex, so he made observations necessary to fixing the longitude of the site. As to latitude, by recording an exact thirty-one degrees, he apparently assumed from seeing tents that he was at the parallel. But Ellicott was only then realizing—from an intensive, five-night study of heavenly transits and distances—that the actual boundary lay three miles to the south. Clark, therefore, must have floated across the thirty-first parallel after he thought he did.[4]

He kept his surveying compass close at hand, however, to figure the position of the Red River, a broad, earth-tinted waterway rumored to rise even closer to Santa Fe than the Arkansas River. No known white explorer had yet followed the entire course of the Red, but legend told that its upper watershed teemed with wild horses, bison, great serpents, and unicorns, and that it held metallic deposits glinting like silver. Mindful also that because the Red issued from somewhere deep inside Spanish territory it might prove useful to devious dealings, General Wilkinson wanted to learn more about it. Wishing to close the Red off to others, he would use Fort Adams, "the door to our whole western Country" as he called it, to keep a selfish eye on that area.[5]

Wilkinson was correct, however, in believing that the Red rises not far from Santa Fe. Had Clark been able to scan the western horizon above the treetops, he'd have seen waters from distant and little-known places—Palo Duro Canyon, the Llano Estacado, the Ouachita Mountains—coursing down the last miles of the Red. Were he to look from above and in the opposite direction, he would have spied a Natchez planter named William Dunbar and (once again) Thomas Power, two of the future explorers of southwestern regions. So would be Ellicott and his chief surveyor, Thomas Freeman. All of them were gifted men, but Dunbar and Power, being Spanish subjects, were preparing with other members of the Spanish Boundary Commission to join the American party and get to work on marking the parallel. Little did Clark (or they) realize how soon they were all to meet.

* * *

Near the mouth of the Red River, part of the Mississippi flowed unimpeded into the Bayou Atchafalaya. To avoid getting pulled onto it and carried through an almost uninhabited land of swamps and sluggish streams to the Gulf of Mexico, boatmen had to hug the eastern shore of the Mississippi. Clark must have done just that as he navigated past what he designates on his map as "Chaflay," but he did not mention it in his daily entry. By nightfall he reckoned he was fifty river-miles closer to New Orleans than he'd been that morning.

If only that figure were the same in land-miles! On the contrary, somewhere around the international boundary, Clark was entering one of the longest and most exaggerated series of loops on the entire Mississippi.

When he reached the end of it the following afternoon, he had traveled fifty-four river-miles in order to gain a paltry five terrestrial miles. Because such extreme twists and turns, if drawn to scale, would not fit on his journal pages, he sketched them narrower than they really were.

At four in the afternoon of April 18, 1798, he pulled ashore at Pointe Coupée, a settlement named for a diversion channel cut years earlier by French Canadian traders wanting to shorten the river some twenty miles. Although Pointe Coupée was the seat of a district holding perhaps eleven thousand residents, it had little more than the ruins of a fort to protect it. But the area was prodigiously fertile; here the Mississippi emerged from hundreds of miles of shadowy forests to link a succession of settlements with fields producing rice, cotton, sugar cane, and tobacco. Grand, prosperous plantations lined the banks from Pointe Coupée to below New Orleans, orange trees in blossom freshened the breeze, and frame dwellings on pilings balanced above the floodplain. For the first time since leaving Natchez, Clark had reason to feel he was back in civilization, but he writes no more of Pointe Coupée than he did of that earlier stop. On his map, though, he began adding numerous small triangles to indicate natural levees on the banks of the Mississippi; such information could be useful to the orientation of visitors or of invading forces.[6]

Clark left town early the next morning. Soon he drifted into a headwind that forced him to tie up until noon beneath some low hills. After making further progress that day and pulling ashore for a time below Thompson's Creek, he and the deckhands experienced "a violent Storm of wind & rane." Clark also watched a keelboat inch against the current as her crew rowed, poled, or warped her toward the Arkansas River. No doubt he appreciated the supreme effort required to complete such a journey, one less arduous than the voyage he was to undertake six years later against the swifter, trickier Missouri. He also spied a boat he termed a "barge" being worked against the current, evidence of the tremendous demand upriver for Louisiana goods.

Despite more wind the following day, April 20, 1798, Clark reached what he called "Battinrouger." He stayed only an hour—long enough to show his passport, obtain permission to proceed downriver, and perhaps to check the local Spanish fort. It stood on an Indian mound, the highest elevation in the area. Shaped in a perfect six-pointed Magen David, the decaying outpost housed Commandant Jacobo Dubreuil and perhaps fifteen soldiers. Spain expected Baton Rouge to buffer not just New Orleans but also the posts of Mobile and Pensacola, which, despite their distance, connected with the Mississippi by way of Bayou Manchac, the Amite River, the lakes Maurepas, Pontchartrain, and Borgne, and the Gulf of Mexico. As if afraid to comment on the sorry defenses before his eyes, Clark notes only that he bought tafia, a cheap rum prepared from molasses and unrefined sugar.[7]

Just below Baton Rouge, the Mississippi contorts itself into another series of zigzags, but Clark threaded them without mishap. By dusk he had landed near the settlement named Iberville to honor Pierre Le Moyne, sieur d'Iberville, the French Canadian explorer of the Mississippi delta. "Stay'd all Night" Clark says, adding only that fog kept his boats ashore until nine o'clock the next morning.

High winds continuing on April 23 compelled Clark to proceed with caution. He made the most of the slower pace by scrutinizing his surroundings, especially what he called "Some butiful Sugar farms" along the river. Whether he preferred the splendid residences of the growers or the expanses of cultivated cane he did not indicate, but he found the total effect so appealing that he repeated, "The Sugar Plantations are butifull in this part of the Mississippi." He may have known, however, that agriculture suited only the narrow, well-drained strips of soil near the river. For this reason, what appeared from a distance to be fields deep with crops, on closer inspection turned out to be mere ribbons of cultivation fronting miles of swamp.

Today the Mississippi between Baton Rouge and New Orleans is relatively unrestrained due to a lack of major dams below St. Louis and to many decades of bank protection and flood control projects. In 1798, however, the river roamed the valley at will, bending in so many disorienting loops that Clark began steering by the steeples of Catholic churches, the tallest features he could see. He depicted one of them with a square.

Early on Tuesday morning, April 24, he gave the command to push the boats away from shore and into a fog; it would shroud them and other vessels hastening down the last reaches above their destination. As the mist dried and the world assumed a sharper aspect, the Mississippi took Clark's flatboats south, carried them around another bend, and turned them east. At first he was able to make out the masts of oceangoing ships, then the steeple of the church named for the canonized King Louis IX of France, and finally the rest of that structure and the others surrounding it.

Experienced navigators often deliberately passed those landmarks to ride an eddy taking them back upstream to a landing place. If Clark performed that maneuver it was the last one of his voyage. Despite major damage to one of his boats and the loss of a canoe, he had reached New Orleans, cargoes intact. He was ready to make the effort and expense of his arduous voyage worthwhile.

PART II

Important Connections from New
Orleans to Natchez and Back Again
April 24 to August 15, 1798

14

Was Politely Received and Treated by All

IN order to land, Clark had to pull his flatboats into an open space along the bank or tie them to boats already fastened to it. So many craft were heading to New Orleans that soon the waterfront would be filled with great trains of them hitched together into a vast, bobbing bridge leading to the muddy shore. A few years hence, Irish traveler Thomas Ashe was to report that more than four hundred oceangoing vessels "of all nations" were moored three-deep at New Orleans. Surely Clark saw a variety of ships too, yet he continued recording little beyond his transactions. Even so, those spare jottings—in light of Spanish governmental documents and the accounts of other travelers—outline some of his activities.[1]

He says he was "politely receved & treated by all." This suggests he easily passed the scrutiny of the Spanish official who checked his passport and inquired into the reason for his visit. Of course Clark's cargoes bespoke a commercial mission, but to underscore that impression he may have produced a letter of introduction from his brothers-in-law Croghan and Anderson to their agent, the well-known Daniel Clark Jr. (no relative to William or to them).[2]

William had to make up his mind whether to market his cargoes in Louisiana, ship them for sale elsewhere, or sell some in town and export the remainder. His decision depended in large part on the applicable charges. For example, if he sold goods locally, he'd owe the Spanish government a tax of 6 percent. He could avoid any duty by dispatching his wares to a market abroad, but until a vessel bound for such a port arrived and took them he might spend a great deal of money storing them in town.

To decide his optimal course of action, he had to learn the current prices of tobacco, peltry, and cured pork at New Orleans as well as in foreign cities. Who better to ask for that sort of information than Daniel Clark Jr.? His talent for trading and his long experience linking Kentucky tobacco farmers, Natchez cotton planters, and San Domingue sugar growers with purchasers and investors in the eastern United States and in Europe made him the most knowledgeable person William could hope to consult.[3]

Although neither of them recorded the place or time they met, soon William learned there was more demand along the Eastern seaboard than in Louisiana for burley tobacco, but that, on the other hand, furs, hams, and bacon were selling briskly at New Orleans. Such information convinced him to export the tobacco when proper shipping arrived, and to market everything else in town. Surely he sought tips on related matters: When were vessels bound for Philadelphia or New York likely to show up? Until they did, how much would it cost to store his tobacco in a New Orleans warehouse? If he sold his other goods locally, could he somehow get the tax on them reduced below 6 percent? And, because he must have been tired of sleeping on a damp, rocking boat and eating stale provisions, where might he secure pleasant quarters, palatable meals, and the company of other English-speaking travelers? Soon he had answers, and important doors began opening to him.

One of them admitted him to a building owned by a Mr. Gravier Jr. Judging it suitable shelter for his tobacco, Clark leased a section of those premises before renting twenty horse-drawn carts and hiring eight Negroes to move his remaining fifty hogsheads from the river to Gravier's property. "Commenced unloading my boats, rented a wareHouse for my tobacco at 9 Dollars p.r Month," he comments, as if there was nothing momentous about that transaction.

On the contrary, it was only the fourth of its kind ever to take place. Pinckney's Treaty made it possible; just one week earlier, the Spanish finally began enforcing the provision guaranteeing Americans the right to "deposit their merchandize and effects in the Port of New Orleans, and to export them from thence without paying any other duty than a fair price for the hire of the stores." But because that provision also allowed Spain to know exactly what was being deposited in New Orleans warehouses, Clark probably had to take his tobacco to the customhouse, a dilapidated building not far from the Mississippi. There, it seems, a worker pried the lid off each hogshead and emptied it onto a scale while a Spanish clerk noted the pounds, quality, and condition of the tobacco and the weight of each container (which, in that era before mass production, varied remarkably in size). William must have been happy that few of his hogsheads were rejected: one of them for "rotting in stock," and two others for containing not enough leaves and too many stems (a coarse, unusable part of the tobacco plant).[4]

When the inspection was finished and all the tobacco repacked as before, the clerk wrote in a new, leather-bound ledger the following entry. Translated from Spanish, it reads: "No. 4 By reason of another [petition for deposit], [this one] presented by Mr. Guillermo Clark, neighbor from said establishments [the United States], record is made by this General Administration [the Louisiana Intendancy] of 50 barrels of leaf tobacco brought to this port from the United States, for deposit in the warehouses of Mr. Gravier, Junior." Next came fifty lines detailing the number and identifying marks on each hogshead, then its gross, net, and container weights. Below those entries the clerk inscribed "Nueva Orleans, 24 de Abl. [April] de 1798," and handed the book to William. He signed his customary "W. Clark," adding beneath it an artful flourish.[5]

Afterward he made his way to the Gravier building, which might have been on Gravier Street, just west of the oldest part of the city. Once William's hogsheads were in order, a Spanish official locked the door to them and pocketed the key—a standard practice to prevent anyone from withdrawing and selling the tobacco without paying a duty. But to keep the Spanish from helping themselves to those same leaves, William must have secured the space with his own lock as well.

Soon another important door opened, admitting him to the boarding-house of Margaret Clark Chabaud. No known kin to William or Daniel Clark, she was an Irish-born widow with years of experience lodging and feeding guests, many of whom were American traders. With her family and slaves she lived in the same building, a relatively new, wooden structure of at least two stories. It was located on the northeast side of rue Conti, between Chartres and Front (now called Decatur) streets. William inquired into her rates, found them similar to those charged at Natchez, and rented lodging. It was likely on the second floor; due to the low situation of New Orleans relative to the Mississippi, most people with houses of more than one level lived on the highest of them.

If he arrived at mealtime, he took a place at one of the five large walnut tables in the Chabaud dining room and had a hearty dinner of the sort of American fare Clark was familiar with. If he came later in the day, he might have gathered with other guests on the shaded, second-floor gallery to enjoy refreshments and the singing of teenager Céleste Chabaud, Madame's vocally gifted daughter. Although unable to read or write, as were many inhabitants of Spanish Louisiana, Madame spoke English and French and probably some Spanish. She ran a lucrative accommodation by providing her guests with comfortable surroundings and amenities such as a well-stocked wine cellar. She decorated in sparing but tasteful style, poured tea from a porcelain set, and served meals on expensive pearlware.

On hot days she kept air circulating as much as possible through the building by opening windows and doors in communal rooms. Guest chambers also having windows, she protected her clientele from mosquitoes by tenting each bed with yards of diaphanous netting. Having stayed at her establishment during the sweltering heat of the previous June, Englishman Francis Baily managed finally to fall asleep by opening both his door and window and stretching out atop the sheet on his bed.

Because the design of the Chabaud house—with individual bedrooms for guests rather than the communal sleeping quarters still common in many American inns—allowed maximum privacy, it prefigured the layout of modern hotels. Such a floor plan, however, would also suit another business to occupy Madame Chabaud's structure after she died. That is, from some time before 1821 and until fire destroyed the premises in February 1822, they were to be rented by a seedy enterprise called the "Rising Sun," quite possibly the very brothel to inspire the popular song "The House of the Rising Sun." If so, William was an early tenant of a legitimate hostelry later to become one of the most notorious bawdy houses in American history.[6]

Daniel Clark Jr. liked to refer visitors to the Chabaud establishment. He planned for his Philadelphia partner Daniel W. Coxe and Coxe's traveling companions to lodge there during the three or four weeks they would be in town. Clark Jr. expected them to arrive any day now, but months had gone by since they had sailed from the Delaware River into the Atlantic Ocean and headed for the West Indies, the first stop on a long voyage taking them to New Orleans. (Alert to reader: During his 1798 travels William dealt with four other Clarks, two of them business partners named Daniel—all of whom were unrelated to him.)

Clark Jr. had also sent Francis Baily to Madame's house. Baily recorded a number of details about its design and operations. Yet he devoted almost as much ink to his fellow boarder Philip Nolan—a close friend of Daniel—and to his tales of capturing wild horses on Spanish lands beyond the Red River. Nolan refrained, however, from mentioning that those rustling missions gave him an excuse to reconnoiter western territory for his benefactor, General Wilkinson.[7]

Daniel was well aware of Nolan's surreptitious activities. In Nolan's absence, and with his permission, Daniel was soon to correspond with Vice President Thomas Jefferson about mustang herds far beyond the Mississippi River. Having learned of those animals from Kentucky senator John Brown (one of Wilkinson's associates in the Spanish Conspiracy), Vice President Jefferson wanted the facts from Nolan, the acknowledged expert on the topic.[8]

In answering for him, Daniel served his own purposes too, by laying the foundation for what he hoped would become a political career if the United States acquired Louisiana. He expected that change to take place before long and was preparing for it by seeking the favor of key people, including Jefferson, Nolan, Boundary Commissioner Andrew Ellicott, and Captain Isaac Guion. Even Madame Chabaud could prove useful to Daniel's scheme; her house was a gathering place for influential Americans and other Anglos whose support he might need. If all went according to his plan, he would swear allegiance to the United States the next time he went to Natchez.[9]

Born in 1766 in Sligo, Ireland, and named for the childless uncle who preceded him to Louisiana and there made a fortune in commerce, Daniel received an English education from that kinsman, moved to New Orleans in 1786, and joined his firm. Soon the novice trader spoke excellent French and Spanish and became acquainted with the important men in town.[10] He also mastered his elder's ways of circumventing the strict commercial laws Spain had put in place in the 1760s to induce Louisiana to trade with other Spanish possessions. Most of these were too distant from her to do so at reasonable rates, however, and for goods such as food and other necessities, Louisiana instead turned to her neighbors, the American colonies along the Atlantic coast, although dealing with them was contrary to Spanish law. With no other feasible means to feed their people, the third and fourth governors of Spanish Louisiana, Luis de Unzaga and Bernardo de Gálvez, opened the way to such extra-legal transactions during the American Revolution. They allowed Daniel Clark Sr. to bring in flour from those settlements and to pay for it with ammunition to use against the British.[11]

A few years later, when Spain tried to influence Louisiana to trade with her ally France and her West Indian possessions, Daniel Sr. modified his practices. He shipped flour and various American goods from the Eastern seaboard to the French island of San Domingue, had the goods loaded onto French and Spanish vessels, and then sent them to New Orleans. There he used the proceeds to buy Louisiana cargoes, packed them with secret stashes of reales, and dispatched them on a return route to the cash-poor United States, having bribed Spanish officials to ignore that he was in fact committing two violations—that of importing American goods and that of exporting royal dollars without paying sufficient taxes on them. Gálvez's successors, including Esteban Miró, knew what the trader was doing but allowed him to continue his illicit practices because they were keeping Spanish subjects from starving.[12]

In 1787, when James Wilkinson showed up at New Orleans with a load of hams, tobacco, and butter to sell, he and Clark Sr. became fast friends and business associates. Wilkinson's reverses and Spain's eventual refusal to approve a monopoly for him soon curtailed their dealings, but those experiences alerted Daniel and his nephew to the high demand for Kentucky products. For the next several years both Daniel Clarks reaped handsome rewards by facilitating commerce from the Ohio River valley—in ways both lawful and otherwise.[13]

By the early 1790s Daniel Sr. had accumulated enough wealth to put his namesake in charge of the firm and to retire upriver to a plantation just north of the thirty-first parallel. Around the same time, Daniel Jr. formed a connection with Reed and Forde, a prosperous Philadelphia purveyor of foodstuffs, textiles, and furniture for Louisiana and a buyer of pelts, cigars, pieces of eight, and other exports of that province. In 1793 Daniel Jr. became partners with Daniel Coxe, a former Reed and Forde agent and an astute businessman whose brother Tench was an official of the U.S. Treasury. While continuing his uncle's shady practices, Clark Jr.—with the help of Daniel Coxe—expanded their network into Europe and the West Indies, adapting as necessary to the latest wars and alliances. Their business grew. When Spain at last opened the Mississippi River to commerce according to Pinckney's Treaty, the younger Daniel added a lucrative sideline—guiding American traders through the labyrinth of Spanish commercial regulations. By the time William Clark arrived, Daniel Jr. had become the essential mercantile agent in New Orleans.[14]

Talent and family connections notwithstanding, Clark Jr. had an even more powerful advantage over his competitors: he was also a clerk in the

Painted from an engraved portrait by Fevret de Saint-Mémin. Its identifying label, "Clarke," has been thought to refer to Daniel Clark Jr.

records office of the Spanish government. This position giving him a rare view into the royal administration, he knew very well which regulations were ripe for transgression and which officials could be bribed with impunity. His Spanish employment, however, also exposed him to classified information about James Wilkinson's seditions, accomplices, couriers, and the thousands of pieces of eight they smuggled to Kentucky. Although Daniel was not yet sure what to do with that intelligence, he continued gathering it while becoming better acquainted with William Clark.[15]

15

You Know the Nature of This Business

CLARK records nothing about such matters, and little else. In just three words, "finished my work," he sums up his activities of April 26, 1798, and about the next five days writes only "at the City all well." On the Ohio he'd penned an average of sixteen words per day, a rate he doubled on the Mississippi, but once he reached New Orleans his pen almost stopped. Such reserve is especially lamentable, considering he was in a country whose population included Creoles, Indians, Africans, Europeans, and Caribbean islanders, many of whom spoke languages foreign to him and comported themselves in unfamiliar ways. Countless sights and smells of the city were also new to him, but on these topics he records not a word.

Those familiar with Clark's journals know that lengthy, descriptive writing was usually not his style. A few years hence, while striving to comply with the president's instructions about chronicling the western Expedition, he was frequently to write less than Meriwether Lewis did, and seldom to mention subjective impressions. That Clark would set down little on paper about life at New Orleans is therefore to be expected.

But one aspect of his 1798 journal-keeping is strikingly at odds with what had by then become his accustomed practice. Earlier that decade, whether as soldier or civilian, he had penned numerous accounts of previous travels and activities, and in those narratives he so often identified the influential men he encountered as to make the recording of such names seem almost a consistent feature of his journal-keeping. While in or near Spanish territory in 1798, however, the opposite would prove true. That is, from Natchez to New Orleans, Clark was to deal with several men of great wealth or influence, yet he inscribes very little—or nothing—about them. That those same individuals would eventually be remembered for their connections with James Wilkinson or the Spanish Conspiracy only accentuates the mystery as to why William Clark devoted so few words, or none at all, to them. Daniel Clark Jr. was to be such a pretermitted individual. At New Orleans William instead writes mostly about his monetary exchanges, listing sums paid for a haircut and a shave, for having his laundry washed, and for buying underclothes, shoes, trousers, oranges, an umbrella, and paper.

He strolled a few blocks north of the Chabaud boardinghouse to Le Spectacle de la Rue Saint-Pierre, the original and only theater in town, and put down the equivalent of one dollar and twenty-five cents for a ticket. He does not name the production but it was surely in French, a language he never learned. A few nights later he retraced his steps and paid the equivalent of one dollar and fifty cents to see another show. Clark loved the thespian arts (in later years he would help found a theater in St. Louis), but he must have noticed a number of empty seats in the recently expanded playhouse. It had been in operation for almost six years but had yet to turn a profit. Trying to increase ticket sales by holding the first-ever lotto game in Spanish Louisiana, the owners of the theater had on another occasion drawn crowds—and defied the convention of racial segregation on stage—by adding West Indian quadroon actresses to a heretofore all-white cast.[1]

Or perhaps Clark came to see women who were *not* onstage. Playhouses of that era often permitted prostitutes onto the premises to solicit business, even reserving a separate section for residents of local bordellos and their clients. Whether Le Spectacle allowed that is unknown.[2] Clark also does not mention what he did after the performance. He may have followed other members of the audience to ballrooms—to dance quadrilles, drink tafia, and play games of chance. Or, possibly he went to the Swamp, a New Orleans district favored by Kentucky boatmen. Bounded by the present streets of Girod, Julia, South Liberty, and South Robertson, it was a rough area of taverns, bordellos, and gambling houses.

Some of the expenses William Clark recorded at New Orleans, from page A22 of his 1798–1801 Notebook.

Not long thereafter, Clark says he "paid a woman [one dollar] for - - - - ," as if the ellipsis refers discreetly to a sexual liaison. That he seldom writes, even euphemistically, of such matters does not indicate inactivity or lack of interest on his part; his letters show he courted women whenever possible. Indeed, biographer Landon Jones suggests that while on the epic western exploration, William engaged in physical intimacy with the agreeable and "handsome" Indian women he met, especially those from tribes on which the Corps of Discovery depended.[3]

On Clark's third day in New Orleans he paid off Robert Kates, the deckhand hired at Natchez. The following week, Clark compensated the seven other departing crewmen, paying a total of 310 dollars for the services of all eight men from the places where they'd first come aboard to work for him. He also notes giving three dollars to a man "for takin Care of my boat," which still held nearly a full load of bacon, hams, furs, and skins. As Clark had not yet sold more than a fraction of his cargoes, he must have borrowed money to meet these early obligations.

He also begins recording the prices of goods traded there. Noting the cost of tobacco at between four and seven dollars per hundredweight, he goes on to list the amounts given for American products, including deer and bear skins, beaver pelts, otter furs, hemp, cordage, bacon, whiskey, and "cyder." He writes the prices of products he might want to invest in: cotton, rice, white and brown sugars, Havana and Jamaica coffee beans. He pays special attention to the cost of alcoholic beverages—French brandies, tafia, rum, "Clarret," and wines from Málaga, "Burdo" [Bordeaux], and Tenerife. For reasons unknown he jots down the expenses of equipping a sugar refinery, as if he were interested in bringing that technology to Kentucky.

On May 1, 1798, he declared the items he planned to sell locally. A Spanish clerk examined those pelts and cuts of meat and assigned them values (most of which, in keeping with the Spanish policy of encouraging trade with Americans, were a good deal *less* than their true worth), then multiplied the figures by 6 percent. The entry, translated from Spanish, follows.:

Appraisal of the cargo of a Flatboat arrived at this Port, proceeding from Louisville, one of the American establishments upriver, composed of the following goods, to wit:

	For Guillermo Clark	Silver Reales
at fifty reales per hundred-weight	Five hundred pounds of Pork, in the form of smoked bacon	250—"
at one real per pound	Twenty-seven Packets, with 1,479 pounds of deer skins in hair	1,479—"
at five reales per pound	Fifty pounds of beaver skins	250—"
at four reales per pound	Ten pounds of otter skins	40—- "
at four reales per skin	Sixty-six bear skins	264—- "
(at one- and one-half real per pound, that is twenty-five reales.)	Seventeen doe skins	27—-17
		2,310—-17

The appraised value amounts to two thousand, three hundred ten and one-half silver reales [$288.77 in U.S. money] and the duty at 6% amounts to 138-1/2 reales [$17.32].

In other words, William owed the Spanish government a relatively low sum, the equivalent of seventeen dollars and thirty-two cents.[4]

Probably to defray this cost he sold the declared bacon within a short time. Although he did not record his proceeds, from other figures he kept we can estimate they were slightly more than seventy dollars, or fourteen dollars per hundredweight; according to him, that was nearly the highest rate then given for bacon. Next, he paid the 6 percent tax (four dollars and twenty-five cents) due on the sale, thereby discharging almost one-fourth of the total tax on all the declared goods. Afterward he gave the officers of the notoriously corrupt customhouse eight hams, and soon, four dollars. He also passed certain inspectors wine and twice slipped them a cash "bri-ab"—for what, he does not mention. All of this, effectively, covered the debt he had to pay for selling his goods in New Orleans. He may also have borrowed funds for this purpose, perhaps from Daniel Clark Jr.

If William was indeed prevailing on customhouse officials to ignore the balance of his debt to the royal treasury, he was only following principles set down by the master of the well-placed douceur. "You know the nature of this business," Clark Jr. wrote a third party about an American associate of theirs who evidently accepted a trove of reales but refused to reimburse the costs of smuggling them past port authorities. Adept at buying the cooperation of government employees policing various aspects of international trade, Daniel was planning to load Daniel Coxe's fleet with thousands of Spanish dollars and spirit them out of Louisiana.[5]

Clark Jr. was also stockpiling legitimate goods to send back to Philadelphia. Since early in the year he'd been purchasing tons of cotton and peltry, expecting both those commodities to sell profitably along the East coast. Tobacco had been less promising since 1791 when Spain nearly stopped buying it. With the price of tobacco low, William learned he might have to wait a long time before he received an agreeable offer on his.

That was probably not the case with his furs and skins. As Daniel Clark was amassing prodigious quantities of them for Coxe and others to freight to American ports, he likely bought William's. Not only did Daniel expect pelts to rise in value, he knew that each bundle of them could provide a hiding-place for some of the pieces of eight he planned to smuggle out of Louisiana. So candid was he about this method, and so favorably impressed was he with William, Daniel may well have revealed the system to him.[6]

* * *

Once William disposed of his boats, paid off the deckhands, and sold or stored the goods he had brought from Kentucky, he surely considered how to inspect the defensive works of New Orleans without drawing notice from the Spanish forces guarding them. Basic details about the five forts were easy to come by. While on a walk in 1797, visitor Francis Baily, a young man of no martial experience, sketched them and took their compass bearings. Any Army veteran could easily have gathered the same intelligence, but an experienced observer with an abiding interest in such things, as was Clark, was sure to collect even more. But because the name of George Rogers Clark still made Spanish authorities uneasy and the memory of General Victor Collot's imprisonment and expulsion for espionage was still fresh, William would have to be extremely circumspect in his reconnaissance.[7]

He realized that General Wilkinson, as U.S. commander in chief, could use such information for legitimate purposes related to the security of American territory—the international boundary lying only seventy-five miles to the north. But Clark may well have heard rumors that Wilkinson also had self-serving reasons—and perhaps even treasonable ones—for desiring this sort of data. And Wilkinson certainly did desire it. Away from Louisiana during the recent military buildup, he wanted to learn the strengths and weaknesses of the province in order to determine whether his advantage lay in working with or against the Spanish. The most coveted part of Louisiana was New Orleans, and its defenses were essential to his decision. Although it seems out of character for Clark knowingly to further Wilkinson's treasonable designs, he quite possibly was still under his influence.[8]

Even from a distance, Clark could observe that most of the military works in town were of recent construction. Founded by the French in 1718, the city lacked fortifications of any sort until 1729, when the Indian attack on Fort Rosalie at Natchez prompted New Orleans residents to surround their town with a palisade. Later they added a powder magazine, but over the next four decades those structures fell into decay as the population grew. To protect the community from British invasion, the French governor in 1762 devised plans for a sophisticated system of defenses, but France ceded Louisiana to Spain before most of them could be built. Spain, in turn, lacked a comprehensive plan for defending the province until rumors of incipient invasion—by the forces of George Rogers Clark and their French allies, and later by the British—prompted Governor Carondelet to action. During most of his time in Louisiana, he concentrated on strengthening forts in the Mississippi valley. He especially devoted great sums to protecting New Orleans from a naval assault coming up from the delta, placing barriers around most of the city and erecting a bastion at every angle of the five-sided Vieux Carre, the oldest section of the city.

Fort San Carlos, the largest and most formidable of these works, stood at the foot of what is now Esplanade Street; of the original part of town, this is the first point to be reached from downstream. The fort had barracks for 150 men, a dozen or more cannons aimed at the river, a powder magazine, a brick parapet, and a secure jail for enemies of Spain. Nearby, in front of the plaza that would become Jackson Square, four huge cannons covered the river. Farther upstream and along the front edge of the city stood Fort San Luis. Almost as large as Fort San Carlos, it was three blocks from the Chabaud house and protected the southernmost parts of New Orleans. Three smaller posts guarded the back side of town. Two named for Saints John and Ferdinand and one for the Burgundy dynasty of France, they held cannons and barracks for a hundred men. Connecting those bastions with the two forts nearer the river were a wooden palisade and a moat containing several feet of water.

Because Carondelet ran out of funds during the construction project, however, the palisade was too low to afford much protection from gunfire and a deficiency of cannons left many locations around town vulnerable to attack. Not only were the three rear bastions quite small, but an enemy could fire from some of them onto the others and could shoot into the city from all five of them. It was therefore evident that even a minor force might take New Orleans by sneaking up on the inland side of town.[9]

William no doubt surmised as much. Instead of putting down his impressions in words, though, he added the five forts to his map, calculating that they lay 904 miles from the mouth of the Ohio. He also recorded the latitude and longitude of New Orleans. Given the technological limitations of this era, especially in computing longitude, his geographic position is remarkably accurate.

Afterward he prepared a final draft of all the coordinates—thirteen in all, four of them described in terms so seemingly non-specific as to allay the suspicion of any wary Spaniard—he had gathered along the Mississippi. Rather than keep those numbers in the order of one traveling downstream, he reversed the arrangement, heading his list "Sundry Latitudes & Longitudes taken on the Mississippi *ascending* [emphasis added]." As he understood very well, few civilians went to the trouble and expense of navigating against the tremendous current of the river for more than a short distance. Clark had no plan to do that, either.

He says nothing about his intentions for the list. Surely unaware of James Wilkinson's secret identity as Agent 13 for Spain, Clark realized that in order to defend the nation, Wilkinson must have data of this sort. Yet how much Clark may have known about the general's desire to use such intelligence for devious or even treasonable purposes can only be conjectured.

16

An Alarm about a British Frigate

BY surrounding New Orleans with military works, Governor Carondelet aimed not just to protect the ten thousand inhabitants of the
city but also to safeguard deliveries of the all-important subsidy, the
Spanish money that kept the entire province functioning. For more than
two decades those funds had been coming to Louisiana in periodic shipments containing hundreds of thousands of dollars in coined silver. Spain
intended the subsidy to stimulate economic growth and, in return, to produce revenues, but it always fell far short of these goals. Instead, Louisiana
remained a parasite on the royal treasury, drawing from it nearly all her
financial sustenance.

Installments of the subsidy originated in New Spain—most of which
would soon become Mexico—but were sent first to Havana. There the
captain general of Cuba, the superior of the Louisiana governor, withdrew
the amounts he needed to keep the economy of his island operating, then
forwarded the balance across the Gulf of Mexico and up the Mississippi
to New Orleans. As Cuba was to defend Louisiana in case of attack, that
order of priorities made a certain amount of sense.[1]

In 1796, however, war between Spain and Britain began to delay the
subsidy deliveries. Intent on revenge against her former ally Spain for rec-
onciling with the enemy French Republic, Britain started patrolling the
shipping lanes of the West Indies and the Gulf of Mexico for Spanish
booty, especially the hard cash destined for Louisiana. So rich was the potential plunder, the British Navy sometimes blockaded parts of the Gulf
to intercept the vessel commonly called the "Money Ship"—any of several

craft sometimes used to transport the treasure. The captain general responded by keeping the pieces of eight in Cuba for long periods, thereby granting himself additional opportunities to dip into them. To make matters worse for Louisiana, once the Money Ship and her armed escorts went to sea, they often avoided pirates by sailing an indirect course.[2]

The consequent shortage of capital pinched especially hard at New Orleans. Often, when subsidy deposits started to run out, Governor Gayoso de Lemos postponed paying all but the most important obligations, borrowed from local merchants, and temporarily appropriated revenues from other administrative departments. If the scarcity of funds continued long enough to jeopardize governmental functions, he printed credit certificates. Exchangeable for Spanish dollars after the Money Ship arrived, they were like IOUs, but they quickly depreciated, causing prices to rise. For this reason, Gayoso preferred to exhaust present sources of revenue, even his own income. By 1798 he had applied so much of it to the expenses of state that he, too, was verging on bankruptcy.[3]

The ongoing financial crisis of Louisiana strengthened his determination not only to continue fortifying the province but also to resuscitate the Spanish Conspiracy. Realizing that Wilkinson, Sebastian, and their confederates were mercenaries at heart, Gayoso begged his superiors for enough money to keep those conspirators from going to work for the enemy. He explained: "In Kentucky there are agents of Britain, and that nation always backs up its negotiations with the most powerful force there is—money. Without the same means, we cannot compete."[4]

Such were affairs in New Orleans when William Clark arrived. So long overdue was the Money Ship, it had yet to bring the last portion of the subsidy for 1797 and any amount for the current year. To protect all specie bound for Louisiana, Gayoso posted to the delta Captain Manuel García's division of the freshwater navy.[5]

At last, on April 25, 1798, the Money Ship—in the form of the royal corvette *La Diligencia*—and its companion vessels began entering the Mississippi. Four days later they reached New Orleans. On April 30, *La Diligencia* discharged into the royal strongboxes 1,985,760 reales (worth 248,220 U.S. dollars). Despite the magnificence of this deposit, nearly half of it was for settling old debts unrelated to the subsidy, and the remainder was the balance for 1797. Nothing came yet for 1798; based on the experience of previous years, Gayoso could expect around four hundred thousand dollars in 1798.[6]

Nevertheless, he finally had the means to begin complying with the international boundary project, a term of Pinckney's Treaty still unfulfilled. Although it called for a shared effort on the part of Spain and the United States, lack of funds had thus far kept the Spanish commission away from the thirty-first parallel, the focus of most of the work. As a result, the American commission had for three weeks been laboring alone, much to the chagrin of their leader, Andrew Ellicott. Having previously waited more than a year for Spain to evacuate the Natchez District so the boundary work could get under way, Ellicott believed that the Spanish had no intention of carrying it forward.

To assure him otherwise, Gayoso sent word on April 30: "The money arrived last night; therefore tomorrow I'll embark the effects for the [boundary] Line & in the course of the present week the Galley [with supplies and most members of the Spanish commission] will sett off to join your Camp. As soon as they sail, I'll follow to meet you & do every thing in concert that may be for the good of our Nations."[7] Gayoso decided to take *La Diligencia*, the swiftest naval vessel in the province, up the Mississippi to the thirty-first parallel. With the money shipment secure in royal coffers and no sign along the coast of the British Navy, he ordered Commander García and the delta patrol to return upriver. Meanwhile William Clark continued to settle in at New Orleans.[8]

At daybreak on May 1, lookout Juan Delacroix spotted a frigate anchored in the Gulf, not far beyond the last waters of the Mississippi. Delacroix served at the Baliza, a fortified Spanish pilot station and lighthouse situated near the place where the river divides into chutes to empty into the Gulf. Being several miles away from the vessel, he was unable to make out her name clearly or to discern her nationality, but he could see she was a fully equipped man-of-war.

He then noticed that, although she remained where he'd first spotted her, two of her longboats were heading into the Mississippi. As they drew closer he could see that each of them carried perhaps twenty men and an

Watercolor-on-ivory portrait of Manuel Gayoso de Lemos, governor-general of Spanish Louisiana and West Florida, by an unidentified artist, circa 1790.

ample supply of weapons, particularly pistols, sabers, and muskets. When the longboats reached the main channel of the river, they proceeded toward the *Recovery*, an American commercial brig anchored in front of the Baliza. Before the crew of that vessel realized what was going on, the armed visitors stole aboard and took control, confiscating fresh water and provisions.

They also sized up the military works of the Baliza and inquired about those upstream but refused to identify themselves. Instead, a lieutenant with a noticeable English accent warned that British warships were in the area and might soon enter the Mississippi. In silent but eloquent testimony of the war with Spain, he unloaded from his firearm four cartridges and handed them to the captain of the *Recovery*, saying they were for the Spanish governor. Then the lieutenant and the other intruders returned to their longboats and slipped back downstream to the warship; it carried forty cannons.

Delacroix immediately summoned the American captain to the Baliza station and asked what had occurred. Alarmed to hear that the uninvited callers were evidently from the British Navy, Delacroix expedited a report some twenty-five miles upriver to the heavily fortified outpost of San Felipe de Placaminas. The message arrived at midnight. On receiving it,

Commander Pedro Favrot added his own words to Delacroix's and dispatched those communications posthaste to New Orleans.[9]

The communications arrived on May 3, causing a panic. The proximity of enemy men-of-war was alone cause for alarm, but the easy penetration of the Mississippi and the capture of a neutral vessel boded grave danger for the province. If the British came back, any maritime skirmishing to take place with the allied forces of Spain and France would likely explode into war fought in Louisiana. And if such a conflict involved another American ship, the United States would no doubt take part, inadvertently creating the sort of turmoil General Wilkinson wished to exploit for selfish reasons.

Suspending other activities to devote full attention to the crisis, Governor Gayoso ordered Manuel García and his squadron back to the delta, then set off in that direction aboard *La Vigilante*, the same single-masted, cannon-equipped craft William Clark had sketched after their 1795 meeting at New Madrid. But Clark does not mention whether he witnessed Gayoso's hurried departure from New Orleans; he says only that the penetration of the delta by the English military caused "an allarm of British frigat off the Mouth of the River."[10]

No matter what he thought of those events he knew that, should the British Navy return, Louisiana might well become a battleground, and New Orleans a prize fought for by his own countrymen. Pinckney's Treaty would no longer be in force, leaving Spain free to close the Mississippi to Americans and to seize their goods as the spoils of war. Whether or not he realized that such an outcome would suit the aspirations of General Wilkinson, Clark surely knew it could imperil his own life and property and keep him in Louisiana much longer than he cared to stay.

He became more reticent than ever in his journal. Writing only that "nothing Extroordinary" happened during the next three days, he reduces that comment down to "nothing Extra." to describe the following four. It seems likely that he varied little from the routine he had established, taking meals and spending nights at Madame Chabaud's house.

More significant, he followed the shipping reports. Every day or two, officials at the Baliza sent word upriver about the latest maritime arrivals and departures, and each Monday that information appeared in the weekly *Le Moniteur de la Louisiane*, the only newspaper in the province. From such authorities Clark could gather that in the last days of April, despite the alarm caused by the British ship, commercial vessels continued arriving at the mouth of the river. From other sources and from the evidence of his own eyes, he knew not only that the majority of those craft would remain in port until they might sail in convoys for their own protection but also that many of them carried artillery to defend against privateers. Clearly, the wars of Europe were taking a toll on traffic in the Gulf of Mexico.[11]

The sinister English frigate that had almost touched off a war in Louisiana stayed away, having disappeared into the southern horizon shortly after the longboats and men returned to her. Governor Gayoso suspected that she belonged to the squadron commanded by Alexander Cochrane, a forty-year-old Scotsman notorious for capturing French privateers. Unless she or other enemy vessels reappeared, though, there was little Gayoso could do in the delta. He made his way back up the river, enjoining the commanders of the Baliza and Fort San Felipe to send immediate notice if any questionable ships sailed within view.[12]

Gayoso resumed his regular duties at New Orleans. He paid special attention to furnishing the royal boundary commission with equipment and supplies, taking care to obtain as many such items as possible from sources within the Spanish empire. Because neither Spain, France, nor any neutral country (including the United States) produced scientific instruments as accurate as those of Britain, he was in the uncomfortable position of having to order from that enemy an astronomical circle, a device useful for deriving terrestrial positions from those of the heavenly bodies. To mask what he was doing, Gayoso ascribed the purchase to astronomer-for-Spain William Dunbar, a native of Scotland, and had the instrument shipped to his Natchez home.[13]

The precarious situation of Louisiana, however, was never far from the Gayoso's mind. He continued asking his superiors for resources to improve the military readiness of the coastline and the Mississippi valley. Having come to expect that Spain would either refuse his requests or postpone providing most of what he asked, he searched for other, less costly ways to protect the province. On one occasion he sought permission to apply local taxes to building a small dock near Fort San Luis; on another, he volunteered, as a former naval commander, to lead a newly organized body of maritime officers.[14]

But even if Spain sent enough money to make Louisiana the most impregnable corner of the realm, it would still be hopelessly insolvent. Its productions were utterly insufficient for the needs of its people, that is, unless Carondelet's variation on the Spanish Conspiracy paid off. The odds against drawing Kentucky out of the Union and attaching her to Spain were high, but Gayoso knew that, if those events were to happen, they would erase the deficit of Louisiana by introducing to her a seemingly boundless supply of lucrative goods from the Ohio valley.[15]

It may seem puzzling that Gayoso still considered General Wilkinson the key to such a breakthrough. Ever since Pinckney's Treaty opened the Mississippi to American trade, Wilkinson had been a sleeper, shrinking from contact with Spain except to send coded reminders of sums owed him. But Gayoso realized that Wilkinson's legitimate duties as commander in chief of U.S. land forces were soon to take him down the river, almost to the thirty-first parallel. By establishing Army headquarters near that international border, he would be in an extremely convenient location to resume betraying the interests—and secrets—of the United States.

To put him in a proper frame of mind to do so, Gayoso had to settle their accounts. The one Wilkinson seemed most concerned about was the 640 dollars he'd used to reimburse Power's smuggling expenses in 1796. Because of the Money Ship, Gayoso at last had the wherewithal to pay off that debt *and* to enlarge it, if he saw fit to do so, with thirty dollars of interest. Such a bonus would not only show faith in Agent 13, it would also tantalize him with a tiny sample of what he might expect for renewing clandestine activities on behalf of Spain. The timing could not have been better; as spokesman for Wilkinson and the other Kentucky intriguers, Judge Benjamin Sebastian was soon to reach New Orleans. So also was Samuel Montgomery Brown, a conspiratorial associate with his own boat.

17

An Uproar about a War

AROUND the same time as Sebastian showed up, a panic even more profound than the one caused by the British infiltration of the delta swept the city. So potentially disastrous to Clark's interests was this latest alarm that on May 11, 1798, he interjected mention of "an upror about a War with the United States & Spain france &c." among what would become a litany of journal entries saying nothing was happening. But the truth, according to newly arrived reports, was that the French had spurned the latest American peace effort. For the first time since the Revolutionary War, the United States stood at the brink of armed aggression against a European opponent. Many expected Franco-American hostilities to spread to Spanish Louisiana, so the news was especially grim for New Orleans.

Yet it was not a total surprise. Since the French Revolution relations between the United States and France had been strained, and particularly so after America put into effect Jay's Treaty, thereby granting Britain favored trading status. Incensed by that agreement, France suspended diplomacy with the United States, motivating President John Adams to send to that republic fellow Federalists John Marshall, Elbridge Gerry, and Charles Cotesworth Pinckney (brother of Thomas, negotiant of the Treaty of San Lorenzo), to seek terms of commerce and amity.

Those envoys reached Paris in October 1797 and presented their credentials but were denied an audience. For many days they tried to open discussions, but French foreign minister Charles-Maurice de Talleyrand-Périgord and his trio of agents—later denominated "X, Y, and Z" by the Adams administration—demanded a substantial loan and a bribe of a quarter-million dollars as the cost of diplomacy. The Americans refused to pay any amount, and the French then turned down American requests to outlaw the plunder of U.S. shipping or to make amends for past maritime depredations. In late October, Marshall, Gerry, and Pinckney began sending Adams coded messages about the failure of their mission.[1]

The first of those communications arrived in March 1798. Fearing that disclosure would lead to an outcry for war, the president kept the correspondence to himself until the House of Representatives called for it in early April. Adams turned it over on the condition that it remain confidential, but the legislators leaked it to the press anyway.

Publication of the dispatches touched off the firestorm of resentment Adams had foreseen, but it also made him appear a bulwark against foreign aggression. Grateful Americans flooded him with messages of support and encouragement; young men turned out in numbers to offer him their military service in case of war. People across the nation began lifting glasses and uttering Charles C. Pinckney's famous—if only alleged—response to Gallic extortion, "Millions for defense, but not one cent for tribute."

A sizable minority of Americans still hoped for a diplomatic resolution of the troubles. Even the president and his cabinet embodied a wide range of reactions to the XYZ sensation. At one extreme was Timothy Pickering; he wanted not just war with the French Republic but also an alliance with Britain. Less militant comrades—Secretary of the Treasury Oliver Wolcott and Secretary of War James McHenry—favored limiting Franco-American hostilities to the high seas. John Adams, a moderate Federalist, looked for ways to avoid open conflict but did not rule out the possibility. The only other member of his administration, Vice President Thomas Jefferson, a francophile who had lived in Paris from 1785 to 1789, was not a Federalist at all but, rather, the driving force behind the opposition. As spokesman for the emerging Democratic-Republican party, he altogether disapproved of going to war with the French Republic.[2]

Newspapers fed the controversy. In Philadelphia, William Cobbett's influential *Country Porcupine* urged readers to demonstrate their Federalism by adding a black cockade—a rounded badge of ribbon—to their hats, in the style of Continental soldiers during the Revolutionary War. Democratic-Republican papers, on the other hand, directed readers to trim their hats with the blue, white, and red cockade of the French Republic. (Some exceeded that style—and parodied the Federalist one—by attaching chips of dried cow dung to their hats.) Within a short time, men all over the country were tearing cockades off the hats of their political opponents.[3]

The rowdiness spread to theaters. Philadelphia Federalists cheered, waved their black-cockaded hats, and demanded encores as house musicians played "President's March" or "Yankee Doodle" but hissed if they struck up "Ça Ira," the "Marseillaise," or other French airs. In turn, Democratic-Republicans bribed orchestra members not to play Federalist music, pelting them with garbage and smashing their instruments if they did.[4]

Hoping to end such brawling, the president declared a national day of prayer and fasting, but observance of that event only deepened the discord. Clergymen of Federalist sympathies likened the French—and their Jeffersonian friends—to the pagan tormentors of ancient Hebrews. Meanwhile, Democratic-Republicans in Stamford, Connecticut, avoided church services in order to tar, feather, and burn an effigy of President Adams. Even his Philadelphia neighborhood became a center of turmoil on the designated holy day, as a large number of young men wearing "French" cockades gathered outside his house and refused to disperse. Adams sent to the War Department for chests of arms to use in case the visitors became unruly, but a superior force of Federalists drove the men off before a shot could be fired.[5]

As time passed, the XYZ revelations—which continued as each successive dispatch was received and published—swelled the ranks of the Federalists. According to Jefferson, by the end of April 1798, enough "wavering characters" from his own faction had joined the "war party" to give it control of both the Senate and House of Representatives. Soon those politicians began enacting laws preparatory to military action: authorizing construction of up to a dozen gunboats, adding a regiment to the Army, establishing a naval department, and providing for the fortification of ports and harbors and for the building of armed galleys. They also created a ten-thousand-soldier "Provisional Army" to be called out in case of war with France. Lacking revenue on hand to fund all those enactments, Congress called for increased taxation.[6]

The large number and steep cost of the new measures inspired debate, but none of them stirred as much controversy as did the Alien and Sedition acts, four pieces of legislation produced late that session. The first three such laws curtailed the civil liberties of foreign (that is, French) nationals. The last law stifled dissent among U.S. citizens by making a high misdemeanor of anti-governmental speech or activity.[7]

In the faraway Mississippi Territory, Daniel Clark Sr. explained to Boundary Commissioner Andrew Ellicott the effect a Franco-American war would likely exert on Louisiana:

> This Country is now at a Crisis which will for ever decide its fate. Should the Spaniards join the [French] Republic against whom I am told the U.S. have declared war, Your [boundary] line will be Curtailed. [New] Orleans must fall to your [American] Arms, and if the British an[d] Americans are in alliance it will be impossible, nay, it will be idle in Spain ever to attempt to repossess her Self of the mouth of this great River.[8]

In Philadelphia, Alexander Hamilton reached the same conclusion. As acting commander of the newly formed Provisional Army, he deliberated how to bring about war with France in order to draw in Spain, thereby creating a reason to invade Spanish Louisiana and West Florida. Unfamiliar with those provinces, he resolved to consult on their topography and defenses with General James Wilkinson, the expert on such topics.[9]

* * *

As the XYZ turmoil raged, George Rogers Clark—now a major general in the Army of the French Republic—left Mulberry Hill and traveled to Philadelphia. There he inquired into what he called "the source of these astonishing complaints and griefs" he had heard against France, "the generous nation to which every true American owes his liberty." Deciding the federal government was to blame for the unrest across the land, George notified Samuel Fulton, his liaison in France, that the Adams administration had betrayed the interests of its own citizens for "English gold."[10]

Such talk defied the Sedition Act and put George—whose French citizenship also made him an undesirable alien—under governmental suspicion. Threatened with imprisonment unless he resigned his French military commission or left the country, George tried without success to secure a place of refuge in France. He then sought aid from the Spanish minister to the United States, Carlos Martinez de Irujo. According to George, Irujo:

> quickly offered me all the protection that a friend and ally of France could accord to one of her officers, and he even asked me to go to St. Louis on the Mississippi and there cooperate with the Commandant of that territory in undoing all the hostile undertakings which the common enemy [Britain] might attempt against Spanish concerns on the Mississippi, remaining there until I receive instructions from the Executive Directory [the governing body of the French Republic].

Irujo was wagering that France would honor its Spanish alliance and not order George to seize Louisiana. But George was hoping to do that very thing, especially during his period of asylum. On his way west, as he paused in Kentucky to safeguard a stockpile of munitions for use against Louisiana, George learned that a federal deputation had arrived to arrest him. With the help of friends he eluded capture and soon slipped across the Mississippi River.

In Spanish St. Louis he paid special attention to the same military works William had studied the previous fall. Taking into consideration the thin distribution of soldiers from the Louisiana Regiment, George realized that the province was almost defenseless. He alerted Fulton: "This country is not able to resist an invasion—neither the military nor the inhabitants are attached to Spain; there are scarcely two thousand troops here; in case of a rupture with the United States, Louisiana will become an easy prey for them and it would be difficult to take it from them."

In other words, conditions were ideal for George to launch the coup that for years he'd been wanting to carry out. Ignoring his promise to help protect Spanish territory, George sought permission to attack it. "If the Executive Directory wants to possess Louisiana," he pressed, "there is no time to lose. In not more than nine months it will be too late; this land will be conquered by America or England."[11]

* * *

Not long before George settled in at St. Louis to await a response, William considered how to get out of lower Louisiana before the fighting started. Having already sold much of his peltry and pork, he wondered what to do with the tobacco. Aware that if war broke out the Spanish might confiscate his hogsheads in Mr. Gravier's warehouse, Clark saw the advantage of conveying all his tobacco as soon as possible. He apparently consulted local mercantile partners Robert Cochran and Richard Rhea but wrote nothing about their meeting or even their names. They proposed to work as his agent, for a fee.[12]

Clark surely mulled over that arrangement as well as the costs of prolonging his time in Louisiana. Even if the area continued peaceful, he knew that the longer he remained, the sooner his expenses—especially the rent he paid to Madame Chabaud and to Monsieur Gravier—would cancel out the profits of his journey. But how to leave? Rather than return home by way of the Mississippi and Ohio River valleys, he must have been curious to experience ocean travel for the first time. He decided that, if possible, he would sail to Philadelphia, proceed overland to visit his brothers Jonathan and Edmund in Virginia, and then continue to Kentucky.

But the streets of New Orleans were full of stories about commercial vessels battling privateers in the shipping lanes linking Louisiana, the West Indies, and the East Coast. In addition, the world's most formidable navies were complicating passage through the same waters. According to recent reports, a British naval squadron had attacked and destroyed part of the Spanish fleet off the coast of Pensacola. As a result of such hazards, not as many American ships as before were sailing to New Orleans and, of those that did, only a few were departing that city promptly.[13]

William had been hearing that Daniel Clark Jr. expected his partner, Daniel W. Coxe, to arrive any day from Philadelphia with several cargo vessels. Clark Jr. wanted to think they would be equipped for war. For months he had been stockpiling goods to send onboard them and had also been hoping that Coxe would purchase artillery, muskets, powder, and shot to defend the ships and their payloads in the privateer-infested waters between the Mississippi delta and the mouth of the Delaware River.[14]

William liked the idea of sailing on a Coxe vessel, especially if it was armed. Even if it was not, though, it would offer the security of a convoy and the convenience of calling at Philadelphia, a city offering stagecoach connections to Fredericksburg, Virginia, the largest town close to Jonathan's and Edmund's farms. What's more, Coxe had unmatchable family ties; until lately his brother Tench had served as commissioner of the revenue, the second-highest position in the U.S. Treasury. Probably for all those reasons, William wanted to travel with the Coxe fleet.

But how long could he wait? Even if the expected war somehow bypassed Louisiana, he knew that seasonal maladies such as "agues" and "fevers" would not. Diagnosed a century later as symptoms of malaria, those disorders usually appeared with the onset of stifling heat and gathered force throughout the summer. So did yellow fever, a deadlier illness that killed thousands in some years but in others left the province untouched. Having first noted sweltering temperatures on May 2, 1798, Clark realized those illnesses were likely to break out soon in New Orleans.

Each hour Coxe did not arrive, therefore, reduced the time Clark had to escape with his health and increased the possibility that Coxe's fleet had been captured by a foreign privateer. Long uneasy about Coxe's tardiness, Clark Jr. grew downright anxious when a ship arriving at New Orleans reported on the escalating war frenzy in the United States and battles at sea between American and foreign ships. Local news was no more promising. On the contrary, Governor Gayoso, having received little response from Spain to his pleas for troops, equipment, and funding, was planning a local conference to devise ways to prepare New Orleans for an onslaught.[15]

Just one civilian vessel was then making ready to leave. She was the American schooner *Active*, a relatively small craft plying alone a regular route between New Orleans and New York. Her master, Nathaniel Wilcox, intended to remain in Louisiana only long enough to discharge cargoes and to receive a new load before returning to the Gulf. Having few or no guns weighing the ship down, Wilcox counted on her being able to outmaneuver corsairs. Clark considered the merits of sailing aboard *Active* rather than continuing to stand by waiting for the flotilla from Philadelphia.

He put off making a choice between the two alternatives until June 17. By that time the *Active* was fully loaded and waiting for a favorable wind and tide to propel her down the river. Of his decision he writes, "I take a passage in the Sckuner *Active*," noting that he gave fifty dollars to sail on her. He also paid thirty-five dollars for provisions, no doubt hoping seasickness would not lay him low.

He turned to packing. We can presume he made space in his trunk and bags for the items he'd bought at New Orleans, but the pieces of eight earned from his sales were more difficult to transport by ship. Keeping them hidden from his fellow passengers would be a challenge, but getting them past any pirates masquerading as international traders might be impossible. As *Le Moniteur de la Louisiane* reminded visitors, there was an additional danger: "Gold and silver specie . . . for no reason whatever can be exported to the American establishments, under pain of confiscation and other penalties of the law." Therefore, if Spanish customs agents found his stash of reales, Clark might have to forfeit them and then face civil and perhaps even criminal penalties.[16]

He looked for a more secure mode of conveying his coined revenues out of the province. A likely scheme, he must have heard, was to take them by horseback to Andrew Ellicott at the thirty-first parallel, or to Captain Isaac Guion at the Natchez fort. Needing hard cash to fund their endeavors, both those men offered to give in return U.S. government drafts almost as versatile as minted silver and much easier to conceal. The only problem with making such an exchange was that a round trip to the boundary or to Natchez required at least ten days, but Captain Wilcox wanted to sail in a matter of hours.[17]

The only other feasible method of smuggling coins was to freight them by boat up the Mississippi and Ohio rivers to Kentucky. Due to the current, not many navigators went in that direction, but their relatively lithe, maneuverable craft made them obvious. If Clark found such a waterman not just willing to carry the concealed lucre but also mindful of the smuggling guidelines set down by Thomas Power, he could rest assured his clandestine cargo would reach its destination.

Yet Clark had more than his own earnings to worry about. On a day he neglected to chronicle, he accepted 670 Spanish dollars, the equivalent of Wilkinson's long-overdue sum, plus interest. That money came from a source Clark did not identify and was to benefit a person whose name he did not record.

18

The Money Is for Mr. Riddle

HAVING given notice that he would miss the May term and perhaps the October term of the Kentucky Court of Appeals, Judge Benjamin Sebastian cautiously descended the Ohio. He liked to say on such journeys that he went in order to check titles to downstream acreage, but real estate had little or nothing to do with his predominant purpose of advancing his lucrative scheming with Spain. Experience had made him adept at eluding detection, particularly by the men General Wayne had ordered to patrol the reaches around Fort Massac. When those soldiers had failed to catch Sebastian on a previous voyage, stories spread that he'd floated by in disguise or had passed at night onboard a compact canoe. Although the dragnet in 1798 was somewhat smaller than before (General Wayne having died and Wilkinson having taken over his command), the judge still could not afford to be caught, especially with the papers he was carrying. Some of them were coded into a seemingly impenetrable series of numbers and symbols, yet they held secrets intended for the eyes of Governor Gayoso and his superiors.[1]

Thus far Sebastian had been fortunate that none of the many treasonous documents he'd sent to Louisiana had gone astray. In November 1796, for example, he dispatched a letter in which he explicitly endorsed abrogating Pinckney's Treaty. In the same missive he went on to ask Gayoso to "point out with precision the object to be pursued, and, if attainable, you shall find my activity and exertions equal to your most sanguine expectations," scrawling 1325 in lieu of his name. Several months later, writing under the pseudonym "Carlos," Sebastian sent Carondelet encrypted suggestions about how Spain should incite western Americans to break away from the Union. Acutely aware that disclosure of such communications would ruin his reputation and lead to the revocation of his judicial appointment, Sebastian nevertheless continued his risky correspondence in order to keep two thousand pieces of eight coming to him each year.[2]

During the winter of 1795–1796 he'd enjoyed the honor of riding downstream from New Madrid on Gayoso's own galiot. Perhaps Sebastian now returned to New Orleans aboard another Spanish vessel. Shortly after arriving at that city, he must have submitted to the royal treasury a request for four thousand dollars—the total of his clandestine salary for 1797 and the current year.[3]

Soon he and the governor commenced a series of meetings. Gayoso had been waiting long months for a definitive answer from Sebastian and his associates to Carondelet's offer of two hundred thousand dollars for the removal of Kentucky from the Union. Having heard of Thomas Power's difficulties in promoting the plan, and of his expulsion from the United States when he revealed it to General Wilkinson, Gayoso could well imagine Sebastian's response. In Gayoso's words:

> Mr. Benjamin Sebastian . . . has repeated that the propositions of the Baron de Carondelet cannot be put into effect, for being untimely, that his friends were of the same opinion, that some [of them] were quite alarmed to hear of the project, especially Nicholas [who] has obliged Innes to sign a letter . . . in which they declare they will not enter into business of this sort [with Spain] nor do they want to accept a [Spanish] salary.[4]

Sebastian also handed him General Wilkinson's most recent encrypted message. It reveals that his avarice exceeded even his considerable dread of being caught conspiring with Spain:

Fort Pitt, March 8 [1798]

> Watched on all sides, I dare not communicate with you nor should you communicate with me. My name has been used . . . and without my consent. . . . Don't trust the people of the West because they are traitors. Fortify your boundaries well. As long as I find myself as I am now, all is secure. I

had buried my cypher but have recovered it. You have had many spies in this Country. In the name of God and of our friendship, I entreat you, *do not speak or write my name* [emphasis added].[5]

Wilkinson had indeed exhumed the pocket dictionary with which he enciphered and deciphered secret messages. He would keep it handy in case he was named governor of the newly formed Mississippi Territory, a position promising numerous opportunities for intriguing with Spain.

Gayoso no doubt also wished for such a turn of events, but not because he had faith in Wilkinson or his cronies. He confided as much to Spanish secretary of state Manuel de Godoy:

Note the strong contradiction in the mistrust which Wilkinson gives rise to regarding the people of the Western Country, and what he has always said of them concerning their inclination in our favor. This arises from the jealous, vengeful spirit of Wilkinson against those who outshine him. He thinks that on extracting himself from the [seditious] business, Sebastian or another Kentuckian will embrace it. . . .

My opinion of the people of the Western Country is that they are unsuited to our placing implicit confidence in them, beginning with General Wilkinson, Mr. Benjamin Sebastian, and however many notables in that Country there are. All of them are mercenary, disposed to take the position which offers the most benefit, and the common people are determined and supremely ignorant, but, by the same token, easy to move to disorder.

Even so, Gayoso considered it crucial to the survival of Spanish Louisiana that he keep bribing members of the Kentucky cabal. Not only did recent intelligence hold that British agents were in that state but Gayoso believed that Britain always supplied its operatives with plenty of cash.[6]

It was equally important to maintain a facade of goodwill toward Wilkinson, Sebastian, and their conspiratorial associates. Doing so with Sebastian was easy; he wrote Gayoso chatty letters warm with greetings for Gayoso's American-born wife, infant son, and mother-in-law. In Gayoso's amiable presence Sebastian surely relaxed enough to air some of his concerns.[7]

One of these concerns regarded land. For a long time Sebastian had been requesting a tract in Spanish territory where he could not only found an agricultural colony made up of American emigrants but also repair to should his duplicity be exposed. Reasoning that a grant of this sort would benefit Spain by helping to people a remote corner of the empire, Sebastian had offered to establish various such settlements—one on the Yazoo River; another, on the Bayou Manchac (in Louisiana); and ultimately, one along the St. Francis River (in present-day southeast Missouri and northeast Arkansas)—but he was still waiting for any of those proposals to be approved. Unfortunately for him, the heyday of Spanish colonization schemes was over; previous years of commotion in the Natchez District among former citizens of the United States had illustrated the near impossibility of transforming Americans into docile Spanish subjects.[8]

Perhaps Sebastian instead asked for an exclusive trade privilege like the one awarded Wilkinson a decade earlier. As all the Kentucky conspirators realized, concessions of this sort—in which Spain guaranteed a few chosen Americans a market for their flour, tobacco, pork, peltry, and other goods—were inequitable to their countrymen but of immense potential profit to themselves. In 1796, word of Pinckney's Treaty stifled a particularly likely monopoly then being concocted for Sebastian; he emerged from the experience determined to secure from Spain another such boon.[9]

Rather than dwell on past disappointments, though, he strove to speak in a positive manner about the future. What better way to do that than to tease with hints of another intrigue? Sebastian must have mentioned that he and his friends had a counterproposal to Carondelet's secession plan, but he wished to unveil it with his partner, Samuel M. Brown, once he arrived from upstream. Gayoso would wait until then.

A few days later, while going by river to the international boundary camp at the thirty-first parallel, Gayoso chanced upon Brown traveling in the opposite direction. They stopped to talk. According to Gayoso, Brown tried to pique interest in the proposal Sebastian had alluded to, handing over "a letter from the Governor of Kentucky, recommending him [Brown] and availing himself of the occasion to open with me a correspondence, which he says he expects to be productive of the mutual prosperity of both nations."[10]

Brown was in New Orleans by June 1, 1798, perhaps putting up at the Chabaud house, the premiere accommodation for English-speaking men of affairs. Curious about the design he was to reveal, Gayoso resolved to confer with him and Sebastian. Meanwhile, Brown declared eighty-two barrels of flour and more than two tons of bacon and ham, all goods for local sale, and paid the appropriate tax. At around the same time, Sebastian collected his illicit salary, and William Clark took delivery of 670 pieces of eight—for someone else.[11]

Soon Sebastian and Clark possessed so many Spanish silver dollars, they needed a reliable plan to get them upriver. Mindful that Power had successfully hidden 9,640 of those coins among cargoes of tropical products he then freighted upstream, Brown must have secured a sleeker, more maneuverable vessel than the one he'd arrived on, and he began loading the new vessel with coopered goods to sell back home. In accord with Power's advice to take an assortment of containers (some holding nothing but mercantile items, and others also carrying sacks of coins), Brown sought to fill the empty spaces on his deck with Louisiana exports. By June 18, he had room for two more barrels.

* * *

Clark continued getting ready to board the *Active*. Having assigned responsibility for the tobacco to Cochran and Rhea and having squared his own account with Madame Chabaud, he obtained a passport and purchased a barrel of sugar and another of coffee, neither of which he intended for himself. He conveyed those loaded containers, along with William Croghan's share of their tobacco income (162 dollars), to Brown. As if acknowledging that the coffee barrel was capacious enough to hold that sum and a larger one, Clark gave permission for almost 265 of Sebastian's pieces of eight (no doubt from Sebastian's illicit income, as he apparently did not sell goods at New Orleans) to be deposited into that container.

Although either Clark or Brown, or perhaps both of them, must have taken the following actions, for the sake of expedience I will describe each step of what occurred as if it resulted from individual effort. That is to say, someone pried the lid off the coffee barrel and scooped out a portion of the contents. Into the remaining beans he inserted cloth sacks containing the coins for Croghan and Sebastian's lucre. He buried at a similar depth within the sugar barrel more bags concealing the 670 Spanish dollars for a recipient whose name Clark did not record. After topping off both barrels with coffee or sugar, someone tightened down the lids on them and made sure they bore markings consistent with a shipment of foodstuffs bound for sale. Last of all, Brown had his accomplices pay their share of the freight expense. Clark gave twenty-four dollars—a charge based on the poundage of his two barrels, their consumable contents, and Croghan's money—but did not help defray the cost of the other coins concealed within them.[12] Humorously affecting a French greeting, Clark wrote to his father:

Mon Zir

In my letter of yesterday by Mr. Sebastian I mentioned forwarding by Captain Brown two Barrels Containing Sugar Coffee &c. you will receve by Mr. Brown a gentleman of my acquaintance & resident of Frankfort Two Barrels marked & Numbered as follow's.
   No. 1 Marked W. Clark, Louisville. Contains 152 1/2 lb. Coffee.
   No. 2 Marked W Clark Louisville, Contains 220 lb. of Sugar of two qualities, and 670 Dollars in Cash.
   I hope the Sugar & Coffee will be of Service to you, the money is for Mr. Riddle. I have nothing new since yesterday.
Permit me to subscribe my self your Dutifull Son

W Clark[13]

The smuggling scheme was set to put in motion. Aware of his own tendency to blurt out the truth when caught off-guard, Sebastian must have been relieved to let the cool-headed Brown carry out the operation.

The essential points of it were as follows: After meeting with Gayoso, Brown and Sebastian would proceed upstream in separate vessels and rendezvous at New Madrid. From there, Brown and the money-laden goods would ascend the Ohio while Sebastian, to avoid detection by any Fort Massac authority who might still be watching for him, would continue up the Mississippi to Kaskaskia, then travel by land to Louisville. Before returning home Sebastian would stop at Mulberry Hill, call on his friend John Clark, and give him William's letters. When Brown reached Louisville some time

A letter from William Clark to his father, John Clark, June 19, 1798.

later, Croghan and Sebastian would retrieve their reales, and Brown would release the coffee beans and the sugar barrel holding 670 Spanish dollars to John Clark. In turn, he would pass along those coins to an agent William called "Mr. Riddle," a name *not* appearing in Spanish records of Americans secretly on the royal payroll but, instead, in correspondence concerning navigators who plied the waters between Spanish Louisiana and Kentucky.

What was he to do with all that money? We can assume he was to deliver it to another person, someone Governor Gayoso deemed deserving but preferred not to designate in writing. Clark never identified "Mr. Riddle" nor clarified his role, a circumspection typical of the various plots of that era between Spain and western Americans. So we must consider other evidence, and the weight of it leads to two well-supported inferences: First, Riddle was probably a boatman, perhaps the same one who a few years hence would transport a special shipment of wine from Louisiana for Sebastian and his judicial brethren. Second, and of much more significance, the nefarious General Wilkinson was likelier than anyone else to be the intended recipient of the money in Clark's sugar barrel.[14]

The reasons for drawing such a conclusion are these: The time for a transaction of that sort was excellent. Wilkinson was still agitating for the 640 dollars, a debt old enough he could expect interest on it, and Brown's arrival—and that of the Money Ship—gave the Spanish government the means to meet such an obligation. Gayoso had plenty of motive to do so too; a payment of 640 dollars was small enough not to compromise urgent needs in Louisiana or to draw attention when smuggled into the United States, yet was sufficiently large to gratify Wilkinson and to lay a foundation for further intriguing with him. The weight of that cache being relatively light, Gayoso could include thirty extra dollars as a bonus without causing the total to become noticeably more cumbersome.

In keeping with Wilkinson's recent plea for secrecy, Gayoso would certainly have kept his identity as confidential as possible. What better way to do that concerning an amount due him, Gayoso might have thought, than to commit it to the care of Sebastian and Brown, fellow conspirators who had already demonstrated their trustworthiness and reliability? If Gayoso not only knew the role Clark was to play in this particular smuggling enterprise but also recalled his 1795 visit to New Madrid when Clark had used his position as General Wayne's messenger to praise that officer's professed enemy General Wilkinson, Gayoso would have cause to believe in Clark's discretion, too.

The most telling evidence that the money was for Wilkinson, a notoriously relentless collector of sums owed him, is that he apparently never again pursued the debt of 640 dollars. As we will see, he was soon to press for a much grander amount from Spain. In the end, if Wilkinson was indeed the one benefiting from those dollars, William Clark may have gambled his honored reputation and drawn in his own father by helping spirit money to a man eventually to become the subject of numerous investigations—some by Congress, others by the military—at least three of which were related to charges of his plotting with Spain against the interests of the United States. We can assume that neither John nor William Clark would have cooperated at all in the smuggling mission had they perceived Wilkinson's history of treachery, especially toward George Rogers Clark, but the fact that not even George himself could prove who had brought about his disgrace testifies to the stealth of Wilkinson.

Having waited as long as possible to book passage on the *Active*—and still hoping the vessels of Daniel Coxe would show up—William likely put off boarding the schooner until further procrastination might result in her sailing without him. But on June 19, 1798, she was ready to depart, and both weather and tide augured a rapid journey down the last hundred miles of the Mississippi and out into the Gulf. At first, Clark little realized that the wind blowing toward the sea was also holding back the very ships he'd been looking for all summer. By the end of the day, however, word arrived that Coxe's vessels—the ship *Star* and brig *Friendship*, each creaking with artillery manned by patriotic Americans—had left the Gulf and were steadily moving upriver toward New Orleans. On hearing of their approach, Clark abandoned all thought of returning to the United States by the *Active* even though not taking her meant forfeiting his substantial expenses. He gathered his belongings and headed back to the Chabaud house.[15]

With a new and better plan, for once he wrote in his journal what it was: "I chan[g]e my rout & Determined to go to Nautchus." Those few words reveal that he deemed losing eighty-five dollars well worth the chance to ride to the border and trade his fifteen hundred pieces of eight for a paper draft much safer and easier to conceal. Further, because Coxe's ship and brig would not be ready to leave Louisiana for three to four weeks, Clark was to have plenty of time to complete his own money-running mission, return to New Orleans and, if he knew of the cunning proposal put forth by Sebastian and Brown, learn how Governor Gayoso reacted to it. If he liked it, Clark might consider investing in the same scheme. And, in the event a war broke out before the *Star* and *Friendship* left New Orleans, he had only to take refuge onboard them to be in the safest place in town. His luck, it seemed, was finally beginning to turn.

Sometime that day, perhaps while proceeding to or from the water-front, he handed the letter for his father to Sebastian. In doing so, Clark attested to his arrangement with the intriguers. It was an alignment that in a few years might threaten to destroy his hope for an illustrious career.

19

A Highly Beneficial but Illicit Monopoly

IN the spring of 1798, before Samuel Montgomery Brown commenced his own flatboat voyage to New Orleans, he received a missive from Harry Innes and his cousin, Thomas Todd. Brown had been expecting to hear from them. So had Sebastian, but he was already downriver and waiting for Brown. The letter reflected discussions that Brown, Sebastian, Innes, and Todd had held among themselves after deciding unanimously not to participate in Carondelet's insurrection project. They all understood that dangerous enterprise could not succeed, Pinckney's Treaty having killed any viable reason for western Americans to leave the United States.

But the allure of two hundred thousand Spanish silver dollars remained irresistible. During the ten months since Power had departed Louisville, those four Kentuckians had been scrutinizing Carondelet's terms, searching for a way to secure such a magnificent amount without fomenting war. At last they had a plan. Calling it a "rational & equitable system of commerce," they shaped it into proper form for presenting to Governor Gayoso, their key to the royal treasury.[1]

Having compiled statistics on Kentucky, particularly on its population, exports, and growth, attorneys Innes and Todd distilled their findings into a concise set of data, arranged the data in logically persuasive order, and transcribed them to the letter for Brown. Drawing from Sebastian's narrative of his 1796 experiences at New Orleans, they added comments sure to resonate favorably with Gayoso. Certainly mindful that if they won his approbation other men (including General Wilkinson and Kentucky governor James Garrard) might want to join their endeavor, they revealed few names, dates, or details, producing a message long on elegantly appealing phrases but short on specifics. Brown received it, memorized its most important points, and took it downriver.[2]

Shortly after reaching New Orleans he and Sebastian must have discussed the proposal and deliberated how each of them would present it. Sebastian probably agreed to entice Gayoso without revealing details. Brown, the partner with the most business experience, would then divulge and explain the entire plot.

The first part of their strategy worked as planned. Intrigued by Sebastian's hints of a new conspiracy, Gayoso set aside June 23 to learn more about it. Whatever William Clark may have heard, he would have to wait until he returned to New Orleans before deciding whether the scheme was worth pursuing.

Brown drew up a three-page-long petition outlining the salient factors of the project. If he planned to follow this document closely, he'd make no reference to previous intrigues—especially those of a violent nature—as if he and his associates wished to divert attention from potentially divisive topics. Instead, Brown opened his remarks with fulsome praise for Gayoso "whose mind, ever active in the pursuit of public good, led . . . [him] to inquire into the advantages that would result from the strictest union being cultivated between our two countries."[3]

After more such flattery, Brown raised the subject of Kentucky. According to the proposal: "It is unnecessary to say anything to your Excellency relative to the fertility of the soil of Kentucky, to make any remarks on the nature of its products, or how far those products are suited to the wants of the inhabitants of Louisiana." Despite such natural blessings, Brown argued, the shortage of hard cash in the American West was making it impossible for Kentuckians to send their goods to Louisiana or to pay taxes on them once they arrived there. Further, that situation was, in the words of Innes and Todd, making Kentuckians "miserable in the midst of plenty," by rendering useless certain rights that Pinckney's Treaty granted them, particularly that of navigating the Mississippi. Brown expanded, saying that duties charged by Spain, though lower than they had been in years, were still excessive. He concluded: "While [the people of Kentucky] will be compelled to acknowledge the bounty of your government, alas, Sir! They will reap but very little benefit from it."[4]

Next, Brown introduced his partnership with Sebastian, Innes, and Todd. He ascribed to it the altruistic purpose of relieving Kentuckians "from the ill-concerted system of commerce which they have hitherto pursued, through which they have been drained of all their circulating wealth." Brown affirmed that he and those associates instead wished to enable their fellows "to enjoy those blessings which, from the fertility of their soil, nature seems to intend for them."[5]

To do this, however, they must have a loan of two hundred thousand dollars, the exact amount Carondelet had dangled before them in 1797. Rather than producing a violent separation of their state from the Union, that sum would enable them to "embrace, for a time, the whole of the commerce of Kentucky, both with respect to export and import." In other words, Brown, Innes, Todd, and Sebastian were offering to funnel to New Orleans the entire output of Kentucky. The petition does not explain how they intended to do so, but it claims that they were able to ship to Louisiana such highly desired products as tobacco, flour, and hemp, all of them "in the greatest abundance."[6]

The petition continues: In return, the Spanish government would send the partners sugar, cotton, indigo, and rice. Because the scheme extended to Cuba as well, that colony was to exchange coffee for Kentucky goods. Additionally, Spain would supply Kentucky with "brandy, wine, Fruit, oil, Salt, and such manufactures as are suited to our wants." There was no reason to fear a disruption of trade if Spain went to war with another European power; Brown stressed that because shipments from Kentucky would descend the Ohio and Mississippi rivers rather than travel by oceangoing vessel, they would be safe from foreign attack. He guaranteed that one of the partners would move to New Orleans in order to direct the business, compile regular reports, and upon request by the Spanish government, open company books for inspection.[7]

Not until Brown was three-fourths of the way through the proposal did he call the scheme what it was. Yet he strove to justify it: "We are aware, Sir, that Monopolies, in general, are considered as injurious to society, but there are cases in which they are highly beneficial, and this we conceive to be one of them." Still, he ignored that this particular monopoly was transparently self-serving and unethical, for it could not succeed unless the partners curtailed their fellow citizens' rights to sell or buy goods at Louisiana.[8]

But was the arrangement illegal? Brown tried to skirt that question, too. He admitted only that the U.S. Constitution prohibits individual states from treating with foreign powers and reiterated the purported need for the monopoly, as "no other mode presents itself" to correct the problems alleged. Even so, he failed to acknowledge that exposure of the project would subject himself and partners to censure, and perhaps even to prosecution, in the United States and Kentucky.[9]

Brown then returned to the subject of the two hundred thousand dollars. Promising full reimbursement in five annual installments, he proposed that the first of those payments not come due until three years *after* Spain advanced the entire amount. That is, he and his partners wanted not just a loan worth a fifth of a million dollars, they also desired eight full years to pay it off. As they all knew, such a period was more than enough time for Louisiana, whether by cession to an ally, sale to another nation, or loss to an invader, to cease being Spanish. By keeping language of such contingencies out of the proposal, Brown gave himself and his confederates an excuse to retain the principal should the inevitable occur within eight years.[10]

Gayoso surely realized that the loan would do nothing to bring about the withdrawal of Kentucky from the Union, and that Brown and company were promising benefits beyond their power to deliver. How could they control the entire output of their state? How might they prevent established traders such as William Croghan and Richard Clough Anderson from continuing to ship goods downriver? For that matter, how would Brown and his partners stop the owners of small farms from taking their flour and tobacco to New Orleans? And, if the monopoly was to stay unknown in the States, how would they account for all the sugar, coffee, rice, and other products they were to receive? Perhaps Gayoso asked those questions, and Brown and Sebastian gave plausible-sounding answers.

Even if they did, they failed to persuade him of the soundness of their ideas or of their own integrity.

Equally unconvincing was Brown's assertion as to what he and the others wished—purportedly for the good of the United States and Spain—from the project:

> Should you see . . . that it will tend to unite and perpetuate that friendship and harmony so necessary to the happiness of the two nations, whose relative situations renders a constant intercourse unavoidable, and whose relative productions nature seems to have fitted, in a peculiar manner, to each other's wants—should it thus strike your Excellency as through you alone they can hope for success, they trust you will take the business under your protection, and represent it at the Court of Spain in the way that you shall judge most likely to insure its accomplishment.[11]

Brown handed over the petition and the letter from Todd and Innes. No doubt promising to submit the documents to his superiors and to send word of their response, Gayoso instead may have just filed them away, not intending to pass them on. More urgent matters required his attention. The latest news held that hostilities between the United States and the French Republic were growing ever more heated. Intent on preparing New Orleans to become a battleground between those powers, Gayoso notified local officials that he was calling a council of war.[12]

20

At Ellicott's Camp on the Line

C LARK made arrangements to travel to Natchez by way of the international boundary camp at the thirty-first parallel. If all went according to plan he would replace his cumbersome reales with a bill of exchange, a single sheet of paper authorizing payment from an office of the U.S. government. Familiar as a soldier with reimbursement by the War Department, he surely knew by now that Tench Coxe, a brother of Daniel Clark Jr.'s Philadelphia partner, had important federal connections that might expedite the process of getting paid. And by traveling overland, William would have more time to reconnoiter that crucial corridor than he did while on the river.[1]

He might also have an opportunity to sharpen his command of terrestrial measurement and celestial navigation. American boundary commissioner Andrew Ellicott and his chief surveyor, Thomas Freeman, resided at the boundary line. Tenting next to their camp was the Spanish contingent; it included Louisiana Regiment major Stephen Minor, an accomplished surveyor and Natchez resident serving as boundary commissioner for Spain, and the ingenious William Dunbar, an amateur astronomer and inventor who owned a local plantation. The secretary and commissary for their group was Thomas Power, onetime secret agent and smuggler for Governor Carondelet.

Eager to set out, Clark spent around a hundred dollars on a saddle, bridle, saddlebags, and two horses—one to ride, the other to carry his silver coins. Bringing another sum to pay his costs of travel, he also packed fifteen hundred of his own pieces of eight (nearly ninety-four pounds of them) to exchange with either Andrew Ellicott or Captain Guion, both of whom sometimes needed hard cash to pay the expenses of their official endeavors. With typical misorthography and journalistic brevity, Clark wrote of June 21, 1798, "Set out for Nauthez," adding nothing about why he was going there or which of the two principal roads he would take. One started on the far side of Lake Pontchartrain and proceeded roughly northwest, avoiding most major settlements and staying clear of the Mississippi. Given his interest in that waterway and strategic points along it, however, Clark probably pursued the other route. Called El Camino Real (the King's Highway), it followed the Mississippi to beyond Baton Rouge before abandoning the river and angling north to Natchez, covering approximately 180 miles.

After traveling seven days without recording a word, Clark emerged at the thirty-first parallel. It was a border like none he'd ever seen. Rather than imposing a wall or a fence on the landscape, or even blazing a succession of trees, the American and Spanish boundary parties were denuding a sixty-foot-wide strip extending eastward from the flooded Mississippi lowlands toward the Pearl River, today the southern boundary between Louisiana and Mississippi.

It was the last Thursday of the month, scarcely a week after the solstice, and the heat that had been retarding the advance of the line was expected to continue for months. To Dunbar, who would soon note the mercury in his thermometer at 120 degrees, each dawn the sun appeared to erupt from the earth, shoot straight up, and spend the rest of the day dropping slowly back to the ground. So high were the daily temperatures that Ellicott and Minor sent the woodsmen out in the early morning, let them rest for most of the afternoon, and had them work on into the evening.[2]

Rough topography and flora coarse enough to dull machetes were further slowing progress. For many miles east of the Mississippi, thick screens of cane—a New World species of bamboo—presented a living barrier of stalks, some more than twelve feet tall. Tangled into that vertical warp was a dense weft of vines, some producing wild hops, grapes, and peas and others leafy with an ivy called the "poison plant" for the blistering and itchiness it caused. Vine tendrils twined around branches and trees and caught hold of others, forming a blanket of matted vegetation that, from above, seemed to dip and rise in waves roughly corresponding to the steep, broken terrain beneath. For one tree to fall, a man often had to chop through a dozen.

Although cutting down the profuse growth was hard work, getting rid of the fallen vegetation was almost impossible without igniting it. Dunbar described what happened when a deliberate burn spread out of control, producing

> a most astonishing line of fire, the flames ascending to the tops of the highest trees and spreading for miles on each side of the line, carried devastation wherever it went; the continual explosions of rarefied air from the hollow cane resembled the re-echoed discharges of innumerable platoons of musketry and mocked every idea that could be formed of the effect produced by the conflict of the most formidable armies. The scene was truly grand, aweful and majestic, and must have been seen to be able to form any just idea of its terrible Sublimity.[3]

No doubt the workers were happy that charring and clearing the land reduced the number of reptiles and amphibians on it. The same spring showers that had earlier impeded Clark's river voyage caused the Mississippi to slop over its lowlands and form numberless pools of stagnant, nutrient-rich water, forming breeding grounds for what Dunbar called the "most disgusting forms and noxious kinds" of animal life—multitudes of toads, frogs, alligators, and hundreds of "Serpents of the waters" (likely including cottonmouths)—sometimes twisting together into fearsome clusters.[4]

Clark was to write more about mosquitoes than about any other of the numerous annoyances he faced during the Pacific expedition; surely he noticed the staggering abundance of flying, crawling, creeping, and blood-sucking insects at the thirty-first parallel. To Thomas Freeman, that section was "the most irregular, hilly, broken & unfinished part of the globe's surface, where every leaf is inhabited by myriads of Moschetoes, gnats, Flies, Ticks, &c. of various kinds so that we may be said for the present to be in a more than Earthly Purgatory." To repel insects, the boundary workers set smoky fires around camp even on the hottest nights.[5]

Despite such precautions, the *Anopheles* mosquito was doing more perhaps than all other natural forces to impede the line work, for it was causing members of both parties to suffer the fluctuating fevers and bone-rattling chills (then called the "ague") characteristic of malaria. As long as anyone could remember, that malady had been pandemic in the Mississippi valley. New cases typically broke out from springtime until the onset of winter, and people already carrying the *Plasmodium* parasite in their livers and bloodstreams suffered relapses throughout the year. Because quinine-rich Peruvian cinchona bark was often an efficacious treatment, both the American and Spanish parties kept supplies of it on hand. In 1804, William Clark and Meriwether Lewis would carry west fifteen pounds of it.

Not until the late nineteenth century did science finally disprove the "bad air" of mosquito-infested lowlands as the source of malaria, but in Clark's time Americans knew such places to be less healthful than drained ones. The link between sickle cell anemia and a partial resistance to malaria would also not be understood for decades. Even so, the fact that people of African ancestry—almost exclusively the carriers of the sickle cell gene—escape full-blown malarial symptoms more often than do those of European blood was well-known then. For this reason, the commissioners were already discussing the possibility of having slaves take over the labors of white workers laid low with chills and fever.[6]

* * *

Atop a hill near the headwaters of Little Bayou Sara, a creek in the southernmost extremity of the Mississippi Territory, Clark tied up his horses and entered the American section of the boundary camp. Two years had passed since he was in such a large encampment, but the odors of cook fires and latrines, of horses, oxen, milk cows, and beef cattle penned nearby, must have reminded him of his Army days. He may not have thought of the boundary endeavor as a military enterprise, but it was; each commission had brought an armed detachment to guard workers from attack by Indians or other hostile forces.

If the American camp was laid out in the order then employed by the U.S. Army, along the periphery were the tents of the enlisted men and their commander, Ensign John McClary. Farther inside were the tall, open-sided fabric marquees of important civilians such as Commissioner Ellicott and his band of surveyors and chain-bearers. Perhaps Clark spied a timber hut with an open roof; it was a makeshift observatory essential to deriving terrestrial coordinates from the movements of the stars—Arcturus, Castor, and Pollux, and constellations such as Pegasus and Corona Borealis. He also observed the weather-beaten tents of slaves and paid workers, a hospital marquee, and fire pits hung with kitchen utensils and kettles of various sizes—smaller ones for cooking, larger vessels for boiling laundry. Wagons guarded the camp perimeter.[7]

Clark was no doubt dismayed by the sight of the men in the American Army escort. They were dressed in ragged remnants of the military styles he had worn—blue coats, white vests and pants, black boots—with civilian clothes making up the rest of their attire. Equally tattered were their tents, having already been subjected to months of hard use sheltering Captain Guion's troops as they waited for the Spanish to leave Natchez.[8]

Clark had only to glance into the adjacent Spanish camp to see tents in better condition and troops outfitted in crisp, new uniforms—blue-trimmed white coats, blue vests and breeches, and white gaiters buttoned a few inches above the knees—and equipped with first-rate gear. Even the privates had .69 caliber muskets and carried sheathed bayonets. Here, Spanish soldiers of all ranks looked superior to their American comrades.[9]

But the civilians in each camp appeared remarkably homogeneous. Other than baker Francisco Cabrera, most of the white, non-military occupants of the Spanish camp, though residents of the Natchez area, were native speakers of English who had Anglo surnames and family roots in the eastern states. So hard was it to tell the members of the Spanish party from the Americans that hat cockades—red for Spain, black for the United States—gave the best clue. To discourage competition and comparisons between the camps, the Spanish had their cook, Steven Williams, prepare the same meals as were served to the Americans and adopted the Americans' pay scale.[10]

Only in scientific apparatus did Ellicott's party have a clear advantage over the Spanish. The Americans possessed up to three versions of every astronomical or technical instrument useful to the boundary project—

sextant, timepiece, compass, zenith sector, theodolite, telescope, and arti-
ficial horizon—some of which Ellicott had built himself. In contrast, the
Spanish had a compass, a sextant, and a type of telescope called an astronomical circle, but none of those devices was capable of precise calibration
or was designed to withstand the heavy wear it would get at the line.[11]

After twilight Andrew Ellicott liked to lie supine on the ground, peer-
ing through the lens of his zenith sector to track the path of particular
stars or even of the satellites of Jupiter. He so loved astronomy that even
after determining data sufficient to keep his woodsmen laboring along the
proper coordinates for the next few miles, he often spent hours studying
the night sky, catnapping during the day to make up for lost sleep. One
may ask whether William Clark conformed his own hours to Ellicott's
schedule in order to learn from Ellicott, the future tutor in celestial navigation of Meriwether Lewis. With seldom a chance to improve his understanding of the sciences, Clark likely took advantage of every feasible
opportunity to do so. If he did, he probably also observed the surveying
techniques of Thomas Freeman, formerly employed by George Washington to plat his lands along the Kanawha and Ohio rivers.[12]

Having joined the Spanish commission to deepen his command of
astronomy, William Dunbar liked to keep late-night vigil with Ellicott.
Around the time Clark arrived, however, Dunbar's malarial symptoms
were making him think of taking to bed at his plantation, "the Forest," less than a day's ride to the north. Soon he went there. But for a
brief interval never to be repeated, three future Jeffersonian explorers—
William Clark, of the Missouri River and beyond; William Dunbar, of
the Ouachita River; and Thomas Freeman, of the Red—trod the same
latitude and longitude. Oh, to have heard their conversation or witnessed
their expertise! However likely such an encounter may have been, if one
took place nobody wrote about it.[13]

But Clark's pen was not entirely idle during those days. "Arrive at Ellicott camp on the line that was cut about 6 miles after about 3 mo: labour,"
he wrote of June 28, 1798, alluding to the inordinate amount of time it
had taken to make such paltry progress on the international border. At
this rate, another twenty-four years and unprecedented funding would

have been necessary to complete the work Congress wanted done and as soon as possible at minimal expense. As Clark might have heard, some people suspected that Ellicott was trying to turn the boundary project into a source of prolonged employment for himself and his son Andy, one of the assistant surveyors.[14]

Whatever the truth of that story may have been, the senior Ellicott was one of the most industrious men on the job. No matter how late he had been up to study the heavens the night before, he usually arose with the sun, trudged to the edge of the cleared boundary, and spent most of the day extrapolating from his nocturnal observations the path of the next segment. He was applying the "tangent offset" method, a technique perfected in the 1760s by English surveyors Charles Mason and Jeremiah Dixon as they laid out the border between colonial Maryland and Pennsylvania along a tangent, correcting it—where necessary—at regular checkpoints. Their work not only ended decades of controversy over where to mark the boundary, it made the "Mason-Dixon" line an honored symbol of scientific achievement long before it became an emblem of the division between northern and southern states.[15]

In 1784 Ellicott saw for himself the effects of their rigorous methodology, when, as a thirty-year-old clockmaker with a flair for astronomy, he joined two other gifted technicians in present-day West Virginia as they extended westward the line of Mason and Dixon. Despite somewhat modifying the method of those famous predecessors, Ellicott and companions—who would also include noted astronomer David Rittenhouse—produced a remarkably precise boundary, completing it in 1785.[16]

Scientific genius notwithstanding, Ellicott was a contentious figure. From 1791 to 1793 he surveyed and marked the ten-mile-by-ten-mile square to become the seat of national government, but when questions arose concerning the accuracy of his work and expense account and about the slow progress of the job, he refused to cooperate with investigators and published charges against his accusers. They responded in kind, adding to previous claims against Ellicott others alleging dishonesty, whoremongering, and adultery. For a while President Washington intervened, but the dispute having progressed too far to be resolved, Ellicott left the project for good. In his place the District of Columbia boundary commissioners hired Thomas Freeman who completed the work to their satisfaction in 1795.[17]

But because Ellicott was still the undisputed master of mathematics and astronomy, President Washington looked past his touchy, sometimes irascible personality and appointed him in 1796 to set the location of the border dictated by Pinckney's Treaty. Exactitude was important; Washington wanted Ellicott's calculations to end decades of friction with the Spanish over territory that would become the states of Mississippi, Alabama, and Georgia. Saying nothing about how the line was to be figured or marked, Pinckney's Treaty specified only that it was to run east along the thirty-first parallel from the Mississippi to the Apalachicola River (in present-day Florida), then down the midpoint of that stream to the Flint River, and straight from there to the headwaters of the St. Marys River, the remainder of which divided American from Spanish territory all the way to the Atlantic Ocean.[18]

An engraved portrait of Andrew Ellicott by an unidentified artist, date unknown.

The entire expanse exceeds six hundred miles, a boundary far longer than any Ellicott had yet worked on. From experience he knew that even if his men remained healthy (a most unlikely prospect, especially during the summer), applying even a modified version of the Mason-Dixon system over such a distance would entail years of effort and exorbitant expense. Even so, he decided the need for precision justified doing that.

Five years hence, Ellicott was to instruct Meriwether Lewis on how to calculate latitude and longitude by means of sextant and chronometer—simpler devices less prone to breakage than zenith sectors and theodolites. The "ten or twelve days" Lewis would first estimate necessary to gain proficiency would stretch into nearly three weeks, after which he would still struggle to figure earthly coordinates, especially longitude. Lacking this sort of expert instruction, Clark was nonetheless to plot hundreds of terrestrial positions during their 1803–1806 western journey, and to draw nearly all the maps of the regions they traversed. How much he may have learned from Ellicott in 1798 we can only guess, but it is likely that Clark took advantage of the opportunity to hone his technique.[19]

He kept in mind a key reason he had left the comforts of New Orleans and ridden to the line: to exchange his silver coins with something easier for him to transport by ship. To this end it seems he presented his fifteen hundred reales to Ellicott, taking in return a draft on the U.S. Treasury. Perhaps because Spain forbade the exportation of her money, Clark did not record explicitly that he had done so.[20]

21

The Nature of the Boundary Business

IN the two months that Ellicott and his party had been working on the boundary they had completed but a handful of miles, yet their expenditures far exceeded the amount originally estimated necessary to carry out the job to this point. As a result, Secretary of State Pickering was having to ask Congress for additional funding. He was also closely scrutinizing Ellicott's expense account.

Quite a few of the outlays noted in it came about in 1797 while Ellicott and his group waited for the Spanish to evacuate their forts north of the thirty-first parallel—but some costs predated September 16, 1796, the day Ellicott, his twenty-year-old son, Andy, and Thomas Freeman, the man who had finished the District of Columbia survey after Ellicott left it, set off together from Philadelphia for Natchez. Among the things the senior Ellicott took with him was a new silver tea service. On trying to collect four hundred dollars for this tea service from the Adams administration, he called the set "absolutely necessary to make a decent appearance" at the line. Additionally, Pickering objected to Ellicott's hiring and transporting Pittsburgh laborers to clear trees and brush from the distant parallel rather than employing men from that locale.[1]

On pausing at Cincinnati as he and his group traveled down the Ohio to the Mississippi, the elder Ellicott made his most controversial acquisition of all: a woman that Freeman would describe as "of the lowest order of garrison prostitutes, and of a filthy appearance" who, according to Freeman, boarded one of the vessels and "proposed . . . to run her chance" with the party. Freeman and Ensign McClary wanted to expel her but Ellicott refused, taking the woman onto his boat. Although her name was Betsy, Freeman and others, mindful of the fictional harlot esteemed by Don Quixote, called her "Dulcinea," a reference William Clark, who revered books, would surely have understood. Any previous harmony between Ellicott and Freeman vanished, and as their fleet drifted downstream, the commissioner began compiling information he hoped to use some-day against his chief surveyor. Ellicott evidently had little idea that Free-man—later to become a friend and supporter of General Wilkinson—was collecting evidence for use against him.[2]

The vessels reached Natchez on February 24, 1797. According to Free-man, Ellicott kept Betsy for himself and Andy, forming a ménage à trois so flagrant that local officials—not wishing to fall afoul of the adminis-tration behind the boundary party—apparently hesitated to speak openly about it. Perhaps for such a reason Captain Isaac Guion reported obliquely that Ellicott "has very much lessened himself and sullied the Commis-sion given him, by his conduct before and since his arrival here—I did not believe it 'till I saw it, and [had] supposed it calumny." Freeman was less inhibited in his expression, calling the elder Andrew "the Beast" and writing about "the Inconsistencies, absurdities, and Brutality of that man, who need only to be known to be despised."[3]

During the thirteen months Ellicott waited at Natchez for the Spanish to depart so that he could begin work on the boundary, he might have gathered data on the weather and on celestial orbits; such information was crucial to precision once the job got started. Instead, he made only a few "thermometrical and astronomical" readings before he put away his in-struments and took up activities *not* covered by his strictly limited, official instructions—to place the international border where Pinckney's Treaty said it should go.[4]

Some of those pursuits were also illegal. Perhaps the one most dan-gerous to the tentative peace of the region was to promise a few friendly Choctaws that the U.S. government would pay their people two thousand annual dollars if they allowed his party to run the line through their coun-try. Not only did Ellicott lack authority to obligate the national treasury in such a manner, but acting as if he was an Indian agent needlessly com-plicated the responsibilities of those who truly were.[5]

Unfortunately, Ellicott also inserted himself into political groups advocating violent or covert methods to make the Spanish leave. Though vested with only narrowly drawn civilian powers to carry out the boundary job, he had nevertheless recruited men for possible military duty against Spain. He even considered having Gayoso kidnapped (but later decided not to carry through with that plan). What's more, in 1797, Ellicott almost precipitated a battle with Spanish forces by persuading U.S. Army lieutenant Piercy Smith Pope to hasten with his troops to Spanish-occupied Natchez, contrary to orders from General Wayne.[6]

Even before Gayoso's forces finally departed that region on March 30, 1798, Ellicott credited himself with having "worried the Spaniards" out of the territory. Captain Guion and others held the opposite opinion, believing that the Spanish had left of their own accord and that Ellicott had brought the area to the brink of bloodshed. Soon Ellicott moved Betsy with him to the thirty-first parallel where he set her up as the laundress for the American party (her flatirons and wash kettles were more than four horses could easily haul). He billed her labor and equipment to the federal government.[7]

By the time Clark rode into camp, the disagreement between Ellicott and Freeman had turned into a feud, splitting the American commission into mutually antagonistic factions. Ellicott and son formed the core of the first faction; Freeman and some of his assistants, joined by Ensign McClary and his men, made up the opposition. For every criticism uttered by the chief surveyor, the commissioner hurled back a countercharge; some of them disparaged Freeman for his Irish birth, others alleged insubordination. Freeman responded by accusing Ellicott of deliberately prolonging his and Andy's paid employment by slowing the boundary effort.[8]

Thinking his clandestine negotiations with the Choctaws would ensure their goodwill, thereby making military protection unnecessary for his party, Ellicott hinted he might tell the soldiers in his escort to put down their arms and instead take up cane knives. To keep this from occurring, Guion properly directed McClary that, "in no instance, or by any directions are the Soldiery to be employed as labourers or drudges, but in that of their duty under Arms. . . . You will keep your Command in frequent exercise of their Arms, and marching and wheeling; and always alert & ready to meet whatever Occasion may present." The ensign did as his captain said. Each morning, the ragamuffin troops paraded to the line where they spent the rest of the day practicing maneuvers when not standing at attention.[9]

In visual contrast with them were three well-attired Choctaws who arrived at camp shortly before Clark did. By the time he showed up it was clear those Indians were inflaming tensions in camp. Yet they were doing so unknowingly, by treating Freeman as if he was the commissioner and having nothing to do with Ellicott.

* * *

The Choctaws were present because a few months earlier Governor Gayoso had received word that a larger group of their people, alarmed that the international boundary line would bisect the Choctaw homeland, was planning to ambush Ellicott's party. According to Gayoso's sources, if the attackers came by night they would remain on the American side of camp, but if they came by day, they would roam the vicinity, killing everyone not wearing the red cockade of Spain, their traditional ally. Wishing no harm to befall the Americans, Gayoso sent notice to Stephen Minor who immediately relayed it to Ellicott. Gayoso advised both commissioners to keep their camps contiguous and their guards on twenty-four-hour duty, and he cautioned Ellicott to stay clear of Choctaw territory until assured of that nation's friendship.[10]

Ellicott made light of both recommendations, asserting that "if there was any reality in the information . . . the sole view of [the] Choctaws was to frighten us and extort large presents from us." He also misinterpreted Gayoso's message as a "political maneuver of the Spanish Government with a view to throw obstructions in his [Ellicott's] way or bring him to a pause, or force him to abandon the [boundary] enterprise." Apparently neither Minor nor Gayoso knew of Ellicott's unauthorized dealings with the Choctaws, a tribe of great power.[11]

For the past thirty years, though, the three major bands making up the Choctaws—spread over thousands of square miles in the present Mississippi, Alabama, and Louisiana—had become so dependent on trade with Spain, they could no longer supply their own needs for weapons, salt, tobacco, or even corn. When a Choctaw warrior in 1798 groomed himself for battle, he likely shaved with an English razor while looking into a manufactured mirror and applied cosmetic paint imported from Europe. Rather than sleeping beneath deerskins, most Choctaws were by then using blankets woven in Britain and paid for with peltry.[12]

For centuries their people had hunted on their own territory, but having recently extirpated the deer on which they relied for subsistence, the Choctaws poached on the trans-Mississippi lands of the fierce Caddos and Osages. Like the Cherokees, Chickasaws, Creeks, and Seminoles, the Choctaws saw their accustomed way of life being strangled by obligations to whites, none of whom were encroaching faster than those from the United States. Once the Spanish Army abandoned Walnut Hills and Natchez to Americans, the people against whom those posts had been built, the Choctaws felt betrayed. Lately they had been quarreling among themselves over whether to continue relations with Spain, to trade with the United States, or simply to deal with the most likely provider of goods and protection.[13]

The heart of southern Choctaw territory lay more than a hundred miles east of the Mississippi River and along the thirty-first parallel, but exactly where that line would pass had yet to be determined. Not only did the Choctaws wonder whether they occupied U.S. or Spanish soil, they also suspected that the international boundary was a step—as indeed it was—toward taking their homeland. Both Spanish and American officials insisted that the project was irrelevant to tribal interests and reflected nothing more than a jurisdictional agreement between the two nations, but many Choctaws remained prudently skeptical.[14]

To learn what was really going on, Choctaws favoring the United States had sent three representatives to the American camp at the thirty-first parallel. One of them was called Otanensatabe by some speakers of English, Ottona Mastubba or Ottamustubbay by others. Another was Pushmakonkicka (also known as Pushaonkicka). Attending them was a mixedblood called John Carnes. Before heading for the boundary line, they had received instructions from Benjamin Hawkins, general superintendent of

Indian Affairs for tribes south of the Ohio River. Mindful of the trouble that Ellicott's extralegal negotiations were causing with the Choctaws and fearing that violence among the tribe would spread to the neighboring Creeks, Hawkins told Otanensatabe and Pushmakonkicka to deal exclusively with Freeman, a man he judged less likely to make rash promises. Hawkins gave the travelers correspondence addressed only to Freeman and then sent them to meet with Choctaw Agent Samuel Mitchell. Angered by the friction caused among his own charges by Ellicott's actions, Mitchell also entrusted the trio with messages for Freeman only.[15]

On their way to the thirty-first parallel the three Choctaws called on Captain Guion at Natchez. Evidently unaware that they'd been instructed to report only to Freeman, he composed a letter for them to carry to Ellicott, advising that they stay at the boundary long enough to become convinced it "is not intended to steal their land, as they have been told." Guion added that special effort was necessary "to win over these people, and make what they have heard from others" seem mistaken. As the ranking military officer in the territory, he was not at liberty—as Hawkins and Mitchell were—to exclude Ellicott, the highest civilian authority there, but Guion was unable to make up for the snubs those men directed at the commissioner.[16]

Once Otanensatabe, Pushmakonkicka, and Barnes reached the American camp they handed over the correspondence, most of it going to Freeman. Ellicott prepared a reply to Guion's letter, assuring that "nothing shall be wanted on my part to explain . . . the nature of our [boundary] business" to the Indians. Not until later did Ellicott realize that the Choctaw visitors were shunning him yet obtaining crucial information from his chief surveyor.[17]

* * *

While at the boundary William Clark must have heard news the trio brought, including word that Winthrop Sargent, secretary and acting governor of the Northwest Territory (in which capacities he had met with Clark in Kaskaskia the preceding autumn) was to govern the Mississippi Territory. In addition, American newspapers held that U.S. citizens believed Spanish officials were deliberately postponing compliance with

Pinckney's Treaty, particularly with the running of the boundary line. According to Stephen Minor of the Spanish camp, such reports only deepened Ellicott's suspicion that Gayoso was craftily trying "to lay the vigilance of the U.S. asleep, lull them into security, and under cover of this mask, draw them into the snares of Treachery." For evidence of such bad faith, Ellicott offered that Gayoso had yet to send proof that Minor, Dunbar, and Power were his duly authorized representatives. If documents to that effect did not come soon, Ellicott said, he would tell the State Department that Spanish cooperation in the boundary effort was "a mere farce and delusion."[18]

But the news of greatest immediate import to the boundary parties came from the American camp when Commissioner Ellicott let it be known he had decided to abandon the expensive, laborious tangent-offset system of determining the line. Once it reached the relatively level pinelands a score of miles to the east, he said, locations would be figured by means of a compass, and labor would be reduced to what Minor termed "blazing the trees and erecting large mounds or prominent marks on the banks of considerable water courses, and on other remarkable places." Thereafter a large measure of Ellicott's technical expertise was to be irrelevant to the boundary job.[19]

Such a prospect gave Freeman additional impetus to discredit the commissioner. In order to do so without revealing the deep strife within the American camp (an event that might cause the Choctaws to lose their illusions about U.S. superiority and send a war party to attack the Americans), Freeman proceeded with the utmost caution. The Choctaws having been led to think he was in charge, he continued pretending to be, acting as though Ellicott was his subaltern. Because some key workers, Ensign McClary, and other soldiers supported Freeman, Ellicott had no alternative but to play along in the charade.[20]

At first he did so without comment, but by the last day of June he could no longer bear the humiliation of taking orders from his subordinate. That morning he sent Freeman concise, written instructions to repair to the line and assist the woodsmen in a job usually performed by the chain carriers. Knowing he would lower himself in the eyes of the Choctaws if he complied, Freeman shot back a refusal. He closed, "The cause of your crusty and unnecessary note of this morning I am at a loss to account for." He was bluffing, of course; he knew Ellicott was trying to regain control. This exchange being confined to written messages, the Choctaws little suspected that a mutiny was afoot. Clark surely knew what was really going on, but he recorded nothing about it or any other matter at the line.[21]

22

The Object of the Plotters

CLARK rode out of camp the next morning and headed north. That evening he wrote, "Arrived at Nautuss [Natchez]," the only diary entry he would make while there. But he started again to record his money transactions, some of them in the broadest possible terms. For example, under the heading "Expenses" he probably lumped the costs of room and board, perhaps at the same house where he lodged while on his way down the Mississippi. Concerning revenues he was more explicit, noting he sold the horses for nearly eighty-five dollars, almost fifteen dollars more than he'd given for them. He laid in supplies of bread and "sundries" and splurged on a hat and blankets. For three dollars he played billiards, likely in the part of town between the top of the bluffs and the Mississippi known as "under-the-hill," a section dotted with taverns, bordellos, and dance halls. Clark had his clothes washed and paid nine dollars to a "poor sick man," apparently performing a magnanimous act of charity no doubt made possible by the sale at New Orleans of his cargoes. He bought a pirogue to paddle back to that city when his mission at Natchez was finished.

Meanwhile, Captain Guion kept the three Choctaw visitors until July 3, bestowing on them gifts of blankets, shirts, rifles, ammunition, sacks of rice, kegs of beef and tobacco, and adornments for the arms, wrists, and hair. As the Indians got ready to go home, they evidently told Guion they now believed the boundary irrelevant to the interests of their people, adding that they would urge them not to oppose it—an attitude that would help bring about the almost wholesale loss of their homeland in the nineteenth century.[1]

To honor the first Independence Day since the Spanish evacuated the Natchez District and Congress organized it as the Mississippi Territory, Captain Guion threw a banquet at his crumbling fort. Whether Clark attended no one recorded, but Guion took pains *not* to invite Don José Vidal, the acting Spanish consul in the area and former secretary to Governor Gayoso.[2] As devoted to serving the interests of Spain as Guion was to serving those of the United States, Vidal employed operatives to bring him newspapers filched from recently arrived flatboats, so that he might scan for intelligence significant to his nation. He explained to Gayoso that, although "Captain Guion is very careful to secure those papers as soon as they arrive . . . at times I manage to read some, then have to return them with the utmost secrecy."[3]

Shortly before Clark reached Natchez such mutual suspicion had spawned an open conflict over one question: Now that Spain had ceded the Natchez District to the United States, could Vidal continue the established practice of having New Orleans–bound American boatmen carry Spanish communications to Governor Gayoso? Guion said no. Soon the word was out that Americans were *not* to transport the mail of Spain.[4]

In the meantime Gayoso heard from sources in St. Louis, New Madrid, Baton Rouge, Natchez, and other points that more than a thousand U.S. soldiers were already on the lower Mississippi. Guion was planning to replace the Natchez fort with a new and better installation at Loftus Heights (the place Clark called Loveless Cliffs), and Colonel John Francis Hamtramck, an officer Clark knew from Fallen Timbers, was soon to depart Walnut Hills for Natchez. In addition, General Wilkinson would shortly commence a downriver voyage to Natchez where he was to review the transition from military to civilian government in the Mississippi Territory. All these stories boded poorly for Spain.[5]

At the thirty-first parallel, Ellicott heard from Secretary Pickering that Switzerland, Rome, Naples, Hamburg, and nearby regions were in danger of being caught in "the fatal grasp of France." He believed only "open war" might save the United States from French aggression. As the infant U.S. Navy had not yet acquired its own fleet, the United States would have to rely for protection against French privateers on armed, privately owned American ships.[6]

While these and other alarming reports circulated in the lower Mississippi valley, people along the eastern shore were considering whether to support America or Spain. The choice was clear in many places but not in Natchez where a large American population had for three decades profited, tax-free, from generous Spanish land grants. Until forced to pick one government over the other, many Natchez residents—and perhaps William Clark—aimed to stay on favorable terms with both nations.

* * *

Back at New Orleans, Gayoso was trying to marshal his shrinking resources in order to get the city ready for armed conflict. From St. Louis, Zenon Trudeau (the same lieutenant governor Clark had dined with the previous autumn) sent word that the federal government was stirring up nearby tribes against the Spanish. And, according to a U.S. newspaper story familiar to Gayoso, an American taking of Louisiana would be the first step toward the conquest of Mexico.[7]

Gayoso's war council convened on July 6. In attendance were the most important representatives of the royal administration in the province: Intendant Juan Ventura Morales, artillery commander Nicolás D'Aunoy, government secretary Andrés López de Armesto, squadron commander Manuel García, and two engineers. Having heard that American troops were on their way to Natchez and the thirty-first parallel, and having experienced the recent scare caused by the British war frigate entering the Mississippi delta, they understood that great sections of Louisiana were unprotected from any sort of invasion.[8]

Gayoso knew it mattered little whether it was France or the United States that attacked, for one of them was almost sure to do so. Without the Spanish navy patrolling the mouth of the Ohio River and the Louisiana Regiment guarding the strategic points between that junction and the thirty-first parallel, the northern and eastern frontiers were the most vulnerable. Although Gayoso suspected the initial assault would proceed from that quarter, he realized it might come from just about anywhere.

All the more reason, he continued, to shore up defenses at crucial points. But how?

Most of the funds arriving on the Money Ship had been spent on other important costs. Of the eighty thousand Spanish dollars remaining, thirty thousand were owed to the Louisiana Regiment for back pay, and almost as many were needed to redeem the paper substitutes for currency that Gayoso had issued to keep the government functioning until the subsidy arrived. And, because of hazards posed by French privateers and the British navy, the next shipment of capital might not leave Cuba for weeks.[9]

Determined that a shortage of funds must not prevent the war council from devising a course of action, Gayoso reminded his listeners that, in spite of monetary shortages, Governor Carondelet had managed a few years earlier to fortify existing defenses and build new ones, thereby preventing a British attack. With proper planning, Gayoso concluded, the province might again protect itself. To a man, the council members voted in support of every suggestion he put forth.[10]

He shaped his ideas into a detailed proposal. He reasoned that defending Louisiana would require an immediate installment of three hundred thousand dollars from the subsidy, along with hundreds of Spanish soldiers. Military recruitment having lagged ever since the beginning of the Spanish regime, he wanted to import troops from regiments in Cuba, the Internal Provinces, and Spain, and to receive increased funding for militias. Additional vessels were also needed, as were naval, infantry, and artillery officers. Expecting enforcement of the Alien and Sedition acts to cause expatriated French officers, including General Victor Collot, to flee the United States, Gayoso put forth the idea of hiring them to defend Louisiana.[11]

On July 30, 1798, he dispatched to Spain a report enumerating the above points and others concerning troop and sailor deployment and the distribution of armaments throughout the province. He wanted in particular to divide the Louisiana Regiment into smaller, more mobile divisions, and to send units of foot soldiers and dragoons upriver to unprotected positions. The royal engineers, he added, would check defenses at strategic places. Gayoso closed on a familiar note:

all this deserves the approval of your Excellency who should be persuaded of the urgency of these arrangements when you consider that from Natchez one can reach Baton Rouge in less than twenty-four hours, and in less than four days one can arrive at the capital of Louisiana. Once [enemy troops are] set up there, regaining [lost ground] seems difficult, and *certain the invasion of the Internal Provinces of New Spain* [emphasis added].[12]

That enormous, underpopulated, and mostly arid region stretched from the Gulf of Mexico toward the Bay of California. Spain valued the Internal Provinces as a buffer zone protecting the mineral wealth of interior Mexico. Although Gayoso lacked hard evidence the U.S. government was planning to attack the Internal Provinces, he could easily guess why Wilkinson, Sebastian, Brown, and their associates were so interested in establishing themselves in adjacent Louisiana.

* * *

Meanwhile, some 253 river-miles up the Mississippi from New Orleans, Andrew Ellicott was engaging in his own campaign to save the United States from the Spanish Conspiracy. He had been suspicious of Wilkinson ever since 1796, when President Washington named him as a person Ellicott should keep an eye on, and especially after hearing rumors later that year about a Spanish agent named Thomas Power bringing large sums of reales to Wilkinson. A few weeks after Power completed that mission by having Philip Nolan smuggle 9,640 pieces of eight from Louisville to Frankfort, Nolan arrived on the lower Ohio while Ellicott's fleet was pulled ashore nearby because of ice. Having no idea what Nolan was truly up to, Ellicott was delighted to make his acquaintance. Nolan enthralled him with talk of capturing wild horses in what is now Texas and with demonstrations of sign language used to communicate with western Indians. Unaware also that Nolan was an accomplished spy using the cover of horse-rustling to gather intelligence for Wilkinson, Ellicott took him onboard his boat and instructed him on points of celestial navigation essential to the terrestrial reconnaissance Nolan secretly planned to carry out in defiance of Spanish law.[13]

After reaching Natchez, Ellicott had stepped up his own espionage, using information from confidential sources to assemble accurate, timely intelligence about the conspiracy. For instance, on June 5, 1797 (the day Power departed Natchez to disseminate Governor Carondelet's grand separatist plot), Ellicott warned the secretary of state:

I have this moment received private information that Mr. Power, who I have mentioned to you in my communication of yesterday, is, by order of the Baron de Carondelet, to proceed immediately through the wilderness to the State of Kentucky. There is every reason to believe that his business is to forward the views of Spain, by detaching the citizens of Kentucky from the Union. It has been hinted to me that Mr. Power will, in the first instance, pay a visit to General Wilkinson, who, we are informed, is now in Cincinnati.[14]

When further spying revealed Power's role in attempting to lure Americans into Carondelet's plan, Ellicott outlined that scheme, using an encrypted, confidential letter he sent Secretary Pickering in November 1797. His information is correct on every major point:

Shortly after the ratification of the late treaty between the U.S. and his Catholic Majesty was carried to Kentucky, Mr. Murray, an attorney at law in that state, proceeded down the Mississippi to visit Govr. Gayoso and the Baron de Carondelet. A few days after Mr. Murray's interview with those gentlemen Mr. Power was despatched up the river apparently upon a trading voyage. He had secreted in a cask of sugar four despatches in cipher, one was directed to Genl. Wilkinson, another to John Brown, Senator of U.S., the third to Judge Sebastian, and the fourth to Mr. Lackasang [La Cassagne] at the rapids of the Ohio. These four men and Mr. Murray receive annual stipends from the Crown of Spain, and several others whose names I have not learned receive occasional payments. Mr. Power delivered the despatches above mentioned himself. He met Gen. Wilkinson at Cincinnati in September last . . . year. They affected for some days to be upon bad terms but were privately closeted at night.

This correspondence in cipher has been carried on for several years, it is ingeniously managed; the letters are deciphered by the help of a pocket dictionary.

The first object of these plotters is to detach the States of Kentucky and Tenesee from the union and place them under the protection of Spain.

If that could have been effected this season the Treaty would never have been carried into effect: and to ascertain the probability of such an event, Mr. Power was sent in the beginning of last June into the States before mentioned.

The design of detaching the western country from the union is but a small part of the general plan which is very extensive and embraces objects of immense magnitude; nevertheless, to ensure success, this point must first be carried, which, being effected . . . a general insurrection will be attempted, and cannot fail of success if the first part succeeds.

Genl. Wilkinson is to proceed from Kentucky with a body of troops through the country by way of the Illinois [Country] into New Mexico which will be a central position—the route has already been explored. Nine-tenths of the officers of the [Spanish] Louisiana regiment are at this time corrupted and the officers of the Mexican regiment which is now in this country are but little better. The apparent zeal of the Spanish officers on the Mississippi for the dignity of the Crown is only intended to cover their designs till the great plan—which is the establishment of a new empire—is brought to maturity.[15]

But Ellicott identified none of his sources and failed to account for his own dexterity with secret codes and ciphers or to explain how he acquired such information. (While on the boundary job a few months later, he was to break open Thomas Power's mail, record important sections of it, reseal it, and pass it along to the unsuspecting Power.) Despite the accuracy of Ellicott's findings about Wilkinson, Sebastian, and Brown, he evidently possessed no idea of their links with William Clark. On the other hand, had Ellicott known that Clark furnished the sugar and coffee barrels used to smuggle a grand quantity of pieces of eight to Sebastian, and an even larger cache to someone assisted by a Mr. Riddle, he would surely not have planned to entrust Clark with a confidential mission when he returned to the line.[16]

23

Mr. Clark, Anxious to Pursue His Journey

O
N Sunday evening, July 8, Clark pushed off from the Natchez landing in the vessel he had recently purchased—probably a broad canoe-like dugout of native cypress, perhaps a smaller version of the pirogues he and the Corps of Discovery would take up the Missouri six years hence. The Mississippi spread wide to the west but he held close to the eastern bank. Hoping to avoid camping in the pestiferous lowlands, he found a house offering overnight accommodation. Of that day he writes only, "Set out down the River in a pireogue, Stay at Mr. Farrows."

Returning to the river the next morning, Clark availed himself of the opportunity to observe once again some of the strategic spots he'd noted back in April. One of the most important of these was Loftus Heights, the promontory on which Captain Guion planned to erect a fort. But if Clark stopped near there he soon pressed on, pulling ashore not far downstream at the landing of the wealthiest man in the Mississippi Territory—Daniel Clark Sr., uncle and mentor of the New Orleans trader. Having consigned business affairs to his nephew, the elder Daniel now split his time between "Clark's Ville," his riverside house some four miles above the thirty-first parallel, and "The Desert," his estate a short ride to the east.[1]

He counted among his friends Captain Guion, Andrew Ellicott, James Wilkinson, and William Clark's brother-in-law Richard Clough Anderson. Lively and personable, Daniel was recovering from a recent hard bout of an intermittent fever. Hoping the United States rather than Spain or France would take possession of the entire Mississippi valley, he wanted Wilkinson to lead an expedition ousting the Spanish from Louisiana and then to serve as its governor.[2]

Having recorded nothing about Daniel Sr. beyond his surname, William left the pirogue behind the next morning and followed a road from Clark's Ville to the boundary camp at the Little Bayou Sara. He could see that, in many ways, nothing there had changed during his absence. Workers and soldiers continued coming down with symptoms of malaria, and William Dunbar, probably suffering from the same disorder, was still at his Natchez plantation. Betsy remained at camp, and the struggle between Ellicott and Freeman raged on. Further, storms that had begun in June kept pounding the area with heavy rain, causing food to molder and tents to rot.[3]

Yet some aspects of life at the parallel were noticeably different from the way they were at William's first visit. The finished boundary, for example, was a mile longer. Having recently arrived to augment the labor force, a crew of slaves was preparing to open the westernmost portion of the line as soon as Dunbar returned to plot the necessary coordinates. And documents reaching Ellicott on or around July 7 satisfied him that Minor, Dunbar, and Power were indeed the authorized representatives of Spain. As Minor wrote to Governor Gayoso about Ellicott:

> the arrival of our commissions has acted like a charm upon his mind and disposition. He is now so fully convinced of your . . . good faith, the uprightness and purity of your views, and so vexed with himself for his incredulity and obstinacy that he can hardly give utterance to his sentiments and the injustice he formerly did . . . in doubting of your sincerity. [It] is now amply made up by the high oppinion he entertains of your integrity and honor, on which he is at present so firmly fixed that nothing less than some signal breach of one or the other could operate an alteration in his sentiments.[4]

But Clark wrote just that he "Went to the line." Omitting mention of an opinion or a conception formed about what was going on there might well have been due in part to habit. Letting pass an opportunity to record the names of important individuals, however, was not.

* * *

Even so, he made the acquaintance of John McKee, a friend of Thomas Freeman. Of wide forehead and florid complexion, McKee could have passed for a kinsman of Clark. Just a year younger, the Virginia-born McKee had a lineage and upbringing that could have been envied by the less formally taught Clark. McKee was first cousin to young Sam Houston, future president of the Republic of Texas, and an alumnus of Liberty Hall Academy (now Washington and Lee University). An early portrait and a later one by artist William Edward West depict an elegantly attired man, with watchful eyes and a slightly mocking tilt to his lips that convey an overall impression of breeding as well as of calculation.[5]

William Edward West's portrait of John McKee, circa 1820.

McKee was at the line because, as a protégé of William Blount (the former U.S. senator from Tennessee, whose plot to raise the value of his own frontier acreage by inciting war on neighboring lands was exposed in 1797), he was suspected of complicity in that scheme. To distance himself from it (although to some extent he had likely been involved in it) and to salvage his political future, McKee aimed to make himself indispensable to the Federalist government. Having promised to "do whatever may be in my power to be useful," he was, at the request of the Adams administration, trying to turn Indian tribes of the southwest frontier against Spain before war pitted that nation and France against the United States.[6]

As if to hedge his bets, McKee was also gathering intelligence. Much of it concerned suspected principals in the Spanish Conspiracy, especially Wilkinson, Sebastian, Nolan, and Power. So familiar was McKee with twists of the various plots between officials of Spanish Louisiana and prominent Americans, he may have suspected Clark's connection with Sebastian, Brown, and the ultimate recipient of the 670 Spanish dollars Clark had sent upriver.[7]

Stifling any misgivings he may have felt about McKee, Clark agreed to accompany him back to New Orleans. Clark wrote only of being "at the line [where I] Sent my pirogue round to Meet me at Tunecow." (He meant Tunica, a downstream landing more convenient to his travels than Clark's Ville was.) He waited for Commissioner Ellicott to finish a letter to the secretary of state. Three weeks having elapsed since Ellicott last wrote Pickering, he now had more information to forward than his opening comment suggests: "I have but little to communicate since my dispatches of the 19th Ultimo . . . which, being very lengthy and *Mr. Clarke, the bearer of this, anxious to pursue his journey*, renders it impossible for me to enclose duplicates [emphasis added]."[8]

As Clark stood by, Ellicott enumerated recent events—Dunbar's prolonged absence, the slow advance of the boundary work, the arrival of the Spanish commissions—and interspersed remarks calculated to resonate favorably with Pickering. Not until midway through the letter did Ellicott write about Freeman's and McClary's recalcitrance, but then he fumed, "Unless the surveyor and commandant of the military escort are to be under my direction, I cannot consider myself responsible for the execution of the work." In other words, Ellicott was threatening to quit if the government failed to confirm his authority over the mutineers.[9]

He closed and sealed the communication, including with it figures on current export duties and tariff reductions, a recent copy of the New Orleans newspaper *Le Moniteur de la Louisiane*, and an earlier issue announcing an auspicious start to the boundary project. He handed the packet to Clark, evidently judging him a more trustworthy messenger than McKee. Ellicott, it seems, also gave Clark a bill promising payment from the U.S. Treasury of the fifteen hundred Spanish silver dollars he had smuggled to the boundary line.[10]

Perhaps Ellicott did not realize that Clark and McKee were carrying mail for the Spanish commission too. Indeed, for the past four days Minor had been writing Gayoso messages detailing what was going on at the line. By July 12 there were six of them, five in fluent Spanish, but none was marked *reservada* (classified) or *sumamente reservada* (top secret). Serving as the cover letter, the one in English identifies the bearers as "Col. McKee and Lieut. Clark."[11]

No doubt aware of Captain Guion's decree forbidding Americans from carrying Spanish governmental correspondence, McKee and Clark nonetheless took Minor's communications and probably one from surveyor Thomas Power, formerly the messenger linking Governor Carondelet with the members of the Spanish Conspiracy. McKee accepted the letters not because he cared to earn favor with Spanish Louisiana but because he was instead determined to lock down his career as a federal bureaucrat. What about Clark? Was he open to the possibility of advancing his own interests by promoting those of Spain? As ever, the Mississippi Journal offers little elucidation on that or other difficult but pertinent questions. For reasons now unknown, Clark failed to write anything about Ellicott, Minor, Freeman, and Power, and he would make only cursory mention of McKee a week or two hence when they sailed from New Orleans on the same ship, although all those men must have impressed him with their knowledge or influence.[12]

He and McKee headed south over a rough road joining the camp with the Tunica landing; there they climbed aboard Clark's pirogue and proceeded downriver. After writing "Set Sale from Tunecow which is about 7 miles from the line," Clark recorded nothing until reaching New Orleans four days later. During that time he may have refined his chart of the Mississippi River, especially at Pointe Coupée; his map shows revisions to the contours of the left and right banks at that strategic position. Lamentably, the only clues Clark left about what he did as the pirogue glided downstream are the faint squiggles of partially erased cartographic lines.

If he and the classically educated McKee looked at *Le Moniteur de la Louisiana* (probably one of the few unsealed documents in their keeping), they could have learned that although "La Goelette [schooner] l'Active, Cap. Nathaniel Wilcox, pour Newyork" had departed on June 21, "le Brig Americain Friendship, Cap. Arnold, de Philadelphie" and "la Fregate Americaine Star," also "de Philadelphie," were getting ready to leave New Orleans. To sail onboard either of these, Clark would have to return promptly to New Orleans.[13]

The newspaper announced, too, that the Spanish government was suspending duties on exported goods but not on silver or gold coins. Therefore, unless visitors had a special exemption, their reales must stay within the Spanish realm "under pain of confiscation, and other penalties by the law." A further article said that King George III had authorized the British navy to seize foreign ships and cargoes departing Spanish possessions. *Le Moniteur de la Louisiane* reported that French privateers continued to capture commercial vessels in the waters between Louisiana and the West Indies. Such accounts gave Clark and McKee fresh reason to wonder whether sailing for Philadelphia was worth the risks.[14]

Somewhere above New Orleans their pirogue came upon a royal Spanish galley carrying upriver Judge Benjamin Sebastian and his son Alfred, a soldier in the Louisiana Regiment. Perhaps rowing close enough to eavesdrop on Benjamin's conversation (probably with Clark), McKee learned the judge had been "treated with marked attention" during his recent stay in the city. McKee also inferred that Benjamin had gone there on clandestine business involving Governor Gayoso. McKee elaborated: "It is said he [Judge Sebastian] was about reviving a correspondence between certain disaffected characters" of Kentucky with Spain, in a plot originally devised to tear "the western country, particularly Kentucky, from the Union."[15]

Whatever Clark uttered, he must have been careful not to let on about his smuggling collaboration with Sebastian and Brown; the glib McKee was to pass along nothing of that nature. And, because Brown and his crewmen were too sick to travel, they and the boat holding William Clark's silver-laden sugar and coffee barrels were so far downstream they likely never came near the pirogue. Yet Sebastian's impressive mode of transport made it clear that he was still important to Spanish Louisiana and gave Clark, if he knew anything about Governor Gayoso's meeting with Sebastian and Brown, reason to believe the monopoly they wanted might yet win royal approval.

24

I Take a Passage on the Ship *Star*

OF July 16, 1798, William Clark wrote only "Arrive at New Orleans," adding nothing about what he did with the pirogue or where McKee went when they got there. Presumably Clark delivered Minor's letters, McKee having earlier run afoul of Gayoso because of the Blount affair. By nightfall Clark was back at Madame Chabaud's. Lacking any cured pork to barter, he agreed to pay cash for room and board.[1]

The house was stirring with other lodgers, many of them having sailed to town on Daniel W. Coxe's ship *Star* and brig *Friendship*. Daniel himself, his kinsman Charles Coxe, and any servants who had accompanied them from Philadelphia were no doubt present. Probably captains Joseph Woodman and Andrew Arnold were too. Whether McKee also stayed there is not known, but soon he decided to sail aboard the *Star* when she returned to Philadelphia.[2]

A year older than William, Coxe was an experienced businessman, having worked for the international mercantile firm of his elder brother, Tench, then for that of Reed and Forde, a pioneer in commerce between the United States and Spanish Louisiana. For the past several years, Daniel Coxe and Daniel Clark Jr. had been trading American goods for those of the lower Mississippi valley and other Spanish territories. Despite occasional setbacks such as war-related slowdowns and losses to privateers, their association was lucrative.[3]

Each partner brought the other unique assets. Coxe owned a string of vessels he accompanied as often as possible and dealt with bankers, politicians, and insurance underwriters eager to profit from facilitating

Etching (1798) made from Fevret de Saint-Mémin's portrait of Daniel W. Coxe.

international commerce. Though lacking his own fleet, Clark Jr. possessed charisma and skill at persuading Spanish officials to relax regulations, especially those involving the smuggling of hard cash or the evasion of export charges. The efforts of the Daniels opened a flow of desperately needed coined money to the Eastern seaboard, connected Louisiana with elite Americans and their European contacts, and made the partners rich.[4]

No doubt Tench Coxe was responsible for some of Daniel's success. In 1790 Tench became a high official in the U.S. Treasury Department, a position enabling him to help his younger brother cash foreign drafts received in payment. Being more interested in formulating a strong economic base for the nation than he was in complying with the routine of government bureaucracy, though, Tench was dismissed in December 1797.

He swiftly cut ties to Federalism and aligned himself with the Democratic-Republican opposition. To tide over his own large family (his wife would bear their eleventh child in 1802) until he secured another public appointment, Tench directed Daniel's business during his long absences. After several years of casting about for government work, Tench was to become purveyor of public supplies for the United States, just after his predecessor, Israel Whelan, provided all manner of goods for the Lewis and Clark Expedition.[5]

Daniel Coxe, however, owed most of his prosperity to Clark Jr.'s expertise in smuggling money out of Louisiana and in placing judicious bribes with corrupt Spanish officials. So long as international relations allowed, the Daniels planned to continue profiting on cargoes, both legal and illicit, shipped from New Orleans to Philadelphia and other ports. Expecting the long-awaited Spanish compliance with Pinckney's Treaty to generate even more business for themselves, Coxe wanted to expand his fleet, the greater part of which was moored not far from the Chabaud house.[6]

William Clark must have been impressed to see the brig and the ship, each painted a warlike black. Fortified with six small but effective cannons, *Friendship* belied the goodwill implicit in her name. Larger and fitted out even more fiercely, the *Star* appeared the equal of all but the most heavily armed privateers. Both vessels were reliable at sea. The three-masted *Star* could haul a payload of 263 tons, and the double-masted *Friendship* had two-thirds her capacity. Like most cargo vessels of her size, *Star* required careful steering when tidal and freshwater currents created shallows over the silty bar separating the Mississippi from the Gulf. At such times, safety depended on cautious loading, but the two vessels occasionally rode low in the water because the partners disliked sacrificing cargoes for freeboard.[7]

The *Star* and the *Friendship* had been riding even lower since Coxe outfitted them with tons of firepower in the spring. The *Star* received eight small cannons capable of shooting six-pound balls, along with a quartet of four-pounders. At the same time the *Friendship* was equipped with a pair of six-pounders and two three-pound guns. Thereafter Coxe continued arming the ship and brig with large artillery and also with muskets, shot, boarding pikes, and langrage to shred enemy sails and rigging.[8]

Coxe took particular pleasure in knowing that all forty crewmen of the ship and the entire twenty-five-man complement of the brig were staunch Americans soon to be trained by a gunner—evidently Richard Clark, Daniel Jr.'s brother. Happy also that no one of French or Spanish extraction booked passage on the ship or brig, Coxe expected his passengers to help defend the vessels if they came under attack.[9]

During June and July the *Friendship* and the *Star* were loaded. The brig took on ten tons of Campeche logwood (valuable for ballast and as a source of purplish-red dye) and hundreds of cowhides. The ship received lead plates and logwood to stabilize her, tin lanterns, indigo, two hundred pounds of tobacco, sacks of peppers, deer hides, and bearskins—perhaps William Clark's. Last of all, bales of cotton went anywhere they would fit.[10]

On July 19, a customs officer came onboard the vessels to appraise their cargoes and compute the export tax owed on them. To do so he also took into account the nautical fare in their larders—brined beef and pork, rice, crackers, red wine, rum, and butter—and six-dozen chickens likely cooped on their aft decks. Despite his detailed notes, he recorded nothing about the most lucrative payload the *Star* would haul—at least 1,351 Spanish dollars nevertheless mentioned in the bill of lading. From this incident, and what we know about the partners' reliance on bribery, we can assume the Spanish official received under-the-table compensation for omitting mention of the money.[11]

No longer wondering how best to leave the province, William Clark wrote, "Take a passage in the Ship Star for Philadelphia preparing untill the 25th for a sale. Wind contrary." He had his clothes washed and purchased a quire of paper, giving sixty cents for the twenty-five sheets. Silent about what he did for three days until July 23, when he had another load of laundry cleaned and bought trousers and more "sundries," he squared accounts one last time with Madame Chabaud and gave eighty-three dollars for passage and provisions on the *Star*. He presented his bags at the customhouse where he received a document signed by Gayoso and promising, in Castilian, free and safe passage out of Louisiana. Then Clark moved aboard the ship, joining others awaiting the right weather conditions to begin the voyage.[12]

On Friday morning, July 27, the wind became northerly, prompting the captains to haul in gangplanks and cables linking ship and brig to the shore. Soon they were gliding down the last hundred miles of the Mississippi. Eager to experience a blue-water voyage, Clark must have watched from the deck of the *Star* as familiar scenes, and eventually the entire city, seemed to dissolve into the horizon. If his slave York accompanied him, he surely watched too.

Because the river near New Orleans runs east in long reaches before angling southward, he began mapping it again in small, disconnected sections, perhaps doing so openly because there were no Spanish onboard. Near the site of the future suburb of Arabi, he calculated having covered 904 miles of the Mississippi from the mouth of the Ohio. Compared with Zadok Cramer's figures of a few years later, Clark's were short by 10 percent, but he continued accurately drawing bends and bayous along the route.[13]

He must have noticed the reemergence of sugar plantations, but those now before him were poorer and smaller than the upstream estates he had so admired in April. Not far below the city, the land became too soggy for agriculture; from there to the Gulf he would see little cultivation of any sort. Although cypresses hemmed the shore for miles around, the farther south they grew, the scrawnier they appeared. But the levees of mud deposited by floods continued beyond the last bend in the river.

Some fifteen miles below New Orleans the brig and ship entered the upper leg of a circle called English Turn; vessels sailing there often slowed because breezes favorable in one section became headwinds in another, sometimes forcing crews to put to shore for a spell. At the terminus of the bend stood the remains of Fort St. Leon, a stronghold erected a half-century earlier, and on the opposite bank were the ruins of an even older outpost called St. Marie; both works had been built by the French to keep British ships from ascending to New Orleans.[14]

Perhaps emboldened by the prospect of leaving Spanish territory, Clark composed his longest entry yet of the journey and resumed his earlier practice of naming noteworthy men: "27th July. Set Sale in the ship Star of 6 guns for Philadelphia Droped down the river the Passengers in the Ship

27th July set sail in the ship
Star of 6 guns for Philadelphia
Dropped down the river the
Passengers in the ship were Mr D
W Lea owns Col. ? Meeker, Mr B
Chew two Mr. Creggs Mr. Martin
Cap Nolin, Cap R. Clark &
about 40 men accompanied
by a brig of 4 guns — Drop.d
down passed the Fort Plick
in the 30th. this fort is strong
and regular, built of Buck
mounting about 12 heavy
cannon a the front & some
small cannon. a small
round fort opposit
is on the West line rover
mounting 16 cannon from
4 to 9 pounders, from this
fort to the Baliza is open
marsh about 30 miles, we
anchored at night found
a Spanish ship Miss. of 16 Guns
& a Brig of same.

William Clark's journal entries as the ship *Star* departs New Orleans, from page 22 of his 1798–1801 Notebook.

was Mr. D W Cox owner Col. J. McKee, Mr. B Chew two Mr. Cregs Mr. Martin Cap. Nolin, Cap Rd Clark & about 40 Men accompanied by a brig of 8 guns."

He may have realized that several of those individuals, including at least one of his fellow boarders at the Chabaud house, were also skilled at surveillance. Daniel Coxe, for instance, had kept clandestine notes during a 1797 river voyage to New Orleans. While claiming to have traveled there to check on goods and markets, he had secretly assayed the prospects for Spanish compliance with Pinckney's Treaty, sending Tench confidential reports about Spanish defenses and the disposition toward the United States of those in charge of the province. In turn, Tench forwarded this intelligence to Secretary Pickering—who released it (without Daniel's permission) to President Adams.[15]

Another shipmate with arcane knowledge was Beverly Chew, an entrepreneur in his mid-twenties who a year earlier had left his home in Fredericksburg, Virginia, for a commercial career in New Orleans. There he became acquainted with the younger Daniel Clark and Wilkinson's operative Philip Nolan, both of them authorities on the various turns of the Spanish Conspiracy. To his friend John McKee (perhaps the most adept spy aboard *Star*), Chew passed details Nolan had gathered about the source of General Wilkinson's illegal reales.[16]

The "two Mr. Cregs" Clark mentions may have been Americans Joseph Craig, a seller of flour and tobacco, and Elisha Craig, a man believing a trusted source who said General Wilkinson held a commission in the Spanish armed forces. The truth is he did not, but he let it be known south of the thirty-first parallel that given enough reales, he would consider commanding Spanish forces.[17]

* * *

Some sixty-five miles below New Orleans, the Coxe flotilla entered a broad curve known as Plaquemines Bend, a name based on the French adaptation of an Indian word for the wild persimmons that once grew there. The vessels soon passed within gun range of Fort San Felipe, the largest, most heavily armed Spanish stronghold in Louisiana. Constructed on marshland from 1792 until 1795, the post completed Governor Caron-delet's design to secure the lower Mississippi River against invaders, par-ticularly the French and their friends (including George Rogers Clark).[18]

Of all strategic locations in Louisiana, this was the one most worth Wilkinson's effort to learn about. He had not yet seen it. Maybe it was also the place Clark referred to in 1797 when he wrote an unidentified Army officer about carrying out their mutual plan. According to that scheme, Clark was to take a load of tobacco to an unspecified downstream destination, thereby to "visit Point Sarlle mearly to See and find out the advantage." (Lacking a Spanish word for persimmon, a New World fruit resembling a European plum, it seems the Spanish could have referred to Plaquemines Bend as "Punto [Point] de Ciruelas," or "Point Sarlle" to Clark's ear.)[19]

The military advantage there was obvious. Fort San Felipe was a mas-sive complex crowned with at least ten large-caliber cannons trained on the Mississippi. Built to shelter up to three hundred soldiers and the hun-dred slaves who worked full-time to maintain it, the outpost stood next to Mardi Gras Creek, site of anchorage for royal war galleys. Because the forces of nature, especially wind, tide, and river currents, often worked in concert to push vessels toward the fort, Carondelet had expected the battery atop it to

> cover the vessels ascending against the current, first from stem to stern, and then broadside, and lastly, from stern to stem. However favorable may be the wind, no frigate can escape drawing the fire of the fort, at least for a quarter of an hour, and if the east wind is not blowing it will be absolutely necessary to anchor under the cannon of the fort of San Felipe.[20]

On the other side of the river stood Fort Bourbon, a smaller installation designed to work in tandem with Fort San Felipe. According to Caronde-let, Fort Bourbon "was for the double purpose of dismasting the up-bound vessels near the shore and thus making them fall under the fire of the fort of San Felipe, and of allowing a protection to the militia who should advance lower down to harass the enemy in their maneuvers and prepara-tions by favor of the thickets and fallen trees which crown the bank in that region." To increase the ability of gunners at Fort San Felipe to blow holes in canvas and to destroy masts and hulls, Carondelet had that site elevated with tons of borrowed earth. A trench twelve feet deep ran around the structure, the better to protect a large powder magazine within it.[21]

As the *Star* drew closer to Fort San Felipe, Clark could see that the center portion of its front wall projected inward as if following a natural cleft in the shoreline, but not until he was downstream might he appreciate how asymmetrical the post really was. Perhaps he noticed a slight sag from the weight of guns, bricks, and beams pressing it into muck. Nevertheless, because it rested on piles driven twenty feet into the earth (and was later reinforced and rebuilt for the U.S. military), it would help defend the southern frontier of the United States for more than a century—except for one year (1861–1862) when Confederate forces controlled it.[22]

Within shooting distance of the most intimidating bulwark he had ever seen, Clark must have been careful upon noting the latitude and strategic features of the site, or penning another lengthy entry: "Dropd Down passed the Fort Pluk in the 30th [parallel]. This fort is Strong and regular, built of Brick Mounting about 12 heavy Cannons {12 to 24 pd.} on the front & Som Small cannon a Small round fort opposit is on the West Side round Mounting 16 Cannon from 4 to 9 pounders, from this fort to the Baliza is open marsh about 30 miles."

Fort San Felipe was also an inspection station where, by law, departing vessels of all registries and sizes were to pause long enough for government officers to check cargoes and papers. Daniel Coxe, however, was unwilling to pay any more officials to overlook his stashes of silver coins. Instead, he had his ships continue downstream before dropping anchor for the night, beyond reach of the cannon-shot of the forts.[23]

25

An Insult to His Majesty

PROCEEDING farther the next day, the *Star* and the *Friendship* traveled beyond Head of Passes, the point where the river splits into chutes to join the Gulf of Mexico. Although a large portion of the Mississippi sluices off to the southwest, the vessels nonetheless followed a course mostly to the southeast. Because neither wind nor tide then favored a safe crossing of the silty bar at the very end of that corridor (called Southeast Pass, the widest and deepest channel then linking fresh with salt water), the ships dropped anchor. Immediately to starboard was the Baliza, the southernmost Spanish station of Louisiana. Officials there sent notice they wished to perform a routine inspection of vessels and passports, but Coxe again refused to allow one.[1]

Such intransigence was dangerous to everyone on his craft. Although the Baliza complex included a lighthouse and quarters for delta pilots, it also garrisoned units of the Spanish army and navy. Those forces possessed several pieces of large ordnance and a streamlined war galley that must have reminded William Clark of Gayoso's *La Vigilante* with its six swivel guns and a much larger cannon. Also at the Baliza was the first in a series of signal cannons enabling troops at the far edge of the delta to send a call for help from Fort San Felipe and to fire warnings which, outpost to outpost, would reach New Orleans in minutes. Although he was surely aware of the potentially hostile military presence around him, Clark made bold to describe it: "This place is in a marsh on rased land about three feet where about 8 Huts & a Block house & lookout, in which is 2 six pds. [pounders, for the weight of the shot they fired] & 4 swivels, a galley with one 18 pd. & 6 swivs, and about 50 Spanish salers & soldiers on the West Side & on an outleat."[2]

He had never been so far south, and seldom in such a brackish or tree-less environment. Both fresh and salt water nourished the plants he be-held—reeds, palmettos, alligator grasses—as well as the shrimp, crayfish, and other underwater creatures he could not see. Attuned to the value of pelts, he must have known that otters, muskrats, and beavers flourished in the marshes. Clark may have watched Eastern brown pelicans—eventual-ly to become the state bird of Louisiana, and then vanish for years because of pesticides—diving for fish. He might have reflected that the Baliza installation was the only distinguishing feature in the vast flatness where oyster grass and black rushes took root on long ribbons of silt tapering out toward the Gulf between currents the color of dusty twilight. So swift was the water here, falling overboard was said to be deadlier than tumbling into the thousand-foot depths a hundred miles beyond.

Daniel Coxe was determined nonetheless to get to sea as soon as pos-sible, Spanish regulations be damned. One of them required him to hire a professional pilot to steer down the last miles of Mississippi and across the bar. A similar rule still applies—not only at this outflowing but also around the world, where navigable rivers join the sea. The law of Spain, however, explicitly forbade anyone but her own officers from performing that duty and related ones such as sounding the depths.[3]

Even so, Coxe refused to take on a pilot and had one of his own sailors gauge the fathoms beneath. To do this, a crewman holding a lead plumb tethered to a long, marked rope walked to the rail and commenced swing-ing the weight in wide circles. He played out the line until, at the right moment, he allowed the heavy pendant to drop into the water and sink to the bottom; afterward he pulled it in and measured the wet section of line. Those acts being impossible to disguise, they drew the attention of Juan Ronquillo, an official who for more than three decades had a monopoly on piloting operations at the Baliza. (Spain had awarded him that concession for captaining the ship which, in 1766, brought the first Spanish governor, Antonio de Ulloa, to Louisiana.) Ronquillo seldom steered vessels any-more, but he supervised numerous assistants, monitored nautical arrivals and departures, oversaw customs inspections, and sent regular reports to New Orleans. He received annually 360 pieces of eight, a much larger salary than what he paid his deputy pilots.[4]

To encourage him to remain at the isolated but strategic post, Spanish officials seldom interfered with his administration, even to counter blatant disobedience. For instance, although ordered to mark the main channel of the river, Ronquillo instead forbade his men to do so, giving the lie to the very name Baliza (derived from *balise*, French for buoy) on the pretext that making the navigation lane obvious would reduce demand for pilotage. During inclement weather he often declined sending his deputies beyond the passes to meet traffic, forcing inbound ships to struggle unassisted across the bar or to remain at sea until the weather cleared. When vessels ran aground, he made extra money by hiring his men out to perform salvage operations.[5]

For the present, though, Ronquillo and the military officers at the Baliza, particularly Lieutenant Francisco Borras of the Louisiana infantry and Lieutenant Bernardo Molina, commander of the war galley Clark noted, grappled with the question of how much defiance they should let pass before enforcing the law against Coxe and his flotilla. There was little precedent to direct them; most Americans in the delta complied with Spanish nautical regulations because they were similar to those of other countries. Unable yet to decide what to do about Coxe's disobedience, Ronquillo, Borras, and Molina resolved to keep an eye on him and his vessels.

* * *

On July 31 (or August 1, depending on whether you believe the date in Clark's journal or the one in Spanish records), a renegade privateer with three American merchant ships under her control sailed out of the Gulf and headed straight for the *Star* and the *Friendship*. Of more than a hundred men to witness this event, William Clark was evidently the only one to leave a complete, surviving narrative of it and of what was to follow. He opens with typical directness: "at the Baliza about 3 oClock arrived in View a French Privutier of 4 Guns & 50 Men, with two American Prises taken in the gulf bound to N. Y. [New York] & C. Town [Charleston,

South Carolina] from   The P.T. [privateer] come up & anchered near us at Dark   all prepared."

The privateer was the schooner *Hennique* (also called the *Creole*), and her commander was François Michel Moreau. Daniel Clark Jr. and Governor Gayoso detested Moreau; the previous year he had seized four American merchant vessels and brought them for condemnation at New Orleans. Because Spain had not then implemented the provision of Pinckney's Treaty allowing the United States to establish a consul in Louisiana, no one there had the standing to hold Moreau's actions to the international protocols regulating privateering. But Governor Gayoso, heartily sick of that practice because it interfered with vital commerce and often threatened to explode into an international dispute, had begun to allow Daniel Clark Jr. (though still a Spanish subject) to act as if he was an American consul. Doing so suited Daniel Jr.; he wished to make a favorable impression on the United States, the nation he expected to acquire Louisiana before long.[6]

Calling himself the American "interim vice-consul," he took Moreau to court over those 1797 captures, getting him to admit having forged a French commission conferring ostensible license to pillage. Moreau also acknowledged ransacking the cargoes of the prizes under his command and putting their captains ashore without papers, supplies, or even a change of clothes, only to recapture them on the streets of New Orleans. Yet the prospect of other maritime plunder was so irresistible to him, he eventually slipped back out to sea.[7]

Now he was returning with fresh captives—the schooner *Apollo* of Charleston, South Carolina, and the ship *Mars* and schooner *Sunbury Packet*, both of them of New York City—along with their payloads of mahogany and logwood. At New Orleans, Moreau planned to commence legal proceedings, which he hoped would yield him the right to sell the booty and keep the proceeds. With him on the *Hennique* were the shackled captains and crewmen of the prizes; steering those craft were Moreau's own sailors. Larger and slower than *Apollo* and *Sunbury Packet*, the *Mars* was still out in the Gulf.[8]

The arrival of the *Hennique* and her captured vessels was William Clark's first direct experience with privateering, an ancient practice that allowed nations without strong navies to commission, through letters of marque, privately owned ships to capture enemy craft. Until some years after the establishment of the Navy Department in April 1798, the United States relied heavily on privateers to protect the Atlantic Coast, commissioning more than a thousand of them during the Revolutionary War and more than five hundred to fight the War of 1812. International law allowed authorized privateers to seize vessels and to have them and their cargoes condemned and sold at auction, the captor receiving the proceeds less a portion allocated to his country. Privateering was outlawed in 1856 by a declaration to which most nations have long since subscribed.

Although in 1796 French vessels protested Jay's Treaty with England by preying on American shipping, such depredations increased dramatically when France declared that neutral craft—such as American merchant ships—holding any item of British origin were fair prizes. England countered with a similar policy against vessels bearing French items. As a result of both orders, captains of that era kept a variety of flags ready in order to disguise the nationality of their ships.

In the waning daylight, Clark observed the *Hennique* bearing down on Coxe's vessels as if intending to seize them. Such obvious aggression alarmed Commander Molina and Lt. Borras, for if the newcomer was truly attempting to take prizes in the river rather than at sea, she was breaking international law and endangering the peace of Louisiana. Molina and Borras could not risk either event happening. To protect Coxe's vessels— and to give Spanish forces room to maneuver the war galley against the *Hennique*—they sent the *Star* instructions in Spanish: Take your craft two or three leagues upstream before the schooner comes nearer.[9]

But Coxe, having refused to allow onboard a pilot or anyone able to translate the message, had no idea what it said and therefore did nothing. His ships stayed put as Moreau's schooner pulled next to them after dusk and dropped anchor. Molina and Borras kept their forces alert and ready to man their guns. So did Coxe's crewmen. "All prepared," Clark says of that uneasy night.

At sunup he heard seamen conversing in a foreign tongue; his haphazard penmanship may refer to it as "Dutch," a common term then for a Germanic language. He recorded the date as August 1—his twenty-eighth birthday—and marked it by joining Coxe and other shipmates paying a visit to the *Hennique*. There Coxe invited the fettered captains—Archibald McCorkill of *Mars*, William Oliver of *Apollo*, and Amariel Williams of *Sunbury Packet*—to breakfast. They accepted and, with Moreau's permission, left the privateer for the *Star*. Clark states tersely, "I go on bord find the Capts. of three A. [American] Vestles taken by her on bord & ther salors in Irons, + two prises then in View off the bar. we envite the {Captive} Captains to brackft. with [us] they axceped the invirtation & the French Cap. Did not Object."

After breakfast, Coxe demanded the prisoners but Moreau refused to free them. Coxe insisted, and finally Moreau suggested they take their dispute to land. Not perceiving the trap being set for him, Coxe assented. Soon he and Moreau were arguing loud enough for the Spanish to overhear Coxe threatening to blow holes in the *Hennique* and liberate her prizes. Such acts if carried out would violate international law and threaten to touch off war with the United States; the Spanish had to intervene.[10]

But what to do? Having never dealt with an American quite like the patently contemptuous but well-connected Coxe, Borras and Molina dispatched an express message to New Orleans, asking Governor Gayoso's counsel. Until they had it, they would keep Coxe, his vessels, and gunner Richard Clark close at hand. But because Moreau had committed no infraction they were commissioned to deal with, they gave him leave to take his schooner and booty upriver. Clark observed as the "Prises Came up under Am: cullors passed us about a miles & anchored." Coxe sent word to New Orleans too, telling his partner of Moreau's reappearance and latest captures. Blind to the problems caused by his own hubris, Coxe promised to cruise the coast for *Mars*, take her by force, and escort her to Philadelphia.[11]

Meanwhile, William Clark kept a lookout. On August 2–3, he found nothing worth noting, but on August 4, he made up for that silence: "At 3 oClock a Sale in Sight from the East. . . . The Wind continu from the rong quarter to allow us to pass the bar wich is about 14 french feet & reguires & Northerly wind to pass it, being narrow Say 50 yards."

Coxe's message reached his partner on August 6, the same day Captains Oliver, McCorkill, and Williams arrived at New Orleans and sought recourse against Moreau. Eager to help them, Clark Jr. wrote Andrew Ellicott, the highest U.S. official he knew in the Mississippi Territory, and asked him to notify the federal government of Moreau's most recent seizures, the "piratical depredations of the French Privateers." The letter closes on an optimistic note, making special mention of William Clark:

> The Ship *Mars*, one of the three vessels lately taken, has not yet got in, and I entertain the pleasing hope that she may yet be met with and retaken by the American Armed Ship *Star* & Brig *Friendship*, which were waiting at the Balize for a wind to proceed to Sea when the two Schooners and the Privateer arrived. These vessels belong to Mr. Daniel W. Coxe of Philada. who is on board the Ship *Star* mounting 16 Guns and has a number of resolute Americans with him among whom are Col. McKee, *Mr. Clark, late of the American Army*, Mr. Chew, and my Brother who goes in order [to] command the Ship in case of coming to action [emphasis added].[12]

Little did Clark Jr. guess, traveling in the opposite direction was an order from Gayoso directing Molina and Borras to apprehend Coxe and Richard Clark and send them to New Orleans. That arrest warrant reached the Baliza on August 7, but before Spanish forces could act on it, Coxe had his vessels set sail for the Gulf. Realizing what they were doing, Molina and Borras stormed aboard the Spanish galley and took off in pursuit, their crews rowing while artillerymen aimed the huge cannon at the slower-moving *Star* and *Friendship*.

Seeing the juggernaut bearing down on his ship and brig, Coxe called a halt just one river-mile from where they had weighed anchor. He reversed direction, ascended the pass, and returned to the Baliza. Gathering around him a cohort including William Clark, Coxe went to the royal blockhouse, intending to remonstrate against being kept in the delta, and to accuse the Spanish of favoring Moreau.

The time for making such points, however, was over; Coxe's attempt to flee forced Molina, Borras, and Ronquillo to deal sternly with him and Richard Clark, commander of the guns that would have been turned on the *Hennique* during the illegal liberation attempt. Rather than being allowed to express indignation, Coxe and Richard were taken into custody and summoned to the capital on charges of insulting the king's territorial right by trying to liberate the prizes. As if unaware that Coxe had flouted numerous regulations, nearly caused a battle with Moreau, and almost provoked the Spanish to sink the *Star*, William Clark makes another long entry: "7th. Drop down about one mile in this act the Spaniards were much alarmed & Came out of Bio [bayou] to the p[o]int with the galley & appeared to be preparing for action, we went to Shore & the officer informed (after our acused him of partialately [partiality] to the F. P. T.) [French privateer] informed us that he had orders to Stop us, this information astonish{d} as we knew of no cause."

Molina and Borras returned the Americans to their vessels, promising to send for Coxe and Richard Clark at midafternoon, and adding that everyone else would then be free to continue the voyage if they wished. Coxe passed the next few hours organizing his legal defense and writing letters, at least one of them to an official of Spanish Louisiana. Soon William Clark saw "4 Men in a yaule [yawl]" row to the *Star*, pick up Daniel and Richard, and take them upstream.

* * *

The next day, August 8, the captured *Mars* stopped just beyond the pass, the wind and tide facilitating outbound traffic. William surely appreciated the irony of at last having ideal conditions to leave the Mississippi and sail into the Gulf, but lacking two people essential to that voyage. A Spanish officer dropped by the following morning and picked up Coxe's letters. In his diary, Clark ascribed the arrests to "a miss representation of the offens at this place in informing the Govr of our insulting him & violateing the rights of his scoverigt." Whether he understood that Coxe provoked the detention by trying to free the prizes—an act that, if successful, would have violated Spain's right to review the legality of Moreau's captures—is not clear.

Later that day, Lt. Borras visited the *Star* to remind those onboard they were free to leave. Although they'd already decided to remain in the delta, at least until learning what had happened to Coxe and Richard Clark, William and six of his fellows boarded a smaller craft, sailed out of the river, and called on the captive *Mars*. William does not say whether he was sizing her up for liberation or just satisfying his curiosity, but on finding her "in possession of about 6 or 8 french and 12 or 14 [Spanish] pilots," he returned to the *Star* and wrote no more about visiting the other vessel.

There was nothing to do as the ship and brig bobbed in the shadeless delta. Quarters below were too hot for restful sleep until late at night, but napping on deck required one to follow the small, fleeting patches of shade. From sunrise to bedtime, passengers had little to anticipate other than meals—which the cook must have continued preparing as though he thought the larder would be restocked before the voyage resumed. A few days later, Clark had a brief respite when the New York sloop *Harriot* arrived outside the pass and dropped anchor while awaiting a southerly wind. Seeing not just a chance to escape the tedium of the *Star* but also to defy Spanish authority with impunity, Clark joined companions he did not name and rowed to the sloop. "We attempted to bord but was ordered not [to] by the pilot We did not mind him," he wrote, adding nothing more of that incident.[13]

He and the others would have been less daring had they realized what was happening to their absent shipmates. First clapped in irons and locked in a dungeon at Fort San Felipe, Daniel Coxe and Richard Clark were then incarcerated in Fort San Carlos once they reached New Orleans. Coxe requested an immediate hearing with Governor Gayoso but learned he would have to wait several days. Daniel Clark Jr. could not help; word had recently arrived that President Adams had chosen another man, William Empson Hulings, as consul for Louisiana. Because months were to pass before diplomatic authorities in the United States and Spain might weigh the legality of Coxe's many questionable actions, his best course for the present was to seek an understanding with the Spanish governor.[14]

Coxe set out to do this. On August 13 he declared to Gayoso that he'd never intended to break the law. Glossing over his many transgressions in the delta, Coxe blamed the unfamiliarity of Molina, Borras, and Ronquillo with English and his own ignorance of Spanish for his inability to disabuse them of the notion that he was trying to free the prize ships (which of course he was). Simplistic and untruthful, his argument was also eminently shrewd, giving Gayoso a pretext for closing the matter amicably while allowing Coxe to continue doing business in Louisiana.[15]

Gayoso embraced that view and ordered the prisoners released and returned to their vessels. Fearing Coxe would complain to the U.S. Congress about his detention, Gayoso asked him to certify in writing his satisfaction with the outcome. Coxe did so and then boarded a Spanish boat to rush him and Richard Clark downstream. The next day—more than two weeks after arriving at the Baliza—they reached the ships, finding them cleared for departure.[16]

For the last time, sailors hauled in anchors tethering the *Star* and the *Friendship* to Spanish territory and got ready to unfurl sails as the vessels glided down the last stretch of river. Ahead was the *Hennique*'s largest prize, but Coxe no longer had an interest in seizing her or in doing anything that might further delay the two-thousand-mile voyage to Philadelphia. At five o'clock in the evening, the ship and brig slipped into the viridian waters of the Gulf and hurried past the *Mars*.

Once free of pilots and of anyone connected with the Spanish regime, Coxe related his experiences. Clark recorded them, penning one of the longest entries in his entire Mississippi Journal, using language and revealing names he had not dared write while on land:

at 8 oClock Mr. Coxe returned, & informed us the Cause of their detainment as follows Viz: insulting the Spanish Comd. of Valias, [Baliza] Lt. Borass & Molenay, in threts to the French Prevater, ordering her prises 2 scuners to come too or the Ship & Brig Would sink her, & other Cowardly complaints Signed by those offcers & Tranquilo [Ronquillo] & all the pilots at this Place, those Gent. that went up was imprisoned at the Pluckomen [Plaquemines] & sent to N. O. & put into the Fort Charls, one night & day.

Perhaps more extraordinary is that the normally terse Clark filled an entire journal page with a word-for-word transcription of the arrest order for Richard Clark:

Being officially informed of the improper conduct that you & Mr. {D W} Coxe have had in the block house of the Valina, Committing an insult

to his Majesty's territorial Right, you & Said Mr. Coxe will immediately
Come up to this Capital to answer for your conduct.

Your vestle may continue to their destination, as the Spanish Nation is in
perfect armony with the U.S.

New Orleans
8 Aug{t}. 1798
Manuel Gayoso de Lemos

Why did Clark go to such trouble to copy a key document from an
incident not directly related to him? Did he consider it of potential use
for himself or someone else to employ, depending on circumstances? As
usual, he fails to elucidate.

Clark's relative verbosity about the arrest and imprisonment of Daniel
Coxe and Richard Clark, however, does not extend to related matters.
That is, nowhere in William's journal does he acknowledge that Coxe's
aggression, rather than hostility on the part of the Spanish, caused the
long delay. Similarly, he neglects to mention that by failing to replen-
ish water and provisions consumed during that interval, Coxe might have
made another calamitous mistake.

PART III

The Homeward Journey
August 16 to December 24, 1798

26

So Reduced I Can Scarcely Walk

EVEN in the long shadows of late afternoon and well beyond the bar, Clark could discern the Mississippi swirling below, infiltrating the Gulf of Mexico with tawny streamers of suspended soils. The disemboguement might have looked the reverse of what he had witnessed eleven hundred water-miles in the opposite direction where the Ohio injects its pellucid currents into the earth-laden Mississippi. But the mingling now beneath him, however, persisted over a far greater distance, lasting hours after he and fellow passengers lost view of the Baliza lighthouse.

If he bothered to peer downward the next day he probably spied fingers of grit still dispersing into the fathoms. Perhaps he focused instead on the horizon, watching for signs of progress and for anything capable of arresting the voyage. Although the majority of foreign ships commissioned for pillage patrolled the Caribbean Sea, enough of them cruised the Gulf to make Coxe and his seamen alert around other craft. With favorable winds, a well-rigged vessel might sail in a week from the delta passes to western Cuba, yet in contrary conditions the voyage took much longer. The waters of that route lack a prevailing channel as forceful as the Gulf Stream flowing up from the tropics to skirt the eastern edge of the United States and traverse the North Atlantic, but they nonetheless move helpfully clockwise. For this reason, even if the air were to go slack, the *Star* and the *Friendship* would sooner or later wash into the Florida Straits and be drawn toward the ocean.

But soon the wind died down, Coxe's flotilla slowed, and its occupants began sighting vessels in the distance. "Discovred a Sale to the leeward in the evening one to the windward," wrote Clark as the *Star* caught a northern breeze on August 16, yet several subsequent days of calm made him wish for more rapid passage. On August 21 he and his companions concluded wrongly when another vessel hove into view: "We all prepared for action sup. [supposing] her to be a Priovteer & bore away."

The newcomer was instead an armed Spanish ship sailing to Havana from what Clark termed Santa Cruz but which was likely Vera Cruz. Because Clark recorded neither her name nor anything specific about her, we have little idea whether she belonged to private interests or to the Spanish navy. We can only guess what she was hauling: tropical hardwoods? food? coined silver? The hundreds of thousands of reales in the royal subsidy for Louisiana were fair game to the British navy, but until the hurricane season ended in October it sometimes kept few naval vessels in the Gulf of Mexico and Caribbean Sea, leaving only commercial vessels to pursue the floating fortune. So long as Spain and France were allies, French privateers had to forgo assaulting the Money Ship, but they owed the *Star* and the *Friendship* neither courtesy nor quarter.

To make matters worse for Coxe, he could expect no protection from his own country; the fledgling U. S. Navy seldom entered the Gulf of Mexico and was not yet able to guard the Atlantic coastline. So bold had corsairs there become that one of them—the French schooner *Croyable*—had ambushed American merchantman *Alexander Hamilton* in Little Egg Harbor, New Jersey, on July 6 and made off with casks of wine and brandy. The following day, Captain Stephen Decatur of the *Delaware* (a former commercial packet fitted out as a U.S. war sloop that William Clark was to admire in a few weeks) made the *Croyable* the first prize of the U.S. Navy.[1]

Soon, however, a more insidious threat, the symptoms of malaria, began afflicting Clark and others aboard the *Star*. Of August 22–28 he writes only sixteen words: "a head Wind I am sick & also severall on bord with the ague & fever." Unaccustomed to recording more about such spells, he may have found this one followed the typical course of malaria. If so, it could have commenced with a feeling of lethargy followed by intense shivering and a sensation of cold giving way to a high fever attended with labored breathing and sweating. Once his temperature returned to normal, Clark may have fallen into a deep slumber from which he awoke exhausted by his body's defense against the microscopic plasmodia.[2]

The first light of August 29 revealed on the horizon the northwest coast of Cuba. Clark called that section of the island Dolphin's Head, perhaps because the jutting shoreline resembled the profile of the game fish often seen leaping from Gulf waters. (He would long remember the dolphin, comparing the shape of its tail to that of a catfish pulled on July 24, 1804, from the Missouri River above the mouth of the Platte.) The northwestern coast of Cuba sheltered pirates so notorious for preying on merchant vessels that, when a pair of ships sailed into view, Coxe and his complement got ready to fight. "We prepared and bore Down & She tacked and bore off," Clark recalled that evening, hale enough to try out some nautical additions to his vocabulary.[3]

On August 30, the *Star* and the *Friendship* dropped below the Tropic of Cancer; at 23 degrees, 27 minutes north of the equator, it is the northernmost point where the sun can shine directly overhead. Within the Torrid Zone for what must have been the only time in his life, Clark began to pay careful, regular attention to terrestrial coordinates, especially the north-south position of the ship. Why those figures were important to him he does not indicate, but they would soon become a regular feature of his maritime journal-keeping. We cannot gauge their accuracy; not only are the logbooks from both the ship and the brig apparently no longer extant, neither is any account of the voyage other than Clark's. His prodigious natural ability as a geographer might suggest that he derived the nautical coordinates on his own, but they must have originated instead with the ship's navigator. Yet we can imagine Clark, during periods of relative health, observing navigational techniques and perhaps trying out scientific instruments.

Although the *Star* probably followed a stretch of the Cuban coast before heading back to sea, she did not stop at the island, even to take on critical supplies of food and water. Havana was the port most convenient to Coxe's route but, according to report, French privateers controlled sea access to the city and blocked American merchantmen from leaving it. As a result, up to eighty such ships were thought to be virtual hostages in the Havana harbor.[4]

Nevertheless, the Coxe vessels came within a short distance of it. On August 30, Clark wrote only "in Lat. 23.15," by which he must have meant 23 degrees, 15 minutes of northern latitude, the southernmost position he would ever record of his own travels. If this measurement is accurate, it indicates a point just a few miles north of Havana. Considering an error margin normal for that time, Clark may have been close enough to make out, through a spyglass lens, both Castillo del Morro and Castillo San Salvador de la Punta, massive military works guarding the harbor entrance. But he chronicled nothing of what he viewed, possibly because he was again within the reach of Spanish justice. The ship turned north, and Clark saw no more of Cuba.

* * *

On the last day of August, he records being eighty-one degrees west of the Prime Meridian. This figure is the sole longitude he notes on the voyage, but because it puts the ship halfway through the Florida Keys when she was almost certainly still west of them all, we must account for the discrepancy. Perhaps the navigator's instruments, particularly his timepiece, were inaccurate; not even the finest chronometer of that day resisted water well or remained unaffected by the rolling of the sea. Possibly the skies were too cloudy, or maybe the navigator erred in his calculations. As Clark and Lewis were to experience on the 1803–1806 Expedition, longitudinal precision depends not just on proper instrumentation but also on human ability to turn measurements, observations, and the arcana of celestial movements into precise figures, a process beyond the ability of most mathematicians then and for years thereafter.[5]

That same day Clark also recorded a latitude of "23.45." It shows the ship was clear of Cuban waters and again outside the Tropics. Captain Woodman stayed on course, and within a few hours the *Star* entered an environment Clark had not yet seen—one of waterless islands and reefs of coral. He responded on September 1 with a disappointing three and a half lines devoid of subjective impression: "At day discovered Some

Small Kees (or Islds.) at abt. 1/2 a mile, 3 fa water we Droped Anchor." If only he had described the panorama before him—perhaps white sand beaches and mangrove thickets fringeing islands thick with ironwood, lignum vitae, and torchwood trees, and teeming with flamingos and turtles—but a wind sprang up and carried the ship and brig away from the little archipelago.

Perhaps aware they were not as far east as the longitude reading indicated, the sailors on the *Star* hailed an unfamiliar vessel to the northeast. "We attempted to Speak [to communicate with the other craft by means of a long trumpet for speaking] but Could not over take her," Clark says after the *Star* gave chase and then fell in behind the stranger. Still unsure if she was foe or friend, he watched the next morning as she drew nigh, made a series of maneuvers, and raised a British flag.

A few minutes later, a lieutenant left the royal ship and boarded the *Star*, announcing he was from "his majestys brig heroe, Capt. Cockburn master," according to Clark. He may have misunderstood the officer's name; it was likely Alexander Cochrane. He was a forty-year-old English captain whom Governor Gayoso suspected of plotting the brief penetration of the Mississippi River delta in early May.

The lieutenant clarified where they all were, his unfamiliar pronunciations probably confounding Clark's already bewildered orthography: "He informed us these reefs was the Dry Tortugas & that we were then Stearing towerd Floriday, in the Bay of Chatha{m} or Punjo [Ponce] & within 35 fathoms water we Sounded & found it the Case." In other words, the vessels were still west of the Florida Keys, and among several large coral islands lacking fresh water but teeming with marine turtles and, at different times of year, a wide diversity of avian life—terns, frigate birds, gulls, pelicans, and cormorants. Of more immediate importance was that, not far beneath, flourished delicious, pincerless lobsters, conchs, and fish species soon to become essential to the survival of those on the *Friendship* and the *Star*.[6]

The *Hero* remained nearby until departing for Cuban waters on the morning of September 3, at which point Coxe's craft proceeded southeast by south for a few hours and then turned almost eighty degrees to starboard. It was a drastic change of direction, but perhaps one helpful to entering the Atlantic by way of the Florida Current, a veritable river of Mississippian swiftness pushing into the Atlantic waters that had already circled some twenty-five hundred miles around the Gulf embayment, starting at the Banks of Campeche. Not long after Captains Woodman and Arnold found the current, the navigator began reporting rapid progress.

Knowing the ship was finally within its pull must have been a joy to Clark, but the speed-increased rolling gave him an upset stomach, an especially troubling condition now that the galley was running out of food. "We are much allarmed about Provisions, having consumed the greater part of our Stock," he writes. The following day brought more cause for concern. Although the *Star* and the *Friendship* were "South of all the States of Floriday," as Clark put it, his mal de mer grew intense. "I am puking all day & Dark." Even so, he managed to note the "Dolfin, Scip Jacks, &c., Grupers Snappers" hauled aboard.

Soon the Coxe vessels rounded the southeastern coast of the Florida peninsula and entered the celebrated Gulf Stream, a three-dimensional highway of water surging at up to six miles an hour into the North Atlantic. If the latitudes Clark recorded are reliable, by September 9, the ship and brig passed the site of what would eventually be called Pompano Beach, Florida, and on September 11 sailed around Cape Canaveral, some 160 ocean-miles closer to their destination. Clark no doubt appreciated greater dispatch, but his nausea grew worse. (This wretched experience may have conferred a degree of tolerance not obvious until November 8, 1805, when he paddled a canoe across high swells at the mouth of the Columbia River yet did not become ill, in contrast with some of his fellow passengers.)[7]

Starting on September 8, 1798, his daily entries become a litany of deteriorating health: "I continu Verry Sick. . . . I continue Verry unwell. . . . I continue Very sick & am so reduced [I] can Scarcely walk." Now and then he mentions agreeable breezes but they did nothing to relieve his distress. In the early hours of September 12, when the *Star* was roughly aligned with Spanish capitals New Orleans and St. Augustine, an atmospheric disturbance blew in, reminiscent of the Mississippi River storm which had so unnerved his deckhands. Unaware that this tempest was to precede several more, Clark begins peppering his recitals of sickness with remarks about the frightful conditions. He continues for eight days:

> Sept. 12th: A Violent Storm all night . . . a Squally day. . . .
> 13th: heavy Squals of wind & rane attended with
> Thunder & lightning. . . .
> 14th: a Squally day with rane. . . .
> 15th: a Squarly Night . . . a Squarly day with
> rane. . . .
> 16th: a Dredfull Nite last of wind & rane. . . .
> 17th: cloudy day with rane. . . .
> 18th: a fair wind which blew violently from the SE,
> acompanied with Storms. . . .
> 19th: a most Dredfull night of wind & Stormy Weather
> obliged us [to] unship our yards. . . .

We can imagine what he does *not* detail: how for hours the *Star* either crashed into watery ridges—each concussion capable of addling the equilibrium and turning cups and compasses, boxes and books into missiles—or rose on walls of seawater only to drop into the troughs behind them. Perhaps Captain Woodman deliberated whether to pursue a straight course by steering directly into the swells or to take them at an angle, thereby reducing the impact of each crash and plunge but protracting time on the ocean. Unfortunately, we have no evidence of the bearing he chose. One of the few certainties of the voyage is that the vessels did not encounter a hurricane, small consolation to Clark and others laid low by the lesser storms.[8]

Limited since early September to three pints of water per day, the crewmen—and certainly some of the passengers—scrambled at every opportunity to catch rain. By September 18 they had caught more than four barrelfuls. The fish they hooked, however, could not make up for the provisions depleted in the delta and not replaced. Disgusted with Daniel Coxe for causing them to go hungry, his sailors began to murmur against him. Clark took note, writing "Provisions Short, men discontented, the greater part of our stores out." Having observed at close range Wilkinson's underhanded effort to discredit General Wayne and having witnessed Freeman's attempt to oust Ellicott from the boundary commission, Clark was attuned to signs of mutiny.

A schooner hauling agricultural products from San Domingue to Philadelphia sailed into view on September 20. Abandoning any pretense of caution, the ship and the brig gave chase until they caught up with her. Coxe arranged a transaction welcome to crew and passengers: "We sent on bord [the other vessel] and got Sugar Coffee & limes Sufficent for our passg." writes Clark.

He was surely happy for the citric protection against scurvy and also for the promise of a hot, sweetened beverage to combat dehydration. But the coffee beans and sugar must have reminded him that just two months earlier he had purchased containers of the same types of goods and had them stuffed with illicit pieces of eight for Judge Benjamin Sebastian and probably for a boatman named Riddle to deliver to someone else. Having entrusted those doctored barrel-loads to Samuel M. Brown, Clark could only guess how far upriver he and Sebastian were by now, and whether they'd yet come upon General Wilkinson making his way to Army headquarters at Natchez.

27

A Thirteen-Gun Salute for Agent 13

URING the first week of June 1798, while Clark had been making preliminary plans to have some of his earnings smuggled upstream from New Orleans, General Wilkinson boarded the barge *Kitty* and, in a convoy of more than two dozen Army vessels, set off from Pittsburgh down the Ohio. Having sufficient water in the river and suitable weather, the fleet put ashore at Cincinnati a couple of weeks later. Wilkinson had been gone from the Ohio valley for much of the past two years; he found matters there in need of attention. He spent the next month at Fort Washington, engaged in licit activities such as fostering Indian alliances and settling local disputes, all the while preparing to continue to Natchez where he was to take command of American forces.[1]

While Clark, saddlebags stuffed with Spanish money, had been approaching the boundary camp at the thirty-first parallel on June 27, 1798, Wilkinson wrote Governor Gayoso de Lemos an official letter, complimenting him on the peaceful evacuation of Spanish troops from the posts at Chickasaw Bluffs, Walnut Hills, and Natchez. Wilkinson enclosed newspapers setting forth what he dramatically called "dreadful scenes impending in Europe which I sincerely implore Heaven, may never be realized on the peaceful Shores of this Continent." Mindful of the general's venality, Gayoso must have suspected that, contrary to his words, he was looking for a chance to bring about, and profit from, war in Louisiana.[2]

On July 20, as Clark awaited favorable conditions for the *Star* to set off down the Mississippi, Wilkinson's convoy stopped at Louisville long enough for the heaviest of cargoes to be offloaded to wagons and hauled around the Falls of the Ohio. Perhaps during that interval the general asked whether Sebastian and Brown were back yet from New Orleans. If Wilkinson indeed made such an inquiry, he must have found out that neither of those conspirators had returned.[3]

By early August, Wilkinson had arrived at Fort Massac. There he took on additional soldiers and supplies and inscribed another official letter to Gayoso. This time he was warning of an American adventurer named Zachariah Cox said to be descending the river with an armed band, perhaps intent on seizing a portion of Spanish Louisiana. He was telling the truth, but the general was again attempting to appear the savior of the province, just as he had done earlier concerning the settlement schemes of George Rogers Clark, New Madrid founder George Morgan, and the South Carolina Yazoo Company. But Wilkinson was also trying to curry goodwill among the Spanish by suggesting his readiness, under certain conditions, to resume acting as Agent 13. He would repeat this message at every opportunity.[4]

Upon leaving Fort Massac he slowed his rate of travel. He had alleged to the secretary of war that low water dictated the delay, but Wilkinson was on the deepest and least obstructed section of the Ohio. The reduced speed, however, allowed him to examine the terrain for a site on which to encamp a vast number of American soldiers whom he hoped to enlist for the purpose of invading Louisiana. Because only armed hostilities there might give him an excuse to do so, he would soon try to bring about those very circumstances, as will be seen.[5]

Covering in five days the same stretch of river that William Clark had floated in eleven hours (including the time necessary to survey an island), Wilkinson entered the Mississippi on August 13, a fitting date for Agent 13 to reach the border of Spanish Louisiana. His arrival, however, went unnoticed by that government, which some time earlier had withdrawn the gunboat patrol and abandoned the docking facility William Clark had sketched in or around 1795. Wilkinson proceeded downstream. On drawing near New Madrid, the depot for most of the thousands of illicit pieces of eight he'd received since secretly pledging fealty to Spain, he had his men fire a greeting he could expect to be described in an official account of the incident.

It was. On August 16, Commandant Carlos Dehault Delassus composed a letter to Gayoso, describing what happened that day as the American fleet passed by the Spanish fort: "At eleven o'clock . . . the convoy approached this post, staying in the middle of the river, and the galley which led the way crossed in front of this fort and saluted this flag with 13 cannon shots, to which I answered shot for shot." Delassus counted a total of twenty-eight vessels, most of them flatboats, and estimated that eleven officers and three incomplete companies were riding aboard them. He also spied at least eight pieces of artillery, four of them of large caliber, two relatively short cannons, and quantities of ammunition.[6]

Meanwhile, Benjamin Sebstian and his son Alfred were heading up the Mississippi on a Spanish galley. Having departed the capital shortly after Samuel M. Brown presented their monopoly proposal to Gayoso, Benjamin had come upon not only William Clark and John McKee but also Governor Winthrop Sargent of the Mississippi Territory as he descended the river to Natchez to assume his duties. Although Sebastian and Sargent had previously met, this time Sargent wanted nothing to do with one so obviously favored by Spain as to ride on a royal barge. Interpreting his circumspection as haughtiness, Sebastian reported that Sargent's "new dignities have made him so stately & consequential that he would make no advances towards an interview . . . of consequence we did not see each other."[7]

Some five hundred river-miles upstream and just below the Chickasaw Bluffs Army post Clark had visited, Sebastian's galley came upon the *Kitty* and companion vessels. Managing to elude the attention of anyone commissioned to spy on him, Wilkinson carefully passed to Sebastian an abundance of intelligence: A Franco-American war seemed unavoidable; French military aggressions throughout Europe were fraying the Spanish alliance and causing Spain to post many thousands of soldiers along her border with France; the Spanish Court had dismissed Secretary of State Manuel de Godoy, allegedly for being too friendly with that republic; the United States was raising twenty-five thousand provisional troops and eighty thousand militiamen to fight the anticipated war with France. Sebastian took careful note; he would forward the same information to his Spanish contacts once he decided how to wring maximum benefit for himself from it. If Wilkinson was indeed the intended recipient of the 670 Spanish dollars in Clark's sugar barrel, Sebastian must have related that because Brown and his rivermen lagged miles below due to illness, the cargoes they hauled might not get to Kentucky until later than originally expected.[8]

Sebastian soon reached New Madrid. With little Spanish money in his possession he stayed there as long as possible as if hoping Brown would rally from his indisposition and catch up with him, but on September 17, he gave up waiting and proceeded upriver. Maybe Sebastian went to Kaskaskia, repeating the detour that a few years earlier had helped him avoid detection at Fort Massac; all we know for sure is that he arrived at Louisville on October 7, 1798.

Knowing that all over the United States, heated protests and even riots had been breaking out in defiance of the Alien and Sedition acts and of recently levied taxes to fund increased military spending, Sebastian reported to Gayoso in March 1799 that "the country [was] involved in tumult and confusion. The Administration of the General Government and the proceedings of the late Congress entirely occupy the public mind and were almost universally reprobated. Nothing was talked of at county meetings but resolutions and remonstrances." Sebastian concluded on an unconvincing note—"I think it much more than probable that a dissolution of the Union will be the consequence"—as if yet hoping to turn such an event into the two-hundred-thousand-dollar bonanza Carondelet had promised in exchange for it.[9]

Sebastian must have realized by this time that Kentucky would not withdraw from the United States, and he knew that a Franco-American war fought in Louisiana would dim the prospects for securing the monopoly he and Brown had asked for. Rather than continuing to pursue it (and the concomitant windfall), he instead concentrated on seeking a grant of acreage to colonize. As he explained:

Independent of the general dissatisfaction with the [U.S.] government, there are many honest, industrious families in this country [Kentucky] who, possessing no land of their own, and, being either unable or unwilling from the great uncertainty of titles here to purchase, would gladly emigrate to Louisiana, provided some respectable characters in whom they have confidence would undertake to lead them.[10]

With a physician named John Watkins (who was later to become mayor of New Orleans), Sebastian formed a company for the purpose of settling expatriated Americans onto what both men hoped would be a grant of three million acres in Spanish Louisiana, between the St. Francis and Mississippi rivers. Sebastian (conducting such business as "Andrew Watkins," one of his pseudonyms) and Watkins sold stock in their scheme—a minimum of six shares at a hundred dollars each per investor. In complex encryptions "Watkins" asked Gayoso how many acres Carlos IV might give them for settling five hundred families? One hundred families? Individuals owning from ten to fifty slaves? As secretary for the concern, Sebastian invested time and ink coding and decoding correspondence about the amount of acreage he and his associates wanted.[11]

Obtaining this grant, however, would require that a company director travel to Spain and present the project to the royal administration. Having already been gone from the Kentucky Court of Appeals for two long stretches, Sebastian instead resumed his judicial duties in hopes no one had noticed that, despite his absences, he was still drawing a full salary. But because it failed to support him and his family in the style they desired, he resolved to continue billing the Spanish regime for his clandestine income and receiving it in payload containers such as the sugar and coffee barrels furnished by William Clark. Unlike Wilkinson, who deemed the risk of collecting such large sums too great to brook, Sebastian kept gambling on not getting caught.

Samuel M. Brown's boat eventually arrived at the Louisville landing. Presumably William Croghan picked up his reales. The coffee beans they had traveled in went to Mulberry Hill, and John Clark took delivery of the sugar barrel with 670 Spanish dollars, passing them along to a boatman named Riddle.

When all those goods were dispersed, Sebastian had his overseer, Joseph George, help unload another barrel, one carted from the riverfront to the judge's Louisville home. Little did George then realize that his impressions from this incident and its aftermath would, with his permission, be made public in 1806 by the *Western World*—a Kentucky newspaper with a Federalist viewpoint, exclusive access to some of the early documents of the Spanish Conspiracy, and an avowed determination to expose the principals of that intrigue. According to a certified statement George was to give the *Western World*, he thought this particular barrel remarkably heavy; moving it required the joint efforts of himself and three other men. Shortly thereafter, on noticing that Sebastian was paying some of his obligations with "Spanish milled dollars, newly coined" and "all of one date," George asked whether the money came from the weighty container. William Sebastian, one of Benjamin's sons, gave him to know that it did.[12]

28

Go, Before It Is Too Late

ON the morning of September 21, 1798, the day after the *Star* took on sugar, coffee, and limes, she sailed within view of what at first appeared to be islands of tall trees crowning the western horizon, but which instead turned out to be part of a continental forest. Soon other vessels fell in with her, evidence they had all found a shipping lane leading to Delaware Bay. Just three days earlier, the forty-four-gun frigate *United States*, followed by the twenty-four-gun *Delaware*, had led two French prizes—the sloop *La Jalouse* and the schooner *Sans Pareil*—along the same route. Now, while Clark was gazing at the U.S. mainland, Captain John Barry of the *United States* was briefing Naval Secretary Benjamin Stoddert about those captures, the first solid blows against French depredations since the beginning of the naval war with France.[1]

At midday Clark watched a pilot get out of a small boat and come on board the *Star*—a scene in sharp contrast with the rejection of the Spanish pilot in the Mississippi delta. But presently the wind shifted and kept Coxe's ships from sailing into the fifteen-mile-broad mouth of the Delaware, and so they remained at sea. Waiting for atmospheric conditions to change, the pilot spread the word about a yellow fever epidemic raging in Philadelphia and other eastern cities.

It was a terrible story. Forty thousand people had already taken flight from Philadelphia. More than two thousand others were dead from the disease. One who had remained in the city to assist the afflicted was Mayor Hilary Baker; he would die of yellow fever on September 25, 1798. Nationally prominent journalists Benjamin Franklin Bache, grandson of Benjamin Franklin and editor of the Democratic-Republican *Aurora*, and his political opponent John Fenno, editor of the Federalist *Gazette of the United States*, were also recent victims. So virulent was the pestilence that entire families were succumbing to it. A Philadelphia resident identified as Henry Bullyberger, on returning from a place of refuge, found seventeen of his relatives dead of the illness. Upon locating his living sister and her husband, Bullyberger contracted the illness. So did they, and soon it killed them all.[2]

Anonymous warnings were being posted all over Philadelphia about the perils of staying there:

> FELLOW CITIZENS! reflect upon your danger before it is too late. One hundred of us are attacked with the fever every day. One half of that number is daily carried to the grave. If we remain in town, it is probable that the fever will continue five or six weeks longer; and, by that time, one-half of our number will have been sick!—and one-fourth of us will be no more! . . . GO, BEFORE IT IS TOO LATE![3]

Home to more than fifty-five thousand people, the metropolitan area was emptying fast. Its wealthy residents sought refuge on country estates, and people of lesser means fled to encampments of tents and wooden huts along the outskirts of town. The federal government suspended operations; most of its departments relocated to Trenton, New Jersey. President and Mrs. Adams retreated to Quincy, Massachusetts, and Vice President Jefferson departed for Monticello, his home in rural Virginia. As people fled Philadelphia, stores closed, stagecoaches stopped running, and streetlights sputtered out because no one refueled them. Among the only active workers in town—other than the valiant doctors and nurses treating the sick—were gravediggers who, to keep pace with the increasing mortality, ceased excavating individual graves and instead opened trenches long enough and deep enough for horse-drawn hearses to drive into them and discharge multiple cargoes.[4]

Not understanding that *Aedes aegypti* mosquitoes—probably arriving on ships from the Caribbean—spread yellow fever, the people staying in Philadelphia tried to avoid contagion by remaining indoors, shutting windows, and fumigating rooms with burning coals, sulfur, and small explosions of gunpowder. The experience of past epidemics taught that the misery would persist until later in the year when average low temperatures dropped below freezing. Unwilling to wait several weeks for this to happen, Clark decided to bypass Philadelphia altogether and go directly to Fredericksburg, Virginia, and the nearby homes of his brothers Edmund and Jonathan.[5]

William paid strict attention to the landscape opening before him. On September 22 he noted that the *Star* pulled close to the Cape Henlopen lighthouse. (It would stand until erosion brought it down in 1926.) The following morning, the ship crossed the Delaware embayment and paused near the village of Cape May, soon to advertise itself as the first U.S. seaside resort offering opportunities to bathe in the ocean, drink superior liquors, and dine on crabs, oysters, and marine fishes. By judging the area "thickly settled," Clark revealed an engrossing but unexplained interest. Just as he had earlier studied the strategic potential of places in the Mississippi valley, from here on he would pay special attention to the number of people and houses in eastern communities.

Within a few hours, a flood tide and a favorable breeze took the *Star* some thirty miles inland, past oyster beds and several narrow, muddy bars, each more than ten miles long, and toward the gentle curve of Bombay Hook ("Bumbohook" to Clark), a low isle soon to come alive with hundreds of thousands of wintering mallards, pintails, teals, and geese. Here the estuary, lined on each side with oaks and poplars soon to be in autumn colors, narrowed to six miles across. The stirring of leaves must have been a more pleasing sound to Clark than the rolling of waves, but he was intent instead on making progress up the Delaware.

Relying successively more on sail power than on the incoming tide to move them, the Coxe ships stopped in the river opposite New Castle, Delaware, the next day. Clark lavished ink on a description of what he saw:

> Cast up in two tides to New Castle, passed a Small Village 12 Miles called port pen about 100 houses, opposit is Rudy Is at this place is a good harbo for shiping from her, a long Ship bound for china lay here, at the port.

> New Castle is a Small Town Containing about 200 houses Thronged with people at present from Philadelphia, which place has the yellow Fever and about 80 p. day Die This place is handsomly Situated & has a good harbr about 40 Sale at present lay opposit, (among which is the U.S. <u>Frigit</u> mounting 47. guns, and Slupe of War cald the Dellaway of 22 guns, & Two French Privateers Prises brought in by those Ships.

The American naval vessels he mentions were Stephen Decatur's *Delaware* and John Barry's *United States*, a vessel with an appropriately American figurehead of a star-crowned woman bearing a spear and wampum in one hand, and the U.S. Constitution in the other.[6]

Almost forty miles downstream from Philadelphia, New Castle was not only the last emporium for ocean-bound travelers wishing to take on garden produce and other provisions but also the place where physicians screened incoming voyagers before letting them return to land. Because Philadelphia was closed to nautical traffic, those who passed the medical inspection had to disembark at New Castle rather than continue upriver. In the early hours of September 25, a doctor boarded the *Star* and began checking passengers and crewmen for signs of yellow fever. He pronounced Clark well in that regard yet his loose clothes bespoke a long bout of seasickness and his recent malarial symptoms suggested he carried the *Plasmodium* parasite in his blood. When satisfied that everyone else was free of yellow fever, the doctor approved the ship for landing. The dreadful voyage lasting more than two months was finally over.

Leaving nine and a half dollars for the cost of the medical examination, his extra expenses on the ship, and a gratuity for the sailors, Clark got off the *Star* as fast as possible. How he must have enjoyed walking again on solid ground and having a choice of where to go! Along the main avenue leading away from the river were shops, taverns, houses historic even then (tradition holds that, in or around 1682, William Penn slept in one of them), and a handsome courthouse built in 1732. Clark inquired about the schedule of the stagecoach line connecting New Castle with the road to Virginia. Christiana Bridge, the town nearest that route, was five miles to the west. He looked into renting a horse-drawn conveyance to take him there and found lodging for the night. Before going to bed he devised a plan to cash his order on the national Treasury and then composed a brief letter to Daniel Coxe:

> Will you be so obligeing as to take charge of the inclosed Bills, drawn on Mr. O. Woolcutt Secty. of the Treasy. for 1500 Dols. and get the Said bills Accepted—and pleas enclose them to me in Baltimore by the male.
>
> I shall stay in Baltimore untill I have the pleasure of hearing from you which I hope you will favor me with as soon as you can make it convenient.[7]

In other words Coxe, who intended to remain with the *Star* and the *Friendship* in order to ensure the safety of their cargoes, including the hidden sacks of reales, would forward the bill to Treasury Secretary Oliver Wolcott. Once Daniel received payment for it, he would send the money on to Clark at Baltimore.

Happy to have such details resolved, Clark handed Coxe the letter, having folded it around the slip of paper representing most of his mercantile income from New Orleans. No one noticed, however, that Clark had forgotten to endorse the bill.

* * *

Finding his shipmates hale the next morning, Clark saw them scatter on their own journeys. John McKee took the secret intelligence he had gathered on Benjamin Sebastian, Samuel M. Brown, and James Wilkinson and set off for Trenton, New Jersey, the office of the War Department during the pestilence in Philadelphia. The Craigs must have headed for Kentucky. Richard Clark no doubt remained nearby until able to join his family in Philadelphia, and Daniel Coxe stayed with his vessels. Having intended all along to visit his family at Fredericksburg, Virginia, Beverly Chew decided to travel with William who must have been happy for the company of such a well-connected young man. The son of Revolutionary War colonel John Chew, Beverly was a protégé of Daniel Clark Jr., a confidant of John McKee, and a trader determined to become a business magnate in New Orleans no matter what happened between the United States and the allied forces of France and Spain.[8]

Clark and Chew rented a horse-drawn carriage for themselves and a cart to haul their heavy belongings. They departed New Castle for the stagecoach route originating in Philadelphia and leading southwest to Baltimore; from there they would switch to the Virginia line. No doubt the weather was more agreeable than the sticky heat they had experienced in Louisiana, but Clark recorded nothing of such matters. Instead he wrote only that Christiana Bridge (now known simply as Christiana) was a town "Small & regular Containing about 90 or 100 houses."

Judging from his logbook at this leg of the journey, one might deem the density of human settlement his main interest, but occasionally he was to write of other matters. He did so on September 26, 1798, noting "the Stage passed at 3 so Crowded We could not get in," perhaps because it was carrying Philadelphians fleeing their stricken city. The next stagecoach was not due to arrive until the evening of September 27, so he decided to spend the night in Christiana Bridge.

There he called on Maxwell Bines, a New Castle native he had served with in the Army. Bines had enlisted in 1791 and taken part in Major General Arthur St. Clair's disastrous Ohio valley campaign in which Miami Indians and their allies killed or injured almost half of St. Clair's troops. Despite such an inauspicious beginning to his military career, Bines became an infantry lieutenant in March 1792, the very month Clark joined the Army and attained the same grade. Both of them served at the Battle of Fallen Timbers. Bines surpassed Clark in rank by becoming a captain, and drew command of Fort Jefferson, near the west-central Ohio town of that name.[9]

Not long after Fallen Timbers, Bines left the Army, perhaps feeling disappointment at not having received the seniority he thought his just entitlement. (Wilkinson was then engendering unrealistic expectations of this sort among junior officers so that, when they failed to receive promotions, furloughs, or other benefits they did not in fact have coming, they would unfairly blame General Wayne for denying them such benefits.) Bines had returned to New Castle where he became county sheriff and laid the foundation for a political career to include appointment as a presidential elector. Recognizing the growing significance of the highways linking Christiana Bridge with Philadelphia, Baltimore, and more distant cities, he secured a license to rent to the public at least one type of horse-drawn conveyance.[10]

After spending the night at his house, Clark and Chew turned in their vehicles from New Castle and procured, perhaps from Bines, another cart and a "chair," a small, open carriage probably of two wheels. Thus equipped, they set out down the road still known as the Old Baltimore Pike. In around four miles they reached a hamlet called Cooch's Bridge, site of the only Revolutionary War skirmish in Delaware, and after a few more miles entered Cecil County, Maryland. By mid-afternoon they pulled into Elkton.

Earlier known as Head of Elk for its location near the place where the broad Elk River, aswarm with herring and raucous with ducks, narrows to a sinuous creek; it was a large village. "Elkton Contains about 100 houses well built of Brick," Clark wrote, indulging again his special interest. Soon the Baltimore stagecoach arrived full, and he and Chew once more looked for lodging. They wound up at a tavern, possibly the one where Irish visitor Isaac Weld had stayed while traveling the same road in 1795. Although Weld declined to name the accommodation, he deemed it typically American because it served communal meals at set hours and put lodgers together in a barracks-like sleeping room rather than in individual chambers.[11]

In the morning Clark and Chew repeated the ritual of turning in their vehicles and hiring another one—this time, an expensive, two-horse carriage—and set off for Baltimore. When dry, the road they followed was often so rutted that stagecoach drivers asked passengers to lean to the right, then to the left, to keep the carriage on all four wheels. Soon the Northeast River branch of Chesapeake Bay came into view, then the port of Charlestown. Three years earlier Weld had counted a score of houses there; now Clark estimated it held almost eighty. A few miles down the road, though, he wrote nothing about the Principio Iron Works, a blast furnace aglow day and night as it cast ore into cannon balls and bar iron to become massive guns for federal warships. Clark's silence on this subject, as well as on the matchless landscapes he'd seen since returning to solid ground, is indeed to be regretted.[12]

In the afternoon he pulled up to a landing where the broad Susquehanna River empties into Chesapeake Bay and boarded a ferry for 140-year-old Havre de Grace, one of the largest settlements in Harford County.

Although Havre de Grace was also a center of banking and trade, Clark recorded about it only the number of residents: "this Town is improveing Containing about 80 or 90 houses." He and Chew again turned in their vehicle and ate supper. Hoping the Baltimore stagecoach would still have seats available, they decided to stay up and wait for it.

At three o'clock in the morning they found room on the Baltimore stagecoach and climbed aboard. At last Clark could enjoy the unaccustomed luxury of relaxing while someone else steered the vehicle and minded the horses, but again he paid little attention to anything but the names and populations of the settlements they passed. Probably referring to the present-day Bush (originally called Harford Town for Henry Harford, son of the last Lord Baltimore), Clark wrote, "a village called Hartford of 50 or 60 hous." Late that morning the stagecoach came to an abrupt stop three miles short of Baltimore. The driver put out all the passengers and explained that the law forbade him from taking them any farther.

29

The Sailors Soon Commenced a Riot

BALTIMORE was closed to vehicles arriving on any route connected to a yellow fever-stricken city. To keep out such traffic, officials at suburban checkpoints stopped inbound conveyances and asked travelers whether, in the last fifteen days, they had been in an afflicted locale. Anyone caught lying or attempting to sneak in faced a hundred-dollar fine.[1]

According to Clark, once he and Chew "were halted Examined & Sworn that we Came from no infexious Town" (New Castle and Christiana Bridge having thus far escaped the pestilence) they gained permission to proceed to Baltimore. They rented another cart for their baggage and set off on foot. As far as we know, Clark had not until this time visited Baltimore; he should have been delighted for the opportunity to see sugar refineries, mills for weaving cotton or producing paper, factories turning out everything from footwear to cordage, and other enterprises applying recently developed technologies. Unlike the streets of Louisville, many streets in Baltimore were paved, flanked with ample sidewalks, and illuminated at night by oil-burning lanterns. Among other marvels of engineering or science were a two-story courthouse built over an arching thoroughfare, a plank bridge across a channelized creek, and an observatory offering telescopic views beyond the mouth of the Patapsco River in Chesapeake Bay. Clark, however, wrote nothing about any of these or other attractions; he was intent on reaching the heart of town.[2]

Along the outskirts he began seeing modestly priced inns and taverns but kept going until they gave way to more elegant accommodations. He stopped at the southeast corner of Baltimore and Hanover streets and entered William Evans's Indian Queen, a deluxe hotel. Having made a fortune running stagecoaches between Philadelphia and Baltimore, Evans had parlayed his earnings into the Indian Queen, equipping it to offer comforts (probably house slippers, shoe-shining, private meals, iced drinks) unknown in most other establishments, and for nearly thrice the rate Clark paid Madame Chabaud for room and board in New Orleans.[3]

After he and Chew checked in, Clark had a load of laundry cleaned, bought a pair of boots and hosiery to wear while breaking them in, and set out to explore the surrounding area. Finding nearby streets disorderly with what he termed "great Contesting about an ellection of a member to Congress," he may have headed north several blocks until coming to St. Peter's Pro-Cathedral, near the site of the present-day Basilica of the Assumption. In the morning he returned for Sunday services, which included the priestly ordination of a French émigré named John Thomas Michael Edward Pierron de Mondesir. Of that day the only other activity Clark mentions is taking supper with a man he identifies as "Mr. Kennedy Merchant."[4]

Perhaps from him Clark learned about the political tumult going on in the neighborhood. A momentous election for U.S. congressman from Baltimore was set to begin on Monday, October 1, 1798, and to continue until the evening of October 4, voting to take place near the Indian Queen. The incumbent was Samuel Smith, a wealthy Revolutionary War hero as well as brigadier general of the Maryland militia and a man of Democratic-Republican principles; his challenger was a youthful, well-connected Federalist attorney named James Winchester. Similar in views on many subjects, the candidates were nonetheless in opposition over the explosive topic of relations with France: Smith was calling for measured diplomacy, and Winchester was advocating war. At stake was not just the course of international dealings or of Maryland politics; the victor would also help decide whether the highly controversial Alien and Sedition acts and the costly measures to increase the American military would stand for long.[5]

Smith had seemed a sure winner until a few weeks earlier when he angered President Adams by commenting that paying the bribe demanded by French envoys "X, Y, and Z" would be less expensive than going to war. Adams responded by impugning Smith's patriotism, and newspapers printed accounts of their exchange, causing Smith's lead to thin. Encouraged by this turn of events, Winchester and his friends tried to make Smith seem such a francophile as to appear un-American, a dangerous reputation to have, in light of the Alien and Sedition acts.[6]

Smith retaliated by calling Winchester an unethical lawyer and a pawn of Britain, then set about campaigning with renewed vigor, consolidating his base with the state militia, and cultivating the rising middle class of tradesmen, artisans, and sailors by opening to them his house and his liquor cabinet. As Smith's popularity rebounded, especially among fractious young men, his rivalry with Winchester turned increasingly acrimonious and often violent. By the time Clark arrived, the contest seemed almost even.[7]

Recently, Smith and a gang of friends had nearly caused a riot by trying to break up a Winchester rally, thereby provoking the election board to banish from the voting area all sticks, bludgeons, and firearms. Afraid that the threat of physical harm would keep his own supporters from the polls, Winchester asked them to turn out anyway but to wear on their hats white cockades rather than the provocative black ones favored by the Federalists. Meanwhile, word spread that Smith's people were preparing to attack Winchester's soon after the voting got under way.[8]

According to Clark, this seems to be what happened on Monday: "The Saylors Soon Commenced a riott which continued all day in torn flags fighting &c. one Killed a horrid Seen for an American as will as a Stranger." The fracas between Smith's and Winchester's adherents erupted at the polls and then spread to the streets. What disturbed Clark perhaps even more than the bloodshed was the spectacle of brother citizens—white men such as him—maiming and murdering each other over political differences.

Tempers continuing high on Tuesday; he avoided the election and instead walked the streets. He came upon an exhibition of a mature lion, perhaps one remaining from the Lailson Equestrian Circus (which had gone out of business in Philadelphia). The creature may have been the first big cat Clark had ever encountered alive and at close range. On that day in Baltimore, he also recorded the name of a married woman he saw, perhaps on stage, but his penmanship and orthography make identification impossible.[9]

On or about Wednesday, October 3, Clark received in the mail the bill of exchange he had entrusted to Daniel Coxe, with instructions to endorse it. Clark did so immediately and sent it back, hoping to take payment on Friday. The next day he wrote his brother Jonathan. Announcing that he was in Baltimore after completing "a Small Adventure of Tobacco" in New Orleans, William said he was heading to Virginia as soon as he received a communication from Trenton. In his logbook he noted that "the Opposition [between the supporters of Smith and those of Winchester was] not so outrageous as yesterday," probably because Smith was by then well ahead in the election.[10]

His lead continuing to grow, he was declared the winner once the polls closed on Thursday. At nightfall a victory parade took to the streets. A volunteer cavalry unit went first, followed by more than a hundred residents bearing lighted candles, then came tradesmen holding lanterns, the most conspicuous of them inscribed "The Constitution Inviolate" (a slogan of opposition to the Alien and Sedition acts) and, in succession, numerous supporters walking six abreast to the accompaniment of musicians and drummers. Behind them came Smith on an armchair probably mounted on poles and carried by his friends; he directed the march through town, past rows of lit-up houses with women and children gaping from windows. More lantern-bearers and another detachment of horsemen followed, then an immense concourse of citizens. Stopping the procession at his own residence, Smith gave the crowd "his most hearty acknowledgments for their attention," according to the *Baltimore Intelligencer*, a supporter of his and a key proponent of his Jeffersonian views. Trying to counter the reputation of Smith's contingent for unruliness, the newspaper continued: "There never was a popular procession of equal magnitude in which peace and harmony was more predominant."[11]

In his Mississippi logbook, Clark recorded one of the few other surviving accounts of the parade: "The Streets ellumonated at Dark, an Arch of lights went in front of Gen. S. who was Seated in a chear, with a Lorrel branch over his head Deckerated . . . light in rear, in This manner he was Carried thro: the Streets for Several hours with Shouts Drums & Instruments of all kind playing after him, &c. &c."

On Friday, October 5, Clark lost his companion of the past two and a half months when Beverly Chew caught the last stagecoach of the week for Fredericksburg. Still waiting for payment from the U.S. Treasury, Clark arranged to spend another night at the Indian Queen and took a stroll. Although the streets were once again orderly they were not yet quiet; supporters of Samuel Smith passed the entire day celebrating his reelection by firing artillery onboard the ship he kept in the harbor.

Reimbursement of the fifteen hundred Spanish dollars Clark had smuggled in his saddlebags from New Orleans to the thirty-first parallel finally arrived on October 6. Clark divided the sum. He kept nearly 250 dollars for himself and forwarded more than 1,250 of the remainder to a firm he called McDonnel and Company, specifying that such payment was "for Mr. Nabb"—perhaps Charles Nabb, a Louisville merchant who may have been a creditor of his brother George. William then booked a seat on the southbound stagecoach leaving on Monday night and arranged to send his trunk ahead to Virginia.[12]

Of Sunday he wrote, "I am visited by an old friend of mine Mr. Flaget a Romon Priest." The caller was French-born Benedict Joseph Flaget for whom Lieutenant Clark, early in his military career, had provided an escort when the missionary traveled from Louisville to Vincennes (at that time part of the immense Baltimore diocese). Having since returned east, Flaget may have recognized Clark at the church services he attended the previous Sunday.[13]

On Monday, Clark purchased some pantaloons (a type of trousers), a thirty-dollar watch, a vest, a heavy overcoat, a lock, saddlebags, and a sack of marbles (probably for Jonathan's children). He settled with William Evans and watched militiamen marching and drilling as they prepared to fight France should Congress declare war. That evening Clark attended the opening of the autumn season at the Holliday Street Theater. There actors who had fled yellow fever in Philadelphia performed in the melodrama *The Natural Son* by British dramatist Richard Cumberland and in the operatic comedy *The Son-In-Law*, by Irish playwright John O'Keeffe. Afterward, Clark returned to the Indian Queen for a brief rest before setting out to catch the late-night stagecoach to Virginia.[14]

* * *

On leaving Baltimore the driver pursued a hilly, unpaved road at times so muddy that vehicles sank beyond the axles and had to be hauled out with the help of passengers or nearby residents. At low places, the stagecoach may have rattled over trees laid crosswise on the mire, but causeways of that sort lasted only until their ribs sank into the muck or broke under wagon wheels.[15]

Seven miles outside town the coach reached a landing opposite Elkridge, an old port at the head of Patapsco River navigation. Fifty years earlier the settlement—then called Elk Ridge Landing—ranked second only to Annapolis in exporting tobacco and indigenous ferrous ore. Since then, however, decades of improvident cultivation had decimated tobacco production, and much of the locally mined iron now went to nearby foundries and became armaments. Some twenty-five miles farther along the Baltimore Pike, Clark once again appraised the habitation and position of settlements: "passed a Village Called Bladensburg containing about 60 houses in a decline."[16]

Later in the day he entered the almost vacant area set aside for the U.S. capital: "Arrived in the Federal City—one Wing of the Capatal nearly finished the Stone Work, this Town much scattered, the Presidents house nearly finished." In the fall of 1798 the ground between Capitol Hill and the edifice later to be known as the White House held just a few straggling buildings and brickyards. Clark paid close attention to the surroundings—unaware that he would return in 1801 to call on an Army friend, Meriwether Lewis, who then would be personal secretary to the newly elected president Thomas Jefferson, or that he would come back again on at least seven other occasions.

The stagecoach continued west to what he deemed the more pleasing terrain of Georgetown. This was a well-shaded, graceful neighborhood on

William Clark's notes on seeing the Federal District for the first time, from page 43 of his 1798–1801 Notebook.

a series of rises encompassing much of the site of Tohoga, an Anacostan Indian village established at the fall line of the Potomac and abandoned in the seventeenth century. Settled again during the early eighteenth century by English, and then Scottish, immigrants wishing to use the deep harbor at that head of Potomac River navigation, Georgetown held many two- and three-story houses, some of fieldstone, others of brick. Clark liked what he saw: "Dined at Georgetown, this place is Small, built of Brick, on the Side of a hill, on the Top is a most ellegunt College [the future Georgetown University]."

Late in the day the stagecoach crossed the Potomac River and reached Alexandria, Virginia. Wishing to transfer that night to the Fredericks- burg line, Clark got off the Baltimore Pike stagecoach. Either that eve- ning or the following day he walked to the harbor. There he studied a pair of privately owned, armed commercial vessels perhaps like the *Star* and the *Friendship*. He sized up their twenty-six guns and heard that tobacco was selling in Alexandria for several dollars more per hundredweight than it had been in New Orleans. He ate supper and remained nearby until the stage arrived at three o'clock in the morning. Following a route that would become part of U.S. Highway 1, the vehicle set off.

At Colchester he noted "a feww retched houses, a ware house a fine bridge," thereby striking a melancholy chord he repeated each time he ob- served a community reduced in population because destructive agricultur- al practices had diminished the crop yields. Such a place was Dumfries, an early settlement in Prince William County. Considering only a tobacco inspection station worthy of mention, Clark estimated that the town con- tained no more than fifty houses despite the hundreds it once had held. Similarly, after dining later that day at the village of Stafford Courthouse, he wrote, "The lands in this County is retchedly pore."

But Fredericksburg was different. Named for Frederick Louis, prince of Wales (he was the son of King George II of England and the father of George III), it was laid out in 1727 at the site of a public ferry on the Rap- pahannock. Fredericksburg had always attracted more settlers than the downstream communities did because its slightly higher elevation made its harbor less likely to fill with silt. The town remained a shipping hub even after tobacco production waned; flour, hemp, flax, and dairy goods became leading exports. By 1798 Fredericksburg was home to almost two thousand people and regularly drew thousands of others who wished to market their crops and to purchase from a wide array of domestic and foreign groceries, dry goods, and luxuries.

George Washington, his mother, and various members of their family had lived for a time in Fredericksburg and had been friends with influential Federalists. Even so, in 1798 the town was a hotbed of opposition to Federalism and its enactments, especially the Alien and Sedition laws. In July of that year, a prominent Fredericksburg lawyer and former U.S. congressman named John Francis Mercer had called out a local militia company to greet Vice President Jefferson as he made his way home to Monticello and, after welcoming him with a sixteen-round salute, escorted him into town for a political rally. Only one of several prominent local men eager to help Jefferson win the presidency, Mercer was soon to gather with them—and William Clark—in Fredericksburg.[17]

30

The Design of the Visit

THE stagecoach from Alexandria rolled through Fredericksburg until it halted at the southwest corner of Caroline and Charlotte streets, in front of the Indian Queen Tavern (an inn sharing a name but unconnected with the Baltimore hotel Clark had just stayed in). He climbed down, grabbed his bags, and headed for the two-story building, the largest structure in a complex filling nearly half a city block with facilities including a carriage house, a granary, a smokehouse, an outdoor kitchen, a forty-stall brick stable larger than many local residences, and a separate edifice for playing billiards.[1]

Over the years such conveniences had drawn George Washington, Thomas Jefferson, and James Monroe, but location on the stagecoach route—which was also the postal road and the main highway linking Philadelphia with Richmond and Williamsburg, Virginia—guaranteed the Indian Queen a succession of travelers willing to pay for genteel accommodations and meals lubricated with distilled spirits or spiked punch. By offering regional delicacies that sometimes included dressed sea-turtle, the proprietor, William Herndon, operated the dining room as a fashionable meeting place for local men of influence. And one of these was William's brother Edmund Clark; he lived not far from Belvoir, Herndon's estate some six miles outside of town.[2]

William had just enough time to check in before setting off for the Fredericksburg Theatre where the drama *Richard III; Or, the Battle of Bosworth Field* and a pantomime called *The Weird Sisters; Or, The Birth of Harlequin* were nearing the end of a paired run, as was a dual attraction appearing on other nights: *Robin Hood; Or, Sherwood Forest* and the farcical *The Mogul Tale; Or, The Descent of the Fredericksburg Cobbler in an Air Balloon.* Without specifying which productions he saw, Clark noted paying a dollar for "1 play tickets," the plural perhaps meaning he reserved a space for himself and a companion, or maybe that he paid to see both shows staged that evening. Because theatergoers often sent servants or slaves early to hold seats, maybe Clark dispatched York to do so.[3]

Although English audiences liked to view the Shakespearean trage-dy—in which the rightful ruler, Henry VII, eventually topples Richard—as vindication of royal succession through the Tudor line, Americans of Jeffersonian views saw it as a warning to Federalists about the wages of unfettered power. If Clark instead saw *Robin Hood*, Leonard MacNally's musical adaptation of the noble bandit legend, he watched fights against medieval injustices, a plot that could also be construed as a challenge to an overreaching federal government.

Just a few weeks earlier, a riot had broken out at the Fredericksburg Theatre when the U.S. envoy and moderate Federalist John Marshall—en route to Richmond after returning from the unsuccessful XYZ negotia-tions in France—showed up to attend a production. The orchestra set out to honor him with a rendition of Joseph Hopkinson's "The President's March," a Federalist anthem. In reaction, Democratic-Republicans in the audience stopped the music, touching off a brawl that spread out into the streets.[4]

On Friday, October 12, William Herndon arranged a special dinner for six prominent men from the area, William Clark, and himself. Blend-ing proper and phonetic spelling, Clark listed the other guests as "Cap Merser . . . & Cap Taylor Mr. Lewis. Green Ford & Coon." Although the omission of Christian names makes certain identification impossible, sources beyond the Mississippi Journal suggest who those men were and why they were gathered together.

"Cap. Merser" must have been John Francis Mercer, the local attorney who had welcomed Vice President Jefferson to town back in July. So op-posed was Mercer to going to war with France, Federalists called him a Jacobin, unfairly implying that he approved of the bloody excesses of the

French Revolution. Mercer was a past member of the Virginia House of Delegates and also of the U.S. Congress. Thinking he might be helpful in gaining recompense from the Virginia Assembly for George Rogers Clark's Revolutionary War debts, William set about winning his cooperation.[5]

He did so in the presence of an even more distinguished dinner guest. John Taylor was a rangy, red-headed Virginia legislator who the previous year had pledged to seek the same reparation for George. Before Taylor had been able to take action, though, a lawsuit against George had temporarily diverted key documents Taylor wanted to lay before the Virginia Assembly. The judicial proceedings having since run their course, Taylor at last had access to crucial evidence, yet he wished to withdraw from the case. Even worse for William, Taylor was not at liberty to explain why.[6]

The reason was that he had recently joined forces with Thomas Jefferson, James Madison, and a select group of Democratic-Republicans meeting secretly at Monticello to defeat the Alien and Sedition laws. Until recently, Taylor propounded that Virginia and neighboring North Carolina should separate from the United States and form their own confederation (unwittingly echoing the secessionist arguments of Wilkinson, Sebastian, and their associates in the early phases of the Spanish Conspiracy), but Jefferson prevailed on Taylor to abandon that position and instead to adopt one calculated to bring down the hated enactments without compromising the Union. They and their group at last devised a plan: Jefferson and Madison would prepare resolutions declaring the Alien and Sedition acts unconstitutional, whereupon John Breckenridge, a Kentucky lawmaker, would introduce Jefferson's resolution in the Kentucky state house, and Taylor would present Madison's draft to the Virginia Assembly. Because the protested measures made criminal offenses of exactly what the four of them were doing, Taylor had to keep their activities absolutely confidential.[7]

He therefore must have directed the dinner conversation away from revealing topics, especially if the man William Clark called "Green" was Timothy Green, founder and editor of the *Virginia Herald*, a newspaper sympathetic to the Adams administration. But because the diners Clark referred to as "Coon," "Lewis," and "Ford" were probably merchants Jacob Kuhn, John Lewis, and Standish Forde, the talk would more likely have turned to international business.

Kuhn kept a local store that sold a variety of products from Irish linen to coarse cottons for clothing slaves. Lewis (a distant cousin to Meriwether Lewis and a relative by marriage of George Washington) had traded for many years in Louisiana goods. John Lewis had also developed a mercantile acquaintance with James Wilkinson; their business relations went back at least to 1788 when Lewis—hoping to benefit from the exclusive trade privilege that Louisiana governor Esteban Miró recommended for Wilkinson—helped to bankroll Wilkinson's early commercial ventures to New Orleans. As we have seen, however, an abundance of tobacco from other sources and the Spanish Court's refusal to grant a monopoly put an end to the advantages Wilkinson hoped to gain, leaving Lewis holding Wilkinson's unpaid promissory notes. Probably to settle that debt, Lewis had recently purchased much of Wilkinson's Kentucky land, including his Frankfort residence prominently situated at the crossing of the streets he had named for himself and Miró.[8]

Lewis derived much of his credit and inventory from Standish Forde, a native Philadelphian who, with John Reed of that same city, had years of experience dealing with merchants in New Orleans and various American cities. Of all Herndon's friends around the table that evening, Lewis and Forde best understood the potential for growing rich from commerce with Louisiana. If they asked William Clark about his months there, he might have related that the *Star*, with Spanish money hidden among her payloads, successfully sailed through privateer-infested waters. He could have recounted the costs of doing business, perhaps mentioning the wine and money he'd slipped the Spanish inspectors of his cargoes. Not only would such talk have been truthful, it might encourage other businessmen to gamble on selling lucrative American goods in Louisiana before it became a battleground. As far as anyone knew, this had not yet happened.[9]

The meal ended before sundown and the diners dispersed. Clark took a walk to explore some of the private gardens for which Fredericksburg was famous. Plots laid out decades earlier by Mary Ball Washington were especially pleasing; perhaps instead he strolled a few blocks north of the Indian Queen to see thirteen horse-chestnut trees—one for each of the original states—planted by her son George. As dusk came on and the temperature dipped, a light drizzle began falling. Clark returned to his room and got ready to leave.[10]

* * *

He had no idea yet that events taking shape in the Mississippi valley were eventually to lure General Wilkinson back into active service as Agent 13, or that Wilkinson's continued intrigues with Spain were going to complicate Clark's life. That series of events began shortly after Wilkinson and his military retinue reached Natchez on September 27, 1798. After announcing his arrival to Governor Winthrop Sargent and relieving a grateful Captain Guion from the duties of command, Wilkinson pronounced the Natchez fort derelict and then descended the river fifty-five miles to Loftus Heights, the place Clark had termed "Loveless Cliffs." Wilkinson found them strategically superior to the Natchez bluffs (not to mention temptingly close to Louisiana, should he dare reprise his role as a paid operative of Spain). On October 5, the day after Clark witnessed Samuel Smith's victory parade in Baltimore, Wilkinson declared Loftus Heights his Army headquarters and ordered construction there of a fortified post.[11]

In selecting this location, he considered more than its potential for defense. Crowning the highest terrain below Natchez, Loftus Heights offered a unique vantage point for stopping naval forces coming up from Spanish territory. In addition, the Heights overlooked the Red River valley, reputedly a route to the fabled wealth of the Interior Provinces of New Spain. So Daniel Clark Sr. reminded Wilkinson in urging him to avail himself of those eminences near the mouth of the Red River, "which you know takes a long course westward into the country of—good stuff." Clark Sr. also wanted Wilkinson to seize New Orleans while French forces were overrunning Europe and thereby distracting the Spanish government from events in Louisiana. Clark Sr., however, was unaware that he was dealing with a double agent and did not realize that Wilkinson had no intention of attacking New Orleans or any part of the Spanish realm, at least not while Governor Gayoso was able to retaliate by releasing proof of his treacheries.[12]

When the general finished reconnoitering Loftus Heights, he paid a call on the international boundary camp, at that time pitched along Thompson Creek, some sixteen miles east of the site William Clark visited earlier that year. Wilkinson and Commissioner Ellicott had much to discuss, and each of them stood to gain a great deal from winning the other over to his views. Ellicott remained prudently doubtful of Wilkinson's fidelity to the United States, but he also felt a degree of gratitude toward him. Not only had the general enabled Ellicott in 1796 to descend the Ohio and Mississippi rivers on one of the Army's most comfortable barges, he had recently offered him the choice of where to meet and then accommodated him by coming to the boundary camp.[13]

Wilkinson arrived on October 14, 1798. He found Ellicott still at odds with Ensign McClary of the military escort and Thomas Freeman who, having failed in his mutiny attempt, was taking ungranted leaves of absence from the work. Wilkinson listened to Ellicott's grievances then proposed to replace McClary and to support the suspension of Freeman from the boundary project. (In a few months Wilkinson would serve his own interests by hiring Freeman to design the Loftus Heights military post; it was to be called Fort Adams, as the one at the Chickasaw Bluffs had ceased going by that name.) In helping Ellicott get rid of the censorious McClary and Freeman, Wilkinson cunningly gained leverage he would use against him a decade later, as we will soon see.[14]

Before departing, Wilkinson asked for a map indicating all roads and points of entry from Spanish terrain to the Mississippi Territory. His position in the Army made this request both legitimate and reasonable, but it also fit exactly into his practice of gathering topographical information about what he called "every critical pass, every direct route & every devious way between the Mexican Gulph & the Tennesse River."[15]

While Ellicott worked on the chart, the general headed back to Loftus Heights to play host to Daniel Clark Jr., another powerful man with grave misgivings concerning his loyalties. Daniel arrived in late October.

Wilkinson was glad to see him for several reasons, but especially because he wished to make sure he remained silent about Wilkinson's sub-rosa salary, a subject he knew of from his part-time employment with the Spanish government. That same occupation, though, had also alerted him to the murder of courier Henry Owen and to the embezzlement of thousands of pieces of eight by courier Joseph Collins. In addition, Clark Jr. knew that Philip Nolan's horse-rustling travels masked espionage carried out for the general. Although Wilkinson could have foreseen that Clark Jr. might acquire some such knowledge from Spanish records, he did not suspect that Thomas Power had also passed on to him further details of Wilkinson's seditions, or that Power had done so to avenge himself for being arrested at Wilkinson's Detroit headquarters and banished to Louisiana in 1797.[16]

Clark Jr. stayed several days at Loftus Heights. Claiming that the Spanish government still owed ten thousand dollars in back payments of his own illicit salary (but never uttering another known word about the 640-dollar debt, which silence strongly suggests he'd received it), Wilkinson asked Clark Jr. to broker a deal in which Governor Gayoso convey to him his Natchez estate rather than sacks of coined silver. Daniel refused to do so but echoed his uncle's plea for a U.S. assault against New Orleans while European conflicts practically guaranteed success. Feigning enthusiasm for the plan, Wilkinson nonetheless declined to take action.[17]

Clark Jr. left discontented and suspicious of Wilkinson. Inferring that the Spanish still wielded influence over the general, he decided to seek payback by revealing evidence of the general's corruption. To do this, Clark Jr. arranged for Ellicott to see a temporarily diverted communication from Gayoso to Power, the acting Spanish boundary commissary and surveyor.[18]

As Clark Jr. expected, Ellicot forwarded those words to Secretary of State Pickering:[19]

> I wonder you could not see the design of Genl. Wilkinson's visit to Mr. Ellicott's and Mr. Minor's camp. It was to fall upon some measures to obtain his [Wilkinson's] papers. They are all safe and never will be made use of against him if he conducts himself with propriety. In fact, the originals are at the Court [in Spain], the copies only are with me. Sebastian and Brown have both been here. They were coldly received.

You may inform them that their papers will be kept safe and secret and will not be made use of to their injury unless their conduct in future should require such a measure.[20]

That is, Gayoso possessed plenty of documents with which to ruin Wilkinson, Sebastian, and Brown if they tried to take unfair advantage of Spain.

Ellicott, however, sent Pickering an accompanying explanation much different in tone from what Clark Jr. hoped he would compose. Rather than raising further alarm about the Spanish Conspiracy, Ellicott made light of it, emphasizing that Wilkinson and his confederates had spurned Carondelet's plot. Ellicott must have known that Gayoso's letter to Power contained further proof of the general's treachery, but he was beholden to him for helping Ellicott get free of Freeman and McClary. Having no such reason to withhold incriminating evidence about Sebastian and Brown, however, Ellicott passed along their names to Pickering, unaware that William Clark—the courier he had entrusted with important messages a few months earlier—was complicit in their smuggling operation. Back at the Indian Queen, William Clark completed preparations to leave Fredericksburg, little suspecting that his own involvement in that money-running mission might someday threaten to become public knowledge.[21]

31

The End of the Journey

THE road leading south from Fredericksburg was dissolving into mud when William Clark and William Herndon set out on the morning of October 13, 1798. Winter was already nipping mountain peaks just beyond the western horizon, prompting Virginians to harvest corn and wheat, dig potatoes, stash cabbages in shallow trenches to be covered with mulch, and turn shoats and young sows out in stubbly fields to root for kernels still on the ground. The smell of swine—whether living or curing—was in the air. People throughout the Piedmont were butchering hogs and salting their parts into bacon, gammon, and middlings, saving other cuts for chops and roasts, and relegating the offal to feed their slaves or to pickle.[1]

Three weeks having passed since the autumnal equinox, the sun was setting earlier each afternoon, prompting Clark to proceed at a smart pace. Perhaps at Belvoir he paused to look over Herndon's impressive stock of horses to select several young mounts for Richard C. Anderson in Kentucky. We may never know exactly what happened that day. Clark wrote only, "a Wet Morning Set out With Mr. Hurndon Road &c to my Brothers, Got to Bro Edms late all well &."[2]

While warming himself that night at Edmund's hearth, William must have reported on his venture to Louisiana and asked about the likelihood of war with France. Rumors were rife in Virginia that the French—with the help of Creole allies in the West Indies—were planning to storm U.S. shores and pillage their way inland. Whether Edmund believed the stories is uncertain, but he paid attention to related developments, and particularly to news of the enormous Provisional Army authorized of late by Congress. As he understood, Lieutenant General George Washington and his chief subaltern, Inspector General (with a rank of major general) Alexander Hamilton, aimed to raise many scores of new officers to command the thousands of soldiers to be recruited.[3]

Edmund would indeed secure such a commission, perhaps because pay in the Provisional Army was set higher than it was in the regular Army. Moreover, Washington and Hamilton were seeking to fill upper echelons with veterans possessing influential connections and Federalist leanings. Edmund had been a lieutenant during the Revolution, came from a respected family, and was unalterably devoted to his country and to the rule of law, but his political views are mostly unknown. Living near Fredericksburg did not make him a Democratic-Republican any more than living closer to Monticello would have; Federalists in that part of the state had recently hoisted a seventy-foot pole inscribed "Independence or Death," an expression of resistance to France and, of course, to Jeffersonian policies.[4]

William continued south the next morning, aware that his brother Jonathan might be away from home—having left his wife, Sarah (called Sally) in charge of their plantation until he came back. Perhaps while he rode, William studied a topography he'd not observed in almost three years. Except along the horizon the ground appeared more or less level, but to his left it gradually descended toward the sea and, on his right, inclined at an almost imperceptible angle toward the distant Blue Ridge. He knew that if Jonathan happened to be on one of his frequent visits to the other side of that cobalt-gray front range of the eastern Appalachians, he could be gone for a week or more.

In him William surely recognized some of his own fascination with travel. When not on the road, Jonathan farmed five hundred acres he had purchased in 1774 from their parents. With his wife and children, he occupied a large dwelling on that tract in the southeast corner of Spotsylvania County and near his residence he housed dozens of their slaves. To support all these dependents, he also invested in land, served as an officer in the Virginia militia, and performed governmental functions that required him to act as a sort of circuit-riding magistrate.

He often set out on those journeys, some of them lasting many days at a time. In a diary he noted where he went (usually to locations within Virginia), the people on whom he called (William Herndon and Edmund Clark were favorites), and his places of lodging, but he recorded few clues as to why he'd left home. The number of Jonathan's travels suggests he enjoyed being on the road, but his minimal notes reveal most of his trips as somewhat brief, routine, and comfortable. Because he seldom ranged far or spread a bedroll on the ground, his journeys formed the antithesis of what from 1804 to 1806 would be the experience of his youngest brother. Even so, William may have modeled some of his own journal-keeping on Jonathan's terse style.[5]

William reached his brother's farm by evening. A subsequent owner of the house was to note that mulberry and catalpa trees shaded the main residence; perhaps they did in 1798. By the time it was razed in the early twentieth century it was an ample, two-story wooden structure heated by five fireplaces, each attached to a massive central chimney. Erected before Jonathan purchased the tract, the house at some point gained five dormers and an east-facing porch. Rather than record details about his arrival, though, William scrawled only, "Came to Bro Jona. foun[d] he was over the ridge all well." Already gone for several days, Jonathan was pursuing an unusually long trip, one taking him across the Potomac and into rural Maryland.[6]

The last William heard before leaving Kentucky, Jonathan and Sally had three boys and two girls (a daughter having died a few years earlier). On arrival at their house in 1798, he met their infant son, George Washington Clark, and became reacquainted with the other children and with Sally. William no doubt made himself as useful as he could. Perhaps in the next few days he also rode back to Fredericksburg to stock up on supplies; he writes that he bought blankets, tack, and warm clothes for the homeward trip. In addition, he engaged a man—whom he called "Goodlove" in one entry and "Goodlar" in another—to drive a string of colts to Kentucky for his brother-in-law Anderson.[7]

Jonathan finally returned on Wednesday, October 24, and remained with his family for a few days before setting off once more on short journeys, William likely accompanying him. On October 29, temperatures dropped as the first snowstorm of the season swept toward the Blue Ridge and the Piedmont beyond, freezing ponds and threatening livestock left out in the open. It was obvious that unless William departed soon for Kentucky, ice and snow might block his way through the mountains until the spring. He got ready to commence the last leg of his travels.[8]

On the second Sunday of November, he bade farewell to Sally and the children and then rode with Jonathan to Edmund's house. Having just completed a letter informing George of developments in the actions related to his war debts, Jonathan gave it to William. As if in deliberate imitation of Jonathan's minimal writing style, William summed up the past month in just seven words: "in Spotsylvania untill Sunday 11th of Novr," adding "Set out for Kentucky."[9]

Perhaps taking the same roads Jonathan liked to follow across the Blue Ridge and northeast through the Shenandoah Valley, William presently reached the home of William Aylett Booth, a speculator in western real estate and a Revolutionary War veteran married to Rebecca Hite, Sally Clark's sister. Booth was not to settle in Kentucky until 1804, yet he visited it so often he was something of an expert on the routes between there and northern Virginia. Maybe he counseled William about the best roads to take across the Appalachians.[10]

Clark comprehended the general course he wished to go, as he had first followed it with his parents and sisters fourteen years earlier and had probably taken it again as a soldier. But since those days, many thousands of travelers had passed that way, opening a myriad of trails across the roughly parallel, geologic rumples including Cacapon Mountain, Sideling Hill, Knobly Mountain, and Red Ridge, and then the innumerable smaller rises slumping toward the Ohio River watershed. Clark surely also wanted to learn which taverns on that route had acceptable food and lodging.

Soon he pressed on. From Allegheny ridges he came down into southern Pennsylvania—crossing the boundary ascertained in the 1760s by Charles Mason and Jeremiah Dixon and run all the way to the western edge of the state by Andrew Ellicott and his associates in the 1780s. Outliers and foothills still dotted the landscape, but it gradually declined to a high, narrow floodplain. When Clark reached Redstone, a Mononga-hela River village later known as Brownsville, he paused for two days, no doubt remembering the winter he and his family had waited there for warmer temperatures to reopen navigation to Kentucky.

He continued overland to Wheeling, the 1770 terminus of a path blazed by Ebenezer Zane, a native Virginian. Zane had since developed Wheeling, extending his trail to the Ohio River and then westward from the opposite shore. In 1796, after the Battle of Fallen Timbers and the Treaty of Greenville quieted the Northwest Territory, Zane received congressional authorization to run the road southwest to an Ohio Riv-er landing across from Maysville, Kentucky. Having also acquired from the federal government large parcels of acreage where the route would cross the Muskingum, Hocking, and Scioto rivers, he opened toll fer-ries at those points while his crews cut the remainder of what was to be known as Zane's Trace. His projects benefited Zane as well as the nation; the Trace would carry most mail to and from the Northwest Territory, sparing taxpayers the higher risks and costs of transporting those loads by water. Settlers followed so rapidly that, in 1798, the land to become Ohio was filling with houses, further prospering Zane and advancing his many highway-related ventures.[11]

Clark must have taken Zane's Trace to the mouth of Paint Creek at the Scioto River. There he stopped a few days at Chillicothe, the creation of another entrepreneurial Virginian, Revolutionary War veteran Nathaniel Massie. Laid out only two years earlier near Mount Logan (a picturesque low rise to the east) and ancient tumuli to be known as the Hopewell Group, Chillicothe was fast becoming a town not so much because of the vistas it offered but because Massie advertised free lots to the first hundred residents.[12]

Clark lingered there but did not note for how long. Having remained a "few days" with Colonel Booth, then paused a while longer at Redstone, Wheeling, and Chillicothe, he was to spend on the road a total of six weeks, more than twice the time it usually took in temperate weather to ride from Fredericksburg to Louisville. He must have expected his parents to be anxious for his return, but there is no known evidence he had written them since the summer.

* * *

While Clark made his way west, Kentucky legislators voted to accept Thomas Jefferson's resolution protesting the Alien and Sedition acts as unconstitutional usurpations of power. John Taylor's Virginia brethren adopted James Madison's similar resolution the following month. In other state houses the debate continued over what, if anything, to do about those controversial laws.

Meanwhile, from his Loftus Heights camp, General Wilkinson dispatched a message to Governor Gayoso, complaining that rumors of their dealings "have been interpreted into the most sinister designs, and falsehoods & fictions have been invented, from Natchez to Philadelphia, to rob me of my Fame & Fortune." At around the same time, Wilkinson received a message from Ellicott saying he'd seen a letter from Power implicating Wilkinson of crimes Ellicott left unspecified. Ellicott added, rather unconvincingly, that he did not believe the general could be guilty of them. Dissembling as ever, Wilkinson replied with holiday greetings on Christmas Eve.[13]

William Clark reached Mulberry Hill on the same date. He wrote "Arrive at my father the 24 of Decr. at Dusk," electing not to mention that he found his mother on her deathbed and his father stricken with grief. And he said nothing about whether George was there or still hiding out in Spanish St. Louis. Realizing that he would likely have to remain home for a long time, William put the Mississippi Journal away. He would not use it again until the spring of 1801.[14]

PART IV

More Hardship and Challenge
1799 to 1807

32

Not the Least Shadow of Succeeding

FOR nearly a half-century, Ann Rogers Clark had guided the family through a long train of difficulties, among them, the war for independence, the deaths of three adult children, the move to Kentucky, and George's heavy financial reverses. Without her, John Clark expected to die before long. Jonathan feared this would happen; he doubted his father was to "pass the remainder of his days with that satisfaction which we could wish," but he hoped he would "submit to the loss with the resignation of [a] Christian, knowing that the dispensation of providence is such that we are to part."[1]

To William, whose burdens began increasing as soon as he returned home, the dispensation of providence must have seemed such that his carefully planned, costly, exhausting travels of nearly ten months might as well have never occurred. Age and bereavement taking a toll on his father, William found himself in charge of John's extensive property, including the 318-acre Mulberry Hill farm. Although neither immense nor opulent, it was costly to maintain, holding, as it did, the Clark residence, slave quarters, barns, stables, sheds, a spring house, detached kitchen, gristmill, smokehouse, slaves, animals, and furnishings.[2]

Agriculture being the principal business at Mulberry Hill, the lives of the Clarks and their labor force revolved around the continual cycles of plowing, sowing, tending, and reaping, and then of marketing, consuming, or grinding the harvest. Every step of the sequence depended not only on proper temperature and rainfall but on the continued health of plants and animals. There were frequent setbacks such as a cutworm infestation in the spring of 1799, yet William continued doing his part to lead the family.[3]

By the summer George was back from his self-imposed exile in Spanish Louisiana, disconsolate because France had again dismissed his offer to conquer New Orleans, and because creditors were redoubling their efforts to collect from him. Making matters worse were tidings from Jonathan who—believing the action for recompense of George's war debts had "not the least shaddow of Succeeding" with a Virginia Assembly more intent on guarding against invasion by the French than on rectifying past wrongs—had withdrawn George's petition. Jonathan was instead consulting Captain John Mercer on whether to sue Virginia for the debt, both of them knowing such an effort would likely fail too.[4]

In July 1799, William rode for Washington County, Ohio, to enforce Jonathan's real estate interests there. Scarcely had he returned when his father developed a cough of increasing severity. Probably with the advice of Benjamin Sebastian, John Clark drew up a will. As the son likeliest to keep the family farm productive, William was to receive it, eight slaves, acreage in Fayette County, Kentucky, and land George had once owned; it lay just north of the Ohio River. Liberal also to Jonathan and Edmund and to the husbands of his daughters (Kentucky law forbade married women to inherit directly), John bequeathed little to George whose creditors stood ready to attach anything of value.[5]

John Clark died on July 29, 1799. After no doubt conferring with fellow executors George Rogers Clark, Richard C. Anderson, William Croghan, Charles Thruston (second husband of his sister Frances), and Benjamin Sebastian, the only executor unrelated to the Clarks, William filed the will in the Jefferson County court on October 1. By then he possessed a good sense of what he was inheriting, having collected debts and examined his father's assets, the largest of which were tracts of undeveloped acreage. But because most of those parcels as yet had little worth and William was also trying to meet George's ever-compounding obligations from expenditures incurred years earlier, he often had to use his own money to make ends meet.

The long-term outlook was grim. Laurent Bazadone—the Spanish subject whose boatloads of merchandise George appropriated in 1786 for his troops at Vincennes—had renewed his suit for damages. The heirs of one of George's subalterns during the Revolution wanted eight thousand pounds to settle another old debt. And Humphrey Marshall, a Kentucky Federalist once linked with George in a land transaction, demanded payment of an additional arrearage.[6]

Several weeks after the river thawed in 1800, William had someone (whose identity is no longer known) dispatch sixty-six barrels of flour to Daniel Clark Jr., asking him to forward the revenue from those goods to a man William identified only as "Mr. Usher of Baltimore." William's letter has not survived but Daniel's carefully worded answer has. By promising to act with "all the caution and discretion the nature of the case requires" and making circumspect mention that Usher might not "be fully acquainted with the Trade of this Country," Daniel implied that he would conceal the coined proceeds among cargoes shipped from New Orleans to Baltimore.[7]

In another missive he proposed helping William procure title to a certain tract of Kentucky land. William was to decline the offer. Still, he could not help but appreciate Daniel's flattering words: "Our acquaintance tho' but short has deservedly placed you so high in my estimation that I should not without regret give up the idea of seeing you again & cementing it more closely."[8]

Daniel Clark Jr. was more determined than ever to oust the Spanish from Louisiana. Perhaps hoping to enlist William in this effort, he wrote him on June 22, 1800, recounting the experiences of William Augustus Bowles, a Maryland-born adventurer. Bowles and his Indian reinforcements had recently bluffed the Spanish commandant of Fort San Marcos de Apalache into surrendering the West Florida stronghold to what he mistakenly believed was a superior force. In other words, the enervated Spanish Army, facing a ragtag band with inferior arms, failed to defend a solidly built and staunchly equipped outpost. Daniel's point was clear: the time had come to rise up against the Spanish.[9]

George Rogers Clark said the same thing, but his recklessly unrestrained drinking disqualified him from leading a coup. "Bro. G," wrote William to Jonathan, "has given up more to that vice which has been so injurious to him than ever." Without the help of George and his troops or of General Wilkinson and those at his command, there was little hope of ending the moribund Spanish regime in Louisiana. Instead it would terminate on October 1, 1800, when Napoleon's agents persuaded those of Carlos IV to cede the province back to France—but to do so in secret. Thereafter the Spanish were to continue administering New Orleans and what would become the Orleans Territory almost until the United States, according to the Louisiana Purchase, formally took possession of it on December 20, 1803.[10]

In May 1800 William Clark rejoined the Kentucky militia, this time as a captain of cavalry. Unlike his first stint, the present one promised little or no Indian fighting, the victory at Fallen Timbers having temporarily quieted the Ohio Valley. Whatever sort of action he expected to see, he did not record.[11]

* * *

Despite helping to settle John Clark's estate, Benjamin Sebastian continued his complicity with Spain. With nearly 265 of his illicit Spanish dollars in William's coffee barrel (and probably many more such coins hidden deep in other containers) reaching his Louisville home by early March of 1799, Sebastian had the wherewithal to advance his intrigues. He decided to concentrate on the one seeking a Spanish land-grant.

To win approval for it he composed a lengthy letter to Governor Gayoso, reporting accurately that the Alien and Sedition acts were embittering western Americans against the federal government. From this point on, though, Sebastian exaggerated, saying those laws were causing large numbers of Kentuckians to seek refuge across the Mississippi from "the oppressions and despotism of this [country]." Asking royal permission to found in Louisiana a major settlement of such expatriates, he closed and scrambled the letter into thousands of numerals and more than twenty cryptic symbols cloaking key words. He added a top-secret postscript:

> As the present voyage is probably the last that Mr. [Samuel Montgomery] Brown will ever make to New Orleans and, of course, the last safe opportunity that will occur for some time at least of transmitting my pension [Sebastian's Spanish salary] to Kaskaskia by the Mississippi, will it be imposing too much upon your goodness to ask you to add to the money obligations which I am allready under, that of sending my pension for the present year by Mr. Brown?[12]

Sebastian gave the communication to Brown who was soon to leave for New Orleans.

As we have seen, Brown was a smuggler as well as a proponent of funneling the output of Kentucky to Spanish Louisiana in order to gain exclusive trading privileges and a loan of two hundred thousand interest-deferred dollars. On February 27, 1799, he had resumed his campaign for those benefits by dispatching downriver a load of flour and Kentucky delicacies including "a Piece of smoked Beef, a Venison Ham, & a Neat's Tongue" to be delivered to Gayoso by a river navigator named Llewellyn Griffith. Shortly after Griffith got under way, Brown followed aboard a new vessel specially designed and built to haul Louisiana exports upstream.[13]

Brown reached New Orleans in June. Finding General Wilkinson at Gayoso's house while awaiting a ship to take him to New York on U.S. Army business, Brown kept quiet about the monopoly, knowing Wilkinson to be a potential rival for it. Instead, Brown dropped off Sebastian's letter, accepted in return an order on the royal treasury, and collected Sebastian's salary of two thousand dollars. Shortly thereafter, Brown succumbed to causes no longer known. At around the same time Gayoso also died, probably of yellow fever.[14]

Griffith eventually took charge of Brown's monetary cargo (most of it having disappeared since his death) and ascended the rivers. To Sebastian he turned over a mere three hundred dollars, allegedly to reimburse the costs of keeping and educating Brown's son while the father went to Louisiana. Sebastian surely was outraged to receive so little of his Spanish pay but, fearing disclosure of its illicit origin, dared not press for more.

He began looking for another courier. After some time he settled on Thomas Bullitt, a Jefferson County trader and relative of Alexander Scott Bullitt, the wealthy grower whose tobacco William Clark had taken to New Orleans in 1798. Thomas's mercantile business lent plausible reason for carrying sugar, coffee, and other Louisiana goods in the sort of containers most useful to smuggling. Rather than revealing to him the unlawful nature of the payments he would be transporting, Sebastian falsely claimed they were profits from a past, legitimate venture he had undertaken with the Spanish government.[15]

* * *

With taxes increasing throughout 1799 and 1800 to pay the high cost of military measures passed in 1798, Americans steadily lost enthusiasm for fighting the French Republic. In northeastern Pennsylvania, an itinerant auctioneer named John Fries embodied the spirit of those times by leading an armed band to harass a number of assessors levying taxes on houses. Fries was promptly arrested, tried, and found guilty of treason. Although President Adams later pardoned Fries, so many Americans publishing or uttering words critical of the Federalists were prosecuted under the Sedition Act, and so many immigrants fled the country because of the Alien Act, those laws became more unpopular than ever.

Yet the resolutions adopted by Kentucky and Virginia failed to inspire similar protest in other states. The opposite occurred in New Hampshire whose legislature held unanimously—and in explicit disagreement with Thomas Jefferson—that only the U.S. court system could weigh the validity of federal laws. In response, Kentucky passed a resolution holding that states can indeed nullify unconstitutional federal enactments. The Virginia Assembly held off from issuing further resolutions, but tempers there ran so high that Alexander Hamilton proposed sending troops to put down anti-Federalist sympathy in that state, despite knowing that a show of force would probably lead to bloodshed. Unwilling to take such provocative measures, even to strengthen his own bid for reelection, Adams continued refusing to call out the Army.[16]

In the meantime, the conflict with France intensified as shipyards along the Eastern seaboard produced vessels for use against privateers. By 1800, the *United States* and the *Delaware* (the frigates William Clark observed at New Castle in September, 1798) had become only a small fraction of the ships guarding U.S. commercial vessels bound for foreign ports. France retaliated by sending her men-of-war to prowl shipping lanes in the Caribbean, but American craft surprised them. By taking the battle to the enemy, the U.S. Navy, with the help of armed, privately owned vessels, gained the upper hand over French corsairs.

Even so, the president still refrained from seeking a declaration of war. In February 1799 he appointed William Vans Murray, President Washington's minister to the Netherlands, to negotiate with France. Thereafter Adams dispatched moderate Federalists Oliver Ellsworth and William R. Davie to share diplomatic responsibilities with Murray. Those actions angered Hamilton and his partisans who were devoted to bringing about a war south of the thirty-first parallel. To neutralize opposition to their goal, Hamilton connived with Secretary of War McHenry and Secretary of State Pickering to block the reelection of the conciliatory Adams.[17]

Hamilton was a novice at intrigue, however, when compared with General Wilkinson, his high-ranking subaltern in the Provisional Army. Unaware that Wilkinson—for his own mercenary purposes rather than for the sake of national expansion—had been hoping to kindle a large-scale, armed conflict in Spanish realms, Hamilton called him east to discuss such a possibility, stipulating he come by way of New Orleans. This being the route most travelers took, Wilkinson must have recognized that those words were a veiled instruction to gather intelligence while there. Gayoso unwittingly advanced the general's efforts by sharing his home with him, then letting him sail down the Mississippi past the mighty Fort San Felipe, which William Clark had studied the previous summer.[18]

At sea when Gayoso grew ill and died, Wilkinson probably learned of his death only when the voyage ended. For more than a decade he and Gayoso had maintained a lively and often furtive correspondence, keeping company whenever possible, and maintaining an amicable appearance that Wilkinson furthered by declaring he would gladly give up one arm if he could embrace Gayoso with the other. But now that Gayoso was dead, the general might relax; there was no one else able to reveal his many crimes if he were to bring an assault against Spanish territory.[19]

In New York, Wilkinson and Hamilton were pleased to learn they both desired such a war. Aiming to bring one about, Hamilton charged the general to assess how western Americans would react to an attack against Spanish Louisiana or Florida and to devise means of supplying U.S. troops in those regions. In addition, Wilkinson was to stockpile munitions, especially artillery key to siege warfare and, of course, to gather intelligence on Spanish military works—a purpose to which William Clark's 1798 notes might ideally lend themselves. As if to goad the Spanish into firing the first shot, Hamilton and Wilkinson devised a plan for moving three thousand soldiers—nearly the entire U.S. Army—down the Mississippi toward Natchez and Loftus Heights.[20]

From that moment on, however, Hamilton's hawkish strategy went awry. After hearing details of his conference with Wilkinson, General Washington, wishing not to provoke the Spanish, forbade Hamilton from stationing large numbers of soldiers along the lower Mississippi. President Adams went further and refused to let the United States launch an offensive against the French-Spanish alliance or to encourage a potential ally, such as Britain, to do the same.[21]

Despite such restrictions, Hamilton found a way to persist in his bellicose pursuits. In a chapter of history almost unknown, probably because numerous related documents were lost when the British burned Washington in 1814, Hamilton and Wilkinson went ahead with their design to found a huge military camp as close as possible to Spanish lands. Rather than concentrate forces on the Mississippi, they would do so instead just a few miles away, along the lowest reaches of the Ohio, on a vast meadow overlooking a chain of rocks slowing river traffic. William Clark had visited the site in 1795 and floated by it in March 1798, and in the summer of 1798 General Wilkinson reconnoitered it the day before firing his thirteen-gun salute at Spanish New Madrid.[22]

His conference with Hamilton completed, Wilkinson set sail from Virginia on December 16, 1799. Back in New Orleans he met the pleasant but lax new governor, the Marqués de Casa Calvo, and shrewdly judged him unlikely to oppose an American military buildup just north of the thirty-first parallel. But before Wilkinson could upset the delicate stability of the lower Mississippi valley by sending forces in that direction, he received orders from the War Department to return east. He sailed out of New Orleans in the late spring of 1800 and arrived in Virginia in July.[23]

Much had changed during his brief absence. Not only was the unfinished City of Washington now the seat of national government, but President Adams, on learning of Pickering's and McHenry's disloyalty, had asked them to resign. McHenry did so immediately; when Pickering did not follow that example, Adams dismissed him. Moreover, ministers Murray, Davie, and Ellsworth were reaching an agreement with the

French to end the undeclared war. In anticipation of this outcome, Congress had voted to disband the Provisional Army and to reorganize the 3,429 members of the regular Army into units deployed for peacetime duty, thereby dooming the plans of Wilkinson and Hamilton to force a conflict in Louisiana. Moreover, congressional caucuses had chosen nominees for the presidential election to take place on December 3. Federalists John Adams and Charles C. Pinckney were to run against Democratic-Republicans Thomas Jefferson and Aaron Burr.[24]

As if expecting those very alignments, Wilkinson reached the District of Columbia well prepared to ingratiate himself with anyone who might eventually command him. For Hamilton, a known philanderer, he brought suggestive accounts of the shapely women he'd met while his ship paused at Cuba, along with Louisiana pecans and orange bushes for the Hamilton family. To curry favor with Mr. Adams and his friends, Wilkinson threw a party enlivened with the music of an Army band. To Jefferson, an enthusiast of western ethnography and natural history, the general delivered "petrifactions, an Indian knife, and a map of the parts of Mississippi Territory," some of those things acquired through adventurer Philip Nolan. But to Burr, a fellow Revolutionary War veteran with dreams of power and glory akin to his own, Wilkinson passed along information about Spanish lands, introducing him to the codes and cyphers with which they would communicate on that enticing topic.[25]

Until Samuel Dexter, the new secretary of war, arrived to take up duties in Washington, Wilkinson was the ranking officer at that department, enjoying full access to documents, even those touching on his double life with Spain. He was still in town on the night of November 8, 1800, when a blaze of suspicious origin broke out in the War Department, consuming records there and practically eliminating any evidence the government might use against him. Whether Wilkinson caused the fire has never been proved, but it further allayed his fear of being brought to justice for plotting against his own country.[26]

33

The Sport of Fortune

JOHN Adams managed to keep the peace yet won only sixty-five electoral votes in the presidential election of 1800. Because each of his opponents, running mates Thomas Jefferson and Aaron Burr, received seventy-three electoral votes apiece, a Constitutional flaw (to be corrected by the Twelfth Amendment) made them rivals with each other for the presidency. Not until thirty-six ballots were cast in the House of Representatives did the deadlock break on February 17, 1801, with Jefferson emerging the victor and Burr his vice president.

During those months of uncertainty over who was to succeed Mr. Adams, Alexander Hamilton, despite having become a civilian when Congress disbanded the Provisional Army, continued with plans for what would come to be called Cantonment Wilkinsonville. The site chosen for it—in present-day Pulaski County, Illinois, on the northern shore of the last great bend of the Ohio River—promised control over a major entrance to the Mississippi, still the western border of the United States. Construction of the camp began early in 1801 and was completed a few months later. By mid-summer it held more than fourteen hundred soldiers, almost one-third of the Army.[1]

Possessing just a modest set of artillery and a layout more typical of a staging ground than of a defensive works, Cantonment Wilkinsonville was evidently not intended to protect the frontier from the Indians, French, or Spanish, none of whom had presented much of a threat since the 1790s. Rather, the installation appeared ideal for striking a blow south of the thirty-first parallel. Such an action would create an excuse for invading what Americans believed was still Spanish territory.[2]

If this was indeed Hamilton's (and Wilkinson's) scheme, it went awry when Jefferson, promising to reduce the Army to a size commensurate with peacetime, was elected president. Under his leadership, Hamilton would be unable to resurrect the Provisional Army or to reenter military life, and Wilkinson had to shelve any hope for an offensive south of the thirty-first parallel. In Washington in March and part of April 1801, Wilkinson was instead obliged to organize lists of officers, their ranks and deployments, in preparation for drastic cutbacks that would also lead to the shuttering of his namesake on the lower Ohio. By August 1801, soldiers posted there began receiving orders to report to other forts, and in April 1802 the Army abandoned Cantonment Wilkinsonville.[3]

In the meantime, to help prune the officer corps and to assist in other ways, Jefferson retained as his own personal secretary Meriwether Lewis, then a twenty-six-year-old Army captain who had grown up near Monticello. At the president's request, Wilkinson released Lewis from military duties but preserved his rank and right to promotion. On April 1, 1801, Lewis reached Washington and began his new assignment.[4]

At around the same time, Clark learned that Laurent Bazadone had at last prevailed in his legal action and was about to levy against George's property. Unless William acted fast, his brother could lose a large portion of acreage, the only asset of value remaining to him. Advised to countersue in a tribunal of the Northwest Territory, where Bazadone had brought his lawsuit, William preferred instead to put the matter before the U.S. Supreme Court, provided it agreed to review a territorial action predating its own founding in 1789. To increase the chance such a hearing would take place, William asked Daniel Symmes, clerk of the Northwest Territory Court, to comb the Bazadone suit for issues appropriate to federal examination.[5]

Then Clark got ready to travel to Washington on his first long journey since 1798. Packing little more than his own necessities and George's papers, he made room for the Mississippi Journal. This time he did not intend to employ it for charting his route or plotting coordinates, and of course there would be no foreign military works along the way to note. Rather, he planned to inscribe in the book a daily total of miles covered, sums spent, and his places of nightly repose, conserving for future use as many as possible of the dozens of blank pages remaining in the volume.

Probably with his slave York he set out on horseback on May 24, 1801, having written a title in the journal, "Memorandon of a Journey, Destane & Expens to the Nothest & back in the Summer 1801." He headed southeast toward the Wilderness Road leading to the Cumberland Gap and stopped by nightfall at the Salt River, some twenty miles from Mulberry Hill. He was passing through a region he knew well from his early years in the militia and from later, when he traveled Kentucky carrying messages and recruiting soldiers for the U.S. Army.

On May 26 he reached Harrodsburg, the oldest, permanent white settlement in Kentucky, then proceeded to Danville where he spent nearly four shillings, probably on supper and lodging. He rode hard May 27 and 28 and forded the Rockcastle and Laurel rivers and Richland Creek. Just west of the Cumberland Gap—of late widened to admit horse-drawn wagons—were the last miles of Kentucky, and beyond them Virginia. He remained on the Wilderness Road (parts of which would become U.S. Highway 58) and slept in a tavern on his first night in Virginia. After sunup he set out again, soon crossing the Holston River.

Near the town of Abingdon his route bent northeastward (paralleling the future course of Interstate 81), splitting the Blue Ridge from the Appalachian chains to the west. He picked up speed, making a daily average of almost forty miles. After riding through a town he called "With Court House" (now known as Wytheville, seat of Wythe County), he crossed the New River, traversed Montgomery County, and continued through the valley.

On June 5 he turned north toward Botetourt County and almost certainly called on William Preston, an Army companion who had also been a special favorite of General Wilkinson and a friend of Meriwether Lewis. Although Clark and Preston may have known about Lewis's current, distinguished duty as President Jefferson's secretary, they little realized they would become brothers-in-law when Clark married Julia Hancock, sister to Preston's spouse. A tale passed down in Clark's family holds that around this time he met both Julia and her cousin Harriet Kennerly, who

The opening of William Clark's 1801 journal entries, page 46 of his 1798–1801 Notebook.

became his wife after Julia's death. If such an encounter then occurred it was brief, for he departed the area the next morning.[6]

Covering forty of the most scenic miles of the journey on that day, he crossed the Rock Bridge (now known as the Natural Bridge), a limestone arch over a gorge more than two hundred feet deep, but he recorded no comment about those landmarks. By sundown of June 7 he was almost out of the mountains. On the following morning he descended into Albemarle County, home to Lewis and birthplace of Clark's brothers Jonathan and George. After pausing at Charlottesville, Clark set an eastward course and later angled toward the north. And so he continued on June 9, riding through the evening to Jonathan's house; according to William it stood 640 miles from his own.

Finding Jonathan at home he stayed for a few days, then forged on to Fredericksburg, catching a stagecoach for Georgetown. There he consulted with attorney John T. Mason about getting the dispute between Bazadone and George into federal court. Asking Mason to keep him apprised of developments in that effort, William proceeded to Washington.[7]

President Jefferson had just marked his hundredth day in office, spending it in much the same manner as he had the previous ninety-nine—carrying out duties while replacing Federalists in government with Democratic-Republicans. Despite the wish of Vice President Burr to take part in the new administration, Jefferson excluded him as much as possible and relied instead on Secretary of the Treasury Albert Gallatin, Secretary of War Henry Dearborn, Secretary of State James Madison, and of course, on Lewis, his secretary and companion in the sandstone residence later to be known as the White House. Rather than interrupt his present travels to call on Lewis, Clark evidently resolved to do so when he returned. He continued to Baltimore and took another stagecoach heading northeast.

By sundown of the following day he was in Philadelphia, his most distant destination. Whether his circumstances allowed for pleasure is not clear, but it seems likely he sought out Daniel W. Coxe who, with the help of Daniel Clark Jr., was still sending to New Orleans oceangoing vessels that then returned with hidden caches of Spanish money. Unfortunately, no known memorandum of such a meeting—or of any of William's activities during this visit to Philadelphia—has survived.[8]

He left town on June 21, 1801, boarding a small vessel he called a "Barkett." He rode it several miles, seeing the Delaware River reaches he'd missed three years earlier because of the yellow fever epidemic. Following his overland route of the earlier trip, he got off at New Castle and took a stagecoach to Baltimore, and then another to Washington. He called at the President's House on June 23.

* * *

Arriving that same day was Andrew Ellicott; Clark had last encountered him along the thirty-first parallel in 1798. Ellicott was trying to collect the unpaid portion of his salary for the Spanish-American boundary project. He had concluded it in the spring of 1800, then returned to Philadelphia where he made his home.[9]

Despite promptly submitting to the federal government his maps and report on the boundary endeavor, and conferring with then-secretaries Pickering and McHenry, Ellicott was unable to obtain either the amount owed him by Congress or a meeting with President Adams. Soon Adams left office. From that point on, Ellicott had little alternative but to seek help from a chief executive elected on promises of frugality, especially concerning debts incurred by the previous administration.[10]

Ellicott nonetheless engaged in a friendly correspondence with Jefferson, his fellow member in the American Philosophical Society, the oldest learned society in the United States. For weeks Ellicott had been passing to him scientific data including printed installments of astronomical observations made along the border with Spanish territory. Not until May 26, 1801, did Ellicott mention his financial straits. Then he waited even longer to send details about them, adding that the cost of transportation from Philadelphia kept him from pleading his case in person. But his long-distance efforts failed to help his cause; without explaining the reasons, Congress continued to ignore his account. By the time he finally decided to visit the City of Washington and growing desperate for money, Ellicott had begun selling off his books and technical instruments, understandably fuming that Spain had munificently and without delay compensated his boundary counterparts Stephen Minor and Thomas Power.[11]

Ellicott came prepared. No longer professing Federalist sympathies, he claimed to be an inveterate Democratic-Republican and brought intelligence he believed Jefferson would welcome. In a private meeting on June 23, 1801, Ellicott revealed that William Jackson, a federal official in Philadelphia, had a few years earlier published a pseudonymous article advocating war with Spain, a policy Jefferson opposed. We can assume the president was happy to know Jackson's identity in order to replace him with someone of more compatible politics, yet he could not have been pleased when Ellicott went on to introduce the subject of General Wilkinson—and presumably also, of Judge Sebastian, Samuel M. Brown, and their intrigues.[12]

Even so, Jefferson allowed Ellicott to continue. While running the boundary line in West Florida, Ellicott explained, he had met Mrs. Tomás Portell and her husband, formerly the New Madrid commander whom Lt. William Clark had dealt with in 1793 and 1795. The Portells told Ellicott of storing in their bedroom at Fort Céleste a trunk laden with 9,640 pieces of eight to be sent to General Wilkinson in 1796. Calling the sum a payment for services traitorous to the United States, Ellicott predicted that, if the federal government kept on supporting the double-dealing Wilkinson, he would sooner or later disgrace it.[13]

Little did Ellicott understand, the president was already inclined to disregard such warnings. Not only did he depend on General Wilkinson to advance his administration by keeping the United States secure, Jefferson also welcomed his gifts of maps, specimens, and artifacts, all of them illuminating American geography or natural history. Consequently Jefferson would follow the example of Adams and Washington by gambling on Wilkinson's loyalty rather than having him investigated.[14]

Meanwhile, probably in a different room from where Ellicott and Jefferson conferred, Clark and Lewis got reacquainted. After sharing information about their lives since parting company (perhaps they had not seen each other since Clark resigned his lieutenancy in 1796), Lewis may have spoken confidentially of an upcoming task. It would require him to grade the political alignment and fitness for command of all 269 officers in the regular Army so that Jefferson might decide which of them to retain when shrinking their numbers. Unacquainted with many commissioned personnel, including those belonging to units in which Clark, but not he, had served, Lewis could have asked about those soldiers; he was later to report that a number of them remained "unknown to *us* [emphasis added]," not recording from whom he derived such information.[15]

Lewis also had a favor to request. As brother-in-law of Richard C. Anderson (chief surveyor of lands allotted to Virginia veterans of the Revolution), would Clark secure the rights of Lewis's family to acreage granted his late stepfather as compensation for service during that war? Clark assented. Perhaps he asked in return that Lewis monitor George's lawsuit if it reached federal court in the District of Columbia.[16]

Once they finished settling these more official matters, did they discuss their personal concerns? William might have inquired how working for the president suited a man so inclined to "rambling," as Meriwether termed his zest for travel. Or, if he recalled Clark's desire to do business in Spanish New Orleans, Lewis might have asked whether he had gotten there yet. In response Clark would certainly hold forth about his 1798 venture, perhaps even referring to the Mississippi Journal for particulars such as the sums given in New Orleans for tobacco, flour, and furs, or the costs of storing cargoes and of procuring lodging and meals.

Considering the scarcity of U.S. coinage in the United States, the topic of Spanish money might have come up. If it did, Clark could have related how he had bribed the royal customs officers or crossed the thirty-first parallel, his saddlebags stuffed with reales to trade for a less cumbersome form of revenue. Had Clark introduced such a topic, though, he would probably not have mentioned helping Samuel M. Brown smuggle back to Kentucky eleven hundred Spanish dollars—especially the portion of them allocated to the care of Mr. Riddle or the other coins going to Judge Sebastian.

Did talk of Clark's 1798 journey inspire Lewis to make the first-ever mention to Clark of Jefferson's long-standing wish to send an exploring party beyond the Mississippi? Clark must have known he wanted to do so. In 1783, Jefferson had asked George Rogers Clark to carry out a western reconnaissance, but George had declined because of the lack of governmental funding and his own financial troubles. Maybe William also realized that in 1790, at the direction of Secretary of War Knox, a friend of the Clarks, Lieutenant John Armstrong, had attempted to set off on a similar undertaking but was forced to stop at St. Louis lest he riled the Spanish. Perhaps William also knew that three years later, Jefferson had retained the French naturalist André Michaux to penetrate the West, unaware that Michaux was secretly involved with George and others in a plot to invade Louisiana for the French Republic. Detected in 1793, the scheme fell apart before Michaux could begin the tour. News of the subsequent, Spanish-sponsored expedition of James Mackay and John Evans up the Missouri River intensified Jefferson's desire to dispatch an American corps up and beyond that waterway. Possibly by the summer of 1801, he was already thinking of sending Lewis.[17]

If Clark therefore had any inkling of the western exploration Lewis was to conduct, he would surely have desired a role in it for himself and a share in the resulting honors and emoluments if it succeeded. Without such a prospect his future was bleak. That is, it would offer little but the same sorts of frustrations and difficulties he had faced since resigning the Army.

Further, Clark had nothing to lose and perhaps a good deal to gain by calling attention to talents and skills that he—but not Lewis—possessed in abundance, having honed them during the 1798 journey. Lewis had never even seen a western river, but Clark had successfully navigated the Mississippi from the Ohio all the way to New Orleans. Moreover, his history of command—both in the Army and the militia and as the civilian captain of a flatboat convoy in 1798—far surpassed Lewis's. Whereas Meriwether, except when in French-speaking parts of the Northwest Territory or while dealing with Indians or foreign visitors to Washington City, seldom heard a language other than English, William had made his way for many weeks in polyglot Louisiana. Of key significance and in further contrast with Lewis, who had never left the United States or lived in an alien culture, Clark had considerably more experience in measuring terrestrial coordinates, drawing maps, and keeping regular diaries—all activities crucial to a western reconnaissance.

In short, to demonstrate that he was ideally suited to help lead a party on an expedition, all Clark need do was open his Mississippi Journal to nearly any inscribed page to show Lewis. In turn, Lewis would have seen proof that Clark had conducted his cargoes and crewmen safely down the river to New Orleans, charted the Mississippi River, reconnoitered Spanish fortifications, thrived during his months in Louisiana, sailed from there to the East Coast, and filled sixty-six pages with diary entries and notes from his 1798 travels. Subsequent events suggest that Clark made those experiences known not just to Lewis but also to President Jefferson and his secretary of war. After a few days at the president's house, Clark took the southbound stagecoach and returned to Jonathan's farm. For most of the next week he waited there for John T. Mason's thoughts on filing George's case against Bazadone in federal court. William sent a reminder to Mason and soon received a reply.[18]

During his remaining time in Virginia, William helped Jonathan and his family advance their plans to move to Kentucky and settle on ground they hoped would be close to Mulberry Hill. Promising his best efforts to secure the tract Jonathan wanted, William set out for Kentucky on July 22, 1801. He followed the same overall route he'd taken in 1798, except for spending a night in southwest Pennsylvania at "Friendship Hill," the residence of Albert Gallatin, before moving on for Wheeling and Chillicothe. At Cincinnati, Judge John Cleves Symmes, father-in-law to future president William Henry Harrison, helped Clark temporarily halt Bazadone's collection proceedings against George. William must have been happy for that outcome; he needed the extra time to organize a defense lest George lose seven thousand dollars' worth of land, a forfeiture that could lead to bankruptcy.[19]

But the closer William got to Jefferson County, the worse his luck turned. Finding the Ohio River too low for shipping ironware for use in his gristmill, he arrived home on August 11 only to discover the mill had been consumed by fire. Ruined also were tools, furnishings, and hundreds of bushels of grain inside the structure. "This is a verry Serious Stroke to me I do assure you," he wrote Jonathan.[20]

"I never went from home any time, but before I returned was informed of Some loss or misfortune," William lamented, no doubt recalling his mother's death when he came back from his long travels of 1798, the last ones he had written about in the journal. By now he may well have associated the journal with bad luck. Concluding, "I am fearfull nature intended me for the Sport of fortune," he put away the handsome book and never wrote in it again.[21]

34

Any Post of Honor and Profit

NOT long after Clark returned from the journey, he must have asked himself whether it would prove worthwhile. Although he was no doubt happy to have met with Meriwether Lewis and the leaders of national government, thus far he had nothing to show except pleasant memories for those encounters. Even more distressing was that George's legal cause seemed no better for William's recent travels; after all, none of the authorities William consulted had assured him of judicial exoneration. If George would not in some way be relieved of liability for the debts Virginia ought to have paid years earlier but instead let fall to George, William might indeed have wasted those eighty days and all the money he spent during those weeks on the road.

Rather than dwell on thoughts of this sort, he tended to more urgent matters, including overdue real estate taxes. Whether he or George owned the encumbered property mattered little anymore because their accounts had become so interlinked that the obligations of one of them affected the other. Further complicating their finances was the ever-increasing number of lawsuits against George. On August 13, 1801, when notice arrived of yet another such proceeding, William had to wonder how long they would be able to keep their home.[1]

Using Jonathan's funds and credit in October 1801, William purchased for him a 410-acre farm—to be called "Trough Spring," for a large seep on the property—just up the South Fork of Beargrass Creek from Mulberry Hill. Two months later, William set out eastward to bring back a crew of Jonathan's slaves who would build him a house. Although William had plenty of blank pages left in the Mississippi Journal he probably left it behind. He may well have neglected to bring anything to write on; no account of these travels is known to have existed. If Clark indeed recorded nothing of this particular journey, he was breaking a habit of many years, for reasons no longer known.[2]

The December trip took him to the City of Washington where he checked on the progress of George's case against Bazadone. Attorney Mason once more recommended having the matter removed to the U.S. Circuit Court in what would soon become the Ohio District and appealing an adverse ruling all the way to the U.S. Supreme Court. William wanted to take his advice but must have wondered how to fund a protracted legal battle.[3]

He probably returned to the president's house. If so he found that Thomas Jefferson and Henry Dearborn were at last ready to submit proposals to Congress on reducing the military, Meriwether Lewis having finished grading the politics and competence of every Army officer but for himself and General Wilkinson.[4]

Back in Spotsylvania County by early January 1802, Clark and the greater portion of Jonathan's slaves set out westward along the same overall route William had followed in 1798 and 1801. From Redstone, Pennsylvania, however, they took a flatboat down the Ohio to Louisville. Work on Jonathan's house commenced, and it proceeded so well that the family moved in on July 14, 1802, around the same time Edmund settled nearby.[5]

Having his brothers close to him gave William great satisfaction but did not resolve his financial problems. It seems that in August a buyer of one of George's tracts failed to pay the balance he owed on it; soon afterward, William had to put Mulberry Hill up for sale. George erected a two-room cabin across the Ohio at a place called Point of Rock, a bluff offering a view of river traffic and proximity to the Falls. (Later that spot would become known as Clark's Point.) Around March 1803, he and William moved there. Determined to earn money, they kept an eye out for bargains in real estate and probably discussed forming a company to dig a navigation canal around the Falls. William, perhaps with George, was to own a long strip of shoreline property they assumed would appreciate as the canal took shape.[6]

From time to time, George presided at gatherings of the officers of his "Illinois Regiment" who oversaw conveyances of acreage Virginia had awarded after the Revolution to members of their unit. Not long after the death of Richard Terrell, surveyor and clerk of that "Illinois Grant," in October 1802, William succeeded him as clerk, thereby gaining access to privileged information about land and the circumstances of those owning it. Decades later, laws would forbid taking advantage of this sort of knowledge, but until then William might use it as he pleased. He looked for opportunities to do so, unaware that his life was soon to undergo a drastic transformation started in 1801, when he evidently alerted the Jefferson administration to his own extensive travels and capabilities.[7]

An early hint of the changes to come was a request from Henry Dearborn for information about Fort Jefferson, George's Revolutionary War outpost on the Mississippi just below the mouth of the Ohio. Pleased to be considered an authority on the subject, William forwarded the notes from his 1795 reconnaissance of that place. Then George sent his longtime friend Thomas Jefferson a letter recommending William—not just for further topographical details but "almost for any business." George added, "If it should be in your power to confur on him any post of Honor and profit . . . it will exceedingly gratify me." The Clarks could not then have realized that this exchange of correspondence coincided with events leading to the Louisiana Purchase.[8]

The first such occurrence took place in April 1802, shortly after Jefferson learned of the secret retrocession of Louisiana. Fearing that Napoleon Bonaparte—who in 1799 had abolished the Directory and named himself the first consul of France—would bar U.S. trade from the Mississippi River, the president directed minister Robert Livingston to ask France for Louisiana and the Floridas. Livingston negotiated as told. But while he did so, Spanish Louisiana intendant Juan Ventura Morales unexpectedly ordered New Orleans warehouses to be closed to U.S. goods, thereby crippling American commerce and nullifying Livingston's efforts.[9]

Word of this development reached President Jefferson in late November 1802. He sent James Monroe as a special envoy to join Livingston in France, instructing them to buy New Orleans and as much of the Floridas as they could. On April 11, 1803, however, just before Monroe's journey ended in Paris, Napoleon abruptly decided to raise capital for his European campaigns by selling the entire province of Louisiana. Livingston immediately expressed interest in buying it and did all he could to enable that transaction, making it easy for Monroe to approve it a few days later. By early May 1803, the details were in place, and the agreement—doubling the area of the United States, for approximately four cents an acre—became final.[10]

Meanwhile, in January 1803, the president asked Congress to fund a plan to enhance "the external commerce of the U.S." by sending a small band of explorers far into the trans-Mississippi. Receiving an initial appropriation of twenty-five hundred dollars, Jefferson expanded the scope of that enterprise far beyond international trade. Picking Meriwether Lewis to lead the expedition *and* to figure terrestrial coordinates, draw maps, and write about natural history and native peoples along the way, Jefferson directed his instruction in celestial navigation, mathematics, botany, mineralogy, medicine, and paleontology.[11]

Lewis made admirable progress in his studies. By the early summer, though, it was evident that in order to carry out his empirical duties he needed the assistance of an officer capable of keeping vessels under way, developing a cohesive crew, recording accurate and systematic notes, and meeting a myriad of contingencies. Who possessed such skills and a temperament compatible with his own? The answer was obvious. By selecting William Clark, his versatile former commander who kept turning up in Washington, Lewis stood to benefit not merely from Clark's practical abilities but especially from his superior experience in navigation, cartography, command, and reconnaissance. Lewis must have also perceived that Clark possessed an unshakeable resolve—honed by years of hard luck and disappointment—to make the epic journey succeed. Truly, Lewis could not have chosen a more suitable partner.

From the time Clark left home to begin their famous journey together until it came to a happy conclusion nearly three years later, he acted in strict compliance with the president's instructions, including a crucial directive calling for the keeping of precise, regular accounts on a full array of topics. To this end Clark brought along a durable elkskin-bound logbook and kept on hand numerous blank sheets torn from various sources. Judging from the dozens of papers used to record his famous "Field Notes," though, we can ask why none of those sheets came from the Mississippi Journal. Did he deliberately leave it behind, and the many blank pages still in it? Did the death of his mother and the destruction of his mill three years later—two major misfortunes attending his return from travels he'd written about in that logbook—make him think it might bring more bad luck?[12]

* * *

Since the death of Governor Gayoso de Lemos, Benjamin Sebastian had been lying low, carrying out his judicial duties while avoiding contact with Louisiana other than to send intermediaries there to collect his clandestine salary and spirit it back to him. They succeeded admirably. Except for the money forfeited because Samuel M. Brown died before he could deliver the full balance for 1799, from then until 1803 Sebastian received most, if not all, of his two thousand pieces of eight each year. But as time went on and the war he had been predicting between American forces and those of France and Spain failed to come about, he did less and less to earn his pay.[13]

He was appalled to hear of the Louisiana Purchase because it spelled the end of his lucrative association with Spain and reminded him that time was running out to acquire from that kingdom the things he most desired—whether land, money, or documents to shroud his disloyalty to the United States. In early 1804, as soon as the ice melted on the Ohio, he dispatched to John Seitz, a Natchez trader who occasionally visited New Orleans, a vaguely worded letter asking him to "inform me of the true situation of the business," no doubt referring to the continuation of his secret salary. Sebastian went on: "for if you succeed, I shall be eased of a great weight of anxiety, and if you do not, I must immediately make the necessary preparations to descend the river myself, for the purpose of collecting proof of my situation, and lay a statement of the business before the minister."[14]

Having no immediate plans to visit New Orleans, Seitz passed the matter along to Stephen Minor, formerly the acting Spanish boundary commissioner whose letters William Clark had carried from the Little Bayou Sara camp in 1798. Minor complied, not only pressing Sebastian's petition but also, at Seitz's suggestion, offering a five-hundred-dollar kickback to secure approval for keeping the Kentucky judge on the royal payroll. Learning—while Lewis and Clark were ascending the Missouri River—that the request had instead failed, Sebastian responded by reducing his contact with Louisiana even further.[15]

James Wilkinson, on the other hand, welcomed the American acquisition of that territory because it furnished the means of resuming corrupt but profitable activities. If he had in fact been the recipient of the 670 pieces of eight smuggled toward Louisville in Clark's sugar barrel, then nearly five years had gone by since he had dared accept such illicit revenue. His chronic improvidence had again led to financial distress.

Appointed by Thomas Jefferson to take delivery of Louisiana, Wilkinson reached New Orleans in December 1803. He conferred with West Florida governor Vicente Folch and also with the former military governor of Louisiana, the Marqués de Casa Calvo, mentioning that for twenty thousand dollars (Wilkinson's estimate of the total salary he had been too afraid to collect), he would divulge intelligence of value to Spain, including "what was concealed in the heart of the President," Mr. Jefferson. Casa Calvo forthwith promised twelve thousand dollars. Regarding that sum as a first installment, but fearful of theft or discovery should he try to have the balance smuggled to him, Wilkinson also asked a monopoly in the flour trade.[16]

To increase the odds of acquiring such a concession, he composed a lengthy dossier known as "Reflections on Louisiana," advice to the ministers of Carlos IV on concentrating power in North America, regardless of the Louisiana Purchase. As Wilkinson had done in earlier, dishonorable memorials, he recommended that the Spanish take a variety of shrewd actions. Some were expensive—reinforcing the Florida and Texas frontiers, for example—but others involved less cost. One measure called for turning back or imprisoning Meriwether Lewis and William Clark as they advanced through lands Wilkinson had just accepted for the United States.[17]

Orders to that effect eventually reached the Spanish commandant at Santa Fe. He dispatched northward several parties of horsemen, but each of them arrived too late to find the explorers. The Spanish failed to intercept Clark and Lewis—who never learned that General Wilkinson had put their mission and even their lives at risk in order to benefit himself.[18]

35

A Distant and Splendid Enterprise

THE tardiness of Spanish soldiers was just one of many lucky occurrences during the grand Expedition, and by the time Lewis and Clark returned to the Great Plains in the summer of 1806 they could begin looking forward to completing their assignment in good order. Not knowing exactly how Congress might recompense them, they must have reviewed the few certainties in their future. Lewis took comfort in having both a close friendship with the president and the prospect of preparing the western journals for publication, but all Clark could count on was moving back in with the increasingly dependent George, and trying to raise enough money from farming, milling, surveying, and speculating in real estate to pay their taxes.

William wished for generous remuneration and eminent employment with the government, yet he knew not to set his hopes for either too high. As the final weeks of the journey passed without mishap, it appeared that most of the "fatiegues" and dangers he had promised to share with Lewis lay behind them, leaving ahead the honors and rewards he had been anticipating since 1803. That Congress would bestow them Clark did not doubt, provided his luck held just a little bit longer.[1]

As he and his companions descended the Missouri River, they began catching up on news they had missed while farther west. Near the area to become Sioux City, Iowa, a passing trader informed them that President Jefferson had won a second term, former Vice President Aaron Burr had shot and killed Alexander Hamilton in a duel, and General Wilkinson, though still a military officer, was, at Jefferson's request, serving as the first governor of the Louisiana Territory, the recent designation for the northern segment of the Louisiana Purchase. Wilkinson's gubernatorial headquarters were at St. Louis where, on September 23, 1806, the Expedition came to a felicitous close.[2]

It was then that Clark and Lewis started hearing of a mysterious plot Wilkinson and Burr were said to be hatching, whether to provoke a confrontation with Spain or to sunder western states from their eastern counterparts was not clear. Those troubling rumors pervaded St. Louis and gave new meaning to a time-honored toast offered at a dinner given there for Lewis and Clark: "The United States . . . may [they] never forget, that *united they stand—but divided they fall.*"[3]

Had the guests of honor wished to learn if those words held a hidden meaning they could not have asked Governor Wilkinson. By order of the War Department he had recently left town to defend Louisiana—and, if necessary, other parts of the country—from Spanish armed forces massing near the Sabine River, the de facto southwestern boundary between the two nations. War seemed imminent, yet no one in the Jefferson administration understood that Wilkinson had brought about those very hostilities by urging in his most recent "Reflections" the Spanish military concentration now in place. Wanting the resultant confusion to open the Internal Provinces and perhaps other parts of Mexico to his own exploitation, he worked to make the American frontier less stable.[4]

He did so with the help of Aaron Burr, a political pariah since killing Hamilton. Having dazzled Burr with talk of invading Spanish territory, then profiting from the consequent chaos (a scheme Wilkinson termed "a distant and splendid enterprise" for the immense wealth it might produce), he drew him into a conspiracy to carry out those goals. Whether Burr understood this particular intrigue had much in common with Wilkinson's earlier ones is not clear, but he little suspected it would go down in history as his own creation.[5]

Burr and Wilkinson delineated their individual duties in the plot and then split up to carry them out. While Wilkinson kept an eye on Louisiana and the Spanish borderlands, Burr spent most of his time in the Ohio River valley, preparing an armed fleet to initiate their military campaign. Not long after Wilkinson became territorial governor, Burr visited him at St. Louis where their enigmatic comments about foreign invasion and their encrypted correspondence increased suspicions against them.

So Clark heard at St. Louis. Shortly after pulling ashore there, however, he wrote Jonathan to report the success of the Expedition. In a subsequent note he asked Jonathan to alert the press to that story. Not yet fully cognizant of the enormous attention being paid to Wilkinson, Burr, and their rumored intrigue, Clark evidently hoped that his and Lewis's accomplishments would become front-page news, disposing governmental leaders to reward them generously.[6]

* * *

But soon Clark learned of the *Western World*, a new Kentucky weekly founded by Federalist writers John Wood and Joseph Street. The paper was supported by the like-minded Humphrey Marshall, General Wilkinson's inveterate foe and one of George Rogers Clark's many opponents in court. Wishing to expose past seditions and to block any current, devious projects, especially of Wilkinson and Burr, Marshall had been feeding the newspaper a stream of innuendo—much of it true—about the controversial pair and their associates, particularly Benjamin Sebastian.[7]

Marshall derived a great deal of information from Joseph Hamilton Daveiss, the U.S. district attorney for Kentucky and a former law student of the late George Nicholas, a prominent, wealthy jurist who for years had secretly connived with Wilkinson, Sebastian, and others in various twists of the intrigue with Spain. In administering Nicholas's estate, Daveiss (whose name is often spelled Daviess) turned up evidence of those and other conspiracies. Further research convincing him that Burr was indeed the general's accomplice in the latest version of his perennial plot to gain wealth and power by undermining the interests of the United States, Daveiss warned President Jefferson accordingly. On receiving from him a timely request for specifics, Daveiss furnished names of suspects—every one of them a Democratic-Republican—whereupon Jefferson all but ceased corresponding.[8]

Incensed by what seemed to be the president's willingness to expose the country to danger rather than investigate members of his own party, Daveiss—with the help of Marshall—released his findings to the *Western World*, and it rushed them to print in a series of exposés. Soon other newspapers were spreading the sensational details in every direction. In St. Louis they increased the unpopularity of Wilkinson who, as territorial governor, often favored the French-speaking gentry whose wealth lay in Spanish land grants (most of them unsurveyed and unrecorded) that American settlers wished to acquire. Determining the validity and value of those tracts was a necessary process but one so hotly contested as to threaten open conflict between former Spanish subjects and the newcomers. Governor Wilkinson, however, frequently made these and other matters worse by surrounding himself with sycophants and by disregarding the decisions of a congressionally created board of land commissioners.[9]

William C. Carr, a St. Louis lawyer disgruntled with Wilkinson, exacted revenge on him by becoming a subscription agent for the *Western World*, thereby ensuring the community steady access to the muckraking gazette and ensuring the paper continuing, unfavorable reports about General Wilkinson. As a result, weeks before Clark and Lewis returned, St. Louisans were following the efforts of Street and Wood to block Wilkinson's future designs and to hold him accountable for a staggering number of past intrigues, as they put it, "TO DELIVER KENTUCKY TO THE SPANIARDS." The journalistic crusade intensified while Clark was in town. Not only did the paper examine the connections of Senator John Brown and Kentucky jurists George Muter, Benjamin Sebastian, and George Nicholas to such seditions, it also accused Wilkinson of treachery to the late General Anthony Wayne, cast doubt on the probity of Kentucky governor Christopher Greenup, and reported the suspicious activities of Aaron Burr.[10]

Years of previous association with Wilkinson and Sebastian should have prepared Clark to hear anew such allegations, but the success of the *Western World* in unmasking their abettors—many of them of high governmental office and heretofore unblemished reputation—may well have made him apprehensive. Through valor and unstinting effort during the

Pacific expedition, he had finally reached the threshold of the fame, recompense, and appointment he'd been seeking for so many years. What might happen to those rewards should his own deep, problematic ties to Wilkinson and Sebastian be revealed?

Ironically, by announcing the return of the Corps, Clark increased the chance that those troubling links would become public knowledge. On October 9, 1806, his report to Jonathan appeared in the *Palladium* of Frankfort, Kentucky, and soon thereafter was reprinted in other newspapers including the *Western World* (which made room for the story by bumping the latest coverage of the "Kentucky Spanish Association" to the following issue). When Clark and Lewis—with a delegation of Mandan and Osage Indians who wished to confer with the president—left St. Louis in late October 1806 and headed toward Washington, word of the completion of their western tour preceded them, due largely to William's missive to Jonathan. But the farther east Lewis and Clark traveled, the more they saw that accounts of their own momentous accomplishments took up far less newspaper space than did stories about seditions against the United States.[11]

Some of those articles must have prepared them for what they found on November 5 when they reached Louisville. That is, up and down the waterfront, dozens of Aaron Burr's recruits were fitting out vessels and loading them with provisions and supplies and, covertly, with munitions and firearms. Although Burr was then in Lexington, Kentucky, his adherents at Louisville and those at other strategic points—Pittsburgh, Pennsylvania; Marietta, Ohio; Blennerhassett Island (a dozen miles down the Ohio River from Marietta); and Nashville, Tennessee—awaited orders to depart for Louisiana. There they were ostensibly to found a colony along the Ouachita River but instead were probably planning to stage the first assault called for by the conspiracy. None of these men knew many details about it, but all of them expected to shove off soon.[12]

Lewis remained around five days with Clark and his family. Continuing to observe local developments and no doubt to stay informed of those reported by the *Western World* (at that time one of the best-selling gazettes in the United States), Meriwether and William could see that the publishers wished to bring down Wilkinson, Burr, Sebastian, and their unprincipled friends. As the newspaper would eventually make clear, some of those men were trying to divert attention from themselves by incriminating others.[13]

Whether Judge Sebastian would do so was yet unknown. His failure to speak on the point must have concerned Clark; he could well imagine his own future if Sebastian admitted that in 1798, payoff for his treasonable association with Spain came to him among Clark's coffee beans. Even worse, what might happen if word got out that Clark had sent his own father a sugar barrel concealing the number of reales Spain owed its master spy, Agent 13, and instructions on getting that sum to the next courier?

Clark, however, had no immediate cause for worry. Rather than accuse his associates, Sebastian quietly joined forces with Harry Innes and John Brown and engaged a writer named William Littell to produce a book supposedly proving the Spanish Conspiracy never existed. But while Littell labored to do that, Humphrey Marshall circulated a broadside charging Sebastian with being on the Spanish payroll. Soon the public demanded action from the Kentucky legislature. Realizing that body would at some time investigate his conduct, Sebastian reopened contact with Louisiana. On October 16, 1806, he penned a letter he hoped would induce Andrés de Armesto, formerly the secretary of Spanish governors, to forward documents making Sebastian's illicit salary appear instead to be lawful compensation for representing Kentucky in commercial dealings.[14]

During that same interval Clark and Lewis discussed traveling separately to Washington so that Meriwether might spend Christmas in Virginia with his kin and William could remain a while longer in Louisville. They decided that Lewis, accompanied at least part of the way by the Osages and Mandans, was to go first; he would pass through Frankfort, and continue into Virginia where he'd visit his mother and then proceed to the City of Washington. Clark, on the other hand, would depart Louisville somewhat later but arrive in Washington before the tributes and festivities planned there for them. Knowing that these events might indeed connect him with politicians to vote on his compensation and appointment to governmental office, Clark had sound reason to get on the road promptly, especially before ice and snow slowed his progress.[15]

So Lewis thought when they split up in Louisville. It seems possible, however, that because his partner in discovery had earlier partnered in a money-running operation benefiting the judge soon to be interrogated in Frankfort about such questionable dealings, he may have wanted to stay clear of that place until the excitement died down. There was no telling yet when that might happen.

36

Standing High with Mr. Jefferson

WHILE Lewis and Clark laid their plans, District Attorney Daveiss mulled over intelligence he had recently gathered at Louisville while seeing for himself what Aaron Burr's followers were up to. Observing that "boats were building" and "an attempt" was being made "to engage men for six months," Daveiss also learned the former vice president's agents were "very busy in disseminating the idea of disunion." What's more, Davis Floyd and John Adair, Burr's leading coadjutors in Kentucky, unwittingly verified to one of Daveiss's informers that the conspiracy called for a series of attacks: first, on Spanish possessions southwest of Louisiana; then, along the Mississippi River frontier; and finally, in the Ohio River valley. Alarmed for the sake of his country, Daveiss decided to stifle the plot before it grew larger. He hurried back to Frankfort.[1]

On November 5, 1806, he asked the federal court to have Burr either arrested or ordered to post a bond high enough to curb the assembling of men, boats, and supplies being undertaken in his name. No crime having yet occurred, Judge Harry Innes properly refused to grant either request, but he let Daveiss call together a grand jury. Daveiss sent appropriate notice to witnesses he wished to examine, counting on compelling the attendance of those necessary to indict Burr. On hearing what Daveiss was doing, Burr hurried to Frankfort to speak in his own defense. Soon hundreds of people from all over Kentucky and elsewhere showed up too, eager for a glimpse of the man who had killed the arch-Federalist Hamilton, an unpopular figure in the heavily Democratic-Republican West.[2]

Daveiss, however, had miscalculated. Although Benjamin Sebastian, John Brown, and other witnesses came to testify, Davis Floyd, the one most important to the prosecution, did not. A lawmaker in the territory to become Indiana, he was allowed to stay in Vincennes until whenever the work of that legislative session might end. Daveiss therefore postponed commencing his proceeding as long as possible but, on November 12, ran out of time and had to admit that without the still-absent Floyd he could not indict Burr. As Judge Innes dismissed the grand jury, the crowd heckled the overreaching district attorney and applauded Burr, once more a free man.[3]

On the morrow, Meriwether Lewis and his exotic charges—Indians of customs, dress, and regalia unfamiliar east of the Mississippi River—reached Frankfort for a two-day visit, yet not a word about them or the famous Lewis appeared in the next edition of the *Western World*. Rather, it reported the failed attempt to incriminate Burr, noting not just that Sebastian had come to testify against him but that Daveiss was expected to call for another grand jury investigation of Burr once Floyd returned. Surely aware also of the pending inquiry concerning Sebastian, William Clark could expect him to remain in or near Frankfort for the foreseeable future.[4]

How Sebastian must have hoped for a man of unimpeachable renown to vouch for him, and soon. Who better to do so, he could have reasoned, than William Clark, celebrated son of his late friend? As if concerned that Sebastian might try to restore his own reputation by calling attention to his role in the smuggling venture of 1798, Clark stayed put in Louisville.

On Saturday, November 22, 1806, the *Western World* reported that a special ten-man legislative panel in Frankfort was to assemble the following week in order to examine evidence of Judge Sebastian's Spanish links. Still awaiting the bogus document he had requested, Sebastian asked for a delay in the hearing until he might secure "from New Orleans or elsewhere . . . such testimony as will operate a complete and satisfactory refutation of the charge." The lawmakers refused, at which point Sebastian resigned his judicial employment. To his shock he learned the inquiry would proceed anyway, but he would not be allowed to call witnesses or to speak on his own behalf.[5]

Thomas Bullitt, William Clark's nephew by marriage and Sebastian's initial courier of Spanish money after Samuel M. Brown died, opened the testimony. He related that twice he had collected at New Orleans two thousand pieces of eight, adding that Sebastian described those sums as lawful payments for his past commercial dealings. Subsequent witnesses spoke of Sebastian's efforts to secure further sums and a royal land grant and of his association with Brown. Even so, no evidence yet produced proved that the judge had committed a crime.[6]

Presently Harry Innes took the stand. He disavowed knowledge of how Sebastian, his longtime friend and client, had laid hold of so many reales. Because Innes's own Spanish nexus was being discussed by some of the same men conducting the current hearing, he must have felt compelled to cooperate with them, yet he could not bear to utter a word against Sebastian. Instead, Innes stalled as long as possible. Then, breaking into sobs until he was crying "like a child," Innes reluctantly handed over papers incriminating to his client.[7]

Sebastian admitted that the charges against him were true, and his interlocutors unanimously pronounced him guilty. Sebastian was to be the only conspirator to tell the truth, to his own detriment. He would never again hold public office. The inquisition closed, leaving undiscovered the role of William Clark in helping smuggle to the former jurist his ill-gotten money.[8]

* * *

On November 27, 1806, the *Western World* sarcastically announced of Sebastian, "The *Glass House* of this *very honorable* Judge . . . is now for the happiness of the Citizens of Kentucky, broken in pieces." That day, Aaron Burr was in Louisville. He was making final preparations to send his armed forces downriver once he thwarted Joseph H. Daveiss's imminent second effort to indict him.[9]

Probably Burr also sought out George Rogers Clark, the undisputed expert at putting together expeditions against Spanish Louisiana. In 1805, while William was on his way to the Pacific Ocean, Aaron and George had likely met during Burr's first visit to Louisville. If so, they must have conferred about building a dam and navigation lock around the Falls of the Ohio, a project Burr embraced because it gave him legitimate cause to frequent the area while secretly preparing for the paramilitary venture he and Wilkinson had discussed launching the following year.

George liked the idea of improving navigation at the Falls; in 1805 he and Burr, with ten others, had subscribed to a proposal to build a canal there. Although no known proof exists that Burr and William Clark ever became acquainted, they may indeed have done so on or around November 27, 1806. By that date Burr would have had tremendous interest in hearing about the Corps of Discovery's penetration of formerly Spanish territory. Clark was certainly curious about the dynamic and influential Burr whose martial intentions were yet unproven and who spoke with enthusiasm of the distant West and of General Wilkinson, the undisclosed author of their scheme.[10]

Little did Burr guess, however, that Wilkinson had already surmised the war on which its success depended would not occur. Spanish leaders were proving as reluctant for active aggression as Jefferson was. In further contrast with Burr, only Wilkinson knew that changes occasioned by the recent death of Prime Minister William Pitt of England decreased the chance that the British Navy would assist the conspirators' forces. And then there was the matter of the *Western World*, which, by focusing attention mainly on Wilkinson, made intriguing riskier for him than for his associates. Consequently he had made up his mind not just to abandon this latest of his plots but also to ascribe it to Burr, a maneuver that would allow Wilkinson to pose as the deliverer of the United States.[11]

He initiated his cunning plan in October 1806 upon deciphering a communication from Burr announcing he was soon to head downstream to open their campaign, perhaps by seizing Baton Rouge. Ignorant of his supposed collaborator's intentions, Burr exhorted him: "The gods invite us to glory and fortune. It remains to be seen whether we deserve the boons." In reaction, Wilkinson sent President Jefferson a letter warning that a "numerous & powerful association" of Americans was dispatching to New Orleans "eight or ten thousand men" on their way to invade Vera Cruz, Mexico. Later messages supplied more details.[12]

On November 27, 1806, just two days after receiving Wilkinson's first alert, Jefferson issued a special communication enjoining Americans from engaging in private military actions against foreign powers. He did not name Burr, but because Burr's project was the only one then in existence, it drew ever more attention as news of the presidential proscription traveled westward. In turn, officials in the Ohio River valley ordered their militias to restrain the activities of Burr's followers.[13]

Still too distant from all these happenings to have any knowledge of them, Burr rode from Louisville to Frankfort where he reappeared in court. Again Daveiss made a tactical error, this time by trying to conduct his own questioning rather than by following the established procedure of leaving that duty to the grand jury. Innes refused to allow the prosecution such latitude. Some of Daveiss's own witnesses recanted their previous statements, and Burr was exonerated and released on December 5. As he traveled to Nashville to coordinate the launching of the various divisions of his river fleet, the *Western World* tried without success to compel an investigation into Harry Innes's rumored Spanish connection.[14]

William Clark remained in Louisville where the waterfront continued to bustle with the increasingly brazen preparations of Burr's men. George Rogers Clark spotted them loading onto boats the sort of crates that typically held cartridges. Dennis Fitzhugh, Frances Clark's third husband, observed Burr's adherents hauling to their fleet the long, heavy boxes usually employed to carry muskets. In short, little that William or his kin saw in fact squared with Burr's purported colonization project nor with his assertion that President Jefferson, possessing full details of his endeavor, regarded it with "complacency." On the contrary, it was becoming obvious that Burr and his men aimed to shatter the fragile peace between the United States and Spain. How would Jefferson react on receiving such news? If only William had the answer to that question, he would understand how to take maximum advantage of the information he and his relatives were gathering.[15]

Accompanied by their upstream brethren, Burr's Louisville contingent finally shoved off into the Ohio River in mid-December and headed for the Mississippi. Soon thereafter, the presidential proclamation reached Louisville, prompting the Kentucky militia to turn out and guard the town. Clark, however, was not among those soldiers. On December 15, or shortly thereafter, he departed on horseback for Washington, having evidently secured Jonathan's promise to send him an updated account of the Burr situation. William must have wanted the latest news in hand when he reported to the president.[16]

Perhaps taking the route he'd followed in 1801, Clark headed southeast for Danville, Kentucky, where his nephews John and Benjamin O'Fallon attended school. After traversing the Cumberland Gap, William paused at Fincastle, Virginia, to woo fifteen-year-old Julia Hancock and to receive acclaim from local citizens for his western exploits. Then he returned to the road, calling several days later at Belle Grove, the Frederick County estate of Jonathan's brother-in-law Isaac Hite. From him or perhaps another friend, William picked up Jonathan's most recent account of Burr's activities along the Ohio River.[17]

During this time Burr and those of his followers who had been able to slip downstream ahead of the chief executive's injunction rendezvoused at the mouth of the Cumberland River, probably on the same island William had surveyed in 1798. With not quite a hundred recruits and only ten boats (far fewer of each than he had before Daveiss's prosecutions and Jefferson's proclamation), Burr planned to unite at New Orleans with General Wilkinson and his soldiers and, later, to join forces in the Gulf of Mexico with the British Navy. In early January 1807, Burr's fleet descended the Mississippi, and on January 10 he landed at Bayou Pierre where he called on Judge Peter Bruin, a fellow Revolutionary War veteran. Expecting to hear that the hoped-for conflict with Spain was under way, Burr instead learned that Wilkinson had betrayed him and that the territorial militia stood ready to take him into custody. He turned himself in, posted bond, and got ready to undergo another criminal investigation.[18]

Meanwhile, members of Congress clamored to learn more of the hostile expedition the president had cautioned about. On January 16, 1807, their demands reached a crescendo as John Randolph of Virginia won overwhelming approval in the U.S. House of Representatives for a resolution asking Jefferson to reveal everything he knew of the Burr affair. Many politicians also wanted to find out why the president had delayed taking action until months after Burr's suspect activities began, and why he did so only at the urging of the artful Wilkinson.[19]

* * *

Clark reached Washington on January 18, 1807, four days after a gala, testimonial dinner took place there to honor him and Lewis for the completion of their western reconnaissance. Having done all he could to postpone the celebration until Clark arrived, Lewis attended it without him, wondering what had happened to that otherwise punctual friend. On hearing he'd stopped en route to court the young woman he wanted to wed, Lewis must have attributed the delay to love, a simplified excuse that nonetheless suited Clark.[20]

President Jefferson was pleased with the intelligence Clark had brought about Burr. By happenstance, on or about the day Clark showed up, so did correspondence from General Wilkinson announcing his efforts to stop Burr and the thousands of armed recruits Wilkinson claimed he might have, lest they "seize on New Orleans, revolutionise the territory, and carry an expedition against Mexico by Vera Cruz." To forestall such evils, wrote the general, he had posted a substantial portion of his troops to New Orleans where he imposed martial law and issued a five-thousand-dollar reward for Burr, alive or dead.[21]

On January 22, Jefferson transmitted to Congress the information sent by General Wilkinson and probably also that provided by Jonathan Clark. The president, however, tainted it with his own desire to protect the general who, as Jefferson planned, would serve as the principal witness against Burr at his trial for treason. In other words, the president, disregarding Attorney Daveiss's early messages to him, unfairly credited Wilkinson with breaking news of the incipient expedition. And, by summarily concluding that Burr, plotting alone, was the "principal actor, whose guilt is placed beyond question," Jefferson evinced a singular wish to see his former running mate convicted. Perhaps echoing such sentiments, Clark on this very day began writing stern words about Burr, referring to him as a "Second Boneparte."[22]

At around the same time, Burr learned of the considerable reward offered for his own capture or assassination. Conscious that Wilkinson was likelier to send a death squad than a bounty hunter after him, Burr jumped bail and fled into the woods. On February 19, 1807, he was apprehended in what is now southern Alabama and through the intervention of local citizens was conveyed in safety toward Richmond, Virginia, for trial. While he traveled, Clark and Lewis continued mingling in the City of Washington with politicians to vote on their compensation for the Expedition and on their future employment. And Clark maintained his tough stance against Burr.[23]

In early March, Secretary Dearborn and U.S. Attorney General Caesar Rodney had Clark join them for a meeting with Major James Bruff, a Revolutionary War veteran of honorable career who had served as the ranking Army officer in St. Louis until the 1805 arrival of General Wilkinson as territorial governor. According to Bruff, Wilkinson thereupon tried to lure him into an enigmatic conspiracy "to make fortunes," only to turn against him when Bruff (who, from reading gazettes such as the *Western World*, suspected Wilkinson of plotting a sedition with Burr) promised instead to expose "any plans or measures which put to hazard the peace and safety of the United States." Having been subsequently court-martialed and suspended from the Army at Wilkinson's behest, Bruff wanted Dearborn and Rodney to restore his pay and active status.[24]

As if to incline them toward doing so, Bruff made various charges against the general. They started with his 1787 trip to New Orleans, covered his first seditious memorial "which," Bruff correctly surmised, "procured him [Wilkinson] exclusive [commercial] privileges from the Spanish Government," and ended with cogent reasons to believe that Wilkinson, not Burr, was a threat to national security. But no proof Bruff offered of the general's rascality seemed to matter to Dearborn and Rodney. They responded that, regardless of evidence, they had to support Wilkinson for he "stood high" with Mr. Jefferson. The lesson to Clark was unequivocal: to ensure the continuation of his own standing in Washington, he must act as though Wilkinson merited the utmost confidence.[25]

But he did not, as Clark surely knew. He need only recall Wilkinson's malevolent efforts to slander the capable General Wayne in order to replace him as commander in chief. The trouble for Clark was that he had nevertheless become such a partisan of Wilkinson, he could not at this point tell the truth about him without appearing to be his confederate or provoking him to retaliate; either outcome was sure to compromise Clark's sterling prospects. And nothing would do so more thoroughly than a revelation that, in 1798, he had sent up the Mississippi River barrels of sugar and coffee stuffed with the illicit fruits of Wilkinson's grand scheme, the top-secret conspiracy with Spain.

Having spent enough time around Wilkinson to appreciate his views on the primacy of self-interest, Clark no doubt realized that his own advantage lay in retaining the approval of Jefferson and his supporters on Capitol Hill. To achieve that end, Clark must oppose Burr, support Wilkinson, and act as if he had never done anything out of keeping with his newly acquired persona as a national hero. He comported himself accordingly.[26]

On March 3, 1807, Congress approved the president's request to grant Clark and Lewis not just sixteen hundred acres apiece, but also double pay for their western service. Within a few days, Secretary Dearborn further notified Clark that at Jefferson's direction he was to serve as agent of Indian Affairs in the Louisiana Territory, earning fifteen hundred dollars annually, and would also lead the territorial militia as brigadier general. Satisfied with these lucrative tokens of governmental approval and having resigned from the Army, Clark left Washington. He rode toward St. Louis where he was to spend the three decades still ahead of him, carrying out his momentous responsibilities with efficiency and devotion to Jeffersonian ideals even after such notions had become as outmoded as the Federalism they once superseded.[27]

And all along, Clark would reveal ever less of himself until at last it appeared even he had forgotten that, in 1798, eager for profit and advantageous connections, he had furthered the interests of prominent Kentuckians receiving grand, secret sums of Spanish money to betray the United States.

Epilogue
The Mammoth of Iniquity Escaped

Whether by design or chance, William Clark never again encountered James Wilkinson. Such a turn of events was indeed favorable for Clark. It allowed him to concentrate on meeting proper obligations—which after his January 1808 wedding to Julia Hancock included her and the children she would bear him.

Clark thrived as a high public servant in St. Louis. With each success, whether as Indian agent or as head of the territorial militia, his professional and political stature grew, creating a legacy that continued long after he died. In this regard he fared much better than did many others touched in some way by Wilkinson's intrigues, especially four men central to our story: Thomas Power, the younger Daniel Clark, Andrew Ellicott, and Thomas Freeman. To see how the general blighted their lives, let us follow a sequence of events starting in Richmond, Virginia, with the preliminary inquiry into the alleged crimes of Aaron Burr.[1]

On March 30, 1807, the captive Burr appeared for the first time before the federal circuit court in Richmond. On the bench was President Jefferson's distant cousin Chief Justice John Marshall, whose duties—like those of his Supreme Court brethren—occasionally required him to hear cases at the trial level. After examining Burr and his deputies, the attorneys for the government framed two pivotal questions: Did Burr commit the crime of treason? Did he commit the misdemeanor of preparing a military project against Spanish territory? Unable or unwilling to attend any of the legal actions against Burr, Jefferson nonetheless was to follow them closely,

313

sending instructions to the prosecutors and having courtroom spectators, including Meriwether Lewis, report back to him.[2]

Burr put together a distinguished team of defenders, and by May 22, 1807, was eager to present arguments for his acquittal. The lawyers for the government, however, were not yet ready for the proceedings to commence. Because indicting Burr would depend almost entirely on the testimony of Wilkinson (then stationed in the Orleans Territory), U.S. Attorney George Hay asked that the hearing be postponed until the general appeared. Marshall acquiesced. In the meantime, the court selected a grand jury to be chaired by John Randolph, a congressional leader who was also a shirttail relative of Thomas Jefferson yet often opposed his administration.[3]

On June 15, 1807, splendid in a uniform he had designed himself (he glittered with medals, gold epaulets, and spurs and carried a full-length sword), Wilkinson at last strode into the courtroom. Randolph immediately had the sword confiscated, explaining he would "allow no attempt to intimidate the jury." Soon he and his fellow jurors detected that the evidence brought forward by Wilkinson, especially Burr's letter announcing he was ready to embark on their campaign of conquest and plunder, had been tampered with; it contained multiple erasures and sections of text in a hand different from Burr's.[4]

Dissatisfied with Wilkinson's excuses for the alterations, Randolph and six of his peers tried to have him charged as an accomplice, but they were unable to do so for lack of a majority. Randolph lamented that the "mammoth of iniquity" escaped legal process, adding that Wilkinson was "the only man that I ever saw who was from the bark to the very core a villain." What Jefferson really thought of him is unknown, except that he believed him essential for the grand jury to indict Burr.[5]

It did exactly that on June 24, 1807, and soon a trial was set on each count. The one on the treason charge came first, taking up nearly the entire month of August, but it concluded with a decision that Burr's activities fell short of the crime as defined by the Constitution. The misdemeanor action, running September 9–15, also ended in acquittal. Yet the case was not over. At the insistence of the president, the government moved to charge Burr once more with treason, this time aiming to have him tried in the Ohio River valley, where he had assembled and launched his fleet. Marshall assented, perhaps aware that Jefferson was talking about having him impeached for his supposed leniency toward Burr.[6]

The new proceeding began promptly. To fulfill its burden of proof, the government had to refute Burr's argument that Wilkinson, not he, was a traitor, and the only way to do this was to have the general testify—a move that might instead cast further doubt on him and ruin the case against Burr. Even so, for five straight days Wilkinson fielded a barrage of questions from enemies including Burr, Major Bruff, and Thomas Power, the former Spanish courier who had perfected the upriver method of smuggling reales to Wilkinson not long before William Clark employed it for his own purposes. Just as the prosecutors feared, the flaws and inconsistencies in Wilkinson's testimony increased suspicions against him. In addition, the anti-Jefferson wing of the press took to calling the protracted hearings "King Tom's Puppet Show." Not until October 10 did these end, Marshall thereafter again ruling that the prosecution had failed to show sufficient cause to hold Burr. Soon Burr was a free man.[7]

Troubles kept multiplying for General Wilkinson, however. Within a short time, John Randolph received a mass of Spanish records from the younger Daniel Clark, since 1806 a congressional delegate from the Orleans Territory. The documents concerned the 9,640 pieces of eight shipped in 1796 from New Orleans, stored in the bedroom of New Madrid commandant Portell, and turned over to Thomas Power—who concealed them in coffee and sugar barrels and took them up the Ohio toward Wilkinson. Randolph released those papers right away to the other legislators. At his urging, they were forwarded to Jefferson, in hopes that he would ask Congress to investigate Wilkinson.[8]

Rather than do so, however, Jefferson sent the evidence to a military tribunal, as the general had requested. Wilkinson wanted that body to examine his Spanish connections in light of an affidavit he'd concocted to make his clandestine salary appear legitimate revenue from tobacco sales. With no way of knowing the document was counterfeit, the board of three colonels—all of whom stood to forfeit their military careers if the vengeful Wilkinson was later acquitted at a court-martial they had recommended—pronounced him blameless.[9]

Vindicated, Wilkinson received orders to repair to New Orleans and take command of two thousand soldiers recently mobilized to protect the region from a threatened British attack. He arrived in April 1809, moving his troops to a nearby locale he had selected. Within a short time the site pooled with rainwater, causing his men—and perhaps himself—to suffer the effects of inadequate drainage and poor sanitation. Many weeks after being ordered to move to more salubrious ground near Natchez, he finally did so. By then nearly half his forces were ill, had deserted, or were dead from disease, the naval attack having failed to take place.[10]

Wilkinson was summoned to Washington to account for this appalling toll and for unresolved issues regarding his past. No longer did he enjoy the unquestioning support of the chief executive; James Madison, one beyond Wilkinson's power to enthrall, had succeeded Thomas Jefferson. Adding to the general's burdens, Daniel Clark had recently published a book entitled *Proofs of the Corruption of General James Wilkinson and His Connexion with Aaron Burr*, and it was renewing interest in these very topics. To address them and the many rumors circulating about Wilkinson, Congress scheduled two investigations.[11]

The first one—concerning his relations with Spain and Burr—commenced in April 1810. It stopped short of completion, however, as Wilkinson had earlier made off with nearly all the papers used against him in the military probe. Late in 1810, a second congressional committee met to examine Wilkinson's role in the heavy mortality of his forces near New Orleans but closed their hearing prematurely when the legislative session ended.[12]

Wishing to compel a military inquiry that would exonerate him once and for all, the general published *Memoirs of General Wilkinson: Burr's Conspiracy Exposed and General Wilkinson Vindicated Against the Slanders of his enemies on that Important Occasion*. As if in response, the War Department called for a court-martial to delve into the same issues the congressmen had left unresolved. The proceeding took place in Fredericktown (now Frederick), Maryland, and began in September 1811.[13]

Again in ostentatious uniform, but for a sword he voluntarily relinquished upon reporting to the court, Wilkinson dodged censure for the loss of so many soldiers. His argument was that an officer of his rank should not be punished for delaying compliance with orders. Burr's acquittal having made irrelevant the charge of complicity with him, Wilkinson prepared to answer the accusations concerning his relationship with Spain by showing his bogus statement of account.[14]

Because witnesses Thomas Power, Daniel Clark, and Andrew Ellicott (all of whom had intersected with William Clark in 1798) could help prove that document fraudulent, the prosecution put their testimony before the court. Wilkinson tore into their arguments and presented their characters in the worst possible light. Consequently Power, who for a time had served as secret agent to Spain and also to Wilkinson, became notorious as one who sold his allegiance to the highest bidder. Daniel Clark Jr., having used bribery and money-running to build an international trade network, came to be thought consummately designing.[15]

To disgrace Ellicott while distracting the court from what he had to say, Wilkinson relied on Thomas Freeman, the surveyor who had objected to Ellicott's keeping Betsy, the prostitute-turned-laundress for the American boundary commission. In a deposition Freeman elaborated about Ellicott, his adult son Andy, and the woman: "It was said, and generally believed, that that extraordinary trio—father, son, and washerwoman—slept in the same bed, at the same time. . . . I was even pressed myself by the old sinner, Ellicott, to take part of his bed with his washerwoman and himself for the night."[16]

Late in December 1811, the inquisition concluded by finding Wilkinson not guilty. The six-hundred-page court transcript went on to President Madison for his consideration. After reviewing the transcript thoroughly, he reluctantly approved the verdict.[17]

Once again Wilkinson obtained a command destined to end in controversy. Ordered to guard the border with Canada during the War of 1812, he instead led his troops to embarrassing defeats along that frontier. Relieved from his duties in April 1814, he underwent another military trial, which again failed to censure him. By the time it was over, he was infamous as the general who never won a battle or lost a court-martial. The Army did not reinstate him.[18]

For several years he and his second wife, Celestine Laveau Trudeau Wilkinson (Ann Biddle Wilkinson having died in 1807), operated a plantation downstream from New Orleans. Between 1810 and 1816 he published a confused and highly selective aggregation of documents, some of them falsified to suit his purposes, titled *Memoirs of My Own Times.* Incredibly, he continued devising, then having younger protégés implement, secret schemes for penetrating the Spanish-speaking regions to the southwest. That area exerted such a pull on him that he spent his last years in Mexico, seeking a land grant in what is now Texas. He never got it, and he died in Mexico City in 1825. His funeral there drew an august group of Americans and Mexicans.[19]

By then most of his enemies had either predeceased him or lapsed into obscurity. Thomas Power may have done both. After Wilkinson disgraced him, he lived out his life so quietly, perhaps in New Orleans, that his demise went nearly unnoticed, even though his clandestine exertions had for years enabled the conspiracy between Spanish and American officials.[20]

Daniel Clark recovered from neither the damage done to his name nor his own disappointment at failing to prove Wilkinson's venality. He gradually withdrew from the mercantile world, dissolved his partnership with Daniel Coxe, and entrusted his accounts to his associates Richard Relf and Beverly Chew (William Clark's 1798 traveling companion from New Orleans to Virginia). Clark Jr. died in 1813. Having learned of her paternity, his putative daughter Myra Clark Gaines challenged his will in 1834. Relf and Chew, who had unjustly enriched themselves on his holdings, forced her to spend the rest of her years proving she was Daniel's rightful heir. In a denouement like that of Charles Dickens's *Bleak House*, she prevailed posthumously in 1891, the estate having dwindled almost to nothing.[21]

In contrast, Andrew Ellicott seemed to rebound from the aspersions made against his character. He spent his last decade working on government surveys and teaching mathematics at the U.S. Military Academy—honorable pursuits capping a distinguished career. He died in 1820. Yet the effects of Wilkinson's accusations seem to have followed Ellicott. Fully qualified to be remembered as a founding father and a technological genius, he instead passed swiftly from public awareness. Today he is almost forgotten.[22]

So is Wilkinson's defender, Thomas Freeman. At President Jefferson's request he directed a reconnaissance of the Red River in 1806. Near the present border between Texas and Oklahoma, however, Freeman and his party were stopped by a large body of Spanish soldiers—alerted because of Wilkinson's surreptitious injunction, the one that could have caused the arrest of Lewis and Clark and the failure of their expedition. Freeman was forced to turn back. In large part because of this occurrence, Congress abandoned plans to dispatch Freeman, or anyone, up the Arkansas River, thus putting an end to Jeffersonian exploration. Freeman thereafter supported himself as a surveyor. He died in 1821.[23]

This is how Wilkinson avenged himself on his enemies Power, Clark Jr., and Ellicott. It is also how Wilkinson's treachery brought down undeserved grief on his supposed friend Thomas Freeman. That is, had Wilkinson not betrayed to Spain the secrets of the United States, Freeman may well have become the William Clark of southwestern exploration and then gone on, as Clark did, to an acclaimed and rewarding government position.

So, Did "Nothing Extraordinary" Happen?

Not long after reaching New Orleans in the spring of 1798, William Clark bribed Spanish officials, dealt with the sly Daniel Clark Jr., and advanced the smuggling venture of Benjamin Sebastian and Samuel Montgomery Brown. Yet William recorded just the monetary effects of those pursuits, burying that data in the ledger section of his journal. His diary entries say nothing at all on these subjects. Indeed, concerning his activities during the month after he paid off his boatmen but before he booked passage on the schooner *Active*, William records only that "Nothing extraordinary happened." Given such obvious reticence on his part, what are we to make of him and the Spanish Conspiracy, a topic about which he left no known reference?

Although I have pointed out certain links of his to major figures in that intrigue—especially Sebastian, Brown, and James Wilkinson—we should consider that some of these connections were legitimate (for instance, those originating in family friendships or in the hierarchy of the military). By the same logic, without further evidence we should not unreservedly assume that in 1798 Clark knew the nearly 265 pieces of eight hidden among his coffee beans were tainted by Sebastian's involvement with the conspiracy. Nor, lacking additional proof, should we necessarily conclude that the 670 such coins secreted away within Clark's sugar barrel were something other than lawful compensation intended for someone else. If we can accept courier Thomas Bullitt's alleged belief that Sebastian's explanation was indeed truthful (the thousands of Spanish dollars due him at New Orleans were honest payment for past work on commercial matters between Spain and Kentucky), we ought then to allow at least for the possibility that in 1798 Clark in good faith accepted a similar story.

Whether he did, of course, depends on what he may already have known of the conspiracy. At this time, lacking any unequivocal writing or testimony by him on the subject, it is well instead to examine his actions and relationships with known conspirators, and to look for clues to his state of mind. Let us do so chronologically.

As we have seen, Clark's 1794 journal demonstrates both his bias at that time in favor of Wilkinson and his scorn for General Anthony Wayne. Was Clark of the same mind a year earlier when, on a secret mission for the Army, he presented himself at Spanish New Madrid at midday rather than passing that fortress by night, as Wayne had instructed him to do? Consider also what occurred in 1795 when he returned to New Madrid on another key mission. Ordered by Wayne to convey no package or correspondence other than that of Wayne to the Spanish authority there, Clark did as told. Yet, according to a report by Governor Gayoso de Lemos, Clark also delivered a glowing, oral account of General Wilkinson's importance to the Army and offered no such words about the acclaimed Wayne, the victor at Fallen Timbers. Although Clark complied with the literal meaning of his orders, one must ask: Was he deliberately deviating from their spirit? And afterward, why did he prepare a seemingly thorough report for Wayne and leave out all mention of the Spanish naval patrol, which Manuel Lisa's convoy had escorted him past, at the mouth of the Ohio River?

Such questions persist even after Clark resigned from the Army in 1796. For example, late that summer and early fall he made his way across Kentucky and north of the Ohio River on a journey benefiting his brother Jonathan. Was William aware of the frequent proximity of Thomas Power, who was then striving to deliver more than nine thousand pieces of eight to Wilkinson? Having told Jonathan that Wilkinson had already departed Cincinnati, did Clark travel there knowing otherwise? If so, why?

Similar concerns dog Clark's 1798 journey. Why—from New Orleans to the boundary camp at the thirty-first parallel and back to New Orleans—did he depart from his early journal practice of naming the key men with whom he dealt? What did he discuss with four of them—Daniel Clark, Andrew Ellicott, John McKee, and Stephen Minor—all of whom knew about the conspiracy? What did William Clark say to Benjamin Sebastian when they came upon each other somewhere on the Mississippi between the thirty-first parallel and New Orleans? And, most strangely, why did Clark compile coordinates of strategically important locations along the Mississippi below the Ohio but list them in the order of one going *upstream*, a progression useless to himself and to most traders of that era—but not to a military force?

Although conclusive answers to these crucial questions and to certain others raised in this book await discovery, the evidence presented herein about the dubious pursuits of William Clark has yet to be refuted. Perhaps it is too late to find definitive resolutions for all these issues, but it is still important to seek them. Not to do so is to deny Clark, whose western Expedition and subsequent public service entitle him to lasting renown, recognition for being the complex individual he surely was.

Appendix A

Dramatis Personae

William Clark's Family

Richard Clough Anderson: Married in 1787 to William's sister Elizabeth (who died in 1795), an officer in the Revolutionary War. Afterward he moved to Kentucky and became a business partner of William Croghan.

Ann Rogers Clark: Wife of John Clark and the mother of ten children, including William, to survive childhood.

Edmund Clark: The brother closest to William's age, he was a Revolutionary War veteran who thereafter engaged in mercantile pursuits and operated a mill in Virginia. He moved to Kentucky in or around 1802.

George Rogers Clark: The most famous of the Clark brothers during the period of this story, he spent much of the Revolution as a general in the Virginia militia, fighting the British and Indians in the Ohio and Mississippi river valleys. His sizable wartime expenses going unreimbursed by Virginia, he became insolvent and dependent on William and the other members of their family.

John Clark: Husband to Ann Rogers Clark and father to William and his siblings, he was a friend of Judge Benjamin Sebastian.

Jonathan Clark: Born twenty years before his brother William, he was a lieutenant colonel in the Continental Army. Afterward he was a Virginia farmer and a man of affairs which often took him on journeys through the state. In 1802 he and his family moved to Kentucky.

William Croghan: Another Revolutionary War veteran from Virginia, he moved to Louisville, Kentucky, after the conflict, obtained a Spanish permit to trade at New Orleans, married William's sister Lucy, and established an estate called Locust Grove, where he operated a land office. With partner Richard Clough Anderson, he sometimes sent to New Orleans cargoes of Kentucky goods for sale.

James O'Fallon: An Irish-born physician who served for the United States in the Revolutionary War, he later migrated to Kentucky. Involved in the South Carolina Yazoo Company and in various questionable projects of James Wilkinson and George Rogers Clark, O'Fallon married William's sister Frances. He died in or around 1794.

Charles M. Thruston: A native of Virginia, he moved to Kentucky in 1788, then formed a mercantile partnership in Louisville. In 1796 he married the widowed Frances Clark O'Fallon. In 1800 he was killed by one of his slaves.

Clark's Downriver Associates Not Conspiring with Spain

Margaret Clark Chabaud: Born in Ireland and unrelated to William, she was a widow who operated a New Orleans boardinghouse catering to English-speaking patrons.

Beverly Chew: Late in the 1790s he moved from Fredericksburg, Virginia, to New Orleans where he went into the mercantile business, at times relying for help on Daniel Clark Jr. Chew was a friend of John McKee and Thomas Freeman.

Daniel Clark Jr.: Another Irish native not kin to William Clark, he bore the name of a New Orleans uncle who grew rich through international trading based in large part on bribery and money-smuggling. Young Daniel joined his uncle in 1781 and a decade later took over their company. Also a part-time clerk in the Spanish government, Clark Jr. had access to intelligence concerning the intrigue between Spanish officials and disloyal Americans.

Daniel Clark Sr.: The Irish-born uncle of his namesake, he lived in 1798 on a plantation just north of the thirty-first parallel.

Richard Clark: Brother to Clark Jr. and nephew of Clark Sr., he also migrated from Ireland. Trained in artillery, he came to New Orleans in 1798 with Daniel W. Coxe aboard his armed ship.

Daniel W. Coxe: A Philadelphian who began working in his father's countinghouse, he became an international businessman, forming a long-distance partnership with Clark Jr. of New Orleans. Thereafter they sent each other regular shipments of goods, many of them onboard Coxe's own craft.

Andrew Ellicott: The astronomer and mathematician who served as American commissioner of the boundary between the United States and Spanish territory. He also monitored the Spanish Conspiracy.

Thomas Freeman: Another native of Ireland, he helped complete the survey of the District of Columbia, then became Ellicott's chief surveyor on the Spanish-American boundary.

John McKee: A college-educated Virginian eager for a federal appointment, he was determined to secure his future in part by revealing information about the Spanish Conspiracy.

Richard Rhea: Business agent at New Orleans for some of William Clark's tobacco.

Spanish Officials

Andrés de Armesto: Secretary to Spanish governors, he decoded and translated into English much secret correspondence between those officials and conspiratorial Americans.

Casa Calvo, Sebastián Calvo de la Puerta y O'Farrill, Marqués de: Acting military governor of Louisiana from 1799 to 1801, he later influenced General James Wilkinson of the U.S. Army to resume activities as a secret operative of Spain.

Carlos III: The Spanish monarch who in 1762 accepted the French cession of New Orleans and the territory west of the Mississippi as a barrier between Americans and the silver mines in what is now Mexico. A just and able ruler, he believed in subsidizing Louisiana although it never produced enough revenue to pay back what it cost Spain.

Carlos IV: The inept son of Carlos III who on his father's death in 1788 inherited the throne. He relied on others, especially Manuel de Godoy, to administer his realm, which included the expensive and unremunerative colonies of Louisiana, West Florida, and Florida.

Carondelet, François-Louis Hector, Baron de: The Flemish-born governor of Louisiana from 1791 to 1797, he fortified it as best he could but proved an easy dupe to the mercenary machinations of James Wilkinson.

William Dunbar: An émigré from Scotland who established himself at a plantation near Natchez, he eventually made enough money from cotton and other crops to devote his attention to scientific pursuits. Accomplished at celestial navigation, he served as astronomer for Spain during the first months of work on the boundary between the United States and Spanish territory.

Manuel Gayoso de Lemos: Spanish-born governor of Natchez from 1789 to 1797, then of Louisiana and West Florida until his death in 1799. He was probably the shrewdest and most even-handed of all high Spanish officials in those territories.

Vicente Folch: Nephew of Louisiana governor Esteban Miró, he served in various military positions. As governor of West Florida in 1804, he encouraged Wilkinson to resume intriguing with Spain.

Manuel de Godoy: Reputedly a lover of Maria Luisa de Parma, queen of Spain and wife of Carlos IV, he became in his mid-twenties the first Spanish secretary of state. Godoy eventually gained the title "Prince of Peace."

Stephen Minor: A Pennsylvania-born settler at Natchez who in 1798 became the acting Spanish commissioner of the boundary with the United States.

Esteban Miró: Governor of Louisiana from 1782 through 1791, he accepted James Wilkinson's ostensible services as a secret agent for Spain, offering in return his efforts to secure Wilkinson an exclusive trading privilege.

Juan Ventura Morales: Acting Spanish intendant from 1796 to 1803, he often performed his duties with zeal and ruthlessness.

Martín Navarro: One of Morales's predecessors as intendant, he supported the earliest phase of the Spanish Conspiracy.

Tomás Portell: He was commandant of New Madrid from 1791 to 1796, and of Fort San Marcos de Apalache when it surrendered to attackers in 1800.

Thomas Power: A Canary Islander who settled in Spanish Louisiana, he carried clandestine messages between officials of that government and James Wilkinson and his conspiratorial associates and developed a reliable method of smuggling coined silver to them. He also served as commissary and surveyor on the boundary line between the United States and Spanish territory.

Juan Ronquillo: Chief pilot at the mouth of the Mississippi River from 1767 until not long before the Louisiana Purchase.

Zenon Trudeau: Commandant and lieutenant governor of St. Louis, he welcomed the visiting William Clark in 1797.

François Vallé: Commandant and leading citizen of Ste. Genevieve, he hosted Clark during an overnight visit to his home in 1797.

José Vidal: The last acting Spanish consul in Natchez.

Some Americans Linked to the Spanish Conspiracy

(Fuller accounts concerning John Brown, Innes, Muter, Nicholas, and Sebastian appear in Chapter 3.)

John Brown: A Virginia-born lawyer who moved to Kentucky where he became a U.S. senator, he was secretly involved in the Spanish Conspiracy.

Samuel Montgomery Brown: As a storekeeper in Frankfort, Kentucky, he accepted shipments of New Orleans goods with Spanish payoffs for James Wilkinson hidden inside them. In 1798 Brown set out to promote a new phase of the Spanish Conspiracy.

Joseph Collins: Once a U.S. Army captain under Wilkinson, he smuggled some of that officer's illicit Spanish revenue to him in 1795.

Harry Innes: The first federal judge for Kentucky, Innes was a Democratic-Republican lawyer who often had James Wilkinson as a client. Innes's friendship with him and Sebastian, however, made him a target of Humphrey Marshall, his perennial rival in court and political opponent.

Michel La Cassagne: A French settler in Louisville, he was one of Wilkinson's many creditors and an early courier of his Spanish money.

William Murray: One of several Kentuckians who, according the Wilkinson, the Spanish could corrupt with a secret salary of two thousand dollars.

George Muter: A Revolutionary War veteran and friend of Wilkinson, he served many years as a Kentucky judge.

George Nicholas: A Revolutionary veteran from Virginia who became a Kentucky attorney, he maintained the appearance of a zealous public servant despite secretly conniving with Spain.

Henry Owen: Reputedly an Irish-born mercenary, he set out to smuggle thousands of Spanish dollars to Wilkinson but was no match for the rowers of his vessel.

Mr. Riddle: Probably an American boatman who at times carried goods and money from New Orleans to Kentucky.

Benjamin Sebastian: A Kentucky Court of Appeals judge who for years accepted thousands of Spanish dollars for working against the interests of his state and country, he nevertheless was the least mendacious of all the Americans conspiring with Spain.

Thomas Todd: Related to Harry Innes, Todd followed him from Virginia to Kentucky where he practiced law and served in various other capacities. Luckier in intriguing than Sebastian, he was appointed in 1801 to the Kentucky Court of Appeals.

James Wilkinson: The architect and prime mover of the Spanish Conspiracy, he was commander of William Clark during Clark's early service in the Kentucky militia and his first stint in the U.S. Army. During the years of our story Wilkinson was a brigadier general.

Americans Opposed to the Spanish Conspiracy

James Bruff: A major in the U.S. Army, he was the ranking military officer in the Louisiana Territory when James Wilkinson arrived in 1805 to govern it.

Joseph Hamilton Daveiss: Brother-in-law to U.S. Supreme Court Chief Justice John Marshall, he became the district attorney for Kentucky in 1799. As a former student of George Nicholas, Daveiss settled his estate, thereby finding among his papers evidence of early phases of the Spanish Conspiracy.

Humphrey Marshall: After serving in the Revolution he left Virginia for Kentucky where he grew rich from real estate speculation, often opposing George Rogers Clark and James Wilkinson in court. A staunch Federalist, Marshall was to join forces with Daveiss in order to expose the principals in the Spanish Conspiracy.

Joseph Street: Editor of the *Western World*, a Federalist gazette founded in 1806 and published in Kentucky.

John Wood: Publisher and editor of the *Western World*, he depended on Daveiss and Marshall to provide much of the information he and Street would print about the Conspiracy.

Appendix B

Our Clark Relics
The Curious Path of the Journal, from Clark to the Present

Why has the story in William Clark's 1798–1801 Notebook not come forth in all its complexity until now? The answer depends in part on who owned the journal after Clark did. And that information may forever remain obscure, no firm evidence of full ownership (that is, the right to possess, manage, and convey the volume) being known to exist from Clark's death in 1838 until May 15, 1923, the day it was purchased by a Missourian who collected historical materials. Because that individual did not record the identity of the seller, we cannot trace its previous provenance any further. Let us therefore work forward from the past, searching for clues—if not to the ownership of the book, then at least to its whereabouts. The trail begins in St. Louis.[1]

Clark arrived there with his bride, Julia Hancock Clark, in late June or early July 1808. They settled into quarters near the busy river landing, and he went to work on his duties, among them serving as head Indian agent for the Louisiana Territory. In August he purchased a tract holding fourteen hundred acres of rolling, forested hills interspersed with lush, wet lowlands; it lay some six miles northwest of the city. He thought the acreage ideal not just as a camping ground for visiting delegations of his native charges but also as his own retreat from the clangor of urban life. In addition, he judged his sprawling parcel a sound investment, expecting it to increase in value as the city expanded in that direction. Although he referred to the entire spread as Marais Castor (Beaver Marsh), he came to call a section of it Council Grove for the meetings he occasionally held there with Indians. Soon his slaves erected a colonial farmhouse at Marais Castor, enabling Clark to spend as much time at the country estate as his responsibilities allowed.[2]

Meanwhile he, Julia, and their first child moved into a new residence not far from their former one in the city. Located on Main Street, the house stood near other town lots that would become important to Clark. One of these was to hold a building in which he would not only negotiate with some of the tribes under his jurisdiction but also exhibit to the public various artifacts he had amassed. Among those things were Indian war regalia, bows, arrows, battle clubs and axes, tribal clothing, a canoe of bark and another of animal hide, and western things such as mineral specimens, animal skins, and petrifactions. The first museum in St. Louis, William's hall of curiosities drew crowds. Several visitors left descriptions of it, naming particular objects on display, but as far as we know, none of those people mentioned his western journals or maps (perhaps because, still needing some of them in order to carry out responsibilities, Clark kept them at his workplace).[3]

But what about his earlier logbooks and documents? There is little evidence of their location at that time. We can, however, assume that, because he could expect to spend the rest of his life in St. Louis and did not retain a residence in the Louisville area (having sold the Mulberry Hill house to his brother Jonathan in 1803), Clark brought most such things with him. He also came to possess numerous other papers, particularly those of his brother George Rogers Clark. A story passed down in William's family holds that he kept his documents "pigeonholed in an old secretary."[4]

By the end of 1818, William and Julia had five children, and she was in failing health. She died in 1820 and was followed in death the next year by their only daughter. In November 1821, Clark wed Julia's cousin, the widowed Harriet Kennerly Radford; she was to bear him two sons, one of whom failed to survive infancy. By the time Harriet died in December 1831, only four children fathered by Clark still lived—all of them male. Three of them were Julia's: Meriwether Lewis Clark, born in 1809; William Preston Clark, born in 1811; and George Rogers Hancock Clark, born in 1816. The youngest was Harriet's: Thomas Jefferson Kearny Clark, born in 1824.[5]

Meriwether shared his father's predilection for sketching, especially architecture, and his medium of choice was pencil. William Preston inherited both his father's love of theater and his uncle George Rogers Clark's weakness for alcohol. Perhaps less artistic but more practical than his elder siblings, George Rogers Hancock would make his way in business. And Thomas Jefferson Kearny—called simply "Jeff"—was a lively fellow, adored by the others. He was the only son not yet an adult when their father died on September 1, 1838.[6]

William Clark's will provided for each son a proportionate share of assets—chiefly slaves, cash, and real estate—but specified nothing about his journals, even the volumes concerning the 1804–1806 exploration. In 1816, two years after the publication of *History of the Expedition under the Command of Captains Lewis and Clark*, Clark had arranged for the American Philosophical Society to receive his Expedition journals and notes. Yet he nevertheless retained five such volumes, apparently deeming the material in them repetitious with that in the donated ones. In 1840, before the distribution of Clark's assets was complete, his son William Preston died, perhaps from the effects of alcohol abuse. His share in the estate went to his three brothers.[7]

Meriwether was then thirty-one years old, married to a woman who would bear him seven children (only one of them was female, and she died at nearly two years of age). They lived in St. Louis. Over the years he worked at various occupations, among them architect, surveyor, civil engineer, and municipal clerk, and he served in the Mexican War. Shortly after his wife died in 1852, he sent his younger boys to be raised by relatives. In a few years his older sons were grown and also gone, and Meriwether was alone.[8]

On a date he did not record, he examined the 1798–1801 Notebook, affixing to the cover a label he filled with a penciled outline—now quite faded—of the subject matter within. Inside the book he inscribed a rudimentary table of contents, and on the opening page of the 1798 travel narrative added comments, precisely penciling beneath them "M. L. C." To several other pages he added sparse notes, particularly about dates he considered significant. So intent, it seems, was Meriwether on the chronology of his father's 1798 travels that he paid no attention to entries about the eleven hundred pieces of eight hidden in coffee and sugar barrels bound upriver to Kentucky.[9]

Meriwether left marks on at least three other journals written by William Clark. One of them dates from a journey to Washington, D.C., in 1809, the second is a record of public accounts spanning the years 1819 to 1825, and the most recent one contains drafts drawn between 1826 and 1831. The first two books bear the same sort of manufactured labels on their covers that the 1798–1801 Notebook has, each of those labels revealing—in what appears to be Meriwether's cramped, meticulous hand—a description of the contents within. The cover of the 1826–1831 journal, however, reveals a discolored patch the size of the labels on the other books; on the flyleaf may be the smudged remains of a penciled "M. L. C." It appears that Meriwether Clark also filled out and affixed such a label to a thirty-page compendium of astronomical data recorded by Meriwether Lewis, the man for whom he was named, and by Robert Patterson, one of Lewis's tutors in such matters.[10]

Meriwether Clark continued to reside in St. Louis as tensions leading to the Civil War escalated. Because he sympathized with the states to form the Confederacy, however, he felt increasingly uncomfortable in his Unionist hometown. He began to think about moving to more agreeable surroundings, perhaps weighing whether to leave his share of his father's historic items behind, in the care of a brother.[11]

Doing so must have seemed a practical course of action, for both George and Jeff, having married local women, were unlikely to leave St. Louis. Their wives were sisters to each other and had grown up near Marais Castor. Therefore, when Thomas Jefferson Kearny Clark wed Mary Susan (Sue) Glasgow in 1849, her sister, Eleanor Ann (Ellen) Glasgow (George's wife since 1841), welcomed her into the Clark family. So close did these couples remain that, after George's death in 1858, Jeff and Sue helped Ellen raise her four children.[12]

By then, Jeff and Sue Clark had plenty of room to do so, their slaves having earlier erected for them a twenty-six-room Italianate mansion on

Photograph of Mary Susan Glasgow Clark and Jefferson Kearny Clark, taken about 1890 by Anita Glasgow.

the crown of a hill at Marais Castor. Topped with a tower to be called the armory for the weapons it held (some of them surely from William's museum), the house would be open not just to the late George's children but also to Meriwether's and a steady succession of guests. Deeming "Council Grove" no longer descriptive of the estate, Jeff took to calling it "Minoma," allegedly an Indian word for the sweet springs on the grounds.[13]

Occasionally Meriwether came to visit, walking to Minoma when he could not afford buggy fare; sometimes he stayed for longer stretches. Jeff stored for him some of the historic things Meriwether claimed from their father's estate, perhaps on the understanding that he would eventually retrieve them. Early in the 1860s, though, Meriwether joined the Confederate Army and went off to fight. After the conflict ended he settled in Kentucky and married a Louisville woman. He died in 1881, having failed to reclaim the relics he had left at Minoma.[14]

By then Jeff and Sue Clark, who had no children of their own, were finished helping to raise those of his brothers. Closer than ever to George Clark's widow, Ellen, Jeff and Sue were especially fond of her eldest child,

Photograph of Minoma, the mansion built by Jefferson K. Clark in 1856 on William Clark's property known as Marais Castor. The house, located in what is now Northwoods, a suburb of St. Louis, was taken down in 1960.

Julia Clark Voorhis, and of Julia's daughter, Eleanor Glasgow Voorhis; both of them showed particular interest in grandfather William Clark's numerous books, papers, and artifacts. In March 1892, an article in the *St. Louis Post-Dispatch* called Jeff's assemblage of such things "one of the most complete and interesting collections of original official and private documents . . . now held outside of the historical museums of America." The paper described the items Jeff considered most valuable. Among them were William Clark's elkskin-bound journal (one of the five Expedition books he had not passed along to the American Philosophical Society), a letter of credit issued by President Jefferson to pay expenses on that journey, a "quaint old colonial desk once owned by Meriwether Lewis Clark," and many documents that had earlier belonged to William Clark and his brother George.[15]

By the time this story appeared, though, Jeff and Sue Clark had already sold the bulk of their real estate to what the *Post-Dispatch* termed "a syndicate of St. Louis capitalists investing in suburban property," having agreed to vacate the house and other structures at Minoma by April 1, 1892. For a while Jeff and Sue lived in the city of St. Louis, but before long they moved to an apartment in New York City. With them they took a sizeable portion of their historic items.[16]

At around the same time, Julia (who for years had been estranged from her husband, Robert Stevenson Voorhis) and her only child, Eleanor, joined the elderly Jeff and Sue Clark in New York. So did a young man named Samuel W. Maguire; at some point Jeff and Sue unofficially adopted him and sent him to law school on the understanding that, as a lawyer, he'd see to their interests. Maguire would do so, eventually going into partnership with a New York attorney named Arthur J. Martin.[17]

* * *

As the twentieth century opened, Meriwether Clark's first-born, William Hancock Clark, liked to think that as "the eldest son of [the] eldest son of William Clark," he was uniquely qualified to speak for his fellow descendants. Also taking for granted that the order of his own birth entitled him to inherit the artifacts his father had left at Minoma, William Hancock Clark began referring to those things as "our Clark relics." Although he suspected his cousin Julia Clark Voorhis might try to waylay them for herself, he had little idea their uncle Jeff Clark had made such exertion on her part unnecessary. That is, in 1896 Jeff Clark amended his will in order to allow his wife, Sue, to convey as she saw fit nearly all his worldly goods—including those once belonging to William Clark and, presumably, to Meriwether.[18]

Shortly after Jeff died in 1900, Sue handed over to Julia most of the historic items they had brought to New York. Adding these to things she'd already inherited from her father, Julia possessed so many portraits, artifacts, papers, journals, and maps once owned by William Clark, and numerous documents of George Rogers Clark, she rented an apartment adjacent to her own to store them in. Having learned that she had received things he considered his birthright, William Hancock Clark waxed indignant but evidently never made good on his threat to sue for them.[19]

No doubt planning eventually to leave her historic legacy to the unmarried, childless Eleanor, Julia negotiated in 1903 and 1904 with editor Reuben Gold Thwaites of the Wisconsin Historical Society. He was preparing a centennial edition of the journals of the Lewis and Clark expedition. Having only recently learned about the Voorhis trove of Clark relics, especially the logbooks not relinquished to the American Philosophical Society, Thwaites considered them essential to the completion of his work. After much effort on his part and a high fee paid her by publisher Dodd, Mead, and Company, Julia consented to let Thwaites examine and quote from her materials. He did so. As a result, the four or five volumes he originally thought necessary to contain his *Original Journals of the Lewis and Clark Expedition, 1804–1806*, swelled to eight. Published in 1904 and 1905, Thwaites's work became a classic of scholarship on the epic exploration.[20]

The *Original Journals* having alerted the public to a legacy of Clark things, Julia was besieged with solicitations from historical societies after Eleanor died in 1919. Julia rebuffed all such inquiries until curator and archivist Nettie Harney Beauregard of the Missouri Historical Society in St. Louis approached her, citing a friendship shared by their forebears in that city. According to Nettie, once she mentioned this link, Julia became "a different person then, was impatient for my visit; any family who had any intercourse with her antecedents were sacred to her." In time, Julia presented several items including two portraits of her ancestors to the society, but refused to say what she would do with the many things remaining to her. Instead, she left that decision to Arthur J. Martin, law partner of Samuel Maguire. Julia died in New York in December 1922, less than a year after the demise of William Hancock Clark in that same city.[21]

Honoring Julia's unwritten wish that the Missouri Historical Society, rather than another institution, would display her Clark treasures in a room dedicated to the memory of Eleanor, Martin obtained the society's promise to do so. In the spring of 1923, he and Maguire began inspecting, classifying, and preparing for shipment hundreds of the Clark relics Julia had inherited. Soon they started sending back to St. Louis crates of things that had once belonged to William Clark and his brother George.[22]

On May 15, 1923, William Clark Breckenridge, a sixty-year-old St. Louisan *not* related to William Clark, paid a dollar and fifty cents to acquire the 1798–1801 Notebook and Clark's three other volumes, which his son Meriwether had inscribed and labeled. For an additional nickel,

Breckenridge purchased the book containing Meriwether Lewis's astronomical figures. Certainly delighted to procure such relics for pennies apiece, Breckenridge nonetheless failed to record the identity of the seller. An honorary member of the Missouri Historical Society and a trustee of the State Historical Society of Missouri (in Columbia), Breckenridge added these books to the thousands of historic volumes and documents kept in his home at 4123 Enright Avenue (almost halfway between William Clark's city residence and his Marais Castor acres).[23]

Perhaps because he had paid so little for the five journals, Breckenridge assigned them no particular importance. He believed instead—as would some of his contemporaries—that sheet music dating to the 1850s and several scrapbooks of historical news clippings were the gems of his collection. He died in December 1927.[24]

The following February, Secretary Floyd Shoemaker of the State Historical Society of Missouri inspected the approximately five thousand historical things in Breckenridge's estate. Although the Breckenridge heirs asked five thousand dollars for that lot of items, the society was unable to offer even half as much money. Shoemaker continued negotiating until they reached an agreement to buy 1,031 key things (including William Clark's four journals and Meriwether Lewis's Astronomy Notebook), for a total of $1,077. The sale took place later that year, and the purchased items came to Columbia, to a section of the University of Missouri Library occupied by the State Historical Society. Shoemaker hoped that the society would buy the remainder of the Breckenridge collection, but it proved unable to do so. Because the Great Depression and the Second World War were to intervene before the society could pay due attention to the items it had bought, for a long time the five journals of Clark and Lewis remained almost unknown in their new surroundings, a building open to the public.[25]

In 1953, when a graduate student named John Louis Loos presented to the History Department of Washington University in St. Louis his dissertation, "A Biography of William Clark, 1770–1813," he acknowledged sources in that city and outside Missouri, but not the journals in Columbia. Evidently lacking knowledge of the 1798–1801 Notebook, Loos had little to say about what his subject did from late 1797 until setting off westward with the Corps of Discovery in 1803. It was as if Clark had lost six years of his life.

In the meantime, the radical alteration of landscapes once known to William Clark accelerated. His Marais Castor acres became successively smaller lots bought by increasingly impecunious buyers, and Jeff Clark's once stately mansion was sold on the courthouse steps at least two times. During the 1930s an elderly woman, perhaps wishing to convert it to a boardinghouse, paid a young couple to rid it of numerous items she deemed worthless. Decades later, that husband and wife recounted throwing out the windows old documents, books, letters, clothing, firearms, china, and even furniture, and burning those things the next day. The house was eventually abandoned and became a target for vandals, thieves, and souvenir hunters.[26]

By the 1950s, Minoma and its environs had been absorbed into the St. Louis County municipalities of Pine Lawn and Northwoods. Around Jeff and Sue Clark's home hundreds of small, tract houses sprang up within a tight network of newly laid out streets. The county proposed turning the historic building into a community center, but so many new dwellings already hemmed it in there was not enough space for a parking lot. The cost of bringing the mansion up to applicable codes proved unaffordable, and it was demolished in 1960. On its footprint six ranch houses went up.[27]

By then many of the city locations familiar to William Clark had been cleared for the development of the Jefferson National Expansion Memorial. Since 1965 its signature monument, the Gateway Arch, has towered over what was once the original core of St. Louis. In that small section William Clark worked, raised a family, and presumably kept some of the historic things that later went to Minoma.

In 1964, the *National Union Catalog of Manuscript Collections*, at that time an annual, printed publication of the Library of Congress, promulgated a brief description of those five volumes, thereby introducing them to the scholarly world. For undetermined reasons, however, that listing made no specific reference to the 1798–1801 logbook and gave only the barest sketch of its contents. Even so, scholars began coming to Columbia to see it and its four companions in the William Clark Breckenridge collection. Discovering in them previously unknown material, they started making their findings known.[28]

John Logan Allen was among the first to do so. In 1975 his *Passage through the Garden: Lewis and Clark and the Image of the American Northwest* was published; it contains a reproduction of a map Meriwether Lewis drew in his Astronomy Notebook. Not long thereafter, Donald Jackson's second edition of the *Letters of the Lewis and Clark Expedition* appeared in print. It includes addenda regarding both the Lewis notebook and Clark's 1809 logbook (which contains information on the expedition journals after Lewis's death that year). In 1977, Jerome O. Steffen wrote the first widely disseminated book—*William Clark: Jeffersonian Man on the Frontier*—to refer specifically to the 1798–1801 Notebook, but such parts focus exclusively on the undated philosophical reflections Clark inscribed on the early pages of the journal.[29]

Not until the twenty-first century did details of Clark's 1798 and 1801 journeys reach a wide readership. In 2002 James Holmberg introduced those travels in *Dear Brother: Letters of William Clark to Jonathan Clark*, corroborating letters Clark wrote from 1798 to 1801 with entries from his Notebook. In 2004, two comprehensive biographies of William Clark— one by William Foley, the other by Landon Jones—augmented that knowledge with many more particulars, most of them from his logbook entries. Four years later, Jay Buckley's study of Clark's Indian diplomacy became the first major work to draw on all four of his volumes at the State Historical Society of Missouri.[30]

It had taken 170 years from William Clark's death, but those journals— and Meriwether Lewis's Astronomy Notebook—had finally emerged from the shadows.

Appendix C

Buried in the Womb of Time
Spanish Sources of This Story

The apparently private ownership of the 1798–1801 Notebook for nine decades after the death of William Clark and the more recent vicissitudes of that journal help explain why the full story in it remained undetected for so long. In addition, the prevalence of Clark's surname, and the custom of his era to substitute titles (such as "Mister" and "Lieutenant") for given names suggest why his dealings with Daniel Clark, Andrew Ellicott, and Daniel W. Coxe lay undiscovered for many years in the papers of those men. Such factors also help illustrate why the Spanish records of William Clark's 1798 transactions drew no special notice for more than two centuries.

The deliberate policy of Spain is the sole reason that these particular documents—and innumerable others in the keeping of that nation—stayed, in James Wilkinson's matchless prose, "buried in the womb of time." That is, having secretly advanced the Conspiracy throughout decades of otherwise peaceable relations with the United States, Spain grew so eager to hide evidence of its own duplicity that for nearly a century after the last scheme ended and all the schemers died, proof of the multifaceted intrigue remained suppressed in Spanish repositories. Unfortunately, so did many thousands of records, including those detailing the lawful activities of American visitors, one of whom was William Clark.[1]

In 1804, the year Wilkinson inaugurated a new phase of the Conspiracy (in part, by betraying the Lewis and Clark Expedition), Spain ordered

347

commandants in the colony of Louisiana to organize and inventory the official records of their jurisdictions. Except for papers related to the inhabitants' personal affairs and property (such documents would be turned over to American administrators), governmental papers were readied for transport to New Orleans. Up the Mississippi River as far as St. Louis and down that stream and her lower tributaries to outposts with now obscure names such as Chapitoulas, Atakapas, Chetimachas, and Pointe du Teiche, functionaries of the shrinking Spanish empire strove to obey. Over the next months most of the requested documents arrived at New Orleans, swelling the archives of the local administration. By the first weeks of 1806, the majority of the transferred records as well as those of New Orleans (except for some treasury files to be sent later) were shipped to Pensacola, the seat of Spanish West Florida. Despite having originated in Louisiana, many of those documents became known as the Florida Occidental papers.[2]

Although Wilkinson was no doubt relieved to learn that numerous documents proving his illicit dealings with Spain had come to rest in remote Pensacola, he still was afraid the intelligence in them might leak out. Seeking to assuage his worries, West Florida governor Vicente Folch sent word that he had already forwarded such records to Havana, Cuba. There they would be so secure, he told Wilkinson, that "before the United States shall be in position to conquer that capital, you and I, Jefferson, Madison . . . and even the Prophet Daniel [Clark, Junior, who shortly before that time had published *Proofs of the Corruption of General James Wilkinson*] himself will have made many day's journeys on the voyage to the other world." Folch was prescient on that point. When the battleship *Maine* blew up in Havana harbor in 1898, giving rise to the Spanish-American War, Wilkinson, Folch, and all those men had been in their graves for decades.[3]

Throughout the first twenty years of the nineteenth century, as Wilkinson underwent judicial investigations, congressional inquiries, and Army courts-martial, the influence of Spain grew ever feebler. In 1811 Paraguay departed the Spanish empire. Three years later Uruguay followed that example, and in 1816 Argentina did so too. In the meantime, great numbers of U.S. citizens continued settling on land that would become parts of Mississippi, Alabama, Georgia, and Florida. Because their runaway slaves often took refuge with the Seminole Indians in Spanish West Florida, a series of aggressive acts known as the First Seminole War occurred, culminating in the seizure of Pensacola by General Andrew Jackson. Soon the United States annexed West Florida. On February 22, 1819, Spain not only renounced its claim to that territory, it ceded East Florida to the United States.

According to instructions from Spain, commandants of those colonies classified their official documents and shipped them to Cuba, still a bulwark of Spanish rule. British corsairs in the Gulf of Mexico intercepted at least one of those paper-laden vessels. Disappointed to find onboard not minted wealth but governmental files, the privateering crew tossed many of them into the sea. Such losses notwithstanding, the transfer of Florida documents to Cuba came to a close in 1819.[4]

Spanish leaders had grown increasingly fearful that any leak of the intrigue with Wilkinson, Sebastian, and their accomplices would sour relations with the United States; they evidently called in more types of records from West Florida than were gathered when Spain relinquished Louisiana. The U.S. government protested, pointing out that Spain was reneging on its agreement to turn over the Florida papers, but to no avail. Although numerous disputed items concerned matters as innocuous as property ownership, Spain kept a tight lid on nearly all of them and from time to time alleged to the Americans that certain of their papers had been "lost in transit." To further that illusion, the Spanish consul at New Orleans advised Cuban officials to turn away a New Orleanian seeking records of his real estate, thereby setting a precedent to last for decades and to affect many Americans.[5]

Meanwhile, the trickle of colonies exiting the Spanish regime became a torrent. Chile left the empire in 1818; Columbia, the next year; in 1821, Venezuela, Mexico, Honduras, Costa Rica, Nicaragua, Panama, and El Salvador separated from Spain. Despite at one time having been the Spanish center of governance for all of South America, Peru declared independence in 1824. Six years later Ecuador did so, and in 1839 Guatemala did too. Soon the American branch of the once vast Spanish domain consisted of little more than Cuba and Puerto Rico.

Even so, Spanish opposition to opening the archives of Louisiana and the Floridas remained nearly adamantine. In recognition not of their places of origin but of the venue of their exile, those collections came to be known as the "Papeles Procedentes de la Isla de Cuba" (Papers Proceeding from the Island of Cuba; hereafter cited as Cuba Papers). They consist of 2,375 bundles (called *legajos*); in all, some 1,250,000 individual records. Just as Vicente Folch had promised Wilkinson, tucked away in that immense tonnage were revelations of his perfidy toward the United States, his pseudonymous correspondence, and papers detailing the thousands of Spanish dollars paid for his nefarious services. So were documents implicating the other conspirators.[6]

The archives of Spanish Louisiana and the Floridas stayed in Cuba for most of the nineteenth century. During that time the United States became a rising power intent on making its presence felt throughout the world, especially in Spanish possessions such as Cuba and the Philippine Islands. Perhaps discerning the first hint of such a threat, the government in Madrid—which for decades had undergone change and disorder after the ineffectual Carlos IV abdicated the throne in 1808—commanded the Captain General of Cuba to transfer the Cuba Papers to Spain. By October 1889, the bulk of the legajos comprising that collection, divided into thirteen shipments, had arrived safely in Seville, Spain.[7]

The document-stuffed bundles were off-loaded, crated, and placed in the Casa Lonja, a large building erected in the sixteenth century as a merchants' exchange. Discovered to be infested with a paper-eating pest known as *Calymmaderus oblongus*, the Cuba Papers were isolated in a section of the Casa Lonja and treated with benzine, then neglected for twenty years.[8]

An American scholar, Roscoe Hill, with funding provided by the Carnegie Institution spent from January 1911 to March 1913 studying the Cuba Papers. He originally intended to calendar individual records pertaining to U.S. history, but in a short time he realized the sheer volume of the collection would not let him complete that plan. Instead, Hill prepared *Descriptive Catalogue of the Documents relating to the History of the United States in the Papeles Procedentes de Cuba deposited in the Archivo General de Indias at Seville*, a 594-page abstract of the legajos he judged relevant to the United States. Published in 1916, this work yet stands as an authoritative overall guide to the extensive collection.

The Cuba Papers, however, comprise just one of twelve components of the Archivo General de Indias (the General Archives of the Indies). Other collections related to the Spanish regimes in Louisiana and the Floridas include the Archivo Histórico Nacional (National Historical Archives), Madrid, and the Archivo General de Simancas (General Archives of Simancas), a town near the Spanish city of Valladolid.[9]

Hill's *Descriptive Catalogue* helped at last to reveal the avarice-driven intriguing of James Wilkinson, Benjamin Sebastian, Samuel Montgomery Brown, John Brown, Harry Innes, George Nicholas, William Murry, George Muter, Thomas Todd, and other corrupt Kentuckians. Of course, by then all of them had died. Sebastian was the only one ever held accountable for conspiring with Spain. The Spanish documents from 1798 that name William Clark are relatively few and reflect his legitimate commercial pursuits. It remains to be seen whether other records may still emerge, shedding further light on his troubling proximity to, and familiarity with, some of those devious men.

Appendix D

Transcription of Diary Entries in the 1798 Journal

Editorial Symbols

Given William Clark's haphazard spelling and capitalization and his frequent disregard for dotting i's, closing o's, and crossing t's, transcribing his entries requires a certain amount of interpretation. The same holds true for his punctuation.

Clark sometimes confused commas with periods, hyphens with colons and even with equal signs. Where he omits punctuation of any sort but instead draws toward the right margin a long stroke of ink from the last letter in a sentence (a mark impossible to reproduce in print), I place a period.

Perhaps because Clark wrote many of his entries while on a moving vessel and probably did so under conditions of poor light, a small number of the marks he made remain ambiguous. Nevertheless, to the extent possible I replicate his exact words, punctuation, and spacing. In cases of ambiguity I render his writing in standard spelling and punctuation. To clarify changes and additions to the text I use the following symbols:

Pencil notes (all by someone other than Clark,
probably Meriwether Lewis Clark):   < >

Words Clark added above the text: { }

Words Clark lined out or wrote over: [ ]

353

<W Clarks first trip to N Orleans was in 1790>
                    <u>Memorandon</u> 1798

9th March Set out from the
Rapids of Ohio at 6 oClock, well
<u>all</u> night <on his 2d trip to N Orleans>
                                    <M. L. C.>

10th Sat: wind blew the greater
part of the evening, on Shore
until at Doe Run.

11th. Wind rose blew & snowed all
the evenning

12th Mon. Continued all Day &
night.

13th: Tues: passed Green River and
the red banks. Continue all night

14th. Wed—passed Waubash,
(a high land on the S. Side opposit
the first Island below) passed
Saline & trade water (high Land
on both Sides of it) wind
rose & obliged us to Land.

15th Thurs: Wind high Land
opposit Cumberland River &
Surveyed the Island on the Left side
opposit the 2 Isd. above is high land
Set out at 3 oClock at Night.

March 16th Friday
Arrived at Fort Massac at
10 oClock, all day & night.

17th Sat: Wind rose continued all
day Set out at 1 oClock at night
in Company with 4 Boats, Mr. Jones,
Brown, Lind & OHarro. I landed &
surveyed the Island near the Mouth
of Ohio, arrived in the Mississippi
at 12 oClock & Landed at chalk
bank about 20 Miles all night.
19th Mon: Wind rose Detained
us untill 12 oClock Set out &
landed opposit Wolf Island. Stayd
all night.

20th Tuesday at 9 oClock landed
at New Madrid wind rose
obliged us to Stay all day. obtain[d]
permission to pass. &c

21st: Wednesday wind continued
one Soldier Deserted. Set out at 4
oclock made 3 miles

22nd Thursday the wind rose obliged
us to put to Shore with great
Dificullty one man Desert from
the Contractors boats and stold
a Number of things.

March 23 Friday the wind rose
verry high obliged us to land with
much Dificulty & Danger the
boates much Scattered, wind con-
:tinue all night Some rane.

24th: Sat: wind blew violently in
the morning Some rane continued
windy all day and night. No account
of the boats to day.

25th Sonday Wind continue, a
Perogue came up from the Bluffs
informed me one boat was one
League below landed, Set out at 12
oclock wind continue blowing a little
a fair evening landed on an Island

2[7]6th Monday a fair morning wind
rose we landed at the 3rd Bluff. Mad
meriment &tc Mr. Jones Sick.

27th. Tuesday a fair morning a large
Boat pass down loaded, a perogue
Passed down arrived at the Bluffs
late in the evening.

28th Wednesday. Wind blew hard as
two flats arrive bound for New
Orleans. All day at the bluffs
wind.

29th. Thursday a windy morn
—ing. Sold one Hhd Tobacco—wind
continue all day & night.

30th Friday rane hard Set out
early wind rose we continue landed
on a Sharp point, a Dangerous part
of the river, one Boat far behind
and caint get in at the pint
one boat behind came late & landed
below, the bank falling in all
night.

31st: Saturday, Set out early a
fog untill 7 oClock rane all day
landed in willow bend before night &
near an Indian Camp, a violent
storm all night, it litiened for
at least 2 hours incesently as
one continued blaze—

1st April <1798> (Sonday) rane Continus
this morning wind rose my boat run
up a Snag which run thro' her bow
then un other which nearly sunk
her & lodged on a third which
hel her fast only injuring the
Stern, here I am at 12 oClock

Canoe Stove, Mr. Linds boat
loaded with Merchandize Sunk
on the 2d. Sawyer that I struk
he lost all but a few {bales & kegs} all the

boats forced to Shore in the
bingle a Verry Dangerous Situ
ation, [a] the Current runs a
=gainst the Shore, the Day
continue Stormey, my hands
fritened, a Stormy evening night
fair continue on the Sawyer

2nd. Apl. Monday Collect all the hans
rase a canooo & push off the snag
and Drop Down 4 Miles, with great
Dificullty Send up my hands to
collect what property of Mr. Linds
which may flote ashore &tc. My
Small boat fall Down

3rd Tuesday at 7 oClock Set out passed
a bad Island in the center of the
River Mr. Lind find som goods
in a bind landed late

4th Wednesday Set out early a fair
morning passed Arkansaw River at 3 oClock
about 300 yards wide, met a french
boat

Ap. 5th Thursday
Set out early (the river verry fast
now just within the banks) land
on the point of an Island.

6th Friday Set out early a verry
unfavourable morning, wind

rose obliged us to land at 6 oClock,
Set out at 9 oClock, ranes, the Wind
obliged us to land at 11 oClock, Some
Indian Canoes overtake us loaded
with peltry, we Stay all night
boats Scattered—

7th Satterday windy morning set
out at 7 oClock landed at 5 oClock
a boat overtake us here. Stay
all night

8th Sonday Set out early a fair
day land above the mouth of
Yauzo. River to wate for the boats
all night

9th. Monday Set out early passed
Yauzo at 6 oClock landed at the
Walnut Hills at 9 oClock Stayd untill
11 Maj. Kersey & two companies & a
Detachment of artilerist & Inft

---

garrisoned at this place, Which they
found at their arrival avaquated
by the Spaniards & left in good
order a Number of new buildings
left, This is a most charming
Situation, Set out at 11 oClock
the wind obliged us to put too
Shore a Violent Storm all day &
night at about 8 oClock at night
a most violent Storm arose from

W. which nearly blew us out of
the river continued about 2 hours

10th Tuesday Apl. The Wind Conti-
—nue this morning, and violintly all day
we oblige to continue here, all the
hands Drunk in the Contractors boat.

11th Wednesday Set out early at 5 Clock
some wind we obliged to land at 1 oClock
on account of the Wind Stay all
night

12th Thursday. Set out early passed
the grand Gulfs at 7 oClock, this
place is Dangerous, on the left the
current runs against the pint of
a rock (under a Hill) & right a

_____

large whorl, also below &
above the rock on the left side
The Wind obliged us to land at BioPierr
at 1 oClock blew all day & night
Violently hard.

13th Friday Set out at 7 oclock the
wind continue tho not hard we
was obliged to land at 10 oClock after
makeing 9 miles. Set out at 1 oClock
wind all day

14th: Saturday Set out early land
[at] {above} the Natchiss at 7 [oClock] {miles} and
that day [thru] night

15th Satt. [landed at the Natchz
a 7 oClock] at the Natchez.

1[6]5th Sond at the N.

1[7]6th. Monday Set out at
12 oClock a fair evening pass
the White Clifts. Landed late
Staid all night—

1[8]7th: Tuesday Set out early met
two large Keel boats the wind
rose early passed two Creeks on the
right & Loveless Cliffs after the

Wind laid, pass Mr. Ellicotts
Camp at the mouth of a Creek
at 12 oClock, passed Red River at
3 oClock & passed two Islands & Land.
Stay all night floted 50 miles, met
at the Mouth of the Red R. a large
Keel Boat.

1[9]8th: Wednesday Set out early met
a Keel boat a 7. oClock one at
10 oClock arrived a point Coupee
and was obliged to land at 4
oClock. Sta all night.

[20]19th Thursday Set out early wind
rose obliged us to land at 9 oClock
Stay untill 12 a large Keel boat
going to O Ark pass us a Mr. {Charles} france
wing obliged us to put at the

Clifts below Thompsons Creek
a violent Storm of wind & rane
continued all night [at] {untill} 7 oClock in
the morning all wet on bored
on Barge come up [last] at Sun
Set

20th. Friday Set out at 7 oClock
the wind continue to blow
We pass two Islands, Stoped
at Battinrouger at 12 oClock. Stayd
one hour the wind continue high.
We landed at Iberville Bio Stay'd
all Night

21st. Satterday a fogy morning lay
to untill 9 oClock on account of the
fog: pass Iberville Bio. a landed near
an Indian Village Stay'd all night.

22: Sonday The fog Violent thick
untill 9 oClock when we Set out
the wind blew all day a
Storm at noon, landed and
Stayd all night

23rd Monday Set out early the
Wind obliged me to land
early 12 miles above the
Town oposit Some butiful
Sugar farms Stay all
night. Mr. Porter on our
other boat come in sight

to say they [were] landed early
the Sugar Plantations are
butifull in this part of
the Mississippi.

24th: Tuesday Set out early
a fog on the river untill 8
land in the City of N Orleans
at 9 oClock — —
  Was politely receved & treated
by all—

25th Commenced unloading
my boats, rented a wareHouse
for my tobacco at 9 Dollars p.r
Month. &

26th Satturday finished my
work &tc

27th, 28th, 29th, & 30th at the City
all well &

May 1st. Tuesday Set of my
Men to Kentucky nothing
material—

2nd Wed: a hot day—

Thursday 3rd May an allarm
of British frigat off the
Mouth of the River.

4th, 5th, 6 nothing Extroordinary

7 8 9 10 nothing Extra.

11 & 12 an Upror about a War with
the United States & Spain france &c

13th, 4, 15, 6 to the 24th. Nothing
extrodeny hapened.

26th. hot Several Small
Vestles arrive within the last
three days under Spanish
colers. 27, 28, 29 30 hot

June 1. Untill the 17th all as usual
as to my self. I take a passage
in the Sckuner Active, Captain
Wilcox, rceve payment for my
Sales of tobacco & engage to
send it by Cap Brown &c.

June 18th. All is well, I get my
Passport. <Paid Mad. Chavous board>

Jun 19th. I chane my rout &
Determined to go to Nautchus

20th purchase horses & equip
my self—

_____

June 21st or 2 Set out for Nauthez

28 arrive at Ellicott camp on
the line that was cut about 6
miles after about 3 mo: labour.

July 1st. Arrived at Nautuss
stay until the 8th in the
evening.

8th Set out down the River
in a pireogue, Stay at
Mr. Farrows,

9th Stay at Mr. Clarks

10th. Went to the line

11 at the line & Sent
my pirogue round to
Meet me at Tunecow

12th. Set sale from Tunecow
which is about 7 miles from
the line

16th Arrive at New Orleans
17 Take a passage in the
Ship Star for Philadelphia
preparing untill the 25th
for a Sale. Wind contrary.

27th July Set Sale in the ship
Star of 6 guns for Philadelphia

Droped down the river the
Passengers {on} in the Ship was Mr. D
W Cox owner Col. J. McKee, Mr. B
Chew two Mr. Cregs Mr. Martin
Cap. Nolin, Cap. R{d} Clark &
about 40 Men accompaned
by a brig of 8 guns—Drop{d}.
Down passed the Fort Pluk
=in the 30th. This fort is Strong
and regular, built of Brick
Mounting about 12 heavy
Cannons {12 to 24 pd.} on the front & Som
Small cannon a Small
round [can] fort opposit
is on the West Side round
Mounting 16 Cannon from
4 to 9 pounders, from this
fort to the Baliza is open
marsh about 30 miles, we
anchored at night found
a Spanish Ship Miss. of 16 Guns
& a Breg ascending

July 31st. At the Baliza about
3 oClock arrived in View a
French Privutier of 4 Guns
& 50 Men, with two American
Prises taken in the gulf
bound to N. Y. & C. Town
from   The P.T. come
up & anchered near us at
Dark   all prepared.

August 1st The privateer
is speaking Dutcn I go
on bord find the Capts.
of three A. Vestles taken
by her on bord & ther
salors in Irons, + two prises
then in View off the bar. we
envite the {Captive} Captains to brackft.
with they axceped the invirtation
& the French Cap. Did not
Object, after brackfast th
Capt. [went] returned & Mr.
Coxe Demanded the prisoners
was refused, the Privateer

saled up the river a few
miles returned at about
4 oClock, in the evening the
Prises Came up under Am:
cullors passed us about
a miles & anchored.

2d & 3rd. Nothing extro:—

4th at 3 oClock a Sale in
Sight from the East,
(This place is in a marsh
on rased land about three
feet where about 8 Huts
& a Block house, & look
out, in which is 2 six pds.
& 4 swivels, a galley with

one 18 pd. & 6 swivs, and about
50 Spanish salers & soldiers
on the West Side, & on an
outleat) The Wind continu
from the rong quarter to
allow us to pass the bar
wich is about 14 french feet
& reguires & Northerly wind
to pass it, being narrow
Say 50 yards.

7th. Drop down about one mile
in this act the Spaniards
were much alarmed & Came
out of Bio to the pint with
the galley & appeared to be
preparing for action, we
went to Shore & the officer
informed (after our acused
him of partialately to the
F.P.T.) informed us that
he had orders to Stop
us, this information astonish{d}
us as we knew of no cause
We concluded to return
to the Ship & Send up
to N.O. to know the cause
Mr. Coxe & Clark accordingly
Set out at about 3 oClock
With 4 Men in a yaule.

8th a fair wind a <u>Ship</u> th
prise to the late P Teer

at the pass a Brig arrive
in sight late & anchor.

---

in the pass

9th at 8 oClock an officer
arrives from the Gov: for
2 letters Sent by Mr. Coxe to
the S. Minister & a letter from
Mr. Coxe accounting for the
Cause of our delay which is
thro a miss representation
of the offens at this place
in informing the Govr of our
Insulting him & violateing
the rights of his scoverigt &c.
at the same time the
Com{d}. of the place came
on bord & gave leave to
go out. 7 of us went down
to the prise Ship, found it
in possession of about 6 or
8 french and about 12 or 14 pilots
We returned in about an hour
lost our best bower Anchor
to day—

10th a fine morning.

11th to 13th [The] a Slupe from N. York
Arived We attempted to bord but
was ordered not by the pilot

We did not mind him.

14th Verry anxious about the
return of Mr. Coxe & Clark

15th of Aug. at 8 oClock Mr. Coxe
returned, & informed us the
Cause of their detainment
as follows Viz: insulting the
Spanish Comd. of Valias, Lt.
Borass & Molenay, in
threts to the French Pre=
=vater, ordering her
prises 2 scuners to come
too or the Ship & Brig
Would sink her, & other
Cowardly complaints
Signed by those offcers &
Tranquilo & all the pilots
at this Place, those Gent.
that went up was impris-
oned at the Pluckomen &
sent to N.O. & put into the
Fort Charls, one night &
day.

Mr. Richard Clark

Being officially informed
of the improper conduct
that you & Mr. {D W} Coxe have had
in the block house of the
Valina, Committing an
[ins] insult to his Majesty's

territorial Right, you &
Said Mr. Coxe will immed-
iately Come up to this
Capital to answer for
your conduct.
Your vestle may
continue to their destination, as the Spanish Nation
is in perfect armony with
the U S.

New Orleans
8 Aug{t} 1798
Manuel Gayoso de Lemos

Set out and left the Mississippi
the 15th at 5 oClock passed the
French prise Marse

16th. Discovred a Sale to the
leeward in the evening one
to the windward

Calm. 18th a Violent gust
at about 8 oClock P.M.

19 & 20 Calm.

21t. of Augt. Discovered a Sale
to the windward we all
prepared for action sup.
her to be a Priovteer &
bore away we Spoke her
at 10 found She was a
Spaniard from Sta. Cruze

to Havannah, a Storm
at Night, I am Sick
as also several pasengers

22, 23, 24, 25, 6.. 27 & 28 a
head Wind I am sick &
also severall on bord

---

with the ague & fever—
Augt. 29th at Day discovered
the Island of Cuby (Dolfins head)
to the SE, and 2 Sales, we
Supposed to e privateers we
prepared and bore Down &
She tacked & bore off

Aug. 30th. in Lat. 23.15.

31st.in lat: 23..45—Lon 81—
bore Northerly—

Septr. 1st. at day discovered
Some Small Kees (or Islds.) at abt.
1/2 a mile, 3 fa water we
Droped Anchor, a wind
Sprung up & wer bore off
N.E called a Sale a [head]
we attempted to Speak but
Could not over take her.
Continue our corse, this Sale
proceed all night.

2nd. at 12 oClock this Sale after
a number of maneuvers came
up hoisted a English flag

We answered, & a Lieut. came
on bord, informed us it was
his majestys brig heroe, Capt.
Cockburn master, &c. &c. &c
he informed us these reefs
was the Dry Tortugas & that
we were then Stearing towerd
Floriday, in the Bay of Chatha{m}
or Punjo & within 35 fathoms
water we Sounded & found
it the Case, the evening
Proven calm. We continued
near each other untill
Sun Set when we Steared
S E By S all night.

3rd. in the Morning this Brig
Who we knew to be a Privateer
or 16 Canon & 150 men bore
off S. We continue untill
4 oClock PM, then bore S.W.
the remainder of the night
We are much allarmed
about Provisions, having con

---

sumed the greater part of
our Stock

4th. Sept. at 12 oClock in Lat
24–28 which we are hapy
to find is the South of all
the States of Floriday—
I am puking all day &
Dark, Catch a no. Of fish
Dolfin, Scip Jacks &c.—Grupers
Snappers &c. &c. a Calm after
twelve A M.

5th a Calm Day, Lat. 24. 2

6th a Squal at 5 oClock. Cloudy
day Lat: 23. 53.

7th Saw 2 Sale S.E, Lat. 24.13.—

8th. Saw the land SE at 5 Legues
Distance, I am taken sick to day
and continue confined.
Lat. 25.6.—-

9th Saw land at 4 P.M. N.W.b W.
at 5 leagues, in Lat 26. 27. I continu
Verry Sick.

10th.a fresh brease tollerably fair
I continue sick Lat: 27.56. N.

_____

11th Sept. (Tuesday) a breze all
day I continue Very sick
                              Lat. 29.10 N.

12th a Violent Storm all night
Obliged us to use great precausion
a Squally day, I continue Verry
unwell   Lat. 30. 18 N.

13th at 5 p.m. heavy Squals of
wind & rane attended with Thunder
& lightning. We caught water that
we much wanted the hands
Being for several days on 3 pints
p day. I continue Very sick
& am so reduced can Scarcely
walk.   Lat. 31. 30 N.

14th. a Squally day with rane
I continue Sick. Lat. 31. 45 N.

15th. a Squarly Night, in 40 Fath{m}.
Water a Squarly day with
rane, [we caught water, which
much wanted & filed 2 Barrels]
Provisions Short, men discont—
=ented, the greater part of our stores
out. I continue Sick.

────────────────────────

16th. Satturday.a Dredfull Nite
last of wind & rane, a jentle
Brese to day from the East—
I continue sick but better to day
            Lat: 32. 14 N.

17th cloudy day with rane cau
ght 2 Barrels of water which

we much wanted, I continue
Verry Sick.   Lat: 33. 12.

18th. a fair wind which blew violently from the SE, acompanied
with Storms. I continue Sick.
              Lat: 34. 21. N.

19th. a most Dredfull night of
wind & Stormy Weather obliged
us unship our yards &c. a
light brese continue today. Saw a
Sale to the E. At 6 oClock, a
Squal at 3. Saw another Sale.
I get better,   Lat: 36. 5. N.
Changed our corse N.W for the
Land. We live almost on fish
having no Sugar Coffee &c. fo 6 Days

20th. Sept Wednesday at day
Discovered a Small Schuner near
the brig bearing our corse, the
Sale we saw yesterday, we bore
Down & spoke her, She was
from Cape Fransway bound
to Philadelphia, loaded with
Sugar, Coffee, & limes we sent
on bord and got Sugar Coffee
& limes Sufficent for our passg.
a Ship in Sight at 6 oClock
to the N. bearing our corse
will to day keep together
all day.

21st. a fresh and fair brese
in Sight of land at 8 oClock &
of Several Vestles, a Pilot
on bord at 12 oClock, wind
Change to N. W b W in the eveng.
Provisions nearly out—

22st. Wind a head but up &
landed opposit the light house
and marshes.

23rd. Sept. Satterday
[landed] Anchored opposit
Cape May, to wate the Tide
this Cape is on the Jersey side
and thickly settled, opposit
is a Small Village, at flod
Tide 8 oClock the Wind fair
we Sat Sale, passed Bumbo
=hook at 10 & anchored to
wate the Tide. This place
is only a remarckable part
of the bay

24th Cast up in two
tides to New Castle, passed
a Small Village 12 Miles
called port pen about 100
houses, opposit is Rudy Is
at this place is a good harbo
for shiping from her, a long
Ship bound for china lay
here, at the port. New Cast

New Castle is a Small Town
Containing about 200 houses
Thronged with people at present
from Philadelphia, which
place has the yellow Fever
and about 80 p. Day Die
This place is handsomly
Situated & has a good harbr
about 40 Sale at present lay
opposit, (among which is the
U.S. Frigit mounting 47.
guns, and Slupe of War cald
the Dellaway of 22 guns, &
Two French Privateers Prises
brought in by those Ships.

25th. Mon: the Doct. Question us
at 7. & We landed at 9 oClk
at the Town, viewed &c. &
rested our Selors, found on
Shore latterly landed 500
Irich famlys. &c.

26th Sept. Tuesday—
at New Castle. all the passengers in
good health—This Town is Small
Containing about 200 or 250 houses
Handsomly situated at the head
of the bay—at 10 oClock Mr. Chew
& my self hired a Carrage & Cart
and Came out to Cristian bridge
5 Miles to Meet the Baltimore

Stage & take it for that place.
This Town is Small & regular
Containing about 90 or 100 houses
the Stage passed at 3 So Crowded
We could not get in, We
Stay all night with an old
friend of mine Cap. Bines.

27th. hired a chair & cart to a
Small Town at the head of Elk
12 Miles, at 6 Miles passed a
Village about 20 houses. Elkton
Contains about 100 houses well
built of Brick, here we wate
for a Stage, it pass at 6 Crowded.

———————————————

Sept 28th Satterday, We hire a
Coach to Haver du grace 17
Miles, pass at 10 Miles an old
Village Called Charlston Containg.
about 70 or 80 houses, Situated
on the bay—Havgrace is on
the West Side of Susquehanah
River at the Mouth, this Town
is improveing Containing about
80 or 90 houses, the River at
this place is 1 1/4 Miles wide
We wate for a Stage that
pass every night—at 11 oClock
it arrive we take passage
& Set out at 3 for Baltimore at
4 1/2 pass a Small Town called
Bush ton. Changed horses &tc

29th at 1 mile passed a village
called Hartford of 50 or 60 hous
at 11 arrived within 3 Miles of
Baltimore where we were halted
Examined & Sworn that we
Came from no infexious Town

Hired a cart to carry our Bags
and Walked, halted at the
Indian Queen Mr. Evins, Saw
great Contesting about an
ellection of a member to Congress.

30th Sunday went to church
Saw a Priest ordained, Dined
With a Mr. Kennedy Merchant.

1st Oct. Monday at 8 oClock the
Poles were opened for Gen Smith
& a Mr. Winchester the Saylors
Soon Commenced a riott
which continued all day in
torn flags fighting &c. one
Killed a horrid Seen for
an American as will as a
Stranger

2nd Tuesday The Ellection &
Confusion Continues, I see a
Lion of about 500 {lbs} of 8 years old
Saw a Mrs Mashurn. Viewed
the Town &c.
                    3rd

3rd of Oct. Wednesday the Ellection
Continue, the Opposition not so
outragous as yesterday

4th. The Ellection continue all
Silent, the first part of the day
Came in Companies from the County
at Night the poles Close & Gen. Smith
was Elected by a Majty. Of 699
Total Votes in City 2223 in County
2298. The Streets ellumonated
at Dark, an Arch of lights went
in front of Gen. S. who was Seated
in a chear, with a Lorrel branch
over his head Deckerated round.
light in rear, in This manner
he was Carried thro: the Streets
for Several hours with Shouts
Drums & Instruments of all kind
playing after him, &c. &c.

5th. Friday Mr. Chew went in the
Stage at 3 oClock for Fredricksbg.
This day the Streets are Still
a Ship of Genl. Smith & skuner

are Draped & firing all day
I walk to view the Town &c.

6th Satturday I recve the letter
that I waited for paid Mssr

McDonel & Co. 1256.25 for
Mr. Nabb in a Bill on W. O.
Woolcut and took my passage
in the Stage for Monday as
no Stage Set out Southerly
Sooner, I engage with Mr. O to send
My trunk out by his Wagons

7th. Sonday I am visited by
an old friend of mine Mr. Flaget
a Romon Priest <{afterwards Bishop Flaget} Bp of Kentucky>

8th I made Some Small purch
is a militia parade, went to the
Play, rose early

9th rose at 3 oClock, & set out
in the stage brackfasted at
a bad tavern, passed a Small
Town called Elkridge, passed
a Village Called Bladensburgh
containing about 60 houses
in a decline at 3oClock

Arrived in the Federal City—
one Wing of the Capatal nearly
finished the Stone Work, this
Town much scattered, the
Presidents house nearly
finished, Dined at George
town, this place is Small,
built of Brick, on the Side of
a hill, on the Top is a most
ellegunt College The federal

City is the Most ellegunt
Situation I ever Saw. Came
on to Alexaneur 8 Miles, this
Town is Small but improvg.
appears to have a considerable
trade of flour & Tobacco—

10th Wed—I am obliged to
Wate in Alex. For the Stage
This Town Stands on a butifull
Situation, a warm Day, here
is fited out by Col. How two
Letters of Mark or Privateers
one of 14 & the other of 12 Guns
Tobacco 7 to 9 Dollars.

11th. Set out at 3 this morning
passed a Small Village
Called Colchester, a feww
retched houses, a ware house
a fine bridge a Cross the
        passed Dumfrease a
Small {old} Town containing 40 or
50 houses here is an inspection
of Tobacco, Dined at Stafford
Courthouse, the lands in this
County is retchedly pore
passed thro Falmouth at
about 3 oclock, passed a
Bridge to Fredricksburgh
Went to a play &c

12th Dined with Mr. Wm.
Hurndon &c. Cap Merser &

Cap Taylor Mr. Lewis. Green
Ford & Coon Went to the
gardens—

13th.a Wet Morning Set out
With Mr. Hurndon Road &c
to my Brothers, Got to
Bro Edms late all well &

14th <{of October 1798}> Sunday, Came to Bro
Jona. foun he was over
the ridge all well.
he returned

In Spotsylvania untill
Sonday 11th of [Oct]<{Novr.}> Set out
for Kentucky—

Stay a few days at Col. Booths. &
a few {2} days at redstone, & at Wheeling
also Chilacother, arrive at my father
the 24 of Decr. at Dusk—<1798>

Abbreviations

People

AE	Andrew Ellicott
BS	Benjamin Sebastian
Clark Jr.	Daniel Clark Junior
Clark Sr.	Daniel Clark Senior
DWC	Daniel W. Coxe
EED	Eva Emory Dye
GDL	Gayoso de Lemos
GRC	George Rogers Clark
IG	Isaac Guion
JC	Jonathan Clark
JW	James Wilkinson
SMB	Samuel Montgomery Brown
TC	Tench Coxe
WC	William Clark
WCB	William Clark Breckenridge
WHC	William Hancock Clark
WS	Winthrop Sargent

American Archival Repositories

HSP	Historical Society of Pennsylvania
IHS	Indiana Historical Society
LC	Library of Congress
MDAH	Mississippi Department of Archives and History
NARA	National Archives and Records Administration
SHSMO	State Historical Society of Missouri

Spanish Archives

AGI, PC	Archivo General de Indias (General Archives of the Indies), Papeles Procedentes de Cuba (Cuba Papers)
AHN	Archivo Histórico Nacional (National Historical Archives); in the following notes always Estado, leg. 3900, apartado 4

Quotations from—and references to—William Clark's 1798–1801 Notebook (also called his Mississippi Journal) are not noted herein. The entries are mentioned in the text with the date they were written.

Notes

Preface: The Unknown William Clark

1. Thomas M. Marshall, ed., "Journal of Henry B. Miller," 268–70; William E. Foley, *Wilderness Journey: The Life of William Clark*, 265.

2. Julia Clark Voorhis, file P-426 (1923), Surrogate's Court, County of New York; Jan Snow, "Lewis and Clark in the Museum Collections of the Missouri Historical Society," 37–41.

3. See William Clark Breckenridge's (hereafter WCB) index card noting contents, price, and date of purchase of journal (Item C-1075), State Historical Society of Missouri (hereafter SHSMO).

1 My Wish Is on the Mississippi

1. William Clark (hereafter WC) to Edmund Clark, 25 November 1794, Lyman Draper Collection, State Historical Society of Wisconsin, Madison, 2L36. Specifics about Clark's boats come mostly from the Mississippi Journal ledger pages. Gary Gackstatter has furnished many details about the technical equipment Clark must have brought on the journey.

2. At an unknown date Clark added five tables of figures concerning an apparently conjectural voyage to an Army volume, which must have come into his possession in 1793. Known as the "Orderly Book from Fort Washington and Fort Hamilton, 1792–1793," the volume belongs to the Cincinnati Museum Center and is cited hereafter as "Orderly Book."

3. Details on the aborted venture come from Clark's draft letter to an unnamed recipient, dated January 1797, in ibid.

4. For an idea of what Clark's boats must have been like and of the work done by his crew, see Michael Allen, *Western Rivermen, 1763–1861: Ohio and Mississippi Boatmen and the Myth of the Alligator Horse,* 67–70.

5. WC to Jonathan Clark (hereafter JC), 4 October 1798, in James Holmberg, *Dear Brother: Letters of William Clark to Jonathan Clark,* 28–29. Information about the tobacco is from Archivo General de Indias, Papeles Procedentes de Cuba, legajo 631, no. 4 (hereafter cited as AGI, PC, with leg. number).

6. Samuel W. Thomas, "William Croghan, Sr. [1752–1822]: A Pioneer Kentucky Gentleman," 48.

7. Ibid., 47–50; Gwynne Tuell Potts and Samuel W. Thomas, *George Rogers Clark, Military Leader in the Pioneer West & Locust Grove: The Croghan Homestead Honoring Him,* 50, 51, 58.

8. Data on the furs, pelts, hides, and pork are from AGI, PC, leg. 502, no. 16.

9. Francis B. Heitman, *Historical Register and Dictionary of the United States Army,* 1:218, 306; Alan D. Gaff, *Bayonets in the Wilderness: Anthony Wayne's Legion in the Old Northwest,* 232.

10. See R. C. McGrane, ed., "William Clark's Journal of General Wayne's Campaign."

11. On Clark's education, see Foley, *Wilderness Journey,* 4–5; Landon Y. Jones, *William Clark and the Shaping of the West,* 17–18; Mathematics Copy Book, William Clark Papers, Clark Family Collection, Missouri History Museum (hereafter WC Papers).

12. See "Journal of Hardin's Campaign," WC Papers.

13. According to a note his son Meriwether Lewis Clark made in the 1798–1801 Notebook, following William's entry of 9 March 1798, the journey beginning that day was "his [William's] 2d trip to N Orleans."

2 Wind Rose, Blew, and Snowed

1. Allen, *Western Rivermen,* 69, 74.

2. Thomas, "William Croghan," 51.

3. Kentucky Secretary of State, Land Office Division, Survey 5687, no. 2.

4. Ibid., Survey 5896.

5. Robert B. Roberts, *Encyclopedia of Historic Forts: The Military, Pioneer, and Trading Posts of the United States,* 266–67.

6. Norman W. Caldwell, "Fort Massac: The American Frontier Post, 1778–1805," 265–78.

7. Jo Ann Brown, "George Drouillard and Fort Massac," 16–19.

8. See Fort Massac Records, Thomas and Katherine Detre Library and Archives, Senator John Heinz History Center, Pittsburgh, Pennsylvania.

9. At Fort Massac on 30 March 1798, Ransom Eastin attested to Zebulon Pike's compensating a boatman for delivering a load of cornmeal. Ibid.

10. Allen Johnson and Dumas Malone, eds., *Dictionary of American Biography* (hereafter *DAB* with volume number and page) 14:3–4.

11. Richard C. Knopf, ed., *Anthony Wayne, a Name in Arms: Soldier, Diplomat, Defender of Expansion Westward of a Nation*, 313–20.

12. Jon Kukla, *A Wilderness So Immense: The Louisiana Purchase and the Destiny of America*, 190–94, 341–49; Arthur P. Whitaker, *The Mississippi Question, 1795–1803: A Study in Trade, Politics, and Diplomacy*, 51–52.

13. Whitaker, *Mississippi Question*, 52–58; Kukla, 206.

14. Whitaker, *Mississippi Question*, 122–25.

15. Norman W. Caldwell, "Cantonment Wilkinsonville," 3.

16. Kentucky Secretary of State, Land Office Division, Survey 5895; "Sundry Latitudes & Longitudes taken on the Mississippi ascending," WC Papers.

17. For a nearly contemporaneous description of the Mississippi River just below the mouth of the Ohio, see Francis Baily, *Journal of a Tour in Unsettled Parts of North America in 1796 & 1797*, 135.

18. Abraham P. Nasatir, *Spanish War Vessels on the Mississippi, 1792–1796*, 154, 254–56, 293–94; "William Clark, 1795," map B, Lewis and Clark Collection, Geography and Map Division, Library of Congress (hereafter LC).

19. Paul R. Cutright, *Lewis and Clark: Pioneering Naturalists*, 37–38.

20. Knopf, 383.

3 Big Little Man

1. Humphrey Marshall, *The History of Kentucky*, 2:165; *DAB* 20:222–26.

2. James R. Jacobs, *Tarnished Warrior: Major-General James Wilkinson*, 1–73; Andro Linklater, *An Artist in Treason: The Extraordinary Double Life of General James Wilkinson*, 1–74.

3. To understand how Wilkinson stealthily supplanted George Rogers Clark as a political and military leader, see Dale Van Every, *Ark of Empire: The American Frontier, 1784–1803*, 97–116; James A. James, *The Life of George Rogers Clark*, 374–81, 417; Temple Bodley, *George Rogers Clark: His Life and Public Services*, 296–97, 300–323, 379–404.

4. Wilkinson's successful twisting of George's actions at Vincennes into a source of Spanish income for himself is well documented. See Arthur P. Whitaker, "James Wilkinson's First Descent to New Orleans in 1787," 82–97; William R. Shepherd, "Wilkinson and the Beginnings of the Spanish Conspiracy," 490–506; Kukla, 124–30; Linklater, *Artist in Treason*, 81–89; Jacobs, *Tarnished Warrior*, 77–81.

5. William. R. Shepherd, ed., "Papers Bearing on James Wilkinson's Relations with Spain, 1787–1789," 764–66.

6. Elizabeth Warren, "Benjamin Sebastian and the Spanish Conspiracy in Kentucky," 107–30; Benjamin Sebastian (hereafter BS) to William Croghan, 30 April 1795, Draper Mss., 1N22; Margery Hill Webb, *Our Sebastian Heritage*, 23–27; *DAB* 16:543–44; John E. Kleber, ed., *The Kentucky Encyclopedia*, 572–73; also H. Levin, ed., *The Lawyers and Lawmakers of Kentucky*, 63–64.

7. Thomas Speed, *The Political Club: Danville, Kentucky, 1786–1790*, 42–45; *DAB* 9:485–86; Kleber, 452–53.

8. Speed, 63–65; *DAB* 3:130–31; Kleber, 128–29; Patricia Watlington, "John Brown and the Spanish Conspiracy," 52–68.

9. Speed, 47–50.

10. Ibid., 159–62; *DAB* 13:482–83; Kleber, 680–81.

11. George Rogers Clark (hereafter GRC) to JC, 2 September 1791, Draper Mss., 2L50.

12. Linklater, *Artist in Treason*, 90–102; Jacobs, *Tarnished Warrior*, 85–93; Warren, 115.

13. Jacobs, *Tarnished Warrior*, 86–107; Linklater, *Artist in Treason*, 98–107; Kukla, 132–33.

14. Linklater, *Artist in Treason*, 107; Jacobs, *Tarnished Warrior*, 110–12; Foley, *Wilderness Journey*, 23–27; Jones, 55.

15. "Journal of Gen. Charles Scott's journey, Ohio River to Louisville," WC Papers; John L. Loos, "A Biography of William Clark, 1770–1813," 16–18; Jacobs, *Tarnished Warrior*, 112–13.

16. Jacobs, *Tarnished Warrior*, 111–15; Michael A. Carter, "'Fighting the Flames of a Merciless War': Secretary of War Henry Knox and the Indian War in the Old Northwest, 1790–1795," 98–102.

17. Heitman, 1:1037.

18. "Journal and Memorandum Book, 1792–1794," WC Papers; Foley, *Wilderness Journey*, 28.

19. Richard H. Kohn, "General Wilkinson's Vendetta with General Wayne: Politics and Command in the American Army, 1791–1796," 361–72; Wilkinson (hereafter JW) to Gayoso de Lemos (hereafter GDL), 22 September 1796, AGI, PC, leg. 2375, no. 8.

20. Kohn, 363–72; Timothy Rusche, "Treachery within the United States Army," 478–91.

21. Jacobs, *Tarnished Warrior*, 92; McGrane, 418–19.

4 No Sort of Trick Is Involved

1. Having published extensively on George Rogers Clark and Fort Jefferson, Kenneth C. Carstens may know those subjects better than anyone since George himself. For a synopsis of this knowledge, see Kenneth C. Carstens and Nancy Son Carstens, *The Life of George Rogers Clark, 1752–1818: Triumphs and Tragedies*, 116–33.

2. Bodley, 335–37.

3. James, 402–7; John C. Parish, "The Intrigues of Doctor James O'Fallon," 230–63; Jacobs, *Tarnished Warrior*, 103–5; Kukla, 164.

4. Dan L. Flores, ed., *Jefferson and Southwestern Exploration: The Freeman and Custis Accounts of the Red River Expedition of 1806*, 51n71.

5. "Sundry Latitudes & Longitudes taken on the Mississippi ascending," WC Papers.

6. Roberts, *Historic Forts*, 455; Georges Henri Victor Collot, *A Journey in North America*, 2:16–19; Baily, 135–39; Nasatir, 177–84.

7. William E. Foley, *The Genesis of Missouri: From Wilderness Outpost to Statehood*, 61.

8. Ibid., 61–63; Max Savelle, "The Founding of New Madrid, Missouri," 30–56; Collot, 2:16–19; Nasatir, 56n65, 177–84.

9. Collot, 2:16–19; Nasatir, 135n8, 154n5, 255–56n43.

10. Knopf, 241–43; Gaff, 116–17; James R. Atkinson, *Splendid Land, Splendid People: The Chickasaw Indians to Removal*, 156–63, 283–84n39.

11. Nasatir, 69–70; Jones, 70.

12. Knopf, 246–47. See also Anthony Wayne to WC, 18 June 1793, Wayne Papers 27, no. 48, Historical Society of Pennsylvania (hereafter HSP).

13. "Journal and Memorandum Book, 1792–1794," WC Papers.

14. Gaff, 116–17; Wayne to WC, 18 June 1793, WC to Wayne, 1 September 1793, Wayne Papers 27, no. 48, and 28, nos. 112–13, HSP.

15. Portell to Carondelet, 5 July 1793, AGI, PC, leg. 27A, no. 378; translated with the assistance of Ralph Lee Woodward Jr.

16. Ibid.; Jones, 71; Knopf, 274; Gaff, 142–43.

17. Knopf, 274.

5 A Grand Tribute to General Wilkinson

1. Portell to Carondelet, 5 July 1793, AGI, PC, leg. 27A, no. 378; Potts and Thomas, 72. That Wayne was well aware of William's close kinship to George, see Knopf, 42.

2. Nasatir, 70–72.

3. James, 417–24; Carstens and Carstens, 231, 237–42; Nasatir, 70–73.

4. Stanley Elkins and Eric McKitrick, *The Age of Federalism*, 330–36; also Carstens and Carstens, 239–42; Kukla, 163–66, 174–77.

5. Elkins and McKitrick, 330–36, 347–52.

6. Arthur P. Whitaker, *The Spanish–American Frontier, 1783–1795: The Westward Movement and the Spanish Retreat in the Mississippi Valley*, 196–97.

7. Jacobs, *Tarnished Warrior*, 152; Percy W. Christian, "General James Wilkinson and Kentucky Separatism, 1784–1798," 309–13; JW to Carondelet, 30 April 1794, AGI, PC, leg. 2374, no. 136; Carstens and Carstens, 242.

8. AGI, PC, leg. 2374, no. 136.

9. Nasatir, 112–14, 119–23.

10. Kohn, 363–67; Paul D. Nelson, "'Mad' Anthony Wayne and the Kentuckians of the 1790s," 1–17; McGrane, 418–19; also M. M. Quaife, ed., "General James Wilkinson's Narrative of the Fallen Timbers Campaign," 81–90.

11. Jacobs, *Tarnished Warrior*, 137–38; Linklater, *Artist in Treason*, 143–45.

12. Jacobs, *Tarnished Warrior*, 148–50; Linklater, *Artist in Treason*, 149–53.

13. Knopf, 453–54, 456–60; Wayne Papers 42, no. 106, HSP.

14. Foley, *Wilderness Journey*, 38–39; Jones, 88–89; Samuel W. Thomas, ed., "William Clark's 1795 and 1797 Journals and Their Significance," 277–85.

15. Wayne to WC, 10 September 1795, reel 15 of Mic. 41, Wayne Manuscripts, 1792–1796, Ohio Historical Society (originals at HSP).

16. Jacobs, *Tarnished Warrior*, 149–52; Nasatir, 119–24, 285.

17. GDL to Carondelet, 3 October 1795, AGI, PC, leg. 2364, no. 21, Reservado; Walter B. Douglas, *Manuel Lisa*, 10–12; "Report to General Wayne on de-

scent of Ohio with dispatches to New Madrid, 4 November 1795," WC Papers. See also Thomas, "Journals," 278–85.

18. "Report to General Wayne on descent of Ohio with dispatches to New Madrid, 4 November 1795," WC Papers.

19. GDL to Carondelet, 3 October 1795, AGI, PC, leg. 2364, no. 21, Reservado; Kenneth Carstens, "The 1780 William Clark Map of Fort Jefferson," 26–31; Nasatir, 293–94n16, 319.

20. GDL to Carondelet, 3 October 1795, AGI, PC, leg. 2364, no. 21, Reservado.

6 These Infernal Bluffs

1. Baily, 141; Fortescue Cuming, *Sketches of a Tour to the Western Country, Through the States of Ohio and Kentucky, 1807–1809*, 290.

2. This Fort Adams should not be confused with the many other military installations (at least eight of them) named for the second or fourth president. Such posts include a Fort Adams in Mississippi (see chapter 30). See also Jack D. L. Holmes, "The Ebb-Tide of Spanish Military Power on the Mississippi: Fort San Fernando de las Barrancas, 1795–1798," 42–43.

3. Whitaker, *Mississippi Question,* 52–58.

4. Holmes, "Ebb-Tide," 36–40; Roberts, *Historic Forts,* 745.

5. J. F. H. Claiborne, *Mississippi as a Province, Territory and State, with Biographical Notices of Eminent Citizens,* 1:178–81.

6. Isaac Guion, "Military Journal of Captain Isaac Guion, 1797–1799," 36–40.

7. Ibid., 42–44, 48–51.

8. Ibid., 45, 46, 48–51; Holmes, "Ebb-Tide," 42–43.

9. Guion, 52. See Clark's pen-and-ink sketch plan of Fort San Fernando at Chickasaw Bluffs, WC Papers.

10. Guion, 68–73; Holmes, "Ebb-Tide," 42–43.

11. Holmberg, 269, 271–72; Gaff, 200.

12. *Annals of Congress,* Senate, 5th Congress, 3rd session, 2333–35. See T. Lewis, Fort Massac, to James McHenry, 18 February 1798, in Bernard C. Steiner, *The Life and Correspondence of James McHenry, Secretary of War under Washington and Adams,* 272. See also Lewis to McHenry, 19 July 1798, McHenry Papers, William L. Clements Library, University of Michigan.

13. Donald Jackson, *Thomas Jefferson and the Stony Mountains: Exploring the West from Monticello,* 99–100.

7 A Spy for the British, a Spy for the Spanish, and a Spy for Somebody Else

1. Christian, 322–23; Nasatir, 286–87n5; Daniel Clark [Jr.], *Proofs of the Corruption of Gen. James Wilkinson, and of His Connexion with Aaron Burr, with a Full Refutation of His Slanderous Allegations in Relation to the Character of the Principal Witness against Him,* 66–67.

2. Clark, *Proofs,* 66–67.

3. Ibid., 26–27; Jacobs, *Tarnished Warrior,* 137–38; Arthur P. Whitaker, "Harry Innes and the Spanish Intrigue: 1794–1795," 242–43.

4. Clark, *Proofs,* 26–27; Jacobs, *Tarnished Warrior,* 137–38; Whitaker, "Harry Innes," 242–43; Linklater, *Artist in Treason,* 144–46.

5. JW to Carondelet, 11 November 1795, AGI, PC, leg. 2374, no. 162; Jacobs, *Tarnished Warrior,* 148, 272–73.

6. Clark, *Proofs,* 66–71; Jacobs, *Tarnished Warrior,* 150; Douglas, 10–11; contemporary copy of a report to Major General Wayne on descent of Ohio with dispatches to New Madrid, 4 November 1795, WC Papers. See also Thomas, "Journals," 282.

7. Christian, 319–22; Jacobs, *Tarnished Warrior,* 150; Linklater, *Artist in Treason,* 152–53; Whitaker, *Spanish-American Frontier,* 211–12.

8. Jacobs, *Tarnished Warrior,* 149–50; Christian, 321–22.

9. Clark, *Proofs,* 66–71; James Wilkinson, *Memoirs of My Own Times,* 2:app. 40; Jacobs, *Tarnished Warrior,* 150; JW to GDL, 4 November 1795, AGI, PC, leg. 2374, no. 156.

10. JW to GDL, 10 October, 1, 4 November 1795, AGI, PC, leg. 2374, nos. 157, 161, 156; Christian, 323–26.

11. JW to GDL, 4 November 1795, AGI, PC, leg. 2374, no. 156; Christian, 324–26.

12. JW to Carondelet, 28 October, 11 November 1795, ibid., nos. 160, 162.

13. JW to GDL, 1 November 1795, JW to Carondelet, 11 November 1795, ibid., nos. 161, 162.

14. Christian, 323; Clark, *Proofs,* 68.

15. Clark, *Proofs,* 21; Jacobs, *Tarnished Warrior,* 134.

16. Clark, *Proofs, 35.*

17. Ibid., 66–67; contemporary copy of a report to Major General Wayne on descent of Ohio with dispatches to New Madrid, 4 November 1795, WC Papers.

18. In the Orderly Book is, in WC's hand, a sketch captioned "General W's Barge." Although Wayne is known on occasion to have descended the Ohio by barge, Wilkinson often employed that mode of transportation, whenever possible having such vessels fitted up for maximum comfort.

19. Foley, *Wilderness Journey*, 39–40; Jones, 84; Thomas C. Danisi and John C. Jackson, *Meriwether Lewis*, 36.

20. WC to unnamed officer, 27 November 1795, WC Papers; Loos, 57; Paul David Nelson, *Anthony Wayne: Soldier of the Early Republic*, 287.

21. Clark, *Proofs*, 66–71; "affidavit of G. Nicholas, Harry Innes, William Murray, and Ben. Sebastian, 19 November 1795," Benjamin Sebastian Papers, Indiana Historical Society (hereafter BS Papers). See also affidavit of James Dunn, 26 February 1796, Northwest Territory Collection, IHS.

22. "William Clark 1795," map B, Lewis and Clark Collection, Geography and Map Division, LC; Clark, *Proofs*, 69.

23. Warren, 117; "Extract of a Letter from a Gentleman at Cahokia to his friend at Vincennes," 15 March 1796, Northwest Territory Collection, IHS.

24. Warren, 117–18; also five communications of February–March 1796, inviting Sebastian to meetings and social gatherings with the highest officials of the Spanish government and their families, in BS Papers.

25. Warren, 117–18; Clark, *Proofs*, 70; Jacobs, *Tarnished Warrior*, 150–51.

26. Warren, 118; Clark, *Proofs*, 46–48; Wilkinson, *Memoirs*, 2:app. 45.

27. Wilkinson, *Memoirs*, 2:app. 42; Clark, *Proofs*, 43–45; Jacobs, *Tarnished Warrior*, 151; Linklater, *Artist in Treason*, 155.

8 A Spanish Lady Going to General Wilkinson

1. Clark, *Proofs*, 33.

2. *Annals of Congress*, 11th Congress, 2nd session, app. 2316–18.

3. Ibid. Protecting Winters's identity by referring to him as "E____ W____," Wayne passed along his report to Secretary of War James McHenry (committing initials rather than full names to paper was a common method of that era to safeguard the confidentiality of communications). See Knopf, 506–7.

4. Clark, *Proofs*, 33–35.

5. Ibid.

6. Ibid., 36–39.

7. Ibid., 33–39; Linklater, *Artist in Treason*, 158.

8. Christian, 336–38.

9. See WC's draft of a letter dated January 1797, to an unnamed recipient, in the Orderly Book.

10. Nelson, *Anthony Wayne*, 291–94; Kohn, 369; Knopf, 495–97, 506–7.

11. Nelson, *Anthony Wayne*, 294–95.

12. Ibid.; Clark, *Proofs*, 37–38, 72–74.

13. Clark, *Proofs,* 37–38.

14. Ibid., 37–38, 72–74; Christian, 335–36.

9 The Gibraltar of Louisiana

1. Zadok Cramer, *The Navigator*, 193.

2. M. I. Ludington, *Uniform of the Army of the United States (Illustrated), From 1774 to 1889*, 3–4; Guion, 84.

3. Jackson, *Thomas Jefferson*, 100; Flores, 30n41.

4. Clark, "Sundry Latitudes & Longitudes, taken on the Mississippi Ascending, ca. 1798," WC Papers.

5. JW to GDL, 6 February 1790, AGI, PC, leg. 2374, no. 18.

6. Jack D. L. Holmes, *Gayoso: The Life of a Spanish Governor in the Mississippi Valley, 1789–1799*, 145–50; Nasatir, 28–29.

7. Holmes, *Gayoso*, 145–50; Collot, 2:49, 53. See also Lawrence Kinnaird and Lucia Kinnaird, "Nogales: Strategic Post on the Spanish Frontier."

8. Guion, 81.

9. Ibid., 71–72.

10. Ibid., 77.

11. Ibid., 77–78.

12. William Kersey to Isaac Guion (hereafter IG), 3 May 1798, Book D, Guion Letters, J. F. H. Claiborne Collection, Mississippi Department of Archives and History (hereafter Guion Letters); Guion, 80–82, 88–89.

13. Clark, "Sundry Latitudes & Longitudes taken on the Mississippi Ascending, ca. 1798," WC Papers.

10 That Miserable Natchez Fort

1. Claiborne, 33–34, 42–46; Roberts, *Historic Forts*, 449.

2. Collot, 2:57–61.

3. Ibid., 60; Guion, 81.

4. Guion, 77, 96.

5. Ibid., 84–85.

6. Ibid., 97.

7. Baily, 152.

8. Ibid., 27, 38, 149, 151.

9. Ibid., 149, 152.

10. Gary Moulton, ed., *The Journals of the Lewis and Clark Expedition*, 6:58.

11. George W. Kyte, "A Spy on the Western Waters: The Military Intelligence Mission of General Collot in 1796," 440–41.

12. Guion, 80–82.

13. As late as December 1797, Power reports that Wilkinson still "anxiously solicits" the 640 dollars, despite knowing he could not expect it until several weeks after the spring thaw of 1798 opened navigation on the middle Mississippi and Ohio rivers. Clark, *Proofs*, 100.

11 The Most Fortunate and Glorious Commotion

1. Clark, *Proofs*, 72.

2. Ibid., 49–50, 72–74.

3. Ibid., 80–85.

4. Ibid., 83.

5. Ibid., 84–85, 87–88.

6. Ibid., 95–96; Isaac J. Cox, "Wilkinson's First Break with the Spaniards," 51–52.

7. Clark, *Proofs*, 95–96. For Carondelet's terms as reduced to writing by Power, see Power to the Kentucky conspirators, 19 July 1797, Harry Innes Papers, LC.

8. Clark, *Proofs*, 96–97; James R. Jacobs, *The Beginning of the U.S. Army, 1783–1812*, 187–91; Nelson, *Anthony Wayne*, 295–300.

9. Jacobs, *Tarnished Warrior*, 161; Linklater, *Artist in Treason*, 161.

10. Clark, *Proofs*, 97–98.

11. Ibid., 98.

12. Ibid.; Wilkinson, *Memoirs*, 2:app. 48. See also Linklater, *Artist in Treason*, 168–69.

13. Jacobs, *Tarnished Warrior*, 164–65; Clark, *Proofs*, 97; Wilkinson, *Memoirs*, 2:app. 52.

14. Clark, *Proofs*, 97; Thomas, "Journals," 294.

15. Clark, *Proofs*, 95–100.

16. Ibid., 100.

12 I Could Not Carry Our Plan in Execution

1. Robert Clarke, a Cincinnati publisher and noted collector of historical items, donated the Orderly Book to the Historical and Philosophical Society of Ohio in 1891. From that date back to the time of William Clark, there is no known evidence concerning the provenance of the volume. See David A. Simmons, "An Orderly Book from Fort Washington and Fort Hamilton, 1792–1793," 125.

2. Heitman, 1:306; WC to JC, 24 August 1796, Draper Mss., 2L42. See also WC's power of attorney to John Armstrong, 8 September 1796, in Hamilton County, Ohio, John Armstrong Papers, IHS.

3. Collot, 1:152–54.

4. Orderly Book; WC to JC, 24 August 1796, Draper Mss., 2L42.

5. WC to JC, 24 August 1796, Draper Mss., 2L42.

6. Jacobs, *Tarnished Warrior*, 158. If Jonathan shared their brother Edmund Clark's strong dislike of Wilkinson, William may well have wished to give them the impression he would not encounter the general. See Edmund Clark to George Tompkins, 17, 18 July 1807, Bodley Family Papers, Filson Historical Society.

7. See also WC's power of attorney to John Armstrong of Hamilton County in the Northwest Territory, John Armstrong Papers, IHS; Holmberg, 240n6; Orderly Book.

8. Orderly Book.

9. Jacobs, *Tarnished Warrior*, 158–62.

10. WC to Edmund Clark, 22 February, 18 August 1797, Draper Mss., 2L44, 45.

11. WC's Journal, 20 August–9 October 1797, Northwest Territory Collection, IHS. See the published version of this log in Thomas, "Journals."

12. Thomas, "Journals," 287–88.

13. Edgar to Governor Arthur St. Clair, 25 August 1797, Winthrop Sargent Papers, Massachusetts Historical Society (hereafter WS Papers).

14. JW to WS, 6 September 1797, also Captain Bartholomew Shaumburgh to WS, 10 September 1797, WS Papers.

15. JW to WS, 5 September 1797, ibid.

16. James, 117–19; Thomas, "Journals," 289–90; Roberts, *Historic Forts*, 265.

17. Thomas, "Journals," 290.

18. Ibid.; Carl J. Ekberg, *Colonial Ste. Genevieve: An Adventure on the Mississippi Frontier*, 72–74.

19. Thomas, "Journals," 290–91; Carstens and Carstens, 116; Roberts, *Historic Forts*, 257–58.

20. Thomas, "Journals," 290–91; Collot, 1:240.

21. Thomas, "Journals," 291–92, 293; James, 121; Roberts, *Historic Forts*, 257.

22. Thomas, "Journals," 292.

23. Ibid., 292–93.

24. Pickering to WS, 15 September 1797, WS Papers; Linklater, *Artist in Treason*, 169–70. See also Clarence E. Carter, ed., *The Territorial Papers of the United States*, 2:627.

25. Thomas, "Journals," 293.

26. Ibid., 293–94.

27. Ibid., 294; Clark, *Proofs*, 97.

28. Carter, *Territorial Papers*, 2:626–27, 630–31; Jacobs, *Tarnished Warrior*, 166.

29. WC to Edmund Clark, 14 December 1797, Draper Mss., 2L46.

30. GDL to Principe de Paz, 5 June 1798, Archivo Histórico Nacional, Estado, leg. 3900, apartado 4 (hereafter cited as AHN), no. 20, fols. 1211–32, muy reservada.

13 The Door to the Whole Western Country

1. Claiborne, 104–5.

2. Ibid., 198.

3. Andrew Ellicott, *The Journal of Andrew Ellicott*, 177; Treaty of San Lorenzo, articles 2 and 3, in Kukla, 342.

4. Ellicott, 177–78.

5. Flores, 14–17, 80–81; Carter, *Territorial Papers*, 5:216.

6. Baily, 159–60, 298n61, 62; Cramer, 221; Collot, 2:71–73.

7. Collot wrote at length on Baton Rouge, especially its sorry defenses. See Collot, 2:75–81; also Baily, 159–60, 298n64; Holmes, *Gayoso*, 237–38.

14 Was Politely Received and Treated by All

1. Thomas Ashe, *Travels in America Performed in 1806, for the Purpose of Exploring the Rivers Alleghany, Monongahela, Ohio, and Mississippi, and Ascertaining the Produce and Condition of their Banks and Vicinity*, 3:255.

2. Baily encountered the same procedure in 1797; Baily, 162.

3. According to Light Cummins, the Spanish government then charged American traders in Louisiana a tax called the Alcabala. Not technically an import duty, it was instead a sales tax paid by foreign purveyors before their goods were sold locally. Cummins to author, 25 May 2007. For an introduction to Clark Jr., see Richard C. Arena, "Philadelphia–Spanish New Orleans Trade in the 1790s," 436–39; Whitaker, *Mississippi Question*, 91–93.

4. Treaty of San Lorenzo, Article 22, in Kukla, 349.

5. AGI, PC, leg. 631, no. 4.

6. About Madame Claud Chabaud (whom Francis Baily called Madame Chabot) and her establishment, see Baily, 162–63, 167–70. See also Shannon Lee Dawdy, Ryan Gray, and Jill-Karen Yakubik, "Archaeological Investigations at the Rising Sun Hotel Site (160R225), New Orleans, Louisiana," vol. 1. In 2005 Dr. Dawdy led an archaeological excavation of a lot located at what is now 535–537 Conti Street, the site of the Chabaud House. Her findings confirm that Indians occupied the French Quarter at least a generation before the coming of Europeans and that Madame Chabaud kept a service of blue pearlware and costly porcelain tearwares, no doubt to accommodate her Anglo guests. Around 1809 she left the running of the business to her daughter Céleste who, in turn, was the landlady of the Rising Sun Hotel when it burned to the ground.

7. Baily, 171–72, 189, 302n31.

8. George P. Garrison, ed., "[Documents] Concerning Philip Nolan," 308–9.

9. Ibid., 309–11; Whitaker, *Mississippi Question*, 92–93; Elizabeth U. Alexander, *Notorious Woman: The Celebrated Case of Myra Clark Gaines*, 75–77.

10. Michael Wohl, "A Man in Shadow: The Life of Daniel Clark," 18–26; Alexander, 64–65.

11. Alexander, 65–67; Wohl, 7–11.

12. Alexander, 66–67; Arthur P. Whitaker, "Reed and Forde: Merchant Adventurers of Philadelphia," 244–45; Whitaker, *Mississippi Question*, 82–83, 133-34.

13. Jacobs, *Tarnished Warrior*, 85–87; Wohl, 19–21.

14. Arena, 435–42; Whitaker, "Reed and Forde," 247–62; Wohl, 21–27. On Clark Jr.'s efforts to become U.S. consul at New Orleans, see Arthur P. Whitaker, "Despatches from the United States Consulate in New Orleans, 1801–1803," part 1, 801–8.

15. Clark, *Proofs*, 105–9.

15 You Know the Nature of This Business

1. René J. Le Gardeur Jr., *The First New Orleans Theatre, 1792–1803*, 1–33; Foley, *Wilderness Journey*, 261.

2. Claudia D. Johnson, "That Guilty Third Tier: Prostitution in Nineteenth-Century American Theaters," 575–84.

3. Jones, 138–39.

4. AGI, PC, leg. 502, no. 16, translated with the assistance of Gilbert Din, PhD. As to the nature of the tax Clark owed, a tax called the Alcabala, see note 3, chapter 14, above. To compare the commodity values he recorded with those promulgated by the Spanish government, see the voluminous Tarifa that opens volume 1 (17 March 1798–6 February 1807) of "Despatches from United States Consuls in New Orleans, 1798–1807," RG 59, National Archives and Records Administration (hereafter NARA).

5. Clark Jr. to Daniel W. Coxe (hereafter DWC), 19 February 1798, Tench Coxe Section, Coxe Family Papers, HSP (hereafter Coxe Papers).

6. See not only the correspondence between Clark Jr. and Daniel W. Coxe or his brother Tench but also that between "David Pole" and "Jonathan Pole" (pseudonyms evidently used on occasion by Clark Jr. and DWC), Coxe Papers. For an example of Clark Jr.'s candor concerning bribery, see Clark Jr. to DWC, 19 February 1798.

7. Baily, 165–67.

8. A few years hence, Wilkinson would boast of the intelligence he had gathered: "With military Eyes I have explored every critical pass, every direct route & every devious way between the Mexican Gulph & the Tenessee River." See Harold Syrett, ed., *The Papers of Alexander Hamilton*, 26:173–74. For examples of Wilkinson's sway over Clark during his first stint in the Army, see McGrane, which shows that, even after the victory at Fallen Timbers, Clark echoed Wilkinson's views—disparaging Wayne and, at one point, praising an enemy commander who refused to comply with Wayne's reasonable protocols.

9. Both Collot and Baily recognized the vulnerability of New Orleans. See Collot, 2:94–98; Baily, 165–67; also Roberts, *Historic Forts*, 345–46.

16 An Alarm about a British Frigate

1. Whitaker, *Mississippi Question*, 29–30, 82; Holmes, *Gayoso*, 106.

2. Holmes, *Gayoso*, 213–14.

3. Ibid., 106, 214; Whitaker, *Mississippi Question*, 61–62.

4. GDL to Principe de Paz, 5 June 1798, AHN, no. 20, fols. 1211–32, muy reservada.

5. Holmes, *Gayoso*, 213–14, 246.

6. Juan Ronquillo to Juan Ventura Morales, 25 April 1798, AGI, PC, leg. 590, fol. 774; Receipt for deposit of 1,985,760 reales into the royal treasury on 30 April 1798, in AGI, PC, leg. 491-A; James A. Robertson, trans., *Louisiana under the Rule of Spain, France, and the United States, 1785–1807*, 1:179.

7. GDL to AE, 30 April 1798, Andrew Ellicott Papers, LC (hereafter AE Papers).

8. GDL to Santa Clara, 4 May 1798, AGI, PC, leg. 1501-A, no. 137 1/2, fols. 448–52; Holmes, *Gayoso*, 233–34.

9. A narrative of the entire incident at the Baliza appears in GDL to Santa Clara, 4 May 1798, AGI, PC, leg. 1501-A, no. 137 1/2, fols. 448–52, with enclosures from Delacroix to Pedro Favrot, 1 May 1798, and from Favrot to GDL, 2 May 1798. Also see Holmes, *Gayoso*, 246.

10. GDL to Santa Clara, 4 May 1798, AGI, PC, leg. 1501-A, no. 137½, fols. 448–52.

11. Correspondence of Juan Ronquillo, AGI, PC, leg. 590, fols. 771–76; Jack D. L. Holmes, ed. and trans., "The *Moniteur de la Louisiane* in 1798," 230–53.

12. GDL to Santa Clara, 4 May 1798, AGI, PC, leg. 1501-A, no. 137 1/2; Holmes, *Gayoso*, 246. Maritime historians Roy and Lesley Adkins, in an e-mail to author dated 26 January 2008, helped identify Captain Cochrane.

13. GDL to Principe de Paz, 6 June 1798, AHN, no. 21, reservada.

14. GDL to Principe de Paz, 5 June 1798, AHN, no. 20, muy reservada.

15. On the chronic financial problems of Spanish Louisiana, see Ralph Lee Woodward Jr., "Spanish Commercial Policy in Louisiana, 1763–1803"; also Whitaker, *Mississippi Question*, 155–59, 177–79.

17 An Uproar about a War

1. For a comprehensive treatment of events leading up to the XYZ Affair, see Elkins and McKitrick, 549–79.

2. Elkins and McKitrick give a thorough account of reactions in the United States to the XYZ revelations. Ibid., 581–90.

3. John B. McMaster, *A History of the People of the United States from the Revolution to the Civil War*, 2:380–81, 403.

4. Ibid., 376–80.

5. Ibid., 383–84; John C. Miller, *Crisis in Freedom: The Alien and Sedition Acts*, 61–62.

6. Elkins and McKitrick, 588; *U.S. Statutes at Large*, 5th Congress, 2nd session.

7. *U.S. Statutes at Large*, 5th Congress, 2nd session.

8. Clark Sr. to AE, 20 May 1798, AE Papers.

9. Whitaker, *Mississippi Question*, 103–4, 116–21.

10. A small series of letters between George Rogers Clark and Samuel Fulton, his agent in France, is one of the only sources of intelligence about this extraordinary chapter in George's life. All information in this section comes from that correspondence. See GRC to Fulton, 3 Juin and 23 fructidor of 1798 in James, 511–15, translation by James K. Wallace.

11. Ibid.

12. Before long Clark would accept the offer of Cochran and Rhea. See an appraisal dated 2 July 1798, AGI, PC, leg. 502, no. 48, fol. 328; also leg. 620, no. 48, a complementary affidavit of the same date.

13. Clark Sr. to AE, 20 May 1798, AE Papers.

14. See "David Pole" (Clark Jr.) to "Jonathan Pole" (DWC), 3 April 1798; Clark Jr. to DWC, 19 April, 15 May 1798; Clark Jr. to Tench Coxe (hereafter TC), 1, 7 June 1798, Coxe Papers.

15. Clark Jr. to AE, 31 May 1798, AE Papers; Holmes, *Gayoso*, 239.

16. Holmes, "The *Moniteur*," 245–46.

17. In late March, Clark Jr. provided several thousand Spanish dollars for the expenses of Army forces led by Captain Guion, who in return paid him bills of exchange. See Clark Jr. to DWC, 20 April 1798, Coxe Papers; Clark Jr. to Guion, 19 March 1798, Guion Family Papers (#295-2), Southern Historical Collection, Library of UNC at Chapel Hill.

18 The Money Is for Mr. Riddle

1. Extract of a letter from a gentleman of Kaskaskia, 16 February 1796; Pike to Wayne, 24 February 1796; Deposition of James Dunn, 26 February 1796; extract of a letter from a gentleman at Cahokia, 15 March 1796; all in the Northwest Territory Collection, IHS.

2. BS to GDL, 5 November 1796, BS to Carondelet, 15 March 1797, AGI, PC, leg. 2375, nos. 10, 11.

3. Clark, *Proofs*, 69–70.

4. GDL to Principe de Paz, 5 June 1798, AHN, no. 20, muy reservada, translated by author.

5. JW to GDL, 3 March 1798, quoted from ibid.

6. Ibid.

7. BS (writing as 1325) to GDL, 5 November 1796, AGI, PC, leg. 2375, no. 10.

8. Warren, 112, 118; BS to GDL, 5 November 1796, 10 March 1799, AGI, PC, leg. 2375, nos. 10, 42. See also two letters from John Watkins, partner in a clandestine land scheme with Andrew Watkins (a pseudonym of Sebastian), to Governor Casa Calvo, both dated 4 March 1800, AGI, PC, leg. 2366, fols. 235–244.

9. J. Merieult to BS, March 1796, BS Papers.

10. GDL to Principe de Paz, 5 June 1798, AHN, no. 20, muy reservada.

11. See two documents dated 1 June 1798, AGI, PC, leg. 620, no. 35, and leg. 502, no. 35, fol. 315.

12. As to the practice of using cloth bags in smuggling operations, see Clark, *Proofs*, 38–39.

13. WC to John Clark, 19 June 1798, WC Papers.

14. "Riddle" or some variation of that name turns up now and then in accounts of Mississippi River travel, from as early as 1787 to as late as 1806. See Whitaker, "James Wilkinson's First Descent," 95; James Brown to BS, 8 November 1806, BS Papers.

15. Juan Ronquillo to Juan Ventura Morales, 17 June 1798, AGI, PC, leg. 590, fol. 800.

19 A Highly Beneficial but Illicit Monopoly

1. Innes and Todd to Samuel Montgomery Brown (hereafter SMB), April 1798, AGI, PC, leg. 2371, fols. 610–12.

2. Ibid.

3. Proposal of SMB to GDL, 23 June 1798, AGI, PC, leg. 2371, fols. 306–8.

4. Ibid.; Innes and Todd to SMB, April 1798, AGI, PC, leg. 2371, fols. 610–12.

5. Proposal of SMB to GDL, 23 June 1798, AGI, PC, leg. 2371, fols. 306–8.

6. Ibid.

7. Ibid.

8. Ibid.

9. Ibid.

10. Ibid. Through the Treaty of San Ildefonso, Spain was to convey Louisiana to France in secret in 1800.

11. Ibid.

12. BS to GDL, 14 June 1798, AGI, PC, leg. 2371, fols. 664–65; Holmes, *Gayoso*, 239–40.

20 At Ellicott's Camp on the Line

1. For details on TC's career at the Treasury, see Jacob E. Cooke, *Tench Coxe and the Early Republic*, chapters 11–15.

2. Eron Rowland, *Life, Letters and Papers of William Dunbar of Elgin, Morayshire, Scotland, and Natchez, Mississippi: Pioneer Scientist of the Southern United States*, 84.

3. Ibid., 83.

4. Ibid., 82.

5. Thomas Freeman to IG, 24 May 1798, Guion Letters; Rowland, *Life, Letters*, 82.

6. William Dunbar to Diana Dunbar, 23 June 1798, William Dunbar Papers, MDAH; Rowland, *Life, Letters*, 80.

7. Robert J. Moore Jr. and Michael Haynes, *Lewis and Clark, Tailor Made, Trail Worn: Army Life, Clothing, and Weapons of the Corps of Discovery*, 28–30. Sketches of Ellicott's observatory hut appear in his *Journal*, almost midway through the "Folio of Plates and Charts" in the back of the book.

8. AE to Timothy Pickering, 19 June 1798, AE Papers.

9. Ibid.; Jack D. L. Holmes, "Military Uniforms in Spanish Louisiana, 1766–1804," 115–17; Moore and Haynes, 222–29.

10. Secretary and commissary Thomas Power's correspondence on the compensation of the workers for Spain is one of the best sources of information on

the demographics of these "Spanish" employees; see AGI, PC, leg. 538-B, "Demarcación de Límites." See also Power's records of a similar nature in ibid., leg. 576. On the effort to conform the Spanish pay scale and rations with those of the Americans, see GDL to Juan Ventura Morales, 23 April 1798, ibid., leg. 576, fols. 567–69.

11. Ellicott, appendix, 44–48.

12. Frances C. Roberts, "Thomas Freeman—Surveyor of the Old Southwest," 216–17.

13. William Dunbar to Diana Dunbar, 6 June 1798, William Dunbar Papers, MDAH. While convalescing at "the Forest," Dunbar wrote Ellicott on 1, 6 July 1798, AE Papers.

14. Guion and Freeman were two of several prominent individuals who believed (as Freeman put it) that Ellicott "was making a job of his appointment." See Freeman to Guion, 19 April 1798, Guion Letters.

15. Andro Linklater, *The Fabric of America: How Our Borders and Boundaries Shaped the Country and Forged Our National Identity*, 28–30.

16. Ibid., 33–41.

17. Bob Arnebeck, *Through a Fiery Trial: Building Washington, 1790–1800*, 147–52, 155–62, 203–9, 213, 309; Roberts, "Thomas Freeman," 217; Florette Henri, *The Southern Indians and Benjamin Hawkins, 1796–1816*, 217.

18. Treaty of San Lorenzo, Article 2.

19. Donald Jackson, ed., *Letters of the Lewis and Clark Expedition with Related Documents, 1783–1854*, 1:40–41; Danisi and Jackson, 64; Stephen Ambrose, *Undaunted Courage: Meriwether Lewis, Thomas Jefferson, and the Opening of the American West*, 87.

20. A note in the ledger section of Clark's 1798–1801 journal says he brought 1,590 Spanish dollars to Natchez but does not indicate what happened to that money. We can assume he withheld 90 of those dollars, probably for his own expenses, and exchanged the remainder for a paper substitute. Although other documentation about this episode has not yet been identified, we can assume for the following reasons that Ellicott, not Guion, was the recipient of the remaining 1,500 Spanish dollars. Neither Guion's journal (which contains many details concerning his sources of finances) nor his numerous letters mention WC or suggest that such a transaction took place. Those same documents, however, show that when Guion had earlier accepted Spanish dollars he usually wrote drafts on the War Department, not on the U.S. Treasury. Further, Guion's work and expenses were nearing an end whereas Ellicott's were only beginning.

In contrast with Guion, Ellicott included almost no financial details in his journal. Against directions from Secretary of State Pickering, he sometimes charged expenses not to the State Department but to the Treasury, probably to keep Pickering from knowing the extent of his expenditures. WC to DWC, 26 September 1798, Coxe Papers; Carter, *Territorial Papers* 5: 42–44.

21 The Nature of the Boundary Business

1. Ellicott, 1; Catharine Van Cortlandt Mathews, *Andrew Ellicott: His Life and Letters*, 108; AE to Pickering, 29 July 1798, AE Papers; Carter, *Territorial Papers* 5:42–44.

2. Roberts, "Thomas Freeman," 217–18; Wilkinson, *Memoirs*, 2:app. 32; Freeman to IG, 24 May 1798, Guion Letters.

3. Ellicott, 40–41; Guion, 81; Freeman to IG, 19 April 1798, Guion Letters.

4. Ellicott, note of 23 March 1797 on page 17 of the appendix.

5. Henri, 214–15. See also Robert Register, "Andrew Ellicott's Observations while Serving on the Southern Boundary Commission, 1796–1800," 19.

6. John C. Van Horne, "Andrew Ellicott's Mission to Natchez (1796–1798)," 160–85. Claiborne covers the same ground, particularly in chapter 19, but with less equanimity. See also Whitaker, *Mississippi Question*, 59–67.

7. AE to Sarah Ellicott, 10 February 1798, AE Papers; Whitaker, *Mississippi Question*, 59–67; Henri, 213.

8. The documents on the impasse between Ellicott and Freeman are extensive. See AE to Freeman, 30 June 1798, and Freeman's reply of the same date; AE to Pickering, 12, 29 July 1798; AE to WS, 15 September 1798; AE to Sarah Ellicott, 6 November 1798; AE to Pickering, 8 November 1798; all in AE Papers. See also Freeman's letters of 19 April, 24 May 1798 to Guion, Guion Letters; Sargent to AE, 18 September, 24 October 1798, Sargent to Pickering, 3 August 1799, in Dunbar Rowland, *Mississippi Territorial Archives, 1798–1803: Executive Journals of Governor Winthrop Sargent and Governor William Charles Cole Claiborne*, 1:49–50, 73, 162–63.

9. Guion, 89–90.

10. GDL to Stephen Minor, 6 June 1798, AGI, PC, leg. 1501-B, no. 154 and enclosures.

11. Minor to AE, 11 June 1798, AGI, PC, leg. 215-B; Ellicott, 181.

12. Greg O'Brien, *Choctaws in a Revolutionary Age, 1750–1830*, 38, 73–80.

13. Whitaker, *Mississippi Question*, 68–70; James T. Carson, *Searching for the Bright Path: The Mississippi Choctaws from Prehistory to Removal*, 51–53.

14. Carson, 48; Henri, 210–13.

15. Minor to GDL, 1 July 1798, AGI, PC, leg. 215-B; Whitaker, *Mississippi Question*, 77; Freeman to IG, 27 June 1798, Guion Letters; Guion, 95–96; IG to AE, 25 June 1798, AE Papers.

16. IG to AE, 25 June 1798, AE Papers.

17. AE to IG, 27 June 1798, ibid.

18. Minor to GDL, 1 July 1798, AGI, PC, leg. 215-B.

19. Ibid.

20. Freeman to Guion, 29 June 1798, Guion Letters.

21. See Freeman to AE, 30 June 1798, and Ellicott's response of the same date, AE Papers; also Minor to GDL, 1 July 1798, AGI, PC, leg. 215-B.

22 The Object of the Plotters

1. Guion, 95–96, 98. It is ironic that in 1826 Clark, with two other members of a special commission appointed by the U.S. government to persuade the Choctaws to give up their homeland in Mississippi and Alabama, was utterly unable to do so. Under increasing pressure by both federal and state governments four years later, however, the Choctaws would cede their territory. See Jay H. Buckley, *William Clark: Indian Diplomat*, 175; Arthur H. DeRosier Jr., *The Removal of the Choctaw Indians*, 92–93, 116–28; Jones, 289, 304.

2. Vidal to GDL, 11 July 1798, AGI, PC, leg. 50, fols. 914–15.

3. Ibid., 10 July 1798, no. 20, fols. 975–76.

4. See Vidal's 20 June 1798 report, including his translation to Spanish of Guion's challenge to him, in AHN, no. 24, reservada, with enclosures 1 and 2. See also GDL to Principe de Paz, 30 July 1798, ibid.

5. GDL to Principe de Paz, 30 July 1798, ibid.; Holmes, *Gayoso*, 239–40.

6. Pickering to AE, 1 June 1798, AE Papers.

7. GDL to Principe de Paz, 30 July 1798, AHN, no. 24, reservada; Holmes, *Gayoso*, 239–40.

8. Holmes, *Gayoso*, 239–41.

9. Ibid.

10. Ibid.

11. Ibid.

12. Ibid., 239–45; GDL to Principe de Paz, 30 July 1798, AHN, no. 24, reservada.

13. Whitaker, *Mississippi Question*, 58–59, 102–4; deposition of AE, *Annals of Congress*, 11th Congress, 2nd session, appendix to 1st and 2nd sessions, 2302–10; Ellicott, 29–30, 35; Linklater, *Artist in Treason*, 204–5; Wilkinson, *Memoirs*, 2:app. 2.

14. *Annals of Congress*, 10th Congress, appendix to 1st session, 2738.

15. AE to Pickering, 14 November 1797, in Mathews, 161–62.

16. Linklater, *Artist in Treason*, 179–80; Ellicott, 182–83.

23 Mr. Clark, Anxious to Pursue His Journey

1. About Clark Sr., see Alexander, 64, 66, 68–71, 76–77.

2. The correspondence of these individuals with Clark Sr. are in his papers and theirs, some of which are in the Guion Family Papers of the Southern Historical Collection, Library of UNC at Chapel Hill. See also a letter from Clark Sr. to Clark Jr., 2 November 1798, in the Gilpin Papers, HSP; and a power of attorney dated 30 November 1798, by which Clark Sr. names Anderson and another "trusty friend" to convey his Kentucky lands, Anderson-Lathan Papers, Virginia State Archives. In addition, Wilkinson's *Memoirs*, 2:122–23 and appendices 7–13, contain several quotations and letters from Clark Sr.

3. Minor to GDL, 1, 9 July 1798, and Power to GDL, 7 July 1798, AGI, PC, leg. 215-B; AE to Pickering, 12 July 1798, AE Papers.

4. Minor to GDL, 9 July 1798 (quote), also Power to GDL, 7 July 1798, AGI, PC, leg. 215-B.

5. Evidence of transactions linking McKee and Freeman appears in the Natchez Court records, MDAH; *DAB* 12:82–83.

6. For more on the slippery McKee, see Whitaker, *Mississippi Question*, 109, 125–26; McKee to McHenry, 16 May 1798, James McHenry Papers, Ms. 647, Maryland Historical Society; William S. Coker and Thomas D. Watson, *Indian Traders of the Southeastern Spanish Borderlands: Panton, Leslie & Company and John Forbes & Company, 1783–1847*, 226–29.

7. See McKee to McHenry, 24 April 1797, 12 October 1798, McHenry Papers, Ms. 647, Maryland Historical Society.

8. AE to Pickering, 12 July 1798, AE Papers.

9. Ibid.

10. Ibid.; Holmes, "The *Moniteur*," 230–31; Clark Jr. to AE and IG, 13 June 1798, AE Papers. On 17 July 1798 Ellicott again wrote Pickering, this time opening the letter by referring to "my communication of the 12th [carried] by Mr. William Clark," AE Papers.

11. Minor to GDL, 9 July 1798, AGI, PC, leg. 215-B. See also Minor's five letters to GDL at this time—one of 10 July, and four written two days later—in AGI, PC, leg. 50. But for the unnumbered letter dated 10 July, the folio numbers of these communications run from 1122 to 1132.

12. Power to GDL, 7 July 1798, AGI, PC, leg. 215-B. On Minor, see Jack D. L. Holmes, "Stephen Minor: Natchez Pioneer."

13. Holmes, "The *Moniteur*," 243.

14. Ibid., 238–40, 245–46.

15. McKee to McHenry, 12 October 1798, McHenry Papers, Ms. 647, Maryland Historical Society.

24 I Take a Passage on the Ship *Star*

1. Nasatir, 129–30; Whitaker, *Mississippi* Question, 109.

2. Among Daniel W. Coxe's ledger entries of expenses at New Orleans in 1798 is one for three hundred dollars paid to "Chevot" (apparently a phonetic approximation of "Chabaud"), Coxe Papers.

3. Cooke, 64n9, 153, 175–76, 334–36; Whitaker, "Reed and Forde," 239, 247, 252–60; Arena, 434, 436–37.

4. The Tench Coxe Section of the Coxe Family Papers contains many letters that Daniel sent Tench from various ports during this period; Whitaker, "Reed and Forde," 247, 252–60; Arena, 435–38.

5. Cooke, x–xiii, 155, 307, 336–37, 407n45, 414–15; Elkins and McKitrick, 628; Jackson, *Letters*, 1:76–99, 2:397n(c), 422.

6. Arena, 436–38; Wohl, 21–25.

7. DWC to TC, 30 June 1798, Coxe Papers; Entry 1119, "Proofs of Ownership for Registered Vessels 1790–1802," 8:63, 66, RG 36, NARA; *Claypoole's American Daily Advertiser,* 5 December 1798.

8. DWC to TC, 20 May, 30 June 1798, Coxe Papers.

9. DWC to TC, 30 June 1798, ibid.

10. Cargo appraisals of 19 July 1798, in AGI, PC, leg. 502, fols. 170–72; M. Taylor to DWC, 8 October 1798, Coxe Papers. As to the cotton, see in AGI, PC, leg. 631, April entries numbered 1, 8, 9, May entries numbered 3, 8, 9, June entries numbered 2, 3, 4.

11. Cargo appraisals of 19 July 1798, AGI, PC, leg. 502, fols. 170–72; M. Taylor to DWC, 8 October 1798, Coxe Papers.

12. Passport dated 24 July 1798, WC Papers.

13. Cramer, 223.

14. Roberts, *Historic Forts*, 352.

15. DWC to TC, 10 July 1797, Coxe Papers. See DWC to an unnamed recipient, 31 July 1797 (extract); unfinished draft, 29 September 1797; Pickering to McHenry, 7 October 1797, to John Adams, 9 October 1797, to DWC, 9 October 1797; DWC to Pickering, 27 October 1797; all in Pickering Papers, Massachusetts Historical Society.

16. Alexander, 47–49; McKee to McHenry, 12 October 1798, McHenry Papers, Ms. 647, Maryland Historical Society. In the John McKee Collection at the Library of Congress are the crumbling remains of at least five friendly letters written by Chew to McKee between 1798 and 1804.

17. On 20 June 1798, a Joseph Craig from the Ohio River valley asked permission to deposit fifty-seven containers of tobacco for export and, three days later, declared sixty barrels of flour for local sale; AGI, PC, leg. 502, fols. 740, 326. As to Elisha Craig and James Wilkinson, see McKee to McHenry, 12 October 1798, McHenry Papers, Ms. 647, Maryland Historical Society.

18. Nasatir, 68–69; Roberts, *Historic Forts*, 352–53.

19. See WC's draft of a letter dated January 1797 to an unnamed recipient, in the Orderly Book.

20. Robertson, 1:315–19; Collot, 2:100–103; M. Perrin du Lac, *Travels Through the Two Louisianas, and Among the Savage Nations of the Missouri; also, in the United States, along the Ohio, and the Adjacent Provinces, in 1801, 1802, & 1803*, 101.

21. Roberts, *Historic Forts*, 331–32; Robertson, 1:316; Collot, 2:100–103.

22. Collot, 2:100–103; Roberts, *Historic Forts*, 352–53.

23. The Spanish documentation of this and subsequent breaches of their law is extensive (see chapter 25).

25 An Insult to His Majesty

1. One of Coxe's subsequent violations was soon to cause an uproar capable of destroying the uneasy peace between Spain and the United States. Documents concerning that chain of events have little to say about this particular infraction, a relatively minor one. See Guillermo (William) E. Hulings to GDL, 14 August 1798, GDL to Hulings, 16 August 1798, AGI, PC, leg. 1501-B, no. 187, fols.

255–263. About the Baliza, see Collot, 2:103–4. Accounts of the major events of this chapter appear in duplicate form in AGI, PC leg. 178 and 1501-B. Since facsimiles of leg. 1501-B are more readily available in the United States, I cite 1501-B only.

2. James Pitot, *Observations on the Colony of Louisiana from 1796 to 1802*, 98–99; Robertson, 1:324, 332.

3. GDL to Hulings, 16 August 1798, AGI, PC, leg. 1501-B, no. 187, fols. 258–63.

4. Rod Lincoln, "The Balize, 1723–1888," 38–42; Jerome J. Salomone, "Mississippi River Bar–Pilotage: The Development of an Occupation," 42–43.

5. Lincoln, 41; Pitot, 99. For a different view of Ronquillo, see Collot, 2:103–4; William Johnson, "William Johnson's Journal," 39–41. As to one of Ronquillo's salvage operations, see note 8, chapter 33.

6. Treaty of San Lorenzo, Article 19; Alexander, 75–76; John G. Clark, *New Orleans, 1718–1812: An Economic History*, 241–44.

7. Clark Jr. to AE, with enclosures, 7 August 1798, Despatches from U.S. Consuls in New Orleans, RG 59, NARA. Although Clark Jr. was at that date neither a citizen nor a consul of the United States, he would soon become both.

8. Ibid. Ronquillo kept Intendant Morales apprised of the progress of those vessels. *Apollo*, probably the lightest of the three, entered the river first, but *Mars* had to wait many days until the proper combination of wind and tide allowed her to cross the bar. See Ronquillo's reports of August 1798 in AGI, PC, leg. 590. On 26 September 1798, GDL recounted these and other events to the Conde de Santa Clara, ibid., leg. 1501-B, no. 186, fols. 237–41.

9. Borras and Molina to Joseph Woodman, 1 August 1798, ibid., leg. 1501-B, no. 187, fol. 252.

10. GDL to Conde de Santa Clara, 26 September 1798, ibid., fols. 245–49; Julian Francisco Muñoz de Campa to an unidentified party, 26 September 1798, ibid., fols. 264–68.

11. GDL to Conde de Santa Clara, 26 September 1798, ibid., fols. 245–49; Clark Jr. to AE, with enclosures, 7 August 1798, Despatches from U.S. Consuls in New Orleans, RG 59, NARA.

12. Clark Jr. to AE, 7 August 1798, Despatches from U.S. Consuls in New Orleans, RG 59, NARA.

13. For more on the *Harriot* (also called *Harriott* and *Harriet*) see Records of U.S. Customs Service, Record of Drawbacks for Sloop *Harriot*, Master James Sellers, July 1798, RG 36, NARA; Juan Ronquillo to Juan Ventura Morales, 14 August 1798, AGI, PC, leg. 590, folio 832.

14. Julian Francisco Muñoz de Campa to an unnamed party, 26 September 1798, AGI, PC, leg. 1501-B, no. 187, fols. 264–68.

15. DWC to GDL, and GDL to DWC, 13 August 1798, ibid., fols. 250–51, 253–54.

16. Bernardo Molina to GDL, 16 August 1798, AGI, PC, leg. 50, no. 8, fol. 433; GDL to DWC, 13 August 1798, ibid., leg. 1501-B, no. 187, fols. 253–54. Once he became U.S. consul at New Orleans, Clark Jr. reminded the Jefferson administration of the "arbitrary and unjust" treatment Coxe had suffered in 1798 as a result of his decisions at the Baliza; Whitaker, "Despatches," 815–22.

26 So Reduced I Can Scarcely Walk

1. Michael A. Palmer, *Stoddert's War: Naval Operations during the Quasi-War with France, 1798–1801*, 30–31.

2. Danisi has written extensively on the effects of malaria on Meriwether Lewis, William Clark, and other members of the Corps of Discovery. See Danisi and Jackson, chapter 4; Thomas C. Danisi, *Uncovering the Truth about Meriwether Lewis*, chapter 13.

3. Moulton, 2:418.

4. U.S. Navy Department, *Naval Documents Related to the Quasi-War between the United States and France: Naval Operations from February 1797 to October 1798*, 1:432–33; Ian W. Toll, *Six Frigates: The Epic History of the Founding of the U.S. Navy*, 109.

5. Robert N. Bergantino, "Revisiting Fort Mandan's Longitude," *We Proceeded On* 27 (November 2001): 19–26.

6. On the natural history of the region Clark was passing through, see William G. De Brahm, *The Atlantic Pilot*.

7. Moulton, 6:35–36.

8. For an idea of the travails experienced onboard oceangoing vessels of this era, see Médéric-Louis-Élie Moreau de Saint-Méry, *Moreau de Saint-Méry's American Journey (1793–1798)*, 1–27.

27 A Thirteen–Gun Salute for Agent 13

1. JW's Order Book, 31 December 1796–8 March 1808 (hereafter Order Book), NARA; Jacobs, *Tarnished Warrior*, 170–71.

2. JW to GDL, 27 June 1798, AGI, PC, leg. 2375, no. 20, fols. 2083–85.

3. JW to Secretary of War, 20 July 1798 (extract), JW Papers, Chicago Historical Society.

4. Order Book; JW to GDL, 2 August 1798, AGI, PC, leg. 2375, no. 21, fols. 2086–87.

5. JW to Secretary of War, 20 July 1798, JW Papers, Chicago Historical Society; Order Book, Orders of August 7–12, 1798, NARA.

6. Order Book, 13 August 1798, NARA; Carlos Dehault Delassus to GDL, 20 August 1798, AGI, PC, leg. 1501-B, no. 190, fols. 302–4. According to U.S. Army protocol, because Delassus was then a lieutenant colonel, thirteen was likely the proper number of shots for the American convoy to salute him with. "Regulations Respecting Salutes," 19 January 1797, Early Records of the U.S. War Department.

7. BS to GDL, 17 September 1798, AGI, PC, leg. 2371, fols. 694–97.

8. Ibid.

9. BS to GDL, 10 March 1799, AGI, PC, leg. 2375, no. 42, fols. 2179–90 (includes encryption, decoded by means of key in leg. 2373, no. 1, fols. 1532–75). The Library of Congress erroneously attributes this 1799 letter to JW.

10. BS to GDL, 10 March 1799, AGI, PC, leg. 2375, no. 42, fols. 2179–90.

11. Ibid.; Warren, 118; *The Palladium*, 28 August 1798. The quest of Sebastian and Watkins was to persist. See John Watkins to the Marqués de Casa Calvo, 4 March 1800, AGI, PC, leg. 2366, fols. 235–44b.

12. *Western World*, 16 August 1806; see also *Palladium (Frankfort, Kentucky)*, 14 August 1806.

28 Go, Before It Is Too Late

1. Palmer, 23, 32, 40–41; U.S. Navy Department, 1:442; William B. Clark, *Gallant John Barry, 1745–1803: The Story of a Naval Hero of Two Wars*, 423–24.

2. Gary W. Shannon and Robert G. Cromley, "Philadelphia and the Yellow Fever Epidemic of 1798," *Urban Geography* 3, no. 4 (1982): 355–57, 367; Thomas Condie and Richard Folwell, *History of the Pestilence, Commonly Called Yellow Fever, Which Almost Desolated Philadelphia in the Months of August, September, and October, 1798*, 104, xxxiv; Cooke, 345–46.

3. Condie and Folwell, 79.

4. Ibid., 82–85.

5. Ibid., xi–xii.

6. As to the number of guns onboard the *United States* and the *Delaware*, see Palmer, 23, 32; Toll, 96.

7. WC to DWC, 26 September 1798, Coxe Papers.

8. McKee to McHenry, 12 October 1798, McHenry Papers, Ms. 647, Maryland Historical Society; DWC to TC, 12 October 1798, William Coxe to TC, 25 October 1798, Coxe Papers; Alexander, 47–49. Genealogical information on Chew from Robert Levering Chew, courtesy of John Chew.

9. Heitman, 1:218; Gaff, 263, 308.

10. Heitman, 1:218; Kohn, 363–65; Gaff, 232; J. Thomas Scharf, *History of Delaware, 1609–1888*, 1:274, 940; Certificate no. 26, dated 18 September 1799, by John Hale Jr., collector of revenue for New Castle County, Del., Maxwell Bines Manuscript Collection, Historical Society of Delaware.

11. Isaac Weld Jr., *Travels Through the States of North America, and the Provinces of Upper and Lower Canada, During the Years 1795, 1796, and 1797*, 1:27–28.

12. Ibid., 37–39; Duke de La Rochefoucault-Liancourt, *Travels through the United States of North America, the Country of the Iroquois, and Upper Canada, in the Years 1795, 1796, and 1797, with an Authentic Account of Lower Canada*, 3:691–93.

29 The Sailors Soon Commenced a Riot

1. *Federal Gazette & Baltimore Daily Advertiser*, 28 September 1798.

2. For more on the attractions of late-eighteenth-century Baltimore, see Weld, 1:43–46; La Rochefoucault-Liancourt, 3:254–58, 670–76; Moreau de Saint-Méry, 76–81.

3. J. Thomas Scharf, *History of Baltimore City and County*, 2:513–14; Moreau de Saint-Méry, 80.

4. Information about the ordination comes from the archives of St. Mary's Seminary of Baltimore, courtesy of the Archdiocese of Baltimore. See also John Carroll, *The John Carroll Papers*, 2:334.

5. John W. Kuehl, "The XYZ Affair and American Nationalism: Republican Victories in the Middle Atlantic States," 5–7; Frank A. Cassell, *Merchant Congressman in the Young Republic: Samuel Smith of Maryland, 1752–1839*, 81–83.

6. Kuehl, "XYZ Affair," 5–7; Cassell, 81–89.

7. Kuehl, "XYZ Affair," 5–7; Cassell, 87–89; John S. Pancake, *Samuel Smith and the Politics of Business, 1752–1839*, 50–51.

8. *Federal Gazette & Baltimore Daily Advertiser*, 28, 29 September 1798.

9. Thomas C. Pollock, *The Philadelphia Theatre in the Eighteenth Century*, 63–64. On the intertwining theater trade of Philadelphia and Baltimore, see Scharf, *History of Baltimore*, 2:682–83; David Ritchey, ed., *A Guide to the Baltimore Stage in the Eighteenth Century: A History and Day Book Calendar*, 36–42.

10. M. Furman to TC, 1 October 1798, Coxe Papers; Holmberg, 28–29; *Federal Gazette & Baltimore Daily Advertiser*, 4 October 1798.

11. Supplement, 12 October 1798, to the *Virginia Argus*, attributed to the *Baltimore Intelligencer*, 5 October 1798.

12. The Bullitt Family Papers of the Filson Historical Society contain several documents reflecting on Nabb's extensive mercantile transactions.

13. J. Herman Schauinger, *Cathedrals in the Wilderness*, 1–3. In August 1814, while ministering to St. Louis as the first bishop of Bardstown, Kentucky, Flaget baptized Clark's children Meriwether Lewis Clark, William Preston Clark, and Mary Margaret Clark and a motherless toddler named Julia Clark Campbell for whom Clark and his wife, Julia, were then caring. See Schauinger, 116; M. J. Spalding, *Sketches of the Life, Times, and Character of the Rt. Rev. Benedict Joseph Flaget, First Bishop of Louisville*, 134–35; Foley, *Wilderness Journey*, 201, 294n16; email to author, 26 August 2008, from Robert J. Moore Jr., who has researched the baptismal records of the Old Cathedral, St. Louis.

14. Ritchey, 234.

15. Weld, 1:46–48.

16. Ibid.; La Rochefoucault-Liancourt, 3:668–70; Marion J. Kaminkow, *Maryland, A to Z: A Topographical Dictionary*, 125–26.

17. *Carey's United States Recorder*, 12 July 1798.

30 The Design of the Visit

1. Kerri S. Barile, Kerry Schamel-González, and Sean P. Maroney, "'Inferior to None in the State': The History, Archaeology, and Architecture of the Marriott Hotel Site in Fredericksburg, Virginia," 48–54.

2. Ibid.; *Index of Spotsylvania County: WPA Historical Inventory*, 1:209.

3. *Virginia Herald*, 12 October 1798.

4. *Carey's United States Recorder*, 16, 18 August 1798.

5. *DAB* 12:543–44; also J. F. Mercer to James Monroe, 9 July 1798, James Monroe Papers, LC; Tristram Dalton to John Adams, 30 July 1798, John Adams Papers, Massachusetts Historical Society.

6. JC to GRC, 31 August 1797, Draper Mss., 55J44. Mercer would soon agree to represent George; see JC to GRC, 10 November 1798, Draper Mss., 55J46.

7. Henry H. Simms, *Life of John Taylor: The Story of a Brilliant Leader in the Early Virginia State Rights School*, 65–92; Robert E. Shalhope, *John Taylor of Caroline: Pastoral Republican*, 101; Dice R. Anderson, *William Branch Giles: A Study in the Politics of Virginia and the Nation from 1790 to 1830*, 61–65; Julian Boyd et al., eds., *The Papers of Thomas Jefferson*, 30:430–35, 601–2; William E. Dodd, "John Taylor, Prophet of Secession," 223–27; *DAB* 18:331–33.

8. On Kuhn, see *Virginia Herald*, 5 January 1792, 24 March 1798; on Lewis, see Jane T. Duke, *Kenmore and the Lewises*, 183–84; Whitaker, "Reed and Forde," 246–50; Deeds dated 16 March, 30 April 1798, by which James and Ann Wilkinson conveyed to John Lewis of Fredericksburg two lots in Frankfort, Kentucky, and twenty-five hundred acres in Shelby County, Kentucky, Lewis Family Papers, Kentuckiana Collection of Reuben T. Durrett, University of Chicago.

9. Whitaker, "Reed and Forde."

10. Francis Taylor Diary, Southern Historical Collection, Library of University of North Carolina, Chapel Hill.

11. Jacobs, *Tarnished Warrior*, 178–80; Roberts, *Historic Forts*, 441.

12. Cox, "Wilkinson's First Break," 54–55; Wilkinson, *Memoirs*, 2:122, app. 8. See also Clark Sr. to Clark Jr., 2 November 1798, Gilpin Papers, HSP.

13. Jacobs, *Tarnished Warrior*, 180; Ellicott, 6; AE to JW, 6 October 1798, AE Papers.

14. Jacobs, *Tarnished Warrior*, 180–81.

15. AE to JW, 19, 23 October 1798, AE Papers; Wilkinson quoted from Syrett, 26:173–74.

16. Clark, *Proofs*, 105–13; Linklater, *Artist in Treason*, 172.

17. Clark, *Proofs*, 107–8; Elizabeth B. Drewry, "Episodes in Westward Expansion as Reflected in the Writings of General James Wilkinson, 1784–1806," 120–21; Linklater, *Artist in Treason*, 178–79.

18. Linklater, *Artist in Treason*, 178–80.

19. Ibid.

20. Cipher letter from AE to Pickering, 8 November 1798, AE Papers.

21. Ibid.

31 The End of the Journey

1. Francis Taylor Diary.

2. *Index of Spotsylvania County*, 1:207–11; John W. Herndon, "A Genealogy of the Herndon Family (Continued)," 92.

3. J. W. Kuehl, "Southern Reaction to the XYZ Affair: An Incident in the Emergence of American Nationalism," 25–27; William H. Gaines Jr., "The Forgotten Army: Recruiting for a National Emergency (1799–1800)," 267–68; Carlos E. Godfrey, "Organization of the Provisional Army of the United States in the Anticipated War with France, 1798–1800," 129–33.

4. Gaines, 267–69; Charles H. Ambler, *Sectionalism in Virginia from 1776 to 1861*, 72; Godfrey, 129–32. For proof of Edmund's patriotism and his low opinion of James Wilkinson, see Edmund Clark to George Tompkins, 17, 18 July 1807, Bodley Family Papers, Mss. A B668e, folder 236, Filson Historical Society.

5. Holmberg, 8–10; typescript of JC Diary, 1770–1811, Temple Bodley Papers, Mss. A B668, folder 56, Filson Historical Society.

6. Robert E. Gatten Jr., "The Birthplace of William Clark," 6–11; Robert E. Gatten Jr., "Clark Land in Virginia and the Birthplace of William Clark," 6–11; typescript of JC Diary, 1770–1811, Temple Bodley Papers, Mss. A B668, folder 56, Filson Historical Society.

7. John F. Dorman, "Descendants of General Jonathan Clark, Jefferson County, Kentucky, 1750–1811," 26–28. Jonathan and Sally regarded William so highly that in 1792 they asked him to serve as godfather to their daughter Ann; see Holmberg, 26.

8. Typescript of JC Diary, 1770–1811, Temple Bodley Papers, Mss. A B668, folder 56, Filson Historical Society; Francis Taylor Diary.

9. JC to GRC, 10 November 1798, Draper Mss., 55J46.

10. Holmberg, 36n10.

11. Clement L. Martzolff, "Zane's Trace," 299–300, 307–24; John C. Hunt, "The National Road," 24–26.

12. R. Douglas Hurt, *The Ohio Frontier: Crucible of the Old Northwest, 1720–1830*, 259.

13. JW to GDL, 19 November 1798, AGI, PC, leg. 2375, no. 29, fols. 2120–31; Jacobs, *Tarnished Warrior*, 181–82; Wilkinson, *Memoirs*, 2:178.

14. Holmberg, 29–30n4.

32 Not the Least Shadow of Succeeding

1. Foley, *Wilderness Journey*, 45; JC to GRC, 26 March 1799, Draper Mss., 55J48.

2. Foley, *Wilderness Journey*, 45; Holmberg, 32–33n1; Jefferson County Will Book, 1:86.

3. WC to JC, 8 June 1799, Draper Mss., 2L50.

4. James, 457; JC to GRC, 26 March 1799, Draper Mss., 55J48; Kuehl, "Southern Reaction," 25–27.

5. WC to JC, 30 July 1799, Draper Mss., 2L51; Jefferson County Will Book, 1:86.

6. WC to JC, 30 July 1799, Draper Mss., 2L51; Jefferson County Will Book, 1:86; Jefferson County Minute—Order Book, 5:180; Bodley, 358–59.

7. Clark Jr. to WC, 22 June 1800 (the shorter of two letters), WC Papers.

8. Ibid., 15 January 1800.

9. Ibid., 22 June 1800 (the longer of two letters); Whitaker, *Mississippi Question*, 162–72.

10. WC to JC, 8 June 1799, Draper Mss., 2L50; Kukla, 320–23; Whitaker, *Mississippi Question*, 250–53.

11. G. Glenn Clift, comp., *The "Corn Stalk" Militia of Kentucky, 1792–1811*, 104.

12. BS to GDL, 10 March 1799, AGI, PC, leg. 2375, no. 42. The Library of Congress erroneously attributes authorship of this letter to JW.

13. SMB to GDL, 27 February 1799, AGI, PC, leg. 2371, fols. 812–13. About Griffith, see *Report of the Select Committee, to Whom was Referred the Information Communicated to the House of Representatives, Charging Benjamin Sebastian, One of the Judges of the Court of Appeals of Kentucky, with Having Received a Pension from the Spanish Government*, 6; Franklin County Order Book B, 1798–1801, 72–73.

14. GDL to BS, 17 June 1799, AGI, PC, leg. 2375, no. 63, fols. 2239–40; Franklin County Order Book B, 72–73, 105; *Report of the Select Committee*, 6; Holmes, *Gayoso*, 265–66.

15. *Report of the Select Committee*, 3–6; Holmberg, 174–75n1.

16. Syrett, 22:452–54.

17. Elkins and McKitrick, 618–20, 732–40; Alexander DeConde, *The Quasi-War: The Politics and Diplomacy of the Undeclared War with France, 1797–1801*, 259–64, 270–72.

18. Whitaker, *Mississippi Question*, 124–25; GDL to BS, 17 June 1799, AGI, PC, leg. 2375, no. 63, fols. 2239–40.

19. Whitaker, *Spanish–American Frontier*, 212.

20. DeConde, 121–23; Whitaker, *Mississippi Question*, 124–25; Jacobs, *Tarnished Warrior*, 190; Caldwell, "Cantonment Wilkinsonville," 8–11.

21. DeConde, 122–23; Whitaker, *Mississippi Question*, 127–29.

22. Caldwell, "Cantonment Wilkinsonville," 3–10; David P. Mayer, "Cantonment Wilkinsonville, 1801: Burr, Wilkinson, the U.S. Army, and Treason"; Mark Wagner, "Searching for Cantonment Wilkinsonville."

23. Jacobs, *Tarnished Warrior*, 191–93.

24. Elkins and McKitrick, 735–36; Jacobs, *U.S. Army*, 235–36.

25. Linklater, *Artist in Treason*, 188–89; Jackson, *Thomas Jefferson*, 100; Jacobs, *U.S. Army*, 240.

26. Jacobs, *U.S. Army*, 239–41; Linklater, *Artist in Treason*, 189.

33 The Sport of Fortune

1. Mayer, 3–6; Caldwell, "Cantonment Wilkinsonville," 3.

2. Mayer, 13–17.

3. Linklater, *Artist in Treason*, 191–92; Theodore J. Crackel, *Mr. Jefferson's Army: Political and Social Reform of the Military Establishment, 1801–1809*, 38–39; Wilkinson, Order Book, RG 94, NARA; Jacobs, *Tarnished Warrior*, 195; Mayer, 6–9.

4. Jackson, *Letters*, 1:1–4; Ambrose, 59–61; Danisi and Jackson, 38–39.

5. "Opinion for M. Wm. Clarke" by J. Hughes, 16 May 1801; Daniel Symmes to WC, 1 June 1801. These documents and others concerning the Bazadone case are in the possession of Peyton ("Bud") Clark. See also JC to GRC, 7 July 1801, Draper Mss., 55J53.

6. John Preston to Francis Preston, 8 August 1793, Preston Family Papers, Special Collections Research Center, College of William and Mary; Holmberg, 125n8, 133–34n5. On Clark's meeting his future wives, see Jones, 107–8. See also a loosely organized collection of family lore, some of it about the Clarks, based on stories passed down by Kennerly, WC's stepson. William C. Kennerly and Elizabeth Russell, *Persimmon Hill: A Narrative of Old St. Louis and the Far West*, 14.

7. In a letter of 2 July 1801, John T. Mason provides the instruction Clark had requested; in the private collection of Peyton ("Bud") Clark. In 1808 and 1809, as superintendant of the Indian Trade, Mason was to help WC become his St. Louis agent. See Holmberg, 199n6.

8. If such a meeting ever took place, Clark must have learned that Coxe had lately sold the brig *Friendship* but lost the ship *Star* in May 1799 when a hired

Spanish pilot ran her aground in the Mississippi delta, not far from where Coxe had been arrested the previous year for (among other malefactions) failing to hire a Spanish pilot. After salvaging cargoes of paint, frying pans, stills, chairs, garments, and kegs of wine, the crew abandoned the *Star* to slow destruction by natural forces. Entry 1119, Proofs of Ownership for Registered Vessels 1790–1802, 8:63, 66, RG 36, NARA; Ronquillo to Juan Ventura Morales, 13 May 1799, and salvage records kept by Ronquillo from 7 to 14 May 1799, all in AGI, PC, leg. 590, fols. 945–50. See also Johnson, "Journal," 40.

Having insured *Star* against only the risk of capture by French privateers, Coxe fraudulently reported that she fell victim at sea to the aggression of an unknown French ship. He thereby collected to the limits of his policy. This ruse led to a dispute lasting more than a century, as the underwriter and his heirs (lacking knowledge of what really happened) sued the French Republic for indemnification. See "Bayard L. Peck, Administrator d.b.n. of the Estate of Peter Elting, deceased, against the United States," French Spoliation case 4585, RG 123, NARA. The grounding of the *Star* also intensified a power struggle between Governor Gayoso and Acting Intendant Morales. See Morales to Soler, 31 May, 10 July 1799, Audiencia de Santo Domingo, leg. 2615, nos. 28, 31.

Once Clark Jr. became U.S. consul at New Orleans, he called the grounding of the *Star* "shameful beyond description," adding that "everything which could be, was plundered." Whitaker, "Despatches," 819.

9. Ellicott, 298–300. On the voyage to Philadelphia with Ellicott went the prostitute Betsy, who became demented at sea and would have killed herself had his assistants not prevented her from doing so. After landing, one of them wrote that Betsy's derangement having persisted, she was "frantic, and chained in a mad house." Claiborne, 197–98.

10. Linklater, *Fabric of America,* 160; Boyd et al., 34:248–51.

11. Boyd et al., 33:371–72, 580–82, also 34:118–21, 183–85, 248–51; Linklater, *Artist in Treason,* 192–93.

12. Before Jefferson became president, Ellicott gave voice to federalist views, at one point calling the Adams administration "political perfection." AE to WS, 20 October 1798, AE Papers; Boyd et al., 34:419–20; Clark, *Proofs,* 129.

13. Clark, *Proofs,* 124–32. Ellicott's account of his conversation with the Portells is in Ellicott, 239–40.

14. Whitaker, *Mississippi Question,* 103–4; Jackson, *Thomas Jefferson,* 99–100; Flores, 80–81.

15. Donald Jackson, "Jefferson, Meriwether Lewis, and the Reduction of the United States Army," 91–96; "Officers Roster," 24 July 1801, fols. 19697–705, Thomas Jefferson Papers, LC; Boyd et al., 34:629–30.

16. Meriwether Lewis to WC, 27 June 1801, WC Papers.

17. Bodley, 238; Ambrose, 68–71. As to Jefferson's subsequent assertion that, in 1792, the teenaged Lewis had sought the assignment Jefferson gave instead to Michaux, see Jackson, *Thomas Jefferson*, 156–57n3.

18. See WC to Mason, 5 July 1801, Mason to WC, 2 July 1801, photocopies in Clark Family Collection, reference files, box 2, folder 1, Missouri History Museum.

19. Holmberg, 30–34; Daniel Symmes to WC, 1 June 1801, private collection of Peyton "Bud" Clark.

20. Holmberg, 30–34 (32).

21. Ibid., 30.

34 Any Post of Honor and Profit

1. Holmberg, 32, 35n8.

2. On the purchase of Trough Spring, see three promissory notes to Allen Campbell, due 25 December 1802, WC Papers; "An Account of William Clark with Jonathan Clark," ibid.; Holmberg, 38–40, 47n4. Though he would make at least six future journeys to the East, Clark, as far as we know, would keep just one more personal account of his travels, doing so in 1809. We can only wonder whether his learning about the violent death of Meriwether Lewis during that journey helped persuade Clark not to continue chronicling travels.

3. Mason to WC, 23 December 1801, from private collection of Peyton ("Bud") Clark.

4. Jackson, "Reduction of the U.S. Army"; Crackel, 48–53, 196n35; Boyd et al., 36:42–48, 416.

5. Holmberg, 40–47.

6. Ibid., 45, 54n29, 177–78n8; Potts and Thomas, 83–84; James, 458–60.

7. Draper Mss., 61J246–47; Lynn S. Renau, *So Close from Home: The Legacy of Brownsboro Road*, 277.

8. Jackson, *Letters*, 1:7–8. See also Dearborn to WC, 6 July 1802, J. W. Tweedale to Lyman Draper, 9 February 1887, fols. 39, 38, at http://wardepartmentpapers.org.

9. *State Papers and Correspondence Bearing Upon the Purchase of the Territory of Louisiana*, 15–18; Kukla, 230–34, 239–45; Whitaker, *Mississippi Question*, 189, 192–94.

10. Kukla, 246–48, 257–59, 269–83. For specifics on the extent and price of the Purchase, see ibid., 335, 415n6.

11. Jackson, *Thomas Jefferson*, 126–27, 132–37.

12. We can assume that Jefferson's instructions to Lewis applied as well to Clark. See Jackson, *Letters,* 1:61–66. Ernest S. Osgood, ed., *The Field Notes of Captain William Clark, 1803–1805*, 191–326, contains facsimiles and measurements of the sixty-seven documents used for this purpose. None of them matches the dimensions of the pages in Clark's Mississippi Journal.

13. *Report of the Select Committee*, 3–6.

14. Ibid., 4.

15. John Seitz to BS, 11, 27 March, 10 April 1804, Minor to BS, 12 May 1804, BS Papers.

16. Isaac J. Cox, "General Wilkinson and His Later Intrigues with the Spaniards," 794–812; Linklater, *Artist in Treason*, 199–201, 206–8; Jacobs, *Tarnished Warrior,* 205–6.

17. Cox, "General Wilkinson." Although the "Reflections" (in Robertson, 2:325–47) are attributed to Folch, it has since been determined that they were written by Wilkinson. See Cox, "General Wilkinson," 798n11, sup.

18. The Spanish failed to halt the Lewis and Clark Expedition, but Wilkinson's warning helped doom other western explorations (especially those of Zebulon M. Pike and of the Thomas Freeman–Peter Custis tour of the Red River) and no doubt led indirectly to the lack of congressional funding for the planned journey of Dunbar and Freeman up the Arkansas River. See Jackson, *Thomas Jefferson*, 153–54, 226–36, 250–54.

35 A Distant and Splendid Enterprise

1. Jackson, *Letters*, 1:60, 112.

2. Moulton, 8:346–48.

3. *Western World*, 11 October 1806. The words "United they stand—but divided they fall" appear in italics, in sharp contrast with the regular type used in reproducing nearly all of the approximately two hundred words in the seventeen other toasts quoted in that story.

4. Jacobs, *Tarnished Warrior,* 229–31.

5. Ibid.; Flores, 54n76, 77–81.

6. Holmberg, 101–18.

7. Thomas P. Abernethy, *The Burr Conspiracy*, 92–95.

8. Ibid., 88–92. For J. H. Daveiss's lively account of his one-sided correspondence with Jefferson, see "A View of the President's Conduct Concerning the Conspiracy of 1806," 68–96.

9. Abernethy, 92–93; Foley, *Genesis of Missouri*, 162–74.

10. *Western World*, 23, 30 August, 13 September, 27 September through 8 November 1806.

11. Holmberg, 116; *Western World*, 11 October 1806.

12. Holmberg, 116–17n2; Daveiss, 98–101; Abernethy, 95–97.

13. Holmberg, 122n1.

14. Warren, 122; Abernethy, 94; BS to James Brown, 16 October 1806, BS Papers. Brown, a lawyer in New Orleans, was a brother of onetime conspirator John Brown. The results of Littell's effort was *Political Transactions in and Concerning Kentucky.* See Marshall, *History of Kentucky,* 2:379–80, concerning the broadside; Thomas M. Green, *The Spanish Conspiracy. A Review of Early Spanish Movements in the South-West*, 353–54.

15. As it turned out, Lewis and the Mandans departed Frankfort on the southern route to Virginia while the Osages, led by their agent, Jean Pierre Chouteau, followed a more northerly path, which included Lexington, Kentucky. Holmberg, 122n1.

36 Standing High with Mr. Jefferson

1. Daveiss, 98; Abernethy, 95–96.

2. Samuel M. Wilson, ed., "The Court Proceedings of 1806 in Kentucky against Aaron Burr and John Adair," 32–36; Abernethy, 95–97.

3. Wilson, 32–36; Abernethy, 96. Davis Floyd was brother to Charles Floyd, the only member of the Corps of Discovery to die during the western exploration. Davis and his family were well known to and friends with the Clarks. Holmberg, 159n8.

4. *Western World*, 15 November 1806. The story about the arrival of Lewis and the Indians at last appeared in the 22 November 1806 issue of the newspaper, but it consisted of a mere three sentences lifted from rival papers and was buried on

a back page. See also the *Kentucky Gazette and General Advertiser,* 17 November 1806.

5. BS to Speaker of the House of Representatives, undated; 24 November 1806 resolution in the House of Representatives to investigate Sebastian; BS to Governor of Kentucky, undated; 27 November 1806 resolution in the House of Representatives to deny Sebastian's request for a postponement, all in BS Papers.

6. *Report of the Select Committee,* 3–6, Holmberg, 132n2.

7. *Report of the Select Committee,* 6–8; Warren, 122–23; Isaac J. Cox, ed., "Letters of William T. Barry, 1806–1810, 1829–1831," 328. Thomas Power was among the courtroom spectators. He said afterward that, although Innes spoke truthfully, he put Power "in a disagreeable situation." See Thos. Bodley's statement of 5 January 1808, Durrett Collection, University of Chicago.

8. Cox, "Letters of William T. Barry," 328; undated report of House of Representatives finding Sebastian guilty, BS Papers; Warren, 125.

9. Leslie Henshaw, "The Aaron Burr Conspiracy in the Ohio Valley," 131.

10. Aaron Burr to Samuel Gwathmey, Draper Mss., 10J215; Isaac J. Cox, "The Burr Conspiracy in Indiana," 263–65; Potts and Thomas, 81–82.

11. Abernethy, 53–55; Flores, 77–85; John Dos Passos, "The Conspiracy and Trial of Aaron Burr," 74–75.

12. David O. Stewart, *American Emperor: Aaron Burr's Challenge to Jefferson's America,* 159–65; Abernethy, 148–52; Walter F. McCaleb, *The Aaron Burr Conspiracy,* 138–46.

13. *Annals of Congress,* House of Representatives, 9th Congress, 2nd session, appendix, 686–87.

14. Abernethy, 97–100; Wilson, 37–40; Warren, 124.

15. Daveiss, 104; Stewart, 172.

16. Daveiss, 103–4; Abernethy, 108–10; Stewart, 180; *Western World,* 25 December 1806; WC to Croghan, 14 December 1806, Croghan Papers, HSP; Holmberg, 122n1.

17. Holmberg, 119, 122–26; Jones, 154–55; Foley, *Wilderness Journey,* 155–56.

18. Abernethy, 113–18; Stewart, 182–85, 193–95.

19. *Annals of Congress,* House of Representatives, 9th Congress, 2nd session, 334–59; Stewart, 211.

20. Holmberg, 119, 122n1; Danisi and Jackson, 131–32. On Clark's courtly attention to the "fair creatures," see Jackson, *Letters,* 2:694–95.

21. Thomas Jefferson, *The Writings of Thomas Jefferson,* 3:427–37; Wilkinson, *Memoirs,* 2:app. 100; Jacobs, *Tarnished Warrior,* 231–33; Stewart, 188.

22. Jefferson, 3:427–37; Holmberg, 119, 122, 123–24n4.

23. Stewart, 188, 198–203; Herbert S. Parmet and Marie B. Hecht, *Aaron Burr: Portrait of an Ambitious Man*, 280–84; Jones, 155–56; Foley, *Wilderness Journey*, 157–59; Ambrose, 413–16; Holmberg, 119.

24. *Annals of Congress*, Senate, 10th Congress, 1st session, 589–605; Abernethy, 251–53; Jacobs, *Tarnished Warrior*, 218, 226. See also Clarence E. Carter, "The Burr-Wilkinson Intrigue in St. Louis," 450–54.

25. *Annals of Congress*, Senate, 10th Congress, 1st session, 589–605. Clarence E. Carter, "The Burr-Wilkinson Intrigue in St. Louis," 450–54.

26. On setting in motion the first phase of the Conspiracy with Spain, Wilkinson asserted that "interest is the ruling passion of Nations, as well as of individuals, and he who imputes a different motive to human conduct either deceives himself or means to deceive others." Christian, 95.

27. Jackson, *Letters*, 2:377–78, 382–83, 387; Jones, 155–56; Foley, *Wilderness Journey*, 157–59, 287n75. On Clark and his adherence to the principles of Democratic-Republicanism, see Jerome O. Steffen, *William Clark: Jeffersonian Man on the Frontier*.

Epilogue: The Mammoth of Iniquity Escaped

1. For details on how Wilkinson insinuated himself with George Washington, Alexander Hamilton, Thomas Jefferson, and other prominent contemporaries, see Roger Kennedy, *Hidden Cities: The Discovery and Loss of Ancient North American Civilization*, 152–56.

2. Abernethy, 230; McCaleb, 310; Arthur M. Schlesinger and Roger Bruns, eds., *Congress Investigates: A Documented History, 1792–1974*, 1:112; Joseph Wheelan, *Jefferson's Vendetta: The Pursuit of Aaron Burr and the Judiciary*, 102–3; Stewart, 233; Danisi and Jackson, 183–85.

3. Wheelan, 102–5; Stewart, 234–36.

4. Abernethy, 238–40; Stewart, 238–40; Dos Passos, 81. Among the many spectators in the courtroom was Washington Irving, who later lampooned Wilkinson in *Diedrich Knickerbocker's History of New York, from the Beginning of the World to the End of the Dutch Dynasty.*

5. Stewart, 240–41. See also William C. Bruce, *John Randolph of Roanoke, 1773–1833*, 1:303–4; John Randolph to Joseph Nicholson, 25 June 1807, Nicholson Papers, LC.

6. Stewart, 242, 247–58, 260–63.

7. Ibid., 259–70; Abernethy, 250–60; Wheelan, 247–56.

8. Schlesinger and Bruns, 1:113–15.

9. Ibid., 115–17; Jacobs (*Tarnished Warrior*, 269–71) shows how this affidavit, so useful to Wilkinson after the Aaron Burr trials, came about in 1796 through the help of Thomas Power. Wilkinson, *Memoirs*, 2:12–13.

10. Schlesinger and Bruns, 1:117; Linklater, *Artist in Treason*, 280–87.

11. Schlesinger and Bruns, 1:117–19; Linklater, *Artist in Treason*, 288–92; Jacobs, *Tarnished Warrior*, 263.

12. Schlesinger and Bruns, 1:119–20; Jacobs, *Tarnished Warrior*, 263–65.

13. Jacobs, *Tarnished Warrior*, 264–67; Linklater, *Artist in Treason*, 291–92.

14. Jacobs, *Tarnished Warrior*, 267–71.

15. Ibid., 269.

16. Ibid.; Linklater, *Artist in Treason*, 292–93; Wilkinson, *Memoirs*, 2:app. 32.

17. Jacobs, *Tarnished Warrior*, 274.

18. Ibid., 284–315; Linklater, *Artist in Treason*, 302–15.

19. Jacobs, *Tarnished Warrior*, 316–40; Linklater, *Artist in Treason*, 317–28; Flores, 51n71; *DAB* 20:222–26.

20. Thomas Power is listed as a resident of the city in New Orleans directories 1805, 1822, 1823.

21. Alexander, 1–4, 25–27, 50–57, 124–26; Wohl, 33–41, 190–203; Perry S. Rader, "The Romance of the American Courts: Gaines vs. New Orleans," 18–23.

22. *DAB* 6:89–90.

23. *DAB* 7:13–14; Roberts, "Thomas Freeman," 220–30; Flores, 311–16.

Appendix B Our Clark Relics: The Curious Path of the Journal, from Clark to the Present

1. Accession information about the 1798–1801 Notebook (Item C/1075) is in the WCB Collection, SHSMO.

2. Foley, *Wilderness Journey*, 166–67, 174; Jones, 164; Glen E. Holt, "After the Journey Was Over: The St. Louis Years of Lewis and Clark," 44.

3. Foley, *Wilderness Journey*, 174, 232–33; Jones, 237; Holt, 44; John F. Mc-Dermott, "Museums in Early St. Louis," 129–33.

4. Potts and Thomas, 63, 195n44. As to Clark's keeping his private papers in an old desk, see Reuben G. Thwaites, "The Story of Lewis and Clark's Journals," 127.

5. Genealogical details about Clark and his wives and descendants are from the late Frances Galt Schweig, a descendant of Clark's sister Frances.

6. Kennerly and Russell, 56–57, 180–81; Foley, *Wilderness Journey*, 246, 262–63; Frances H. Stadler, "Letters from Minoma," 238; Paul R. Cutright, *A History of the Lewis and Clark Journals*, 118. A miniature watercolor portrait painted by George Catlin and owned by Peyton ("Bud") Clark bears the caption "Wm. Preston Clark as Iago, 1831. Phil. Pa. G.C." See also Foley, "A Family's Ordeal: The Troubling Case of William Preston Clark."

7. WC's last will and testament, Missouri State Archives; Jackson, *Letters*, 2:623; Cutright, *History*, 69–71, 118–19; Schweig genealogical records; Charles Van Ravenswaay, *St. Louis: An Informal History of the City and Its People, 1764–1865*, 319.

8. Schweig genealogical records; Stadler, 238, 243.

9. Item C/1075 in WCB Collection, SHSMO.

10. Items C/1074, C/1076, C/1077, C/1078, ibid.; Moulton, 2:564–65.

11. Stadler, 249–59.

12. Schweig genealogical records. Several references to the children of George and Ellen Clark are in Stadler.

13. Mary Bartley, *St. Louis Lost*, 176–78; *St. Louis Star-Times*, 19 July 1937.

14. Stadler; Schweig genealogical records; William Hancock Clark (WHC) to Eva Emory Dye (EED), 10 May 1905, EED Papers, Oregon Historical Society.

15. *St. Louis Post-Dispatch*, 20 March 1892.

16. Ibid.; general warranty deed from Jefferson K. and Mary S. Clark to Edgewood Park Association, 19 September 1891, box 58, pp. 240–42, St. Louis County Recorder of Deeds.

17. Snow, 37–38; telephone conversation with Peyton ("Bud") Clark on 5 January 2005; *St. Louis Post-Dispatch*, 18 February 1923; Julia Clark Voorhis, file P-426 (1923), Surrogate's Court, County of New York.

18. WHC to EED, 14 April 1901, WHC to George Himes, 8 July 1901, WHC to EED, 10 May 1905, EED Papers, Oregon Historical Society; Codicil of 16 November 1896, Estate of Jefferson K. Clark, City of St. Louis Probate Court.

19. It seems that Julia's brother John O'Fallon Clark also inherited certain historical things. See WHC to EED, 10 May 1905, EED Papers, Oregon Historical Society; Snow, 37–38; Estate of Jefferson K. Clark, City of St. Louis Probate Court.

20. Cutright, *History*, 117–26.

21. Snow, 37–38; Schweig genealogical records; Julia Clark Voorhis, file P-426 (1923), Surrogate's Court, County of New York; *New York Times*, 24 January 1922.

22. Snow, 37–38. Information on the accession of the Eleanor Glasgow Voorhis Collection is in the Clark Family Collection, Missouri History Museum. See also the 25 November 1923 issues of *St. Louis Post-Dispatch* and *St. Louis Globe-Democrat*.

23. See index cards prepared by WCB for items C/1074–C/1078, in the WCB Collection at SHSMO. Alexander N. DeMenil, "Memoirs of Deceased Members of the Society," 124–27.

24. DeMenil, 124–27; Floyd Shoemaker to George Mahan, 8 February 1928, WCB Collection, C/1036, SHSMO.

25. WCB Collection, C/1036, SHSMO; Petition for Order of Partial Distribution, 4 June 1928, Estate of WCB, No. 66595, City of St. Louis Probate Court.

26. Bartley; *St. Louis Star-Times*, 19 July 1937; Holmberg, 26–27n18.

27. *St. Louis Globe-Democrat*, 3 February 1960; clipping from *St. Louis Post-Dispatch*, date uncertain, in "Historic Houses Scrapbooks," vol. 7, Missouri History Museum.

28. *National Union Catalog of Manuscript Collections*, 1964, 87–88.

29. John Logan Allen, *Passage through the Garden: Lewis and Clark and the Image of the American Northwest*, 340; Jackson, *Letters*, 2:724–26, 738; Steffen, 3–4, 11, 15.

30. Holmberg, 28–40; Foley, *Wilderness Journey*, 43–45, 46–47; Jones, 98–108; Buckley.

Appendix C Buried in the Womb of Time
Spanish Sources of This Story

1. Christian, 99.

2. Roscoe R. Hill, *Descriptive Catalogue of the Documents relating to the History of the United States in the Papeles Procedentes de Cuba deposited in the Archivo General de Indias at Seville*, xiii–xviii.

3. Ibid., xviii–xix.

4. Ibid., xx–xxi.

5. Ibid., xx–xxii.

6. Ibid., ix, xi; G. Douglas Inglis of the Texas Tech University Center in Seville, Spain, to author, e-mails dated 30 January, 17 February 2014.

7. Hill, xi.

8. Ibid., viii, xxiv.

9. Ibid., vii–ix, xxiv–xxv. See also William R. Shepherd, *Guide to the Materials for the History of the United States in the Spanish Archives (Simancas, the Archivo Historico Nacional, and Seville)*, 77–78.

Bibliography

Books

Abernethy, Thomas Perkins. *The Burr Conspiracy.* New York: Oxford University Press, 1954.

Alexander, Elizabeth Urban. *Notorious Woman: The Celebrated Case of Myra Clark Gaines.* Baton Rouge: Louisiana State University Press, 2001.

Allen, John Logan. *Passage through the Garden: Lewis and Clark and the Image of the American Northwest.* Urbana: University of Illinois Press, 1975.

Allen, Michael. *Western Rivermen, 1763–1861: Ohio and Mississippi Boatmen and the Myth of the Alligator Horse.* Baton Rouge: Louisiana State University Press, 1990.

Ambler, Charles Henry. *Sectionalism in Virginia from 1776 to 1861.* Chicago: University of Chicago Press, 1910.

Ambrose, Stephen. *Undaunted Courage: Meriwether Lewis, Thomas Jefferson, and the Opening of the American West.* New York: Simon and Schuster, 1996.

Anderson, Dice Robins. William Branch Giles: *A Study in the Politics of Virginia and the Nation from 1790 to 1830.* Gloucester, Mass.: Peter Smith, 1965.

Arnebeck, Bob. *Through a Fiery Trial: Building Washington, 1790–1800.* Lanham. Md.: Madison Books, 1991.

Ashe, Thomas. *Travels in America Performed in 1806, for the Purpose of Exploring the Rivers Alleghany, Monongahela, Ohio, and Mississippi, and Ascertaining the Produce and Condition of their Banks and Vicinity.* 3 vols. London: John Abraham, 1808.

Atkinson, James R. *Splendid Land, Splendid People: The Chickasaw Indians to Removal.* Tuscaloosa: University of Alabama Press, 2004.

Baily, Francis. *Journal of a Tour in Unsettled Parts of North America in 1796 & 1797.* Edited by Jack D. L. Holmes. Carbondale: Southern Illinois University Press, 1969.

Balletta, Patricia Wilkinson Weaver, ed., T*he Wilkinson Book: Being the Ancestry & Descendants of Major General James Wilkinson of Calvert County, Maryland et ux Ann Biddle of Philadelphia, Pa.* Wyandotte, OK: Gregath Publishing, 1994.

Bartley, Mary. *St. Louis Lost.* St. Louis: Virginia Publishing, 1998.

Biddle, Nicholas, ed. *History of the expedition under the command of Captains Lewis and Clark, to the Sources of the Missouri, thence across the Rocky Mountains and down the River Columbia to the Pacific Ocean. Performed during the years 1804–5–6. By order of the government of the United States.* 2 vols. Philadelphia: Paul Allen, 1814.

Bodley, Temple. *George Rogers Clark: His Life and Public Services.* Boston: Houghton Mifflin, 1926.

Boyd, Julian P., et al., eds. *The Papers of Thomas Jefferson.* 41 vols. to date. Princeton: Princeton University Press, 1950– .

Brown, Jo Ann. *St. Charles Borromeo: 200 Years of Faith.* St. Louis: The Patrice Press, 1991.

Bruce, William C. *John Randolph of Roanoke, 1773–1833.* New York: G. P. Putnam's Sons, 1922.

Buckley, Jay H. *William Clark: Indian Diplomat.* Norman: University of Oklahoma Press, 2008.

Carroll, John. *The John Carroll Papers.* 3 vols. Edited by Thomas O. Hanley. South Bend, Ind.: University of Notre Dame Press, 1976.

Carson, James Taylor. *Searching for the Bright Path: The Mississippi Choctaws from Prehistory to Removal.* Lincoln: University of Nebraska Press, 1999.

Carstens, Kenneth C., and Nancy Son Carstens, eds. *The Life of George Rogers Clark, 1752–1818: Triumphs and Tragedies.* Westport, Conn.: Praeger, 2004.

Cassell, Frank A. *Merchant Congressman in the Young Republic: Samuel Smith of Maryland, 1752–1839.* Madison: University of Wisconsin Press, 1971.

Claiborne, J. F. H. *Mississippi as a Province, Territory, and State, with Biographical Notices of Eminent Citizens.* Vol. 1. 1880. Reprint, Baton Rouge: Louisiana State Press, 1964.

Clark, Daniel. *Proofs of the Corruption of Gen. James Wilkinson, and of His Connexion with Aaron Burr, with a Full Refutation of His Slanderous Allegations in Relation to the Character of the Principal Witness against Him.* Philadelphia: Hall & Pierie Printers, 1809.

Clark, John G. *New Orleans, 1718–1812: An Economic History.* Baton Rouge: Louisiana State University Press, 1970.

Clark, William Bell. *Gallant John Barry, 1745–1803: The Story of a Naval Hero of Two Wars.* New York: Macmillan, 1938.

Clift, G. Glenn, comp. *The "Corn Stalk" Militia of Kentucky, 1792–1811.* Frankfort: Kentucky Historical Society, 1957.

Coker, William S., and Thomas D. Watson. *Indian Traders of the Southeastern Spanish Borderlands: Panton, Leslie & Company and John Forbes & Company, 1783–1847.* Gainesville: University Presses of Florida; Pensacola: University of West Florida Press, 1986.

Collot, Georges Henri Victor. *A Journey in North America.* 2 vols. and atlas. 1826. Reprint, New York: AMS Press, 1974.

Condie, Thomas, and Richard Folwell. *History of the Pestilence, Commonly Called Yellow Fever, Which Almost Desolated Philadelphia in the Months of August, September, and October, 1798.* Philadelphia: Richard Folwell, 1799.

Cooke, Jacob E. *Tench Coxe and the Early Republic.* Chapel Hill: University of North Carolina Press, 1978.

Cox, Isaac J. *The West Florida Controversy, 1798–1813: A Study in American Diplomacy.* 1918. Reprint, Gloucester, Mass.: Peter Smith, 1967.

Crackel, Theodore J. *Mr. Jefferson's Army: Political and Social Reform of the Military Establishment, 1801–1809.* New York: New York University Press, 1987.

Cramer, Zadok. *The Navigator.* 1814. Reprint, Ann Arbor, Mich.: University Microforms, 1966.

Cuming, Fortescue. *Sketches of a Tour to the Western Country, Through the States of Ohio and Kentucky, 1807–1809.* In *Early Western Travels, 1748–1846.* Vol. 4, edited by Reuben Gold Thwaites. 1904. Reprint, New York: AMS Press, 1966.

Cutright, Paul Russell. *A History of the Lewis and Clark Journals.* Norman: University of Oklahoma Press, 1976.

————. *Lewis and Clark: Pioneering Naturalists.* Urbana: University of Illinois Press, 1969.

Danisi, Thomas C. *Uncovering the Truth about Meriwether Lewis.* Amherst, New York: Prometheus Books, 2012.

Danisi, Thomas C., and John C. Jackson. *Meriwether Lewis.* Amherst, New York: Prometheus Books, 2009.

De Brahm, William Gerard. *The Atlantic Pilot.* London: T. Spilsbury, 1772.

DeConde, Alexander. *The Quasi-War: The Politics and Diplomacy of the Undeclared War with France, 1797–1801.* New York: Charles Scribner's Sons, 1966.

Derosier, Arthur H., Jr. *The Removal of the Choctaw Indians.* Knoxville: University of Tennessee Press, 1970.

Douglas, Walter B. *Manuel Lisa.* New York: Argosy-Antiquarian LTD., 1964.

Duke, Jane Taylor. *Kenmore and the Lewises.* Garden City, New York: Doubleday, 1949.

Du Lac, M. Perrin. *Travels Through the Two Louisianas, and Among the Savage Nations of the Missouri; also, in the United States, along the Ohio, and the Adjacent Provinces, in 1801, 1802, & 1803.* Translated from the French. London: J. G. Barnard, 1807.

Ekberg, Carl J. *Colonial Ste. Genevieve: An Adventure on the Mississippi Frontier.* Gerald, Mo: The Patrice Press, 1985.

Elkins, Stanley, and Eric McKitrick. *The Age of Federalism.* New York: Oxford University Press, 1993.

Ellicott, Andrew. *The Journal of Andrew Ellicott.* 1803. Reprint, Chicago: Quadrangle Books, 1962.

Foley, William E. *The Genesis of Missouri: From Wilderness Outpost to Statehood.* Columbia: University of Missouri Press, 1989.

————. *Wilderness Journey: The Life of William Clark*. Columbia: University of Missouri Press, 2004.

Flores, Dan L., ed. *Jefferson and Southwestern Exploration: The Freeman and Custis Accounts of the Red River Expedition of 1806*. Norman: University of Oklahoma Press, 1984.

Gaff, Alan D. *Bayonets in the Wilderness: Anthony Wayne's Legion in the Old Northwest*. Norman: University of Oklahoma Press, 2004.

Green, Thomas Marshall. *The Spanish Conspiracy. A Review of Early Spanish Movements in the South-West*. Cincinnati: Robert Clarke & Co., 1891.

Hay, Thomas Robson and Werner, M. R. *The Admirable Trumpeter: A Biography of General James Wilkinson*. Garden City, N. Y.: Doubleday, Doran, 1941.

Heitman, Francis B. *Historical Register and Dictionary of the United States Army*. 2 vols. Washington, DC: USGPO, 1903.

Henri, Florette. *The Southern Indians and Benjamin Hawkins, 1796–1816*. Norman: University of Oklahoma Press, 1986.

Hill, Roscoe R. *Descriptive Catalogue of the Documents relating to the History of the United States in the Papeles Procedentes de Cuba deposited in the Archivo General de Indias at Seville*. Washington, DC: Carnegie Institution of Washington, 1916.

Holmberg, James J., ed. *Dear Brother: Letters of William Clark to Jonathan Clark*. New Haven, Conn.: Yale University Press, 2002.

Holmes, Jack D. L. Gayoso: *The Life of a Spanish Governor in the Mississippi Valley, 1789–1799*. 1965. Reprint, Gloucester, Mass.: Peter Smith, 1968.

Houck, Louis. *A History of Missouri*. 3 vols. Chicago: R. R. Donnelley and Sons, 1908.

Hurt, R. Douglas. *The Ohio Frontier: Crucible of the Old Northwest, 1720–1830*. Bloomington: Indiana University Press, 1996.

Irving, Washington. *Diedrich Knickerbocker's History of New-York, from the Beginning of the World to the End of the Dutch Dynasty*. 1809. 2 vols. Reprint, New York: Putnam, ca. 1880.

Jackson, Donald, ed. *Letters of the Lewis and Clark Expedition with Related Documents, 1783–1854.* 2 vols. Revised edition, Urbana: University of Illinois Press, 1978.

———. *Thomas Jefferson and the Stony Mountains: Exploring the West from Monticello.* Urbana: University of Illinois Press, 1981.

Jacobs, James Ripley. *The Beginning of the U.S. Army, 1783–1812.* Port Washington, N.Y.: Kennikat Press, 1947.

———. *Tarnished Warrior: Major-General James Wilkinson.* New York: Macmillan, 1938.

James, James Alton. *The Life of George Rogers Clark.* Chicago: University of Chicago Press, 1928.

Jefferson, Thomas. *The Writings of Thomas Jefferson.* Vol. 3. Edited by Andrew A. Lipscomb. Washington, DC: The Thomas Jefferson Memorial Association of the United States, 1904.

Johnson, Allen, and Dumas Malone, eds. *Dictionary of American Biography.* 20 vols. New York: Charles Scribner's Sons, 1958–1964.

Jones, Landon Y. *William Clark and the Shaping of the West.* New York: Hill and Wang, 2004.

Kaminkow, Marion J. *Maryland, A to Z: A Topographical Dictionary.* Baltimore: Magna Carta Book, 1985.

Kastor, Peter J. *William Clark's World: Describing America in an Age of Unknowns.* New Haven, Conn.: Yale University Press, 2011.

Kennedy, Roger G. *Hidden Cities: The Discovery and Loss of Ancient North American Civilization.* New York: Free Press, 1994.

Kennerly, William Clark, and Elizabeth Russell. *Persimmon Hill: A Narrative of Old St. Louis and the Far West.* Norman: University of Oklahoma Press, 1948.

Kleber, John E., ed. *The Kentucky Encyclopedia.* Lexington: University Press of Kentucky, 1992.

Knopf, Richard C., ed. *Anthony Wayne, a Name in Arms: Soldier, Diplomat, Defender of Expansion Westward of a Nation.* Pittsburgh: University of Pittsburgh Press, 1960.

Kukla, Jon. *A Wilderness So Immense: The Louisiana Purchase and the Destiny of America.* New York: Alfred A. Knopf, 2003.

La Rochefoucault-Liancourt, Duke de. *Travels through the United States of North America, the Country of the Iroquois, and Upper Canada, in the Years 1795, 1796, and 1797, with an Authentic Account of Lower Canada.* 4 vols. London: R. Phillips, 1799.

Le Gardeur, René J., Jr. *The First New Orleans Theatre, 1792–1803.* New Orleans: Leeward Books, 1963.

Levin, H., ed. *The Lawyers and Lawmakers of Kentucky.* Chicago: Lewis Publishing, 1916.

Linklater, Andro. *An Artist in Treason: The Extraordinary Double Life of General James Wilkinson.* New York: Walker, 2009.

———. *The Fabric of America: How Our Borders and Boundaries Shaped the Country and Forged Our National Identity.* Walker, 2007.

Littell, William. *Reprints of Littell's Political Transactions in and concerning Kentucky and Letter of George Nicholas to his Friend in Virginia: also General Wilkinson's Memorial.* Louisville: J. P. Morton, 1926.

Ludington, M. I. *Uniform of the Army of the United States (Illustrated), From 1774 to 1889.* New York: American Lithographic, 1890–1909.

Marshall, Humphrey. *The History of Kentucky.* 2 vols. Frankfort: G. S. Robinson, 1824.

Mathews, Catharine Van Cortlandt. *Andrew Ellicott: His Life and Letters.* New York: Grafton Press, 1908.

McCaleb, Walter Flavius. *The Aaron Burr Conspiracy.* New York: Wilson-Erickson, 1936.

McMaster, John B. *A History of the People of the United States, from the Revolution to the Civil War.* 8 vols. 1883–1913. Reprint, New York: D. Appleton, 1924.

Miller, John C. *Crisis in Freedom: The Alien and Sedition Acts.* Boston: Little, Brown, 1951.

Moore, Robert J., Jr. and Michael Haynes. *Lewis and Clark, Tailor Made, Trail Worn: Army Life, Clothing, and Weapons of the Corps of Discovery.* Helena, Mont.: Farcountry Press, 2003.

Moreau de Saint-Méry, Médéric-Louis-Élie. *Moreau de St. Méry's American Journey (1793–1798).* Translated and edited by Kenneth Roberts and Anna M. Roberts. Garden City, N.Y.: Doubleday, 1947.

Moulton, Gary, ed. *The Journals of the Lewis and Clark Expedition*. 13 vols. Lincoln: University of Nebraska Press, 1983–2001.

Nasatir, Abraham P. *Spanish War Vessels on the Mississippi, 1792–1796*. New Haven, Conn.: Yale University Press, 1968.

Nelson, Paul David. *Anthony Wayne: Soldier of the Early Republic*. Bloomington: Indiana University Press, 1985.

O'Brien, Greg. *Choctaws in a Revolutionary Age, 1750–1830*. Lincoln: University of Nebraska Press, 2002.

Osgood, Ernest Staples, ed. *The Field Notes of Captain William Clark, 1803–1805*. New Haven, Conn.: Yale University Press, 1964.

Palmer, Michael A. *Stoddert's War: Naval Operations during the Quasi-War with France, 1798–1801*. Columbia: University of South Carolina Press, 1987.

Pancake, John S. *Samuel Smith and the Politics of Business: 1752–1839*. Tuscaloosa: University of Alabama Press, 1972.

Parmet, Herbert S. and Marie B. Hecht. *Aaron Burr: Portrait of an Ambitious Man*. New York: Macmillan, 1967.

Pitot, James. *Observations on the Colony of Louisiana from 1796 to 1802*. Baton Rouge: Louisiana State University Press, 1979.

Pollock, Thomas Clark. *The Philadelphia Theatre in the Eighteenth Century*. New York: Greenwood Press, 1968.

Potts, Gwynne Tuell, and Samuel W. Thomas. *George Rogers Clark, Military Leader in the Pioneer West & Locust Grove: The Croghan Homestead Honoring Him*. Louisville: Historic Locust Grove, 2006.

Prucha, Francis Paul. *The Sword of the Republic: The United States Army on the Frontier, 1783–1846*. Toronto: Macmillan, 1969.

Renau, Lynn Scholl. *So Close from Home: The Legacy of Brownsboro Road*. Louisville: Herr House Press, 2007.

Ritchey, David, ed. *A Guide to the Baltimore Stage in the Eighteenth Century: A History and Day Book Calendar*. Westport, Conn.: Greenwood Press, 1982.

Roberts, Robert B. *Encyclopedia of Historic Forts: The Military, Pioneer, and Trading Posts of the United States*. New York: Macmillan, 1988.

Robertson, James A., trans. and ed. *Louisiana under the Rule of Spain, France, and the United States, 1785–1807.* 2 vols. Cleveland: Arthur H. Clark, 1911.

Rowland, Dunbar, ed. *The Mississippi Territorial Archives, 1798–1803: Executive Journals of Governor Winthrop Sargent and Governor William Charles Cole Claiborne.* Vol. 1. Nashville, Tenn.: Press of Brandon Printing, 1905.

Rowland, Eron. *Life, Letters and Papers of William Dunbar of Elgin, Morayshire, Scotland, and Natchez, Mississippi: Pioneer Scientist of the Southern United States.* Jackson: Press of the Mississippi Historical Society, 1930.

Scharf, J. Thomas. *History of Baltimore City and County.* 1881. Reprint, 1 in 2 vols., Baltimore: Regional Publishing, 1971.

———. *History of Delaware, 1609–1888.* 2 vols. Philadelphia: L. J. Richards, 1888.

Schauinger, J. Herman. *Cathedrals in the Wilderness.* Milwaukee: Bruce Publishing, 1952.

Schlesinger, Arthur M., Jr., and Roger Bruns, eds. *Congress Investigates: A Documented History, 1792–1974.* 5 vols. New York: Chelsea House Publishers, 1975.

Shalhope, Robert E. *John Taylor of Caroline: Pastoral Republican.* Columbia: University of South Carolina Press, 1980.

Shepherd, William R. *Guide to the Materials for the History of the United States in the Spanish Archives* (Simancas, the Archivo Histórico Nacional, and Seville). Washington, DC: Carnegie Institution, 1907.

Simms, Henry H. *Life of John Taylor: The Story of a Brilliant Leader in the Early Virginia State Rights School.* Richmond: Vir.: The William Byrd Press, 1932.

Spalding, M. J. *Sketches of the Life, Times, and Character of the Rt. Rev. Benedict Joseph Flaget, First Bishop of Louisville.* Louisville: Webb & Levering, 1852.

Speed, Thomas. *The Political Club: Danville, Kentucky, 1786–1790.* Louisville: John P. Morton, 1894.

Steffen, Jerome O. *William Clark: Jeffersonian Man on the Frontier.* Norman: University of Oklahoma Press, 1977.

Steiner, Bernard C. *The Life and Correspondence of James McHenry, Secretary of War under Washington and Adams.* Cleveland: Arthur H. Clark, 1907.

Stewart, David O. *American Emperor: Aaron Burr's Challenge to Jefferson's America.* New York: Simon & Schuster, 2011.

Syrett, Harold C., ed. *The Papers of Alexander Hamilton.* New York: Columbia University Press, vols. 1–27, 1961–1987.

Thwaites, Reuben Gold, ed. *Original Journals of the Lewis and Clark Expedition.* 8 vols. New York: Dodd, Mead, 1904–1905.

Toll, Ian W. *Six Frigates: The Epic History of the Founding of the U.S. Navy.* New York: W. W. Norton, 2006.

Van Every, Dale. *Ark of Empire: The American Frontier, 1784–1803.* New York: William Morrow, 1963.

Van Ravenswaay, Charles. *St. Louis: An Informal History of the City and Its People, 1764–1865.* St. Louis: Missouri Historical Society Press, 1991.

Webb, Margery Hill. *Our Sebastian Heritage.* Lima, Ohio: published by author, 1989.

Weld, Isaac, Jr. *Travels Through the States of North America, and the Provinces of Upper and Lower Canada, During the Years 1795, 1796, and 1797.* 2 vols. London: John Stockdale, 1800.

Wheelan, Joseph. *Jefferson's Vendetta: The Pursuit of Aaron Burr and the Judiciary.* New York: Carroll & Graf Publishers, 2005.

Whitaker, Arthur Preston. *The Mississippi Question, 1795–1803: A Study in Trade, Politics, and Diplomacy.* 1934. Reprint, Gloucester, Mass: Peter Smith, 1962.

———. *The Spanish-American Frontier, 1783–1795: The Westward Movement and the Spanish Retreat in the Mississippi Valley.* Boston: Houghton Mifflin, 1927.

Wilkinson, James. *Memoirs of General Wilkinson: Burr's Conspiracy Exposed and General Wilkinson Vindicated against the Slanders of his enemies on that Important Occasion.* Washington, DC, 1811.

———. *Memoirs of My Own Times.* 3 vols. and atlas. Philadelphia: Abraham Small, 1816.

Articles

Arena, C. Richard. "Philadelphiia–Spanish New Orleans Trade in the 1790s." *Louisiana History* 2 (1961): 429–45.

Bergantino, Robert N. "Revisiting Fort Mandan's Longitude." *We Proceeded On* 27 (November 2001): 19–26.

Brown, Jo Ann. "George Drouillard and Fort Massac." *We Proceeded On* 25 (November 1999): 16–19.

Caldwell, Norman W. "Cantonment Wilkinsonville." *Mid-America, an Historical Review* 31 (January 1949): 3–28.

———. "Fort Massac: The American Frontier Post, 1778–1805." *Journal of the Illiniois State Historical Society* 43 (Winter 1950): 265–81.

Carstens, Kenneth C. "The 1780 William Clark Map of Fort Jefferson." *Filson Club History Quarterly* 67 (January 1993): 23–43.

Carter, Clarence E. "The Burr-Wilkinson Intrigue in St. Louis." *Bulletin of the Missouri Historical Society* 10 (July 1954): 447–64.

Carter, Michael A. "'Fighting the Flames of a Merciless War': Secretary of War Henry Knox and the Indian War in the Old Northwest, 1790–1795." *Journal of the Indian Wars* 1.2 (1999): 93–122.

Cox, Isaac Joslin. "The Burr Conspiracy in Indiana." *Indiana Magazine of History* 25 (December 1929): 257–80.

———. "General Wilkinson and His Later Intrigues with the Spaniards." *American Historical Review* 19 (1914): 794–812.

———."Wilkinson's First Break with the Spaniards." *Biennial Report of the Department of Archives and History of the State of West Virginia, 1911–1912, 1913–1914.* Appendix, 49–56. Charleston: State of West Virginia, 1914.

Cox, Isaac Joslin, ed. "Letters of William T. Barry, 1806–1810, 1829–1831." *American Historical Review* 16 (1911): 327–36.

Daveiss, J. H. "View of the President's Conduct Concerning the Conspiracy of 1806." 1807. Reprint. In *Quarterly Publication of the Historical and*

Philosophical Society of Ohio 12 (April–June, July–September 1917): 50–154.

DeMenil, Alexander N. "Memoirs of Deceased Members of the Society." *Missouri Historical Society Collections* 6 (October 1928): 124–27.

Dodd, William E. "John Taylor, Prophet of Secession." *The John P. Branch Historical Papers of Randolph-Macon College* 2 (June 1908): 214–52.

Dorman, John F., III. "Descendants of General Jonathan Clark, Jefferson County, Kentucky, 1750–1811." *Filson Club History Quarterly* 23 (January 1949): 25–33.

Dos Passos, John. "The Conspiracy and Trial of Aaron Burr." *American Heritage* 17 (February 1966): 4–9, 69–84.

Foley, William E. "A Family's Ordeal: The Troubling Case of William Preston Clark." *We Proceeded On* 34 (May 2008): 8–19.

Gaines, William H., Jr. "The Forgotten Army: Recruiting for a National Emergency (1799–1800)." *Virginia Magazine of History and Biography* 56 (July 1948): 267–79.

Garrison, George P., ed. "[Documents] Concerning Philip Nolan." *Quarterly of the Texas State Historical Association* 7 (April 1904): 308–17.

Gatten, Robert E., Jr. "The Birthplace of William Clark." *We Proceeded On* 19 (May 1993): 6–11.

———. "Clark Land in Virginia and the Birthplace of William Clark." *We Proceeded On* 25 (May 1999): 6–11.

Godfrey, Carlos E. "Organization of the Provisional Army of the United States in the Anticipated War with France, 1798–1800." *Pennsylvania Magazine of History and Biography* 38 (1914): 129–82.

Guion, Isaac. "Military Journal of Captain Isaac Guion, 1797–1799." In *Seventh Annual Report of the Director of the Department of Archives and History of the State of Mississippi, from October 1, 1907 to October 1, 1908.* Nashville: 1909, 23–113.

Henshaw, Leslie. "The Aaron Burr Conspiracy in the Ohio Valley." *Ohio Archaeological and Historical Publications* 24 (1915): 121–37.

Herndon, John W. "A Genealogy of the Herndon Family (Continued)." *Virginia Magazine of History and Biography* 10 (June 1903): 92.

Holmes, Jack D. L. "The Ebb-Tide of Spanish Military Power on the Mississippi: Fort San Fernando de las Barrancas, 1795–1798." *Publications of the East Tennessee Historical Society* 36 (1964): 23–44.

———. "Military Uniforms in Spanish Louisiana, 1766–1804." *Military Collector and Historian* 17 (Winter 1965): 115–17.

———. "Stephen Minor: Natchez Pioneer." *Journal of Mississippi History* 42 (February 1980): 17–26.

Holmes, Jack D. L., ed. and trans. "The *Moniteur de la Louisiane* in 1798." *Louisiana History* 2 (Spring 1961): 230–53.

Holt, Glen E. "After the Journey Was Over: The St. Louis Years of Lewis and Clark." *Gateway Heritage* 2 (Fall 1981): 42–48.

Hunt, John Clark. "The National Road." *American History Illustrated* 5 (August 1970): 24–31.

Jackson, Donald. "Jefferson, Meriwether Lewis, and the Reduction of the United States Army." *Proceedings of the American Philosophical Society* 124 (April 1980): 91–96.

Johnson, Claudia D. "That Guilty Third Tier: Prostitution in Nineteenth-Century American Theaters." *American Quarterly* 27 (December 1975): 575–84.

Johnson, William. "William Johnson's Journal." *Louisiana Historical Quarterly* 5 (January 1922): 34–50.

Kinnaird, Lawrence, and Lucia B. Kinnaird. "Nogales: Strategic Post on the Spanish Frontier." *Journal of Mississippi History* 42 (February 1980): 1–16.

Kohn, Richard H. "General Wilkinson's Vendetta with General Wayne: Politics and Command in the American Army, 1791–1796." *Filson Club History Quarterly* 45 (October 1971): 361–72.

Kuehl, John W. "Southern Reaction to the XYZ Affair: An Incident in the Emergence of American Nationalism." *Register of the Kentucky Historical Society* 70 (January 1972): 21–49.

———. "The XYZ Affair and American Nationalism: Republican Victories in the Middle Atlantic States." *Maryland Historical Magazine* 67 (Spring 1972): 1–20.

Kyte, George W. "A Spy on the Western Waters: The Military Intelligence Mission of General Collot in 1796." *Mississippi Valley Historical Review* 34 (December 1947): 427–42.

Lincoln, Rod. "The Balize, 1723–1888." *The Deep Delta* 2 (February 1984): 38–42.

Marshall, Thomas M. "The Journal of Henry B. Miller." *Missouri Historical Society Collections* 6 (1931): 213–87.

Martzolff, Clement L. "Zane's Trace." *Ohio Archaeological and Historical Quarterly* 13 (July 1904): 297–331.

McDermott, John Francis. "Museums in Early St. Louis." *Bulletin of the Missouri Historical Society* 4 (April 1948): 129–38.

McGrane, R. C., ed. "William Clark's Journal of General Wayne's Campaign." *Mississippi Valley Historical Review* 1 (December 1914): 418–44.

Nelson, Paul David. "'Mad' Anthony Wayne and the Kentuckians of the 1790s." *Register of the Kentucky Historical Society* 84 (Winter 1986): 1–17.

Parish, John Carl. "The Intrigues of Doctor James O'Fallon." *Mississippi Valley Historical Review* 17 (September 1930): 230–63.

Quaife, M. M., ed. "General James Wilkinson's Narrative of the Fallen Timbers Campaign." *Mississippi Valley Historical Review* 16 (1929–1930): 81–90.

Rader, Perry S. "The Romance of the American Courts: Gaines vs. New Orleans." *Louisiana Historical Quarterly* 27 (1944): 5–322.

Register, Robert. "Andrew Ellicott's Observations while Serving on the Southern Boundary Commission, 1796–1800." *Gulf Coast Historical Review* 12 (Spring 1997): 6–43.

Roberts, Frances C. "Thomas Freeman—Surveyor of the Old Southwest." *Alabama Review* 40 (July 1987): 216–30.

Rusche, Timothy M. "Treachery within the United States Army." *Pennsylvania History* 65 (Autumn 1998): 478–91.

Salomone, Jerome J. "Mississippi River Bar-Pilotage: The Development of an Occupation." *Louisiana Studies* 6 (Spring 1967): 39–52.

Savelle, Max. "The Founding of New Madrid, Missouri." *Mississippi Valley Historical Review* 19 (June 1932): 30–56.

Shannon, Gary W., and Robert G. Cromley. "Philadelphia and the Yellow Fever Epidemic of 1798." *Urban Geography* 3 (1982): 355–70.

Shepherd, William R. "Wilkinson and the Beginnings of the Spanish Conspiracy." *American Historical Review* 9 (April 1904): 490–506.

Shepherd, William R., ed. "Papers Bearing on James Wilkinson's Relations with Spain, 1787–1789." *American Historical Review* 9 (July 1904): 748–66.

Simmons, David A. "An Orderly Book from Fort Washington and Fort Hamilton, 1792–1793." *Cincinnati Historical Society Bulletin* 36 (1978): 125–44.

Snow, Jan. "Lewis and Clark in the Museum Collections of the Missouri Historical Society." *Gateway Heritage* 2 (Fall 1981): 36–41.

Stadler, Frances Hurd. "Letters from Minoma." *Bulletin of the Missouri Historical Society* 16 (April 1960): 237–59.

Thomas, Samuel W. "William Croghan, Sr. [1752–1822]: A Pioneer Kentucky Gentleman." *Filson Club History Quarterly* 43 (January 1969): 30–61.

Thomas, Samuel W., ed. "William Clark's 1795 and 1797 Journals and Their Significance." *Bulletin of the Missouri Historical Society* 25 (July 1969): 277–95.

Thwaites, Reuben Gold. "The Story of Lewis and Clark's Journals." *Annual Report of the American Historical Association.* Washington, DC: USGPO, 1903, 107–29.

Van Horne, John C. "Andrew Ellicott's Mission to Natchez (1796–1798)." *Journal of Mississippi History* 45 (August 1983): 160–85.

Warren, Elizabeth. "Benjamin Sebastian and the Spanish Conspiracy in Kentucky." *Filson Club History Quarterly* 20 (1946): 107–30.

Watlington, Patricia. "John Brown and the Spanish Conspiracy." *Virginia Magazine of History and Biography* 75 (1967): 52–68.

Whitaker, Arthur Preston. "Despatches from the United States Consulate in New Orleans, 1801–1803." Part 1. *American Historical Review* 32 (October 1926–July 1927): 801–24.

———. "Harry Innes and the Spanish Intrigue: 1794–1795." *Mississippi Valley Historical Review* 15 (June 1928): 236–48.

———. "James Wilkinson's First Descent to New Orleans in 1787." *Hispanic American Historical Review* 8 (1928): 82–97.

———. "Reed and Forde: Merchant Adventurers of Philadelphia." *Pennsylvania Magazine of History and Biography* 61 (July 1937): 237–62.

Wilson, Samuel M. "The Court Proceedings of 1806 in Kentucky against Aaron Burr and John Adair." *Filson Club History Quarterly* 10 (1936): 31–40.

Woodward, Ralph Lee, Jr. "Spanish Commercial Policy in Louisiana, 1763–1803." *Louisiana History* 44 (Spring 2003): 133–64.

Manuscript Collections

Chicago Historical Society
    James Wilkinson Papers
Cincinnati Museum Center
    Orderly Book from Fort Washington and Fort Hamilton, 1792–1793
College of William and Mary, Special Collections Research Center
    Preston Family Papers
Filson Historical Society, Louisville, Kentucky
    Bodley Family Papers
    Bullitt Family Papers
    Clark-Hite Collection
George Mason University
    War Department Papers, courtesy of the Center for History and New Media. http://wardepartmentpapers.org
Senator John Heinz History Center, Pittsburgh, Pennsylvania
    Thomas and Katherine Detre Library and Archives
    Fort Massac Records
Historical Society of Delaware
    Maxwell Bines Manuscript Collection
Historical Society of Pennsylvania, Philadelphia
    Coxe Family Papers

Croghan Papers
Gilpin Papers
Anthony Wayne Papers
Historic New Orleans Collection
City of New Orleans Directories
Indiana Historical Society
John Armstrong Collection
Northwest Territory Collection
Benjamin Sebastian Papers
Jefferson County, Kentucky
Court Minute-Order Books
Deed Books
Will Books
Kentucky Secretary of State, Land Office Division
Old Kentucky Patents
Library of Congress, Washington, DC
Andrew Ellicott Papers
Geography and Map Division
Harry Innes Papers
Thomas Jefferson Papers
James Monroe Papers
Nicholson Papers
Maryland Historical Society
James McHenry Papers
Massachusetts Historical Society
John Adams Papers
Timothy Pickering Papers
Winthrop Sargent Papers
Mississippi Department of Archives and History
J. F. H. Claiborne Collection
William Dunbar Papers
Natchez Court Records
Missouri History Museum, St. Louis, Missouri
Clark Family Collection

Missouri State Archives
    Probate File of William Clark
National Archives and Records Administration, Washington, DC
    Adjutant General's Office: Record Group 94
        Gen. James Wilkinson's Order Book, December 31, 1796–
        March 8, 1808.
    Court of Claims: Record Group 123
    Customs Service: Record Group 36
    State Department: Record Group 59
        Despatches from U.S. Consuls in New Orleans, 1798–1807
New York Surrogate's Court, County of New York
    Probate records
Ohio Historical Society
    Anthony Wayne Papers
Oregon Historical Society
    Eva Emery Dye Papers
Saint Louis City, Missouri
    Probate Court
Saint Louis County, Missouri
    Probate Court
    Recorder of Deeds
State Historical Society of Missouri
    William C. Breckenridge Collection
State Historical Society of Wisconsin, Madison
    Lyman Draper Manuscripts
University of Chicago
    Innes Letters
    Kentuckiana Collection of Reuben T. Durrett
    Lewis Family Papers
University of Michigan, William L. Clements Library
    James McHenry Papers
University of North Carolina at Chapel Hill, Southern Historical
    Collection

Guion Family Papers
Francis Taylor Diary
Virginia State Archives

Online Resources

Early Records of the U.S. War Department http://wardepartmentpapers.
org

Theses, Dissertations, and Reports

Barile, Kerri S., Kerry Schamel-Gonzalez, and Sean P. Maroney. "'Inferior to None in the State': The History, Archaeology, and Architecture of the Marriott Hotel Site in Fredericksburg, Virginia." Prepared for the City of Fredericksburg by Dovetail Cultural Resource Group, April 2008.

Christian, Percy W. "General James Wilkinson and Kentucky Separatism, 1784–1798." PhD diss., Evanston, Ill.: Northwestern University, 1935.

Dawdy, Shannon Lee, Ryan Gray, and Jill-Karen Yakubik. "Archaeological Investigations at the Rising Sun Hotel Site (160R225), New Orleans, Louisiana." Vol. 1. Prepared for the Historic New Orleans Collection by Dawdy and students at the University of Chicago, Department of Anthropology, June 2008.

Drewry, Elizabeth B. "Episodes in Westward Expansion as Reflected in the Writings of General James Wilkinson, 1784–1806." PhD thesis, Ithaca, N.Y.: Cornell University, 1933.

Loos, John L. "A Biography of William Clark, 1770–1813." PhD diss., St. Louis, Mo., Washington University, 1953.

Mayer, David P. "Cantonment Wilkinsonville, 1801: Burr, Wilkinson, The U.S. Army, and Treason." Unpublished manuscript in the possession of the Center for Archaeological Investigations, Southern Illinois University, Carbondale, 1985.

Porter, David Orin. "James Wilkinson: Spanish Agent or Double Agent?" PhD diss., Washington, DC, George Washington University, 2007.

Rusche, Timothy. "The Battle of Fallen Timbers: Securing America's Western Frontier." Thesis, Philadelphia: University of Pennsylvania, 1997.

Wagner, Mark. "Searching for Cantonment Wilkinsonville." Unpublished manuscript in the possession of the Center for Archaeological Investigations, Southern Illinois University, Carbondale, 2004.

Wheeler, Austin T. "The Scandalous General James Wilkinson and His Connection with the Spanish, Aaron Burr, and Daniel Clark." Thesis, Lubbock: Texas Tech University, 2009.

Wohl, Michael. "A Man in Shadow: The Life of Daniel Clark." PhD diss., New Orleans: Tulane University, 1984.

Newspapers

Baltimore Intelligencer
Carey's United States Recorder, Philadelphia
Claypoole's American Daily Advertiser, Philadelphia
Federal Gazette and Baltimore Daily Advertiser
Kentucky Gazette and General Advertiser, Lexington
Le Moniteur de la Louisiane, New Orleans
New York Times
Palladium, Frankfort, Kentucky
St. Louis Globe-Democrat
St. Louis Post-Dispatch
St. Louis Star-Times
Virginia Argus, Richmond
Virginia Herald, Fredericksburg
Western World, Frankfort, Kentucky

Government Documents in the United States

Annals of the Congress of the United States, 1789–1824. 42 vols. Washington, DC: Gales and Seaton, 1834–1836.

Carter, Clarence E., ed. *The Territorial Papers of the United States.* Vols. 2 and 3, *The Territory Northwest of the River Ohio, 1787–1803* (1934). Vol. 5, *The Territory of Mississippi, 1798–1817* (1937). Washington, DC: USGPO, 1934–1962.

Franklin County (Kentucky) Order Book B, 1798–1801.

Index of Spotsylvania County: WPA Historical Inventory. Vol. 1.

Jefferson County (Kentucky) Will Book. Vol. 1.

Jefferson County (Kentucky) Minute—Order Book. Vol. 5.

Kentucky Secretary of State, Land Office Division.

National Union Catalog of Manuscript Collections. 29 vols. Washington, DC: Library of Congress, 1961–1993.

Report of the Select Committee, to Whom was Referred the Information Communicated to the House of Representatives, Charging Benjamin Sebastian, One of the Judges of the Court of Appeals of Kentucky, with Having Received a Pension from the Spanish Government. Frankfort (KY.): J. M. Street Press, 1806.

State Papers and Correspondence Bearing Upon the Purchase of the Territory of Louisiana. Washington, DC: USGPO, 1903.

Treaty of San Lorenzo. Also known as Pinckney's Treaty.

U.S. Navy Department. *Naval Documents Related to the Quasi-War between the United States and France: Naval Operations from February 1797 to October 1798.* Vol. 1 of 7. Edited by Dudley W. Knox. Washington, DC: USGPO, 1935.

U.S. Statutes at Large. Washington, DC, 1850.

Archival Collections of Spain

Archivo General de Indias (General Archives of the Indies).
    Papeles Procedentes de Cuba (Cuba Papers)
Archivo Histórico Nacional (National Historical Archives).
    Papeles de Estado (State Papers)
Audiencia de Santo Domingo (Court of Santo Domingo).

Acknowledgments

Thanks go to Kerri Barile, Deborah Breckenridge, Kenneth Carstens, Shannon Dawdy, William Foley, Ronald Goldbrenner, James Holmberg, R. Bruce McMillan, Kristine Sjostrom, and Ralph Lee Woodward, Jr. for providing crucial, material help, and to Shannon White, Aaron Kale, and Marta Payne for their work on the maps of Clark's river route.

I am indebted to the State Historical Society of Missouri and its staff, especially Gary Kremer, Anne Cox, Todd Christine, Kimberly Harper, and John Konzal, and to Jaime Bourassa, Carolyn Gilman, Molly Kodner, and Dennis Northcott of the Missouri History Museum. Thanks go as well to University of Missouri librarians Sara Bryant, Eric Cusick, John Dethman, June DeWeese, Tyler Dwyer, Piana Edwards, Karen Eubanks, Gwendolyn Gray, Esther Schnase, David Shay, and Cindy Shearrer, and to Nina Sappington at the Daniel Boone Regional Library.

Others deserving of thanks are: Shirley Ackerman, Kandie Adkinson, Edgar Ailor, David Angerhofer, Pamela Arceneaux, Stephen Archer, Carolyn Autrey, Carol Bartels, Ray Benson, Robert Bergantino, Trey Berry, Rhonda Bickerstaff, Siva Blake, Matthew J. Brown, Philip A. Brown, Jay Buckley, Steven Bychowski, Art Carpenter, Paul Cary, Mark Cave, John Chew, Edward Chichirichi, Bud Clark, Bonnie Coles, Mary Condy, Brian Coutts, Light Cummins, Thomas Danisi, Gilbert Din, Scott Dine, Rita Dockery, Lesley Douthwaite, Jeffrey Edmunds, Steven Edwards, Ernest Emrich, Jay Feldman, Mark Fernandez, Mary Frye, Gary Gackstatter, Jill Gage, Kira Gale, Robert Gatten, William Glankler, Ronald Goldbrenner, John Gordon, Chuck Gray, Suzanne Hahn, Kirsten Hammerstrom,

Neal Hammon, David Haugaard, Donald Hickey, Paul Hoffman, Hilary Holladay, Scott Howard, Galvin Humphries, G. Douglas Inglis, Mimi Jackson, Jonathan Jeffrey, Landon Jones, Jill Larson, Dan Lashley, Alfred Lemmon, Wally Mading, Maurice Manring, Sean Maroney, Heather Merrill, Joseph Mertzlufft, David Morgan, David Moore, Robert Moore, Lynn Morrow, William Morton, Steve Murray, Stanley Nelson, Greg O'Brien, Dustin Oehl, Toy O'Ferrall, David Pavelich, Julie K. Brown Petersen, Ed Redmond, Robert Register, Lynn Renau, Hugh Ridenour, Timothy Rusche, Rena Schergen, William Shansey, Anne Shepherd, Monica L. Smith, Greg Spies, David O. Stewart, Heather Stone, Robert Ticknor, Gary Venable, Dora Vigil, Mary Wade, Mark Wagner, James Wallace, Kathryn Wallace, Minor Weisinger, Barbara Willis, Sue Willis, Ben Windham, Jack Wolcott, and W. Ray Wood.

I am also grateful to Mary Conley, Sara Davis, Kirk Hinkelman, Pippa Letsky, and Clair Willcox, all of them with the University of Missouri Press.

Illustration Credits

1. Courtesy of Independence National Historical Park
2. Courtesy of the State Historical Society of Missouri
3. Courtesy of the State Historical Society of Missouri
4. Courtesy of Shannon H. White, Aaron Kale, and Marta Payne, all of the Missouri Geographic Alliance
5. Land Office Division of the Kentucky Secretary of State
6. Courtesy of the State Historical Society of Missouri
7. Courtesy of Independence National Historical Park
8. The Byron R. Lewis Historical Library, Vincennes University, Indiana
9. Courtesy of Shannon H. White, Aaron Kale, and Marta Payne, all of the Missouri Geographic Alliance
10. Missouri History Museum, St. Louis
11. Courtesy of Shannon H. White, Aaron Kale, and Marta Payne, all of the Missouri Geographic Alliance
12. The Historic New Orleans Collection, Acc. No. 1974.25.27.75.
13. Courtesy of the State Historical Society of Missouri
14. Courtesy of the Collections of the Louisiana State Museum.
15. Missouri History Museum, St. Louis
16. Prints and Photographs Division, Library of Congress
17. Alabama Department of Archives and History, Montgomery, Alabama
18. Coxe Family Collection, The Historical Society of Pennsylvania
19. Courtesy of the State Historical Society of Missouri
20 Courtesy of the State Historical Society of Missouri

21. Courtesy of the State Historical Society of Missouri
22. Missouri History Museum, St. Louis
23. Missouri History Museum, St. Louis

Index

Wilcox, Nathaniel, 149–50, 196
Wilderness Road, 280
Wilkinson, Ann Biddle, 29, 317
Wilkinson, Celestine Laveau Trudeau,
317–18
Wilkinson, James, 20, 95, 162, 177, 190,
191–92, 194, 205, 228, 231, 232, 239,
277, 313; background and education,
29–33, 255; betrays Lewis and Clark
expedition, 294–95, 319; and "Burr"
plot, 297–98, 306–11, 314–15;
commercial aspirations of, 35–36, 41,
43, 124, 255; conspires with Spain,
13, 32–35, 44, 49–50, 60, 61, 65–70,
71, 82–83, 85, 93, 126, 137, 230,
256–59, 294–95, 350–55; as governor
of Louisiana Territory, 296–97, 298,
299, 310; interest in maps and data
on Spanish territory, 23, 28, 41, 63,
81, 112, 123, 133, 135, 146, 188,
256, 257, 277; investigated by U.S.
Army and Congress, 314–17; and
Kentucky politics, 35–37; maligns
George Rogers Clark, 5, 13, 31–32,
50, 78, 160; secret correspondence
and documents of, 33, 53, 55, 73,
97–98, 153–54, 189, 265, 277, 306,
314, 348; Spanish pay of, 65–70, 73,
74–78, 94, 99, 101, 151, 159–60,
188, 204, 233, 284, 315, 317; under
suspicion, 8, 77, 96–97, 108, 188,
189–90, 204, 265, 299, 300–301,
306; in U.S. Army, 36–37, 60,
96–98, 103–5, 107, 108, 109, 111,
142, 152, 185, 229–31, 273, 276,
279, 280, 290, 297–98; vendetta
against Wayne, 9, 37–38, 45, 51,
52–53, 76, 101, 102–3, 227, 240, 310;
war aspirations of, 23, 107–8, 140,
229–30, 275–76, 318; and William
Clark, 44, 56, 70, 160
Williams, Amariel, 212–13
Williams, Steven, 171
Winchester, James, 244, 245, 246
Winters, Elisha, 74–75, 76, 77
Wolcott, Oliver, 144, 239
Wood, John, 298, 299
Woodman, Joseph, 198, 224, 226, 227
Wythe Courthouse (Wytheville), Virginia,
280

XYZ Affair, the, 143–46, 245, 253

Yazoo River, 41, 82, 83, 155
Yellow fever, 149, 235–37, 238, 243
York (slave), 6, 202, 253, 280

Zane, Ebenezer, 264

About the Author

Photo: Edgar Ailor III

Attorney Jo Ann Trogdon lives in Columbia, Missouri, the same city where the 1798–1801 journal of William Clark has been housed, virtually overlooked, in the State Historical Society of Missouri since 1928. She was led to the journal by her research in Spanish archives for her book *St. Charles Borromeo: 200 Years of Faith*. Her articles on history have appeared in publications including *Arizona Highways* and *We Proceeded On*, a publication of the Lewis and Clark Trail Heritage Foundation.